KEEP AUSTRALIA
ON YOUR LEFT

A True Story of an Attempt
to Circumnavigate Australia by Kayak

A TOM DOHERTY ASSOCIATES BOOK
NEW YORK

KEEP AUSTRALIA ON YOUR LEFT

Eric Stiller

Keep Australia on Your Left: A True Story of an Attempt to
Circumnavigate Australia by Kayak

Copyright © 2000 by Eric Stiller

This book is printed on acid-free paper.

Photographs of Eric Stiller courtesy of Tony Brown

Book design by Jane Adele Regina

Map by Anita Karl and Jim Kemp

A Forge Book
Published by Tom Doherty Associates, LLC
175 Fifth Avenue
New York, NY 10010

www.tor.com

Forge® is a registered trademark of Tom Doherty Associates, LLC.

Library of Congress Cataloging-in-Publication Data

Stiller, Eric.
    Keep Australia on your left : a true story of an attempt to circumnavigate
Australia by kayak / Eric Stiller.—1st ed.
        p. cm.
"A Tom Doherty Associates book."
ISBN 0-312-87458-8
1. Kayaking—Australia. 2. Stiller, Eric—Journeys—Australia. 3. Australia—
Description and travel. I. Title.

GV776.89.A2 S75 2000
919.404'66'092—dc21
    [B]   00-028810

First Edition: September 2000

Printed in the United States of America

0 9 8 7 6 5 4 3 2 1

This book is dedicated to my intrepid and inspiring paddle partner, Tony Brown, and my steady-as-she-goes, detail-watching father, Dieter Stiller.

Contents

Acknowledgments

My deepest appreciation goes to the following people who aided and abetted in bringing this "epic" to fruition from planting the seeds of the trip to dotting the last I in the book.

First, a special thanks to my dear friend Dave Klevatt and his wife, Lara Perry, for having the belief and the wherewithal to take a 1,000-page opus and see and extract the true story inside.

Another special thanks to Irene Gallo, who kept the ball alive in the unforgiving court of publishing.

To my editor, Jonathan Schmidt, who challenged me to make the trip come alive again with salt, sand, and wind in the hair.

To the publisher: Tom Doherty and the crew at Forge Books.

To: Karen Stiller, Paul Theroux, David Lee Roth, Howard Rice, Martin Walsh, Radu Teoderescu, Nicole Gallant, Craig Uher, Ralph Diaz, Bill and Janet Lozano, H. S. Walther GmbH, Ryan at Werner Paddles, Limerick Kaye, Harry and Claire De-Roohey, Jersey and Mariane, Dez, Val and Berry, "Blackie," Michael Penn, Sam, Sammie, Phinney, Brent, Caroline, Power Bar, Magellan Industries, Don Jr., Algis Pabaracius, Andre, Eric & Charles and the cast of The Coffee Shop and Live Bait circa 1991. Dierdre Coleman, Kevin, Al Bakker, John Dowd, Calvin and Kelly Klein, Moz, Ron Arias, Rufus Albermale, Voyageur, Michael Gabor, Dee Gillette, Paul Caffyn, Trevor, Tim Lane, Michael Skott, Ian and Rosary Gibson, Phil & Wally, Sue and Dave, Sam Gooch, Carl and Paunch Svendsen, Richard Pops, Barron Eyraud, Eric Gustavsen, Dr. Rogen Draper, Jersey and Marianne, Dot, Kelly, and the TI Bakery and all those wonderful souls who got us up and kept us going.

And in memoriam: Eric Konheim, Jan Lee-Lewes (Tony's mum), and Arthur Nehring, my grandfather.

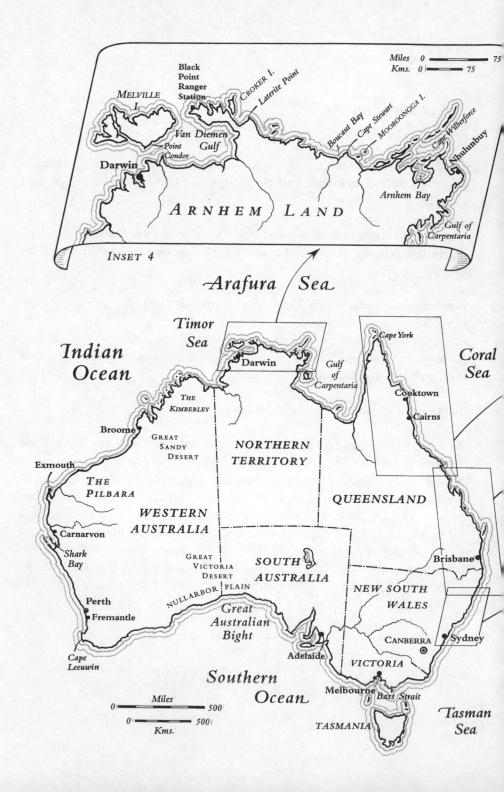

Miles 0 ——— 75
Kms. 0 ——— 75

INSET 4

Black
Point
Ranger
Station

CROKER I.

Laterite Point

MELVILLE
I.

Van Diemen
Gulf

Point
Condor

Boucaut Bay

Cape Stewart

MOOROONGGA I.

Cape Wilberforce

Nhulunbuy

Darwin

Arnhem Bay

Gulf of
Carpentaria

A R N H E M   L A N D

Arafura   Sea

Timor
Sea

Indian
Ocean

Darwin

Gulf
of
Carpentaria

Cape York

Coral
Sea

Cooktown

Cairns

THE
KIMBERLEY

Broome

GREAT
SANDY
DESERT

NORTHERN
TERRITORY

Exmouth

THE
PILBARA

WESTERN
AUSTRALIA

QUEENSLAND

Carnarvon

Shark
Bay

GREAT
VICTORIA
DESERT

SOUTH
AUSTRALIA

Brisbane

NEW SOUTH
WALES

Perth

NULLARBOR   PLAIN

Fremantle

Great
Australian
Bight

CANBERRA

Sydney

Cape
Leeuwin

VICTORIA

Adelaide

Southern   Ocean

Melbourne   Bass Strait

Tasman
Sea

TASMANIA

Miles 0 ——— 500

Kms. 0 ——— 500

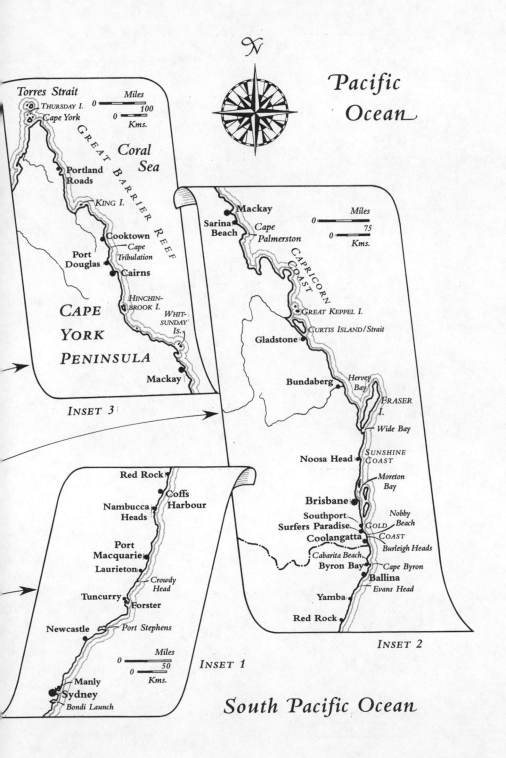

N

Pacific
Ocean

Torres Strait
THURSDAY I.
Cape York

GREAT BARRIER REEF

Miles
0   100
0
Kms.

**Coral
Sea**

**Portland
Roads**

KING I.

Cooktown
*Cape
Tribulation*

**Port
Douglas**

Cairns

*HINCHIN-
BROOK I.*

*WHIT-
SUNDAY
Is.*

**CAPE
YORK
PENINSULA**

Mackay

INSET 3

Mackay
**Sarina
Beach**
*Cape
Palmerston*

CAPRICORN COAST

Miles
0   75
0
Kms.

Great Keppel I.

CURTIS ISLAND/Strait

Gladstone

Bundaberg
*Hervey
Bay*

*FRASER
I.*

Wide Bay

*SUNSHINE
COAST*

Noosa Head

*Moreton
Bay*

Brisbane

Southport
Surfers Paradise
Coolangatta

*Nobby
Beach*

GOLD
COAST

Burleigh Heads

Cabarita Beach
Byron Bay
Cape Byron

Ballina
Evans Head

Yamba

Red Rock

INSET 2

Red Rock

**Coffs
Harbour**

**Nambucca
Heads**

**Port
Macquarie**
Laurieton
*Crowdy
Head*

Tuncurry
Forster
Port Stephens

Newcastle

Miles
0   50
0
Kms.

INSET 1

Manly
Sydney
Bondi Launch

South Pacific Ocean

© A. Karl / J. Kemp, 2000

KEEP AUSTRALIA ON YOUR LEFT

Prologue

"Tony! Let's set the sails!"

He nodded OK.

The mainsail parachuted open and the mainsheet was snapping at the air like the whip of a desperate lion tamer. I reached to the right to grab it and another gust hit, heeling the boat. Water poured into the cabin. Tony deftly fish-poled the line out of the air with his paddle.

"The wind's up a little early today, mate!"

I laughed. "Wants to make sure we are wide awake for this one!" I felt exhilarated. I flashed Tony the thumbs-up. Then the trouble began.

"Tony! It looks like surf is breaking on a shoal up ahead."

"Mate, it sure looks like it goes a long way."

"It looks like a mile. We should take a course around it."

"OK."

I was wrong. Crisscrossing waves broke all around us and as far as the eye could see. Even when perched atop a wave!

"What's going on?" yelled Tony.

"I don't know!" I yelled back.

The five-foot waves became six-. They became steeper and started stacking themselves closer and closer together until we were in a massive corrugated field of seven- and eight-footers. I scanned the shore for a possible landing, just in case. But we had reached Point Condor faster than anticipated. Instead of an accommodating sandy beach, all that confronted us was sheer rock face and not a beach in sight.

A bailout was not possible.

There was no turning back.

Southern Cross was pounded by one wave after another, it was all we could do to keep upright. Hip tilt right. Head tilt left. Hips left, head and shoulders right. We were like a slinky toy trying to stand atop the handlebars of a motocross bike.

The frame of *Southern Cross* suddenly twisted one way left in the bow and bent upward in the stern as the sea clawed at the boat from all directions. We were being spun and counterspun like the needle of a cheap compass. The sails had become a curse. Instead of converting the pressure of the wind into speed and balance, they had become the playground for a troop of invisible monkeys.

Too late. We imploded into an overfalling wave and capsized. Tony managed to sling one leg into the boat, but the cockpit was so cluttered with scattered debris that the other leg dangled half over the side.

The waves looked like ten-feet high. We paddled as hard as possible into the sets. We were hammered every few minutes. My full, forward body lean would be knocked flush against the deck behind me as one large white "paw" toyed with me and pinned me heartlessly.

"How are we going to get out of this?" Tony yelled.

There was barely enough time to breathe, much less talk.

Paddling as hard as we could, we were able to keep *Southern Cross* from being pushed backward into the cliffs. But that was it. We could not make any forward progress at all. We couldn't get any bite on our blades. It was like paddling in foam.

It was possible that we were in some type of freak whirlpool. Maybe it would drop with the tide. Maybe not. We were getting hit very hard in the chest by the overfalling waves.

Our only hope was that we could hold position and keep paddling into the waves and wait for the tide to drop. I did quick, frantic calculations in my head. A six-hour bell-curve pattern. Give or take an hour. *Shit!* We were looking at maybe four more hours of sustained give-it-all-you-have paddling. I knew we could paddle that long under normal circumstances. But this was anything but normal.

For the first time on the trip I thought we were *truly* paddling for our lives.

Manhattan, USA

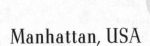 It was past closing time at the Klepper Kayak Shop. I was putting on my coat in the back of the store, preparing to set out into the early autumn night. I had one arm in the sleeve when I heard the door jingle and I headed to the front. A warm glow from the entranceway spotlights welcomed a tall, broad-shouldered presence. I wanted to yell "we're closed" but saw him gravitate to one of our two-person sea kayaks. I approached him with my well-rehearsed greeting.

"Hello. Are you familiar with these boats?"

"I've heard about them. I'm thinking of taking one around my country."

I detected an accent. "Where are you from?"

He slightly puffed his chest and with a quick change in tone proclaimed with mischief and pride, *"Australia!"*

"I hear the Whitsunday Islands are nice. What part of the country do you want to paddle?"

"All the way around, mate."

A gleam in his eye confirmed what he said, but did he have any idea what he was talking about? I had been involved with kayaking and Klepper kayaks since I could walk. For the last eight years since graduating from the University of Colorado with a business degree, I had been outfitting new and experienced kayakers from my father's shop on Union Square in New York City.

I had outfitted JFK Jr. for an expedition to Alaska. I had trained U.S. Special

Forces in utilizing the boats for "re-con and infiltration." I knew all the Klepper legends: Captain Romer's and Dr. Hans Lindemann's solo trips across the Atlantic, John Dowd and company across the Caribbean, Carl Schotts's travels from Germany to India.

Most recently I had helped Howard Rice add his name to the list by training him for his solo rounding of Cape Horn in the smallest boat ever. A fifteen-foot, sixty-pound, single-seat Klepper.

Yes, I thought to myself, this Aussie had found ground zero for kayak expeditions. But Australia? The continent? As big as the United States's lower forty-eight surrounded by notoriously high winds, rough seas, and giant surf?

"Do you have a lot of experience sea kayaking?"

"No, but I've done some white water."

"Oh really, Class three? Class four?"

"Hard to say, I've only done it a few times."

"Do you plan to do it by yourself or with a partner?"

"With my mate, Sam. He helped come up with the idea on a climbing trip in Europe."

"Does he have any experience?"

"No. But he's a great outdoor cook."

That was my cue to get him a brochure, a price list, and a bibliography of past expeditions.

"Here's my card and some material to study. My name's Eric, and yours?"

"Tony."

"What's your time frame?"

"About a year and half."

At least he didn't say next month! I wanted to suggest a trip in the Mediterranean, which would have made more sense, but I didn't. Instead I called his bluff. "That's not a lot of time. When you want to get serious about this I can help you with your boat and give you some paddle training."

"Yeah? How about now?"

Huh? He had raised me. I could fold and say no. Or I could push all my chips to the center of the table. What did I really have to lose? My best hope was to sell a boat. At the very least I had a good excuse to get out of the office and show him a thing or two about paddling.

"Come by the day after tomorrow. We'll go out for a few hours."

"Can I treat you to a drink, mate?"

"Sure, why not."

We went to a bar down the street where he was greeted warmly from behind the bar. Tony instructed me: "It is very important to know the bartender."

The "drink" of choice was Tequila. A few rounds into our bonding ritual I learned that Tony's occupation was international modeling, but his passion was climbing. He typically would work for six months and then meet friends in

Europe where they would camper-van through the Alps from climb to climb. We talked about climbing experiences. The few drinks became several and the next morning had a luster all its own.

The "training" apparently had begun.

I wasn't sure that I would ever see Tony again, and I wasn't sure I wanted to. I didn't think my five-foot-eight-inch frame would handle any more Australian bonding rituals. Nevertheless, I took apart one of the double Kleppers and put it into its two bags . . . just in case.

I knew it would take a day to prepare Dieter, my father, for my possible absence the next day. He tried to run a tight ship that was chronically—terribly—understaffed. He had been managing the New York store for more than thirty years and had a chip on his shoulder about paddling on company time. He looked first at the folded Klepper, then at me.

"Who are you packing that boat for?"

"Dad, I've got a 'live' one who thinks he wants to go on an expedition around Australia. We're going out tomorrow for a little trial by fire."

"Ach, that is ridiculous, you can do it on the weekend."

"No, he's going back to Europe soon and he really wants to give the boat a try. I think he may just pick one up before he goes."

"On *impulse?*"

I hesitated. "Yes."

This was the only way to clear the day for Tony and myself. Dieter had to believe there was a legitimate chance for a boat sale. Klepper boats cost almost four thousand dollars before accessories. It took unusual dedication to sell folding expedition kayaks in Manhattan, where a substantial part of the population does not even acknowledge that they live on an island. Clients needed to have time, money, athleticism, and some mechanical ability. A rare combination.

Moreover, Dieter did not want me to get too excited about paddling and get notions to up and leave the store. He had watched many top kayakers come and go after a few short years of working for him. One of his friends, Eric Seidel, who helped pioneer U.S. kayak racing in Colorado, was his top salesman. He didn't stay for the long haul.

"The racers cannot be businessmen," Dieter would grumble.

Dieter had outfitted hundreds—thousands—of trips all over the world. His roster of clients over the years included the Rockefellers, Bobby Kennedy, the Mellons, and shipping magnate Spyros Niarchos. His dedication to his shop had nothing to do with celebrity. Typically, he would be the last man out of the store on a Friday night if a panicked client needed a three-dollar part overnighted to Mexico.

However, new German ownership was putting pressure on him to sell more and cut costs. They were talking about closing the store.

I believed that more high-profile expeditions—and the publicity generated—

could save the business. My years spent training Howard had resulted in articles in *Sea Kayaker* magazine, *Sports Illustrated,* and keynote speeches at major symposia throughout the country. Howard started a kayak tour business specializing in Klepper boats that operated out of the Bahamas. He also founded the first Klepper Society. I had a sense that Tony might have what it took to pull off another big trip. He had daring and naïveté. A potent cocktail. Given half a chance I could mold him for the task. Or so I thought.

Somewhat surprisingly, Tony showed up the next day at noon dressed in his Blundstones (a slip-on style Australian work boot), cotton sweatpants and tops.

"Ready to go, mate?"

I gave him a blank stare. He had no idea what it took to clear the decks for this "tryout." To begin with, he was improperly—even dangerously—dressed. I got him some synthetic fleece tops and bottoms, as well as wind pants and nylon anorak.

"You'll want to wear these. The water temp is under fifty degrees, and cotton clothing conducts heat away from the body twenty-five times faster when wet."

"Do I really need this?"

"If we capsize, the cotton sweats get very heavy and act like the concrete pants they put on out-of-favor Jersey gangsters."

"We're not going to capsize in one of these!" He pointed to one of the Klepper doubles. "I rowed competitively throughout university. Those boats were much tippier than these."

"It's not likely," I admitted, "but the Hudson River is not a lake or a canal. It's a tidal river with strong currents and winds that can make waves come from all directions. The Mohicans called it Great Waters Constantly in Motion."

Tony reluctantly complied, and I handed him one of the bags with the boat.

"What's this?" he frowned, hefting the bag experimentally.

"We're taking the boats on the subway uptown to Dyckman Street and then paddling downtown to Fourteenth."

"How far is that?"

"You'll see. We call it a half-Manhattan trip."

I figured I would introduce him to all the capabilities of the kayak and to a little extra workload, which I had become all too familiar with when Howard and I trained.

After a twenty-minute subway ride and short walk, we were at the small gravel, sand, and debris launch site. I started unpacking the two forty-five-pound bags. Tony immediately wanted to help put the boat together.

"It's best to watch me put together the first half and then you can help me with the second half."

But Tony was too impatient to watch.

"The front-half parts are marked in red and—"

"The rear half are in blue, right?"

Tony began assembling immediately and we had the job finished in no time. I was going to go through a step-by-step dry-land paddle system, but Tony seemed to learn by doing. I opted for the "get in the boat and follow me" method.

We maneuvered the boat to the edge of the river.

"Acchh!" Tony grunted as his beloved Blundstones flooded.

I took the front seat and put Tony in the back. Part of the reason simply was so Tony could see my stroke and copy it. Another reason is based on boat fit and balance. Tony is six-foot-four and almost two hundred pounds. I am five-foot-eight and a hundred and sixty-five pounds. The seventeen-foot-long "Swede-form" shape of the Klepper Aerius II has a little more buoyancy aft than in the front. A heavy front end can make for a very wet ride when paddling into the waves and cause a plowing effect when riding with waves from astern. More-over, longitudinal ribs inside the boat provide places to brace the feet and pro-vide solid contact for power and control. Ideally, we *wear* the kayak and do not just sit in it. The more we can merge our bodies with the skeleton of the kayak, the more our paddles work like the tail of a fish, directly affecting the movement of the whole animal.

Most self-taught kayakers mistakenly paddle with their arms and shoulders. This is what comes "naturally," but proper paddling form begins with the feet and travels through the legs, which pivot the hips and torso delivering the power to the paddle blade with minimum bending of the arms. It is akin to a graceful golf swing. The difference is that the instant you have reached the high point of your golf swing, you must switch into a perfect downstroke. One stroke after another, over and over and over with a minimum amount of resist-ance or variation.

To coordinate the strokes of two paddlers, to have their paddle blades opti-mally hit the water simultaneously, is like having two golfers standing parallel to each other one yard apart facing the same direction and timing their swings to hit their golf balls at the same time. In Olympic tandem kayaking, for instance— where a two-man crew paddles at a pace of more than one hundred strokes per minute for almost four minutes—one missed hit by either paddler can lose the race.

Obviously in expedition kayaking there is greater margin for error. But not as much as one might think. In long-range expedition kayaking the finish line may be many hours away. Mistimed strokes rob one of energy. Imagine constantly having to interrupt your paddle rhythm to accommodate your mate. It's like the guy who decides to cruise on a tandem bike.

Paddle clashing frays nerves.

I had taken another risk. I had left the foot-control rudder assembly that steers the boat back at the shop. Quite simply, that means that the boat is steered by body English and the thrust of the paddles alone. Forward paddle power has to be balanced with control from the hips through the contact points of the seat, feet, thighs, and lower back. Power without control and vice versa was not going to cut it.

The current was with us and the wind was coming from the side generating a quartering sea. If Tony didn't "get it" I would be in for a long day correcting the boat's course with stronger paddling and hip tilting to the right (windward) to compensate for the boat's natural tendency to "weathercock" (turn toward the wind).

A rudder can disguise or compensate for imbalances, but only in the short run. I had learned that lesson the hard way on a long crossing with a novice kayaking friend years ago. In reaching deeper and deeper over the long distance, one set of muscles in my back worked harder than the other. That side ached painfully for days after.

It is best to learn to balance strokes first, and then use the rudder as a bonus, not as a necessity.

We pushed off and slipped gently into the current.

The boat surged forward with our first strokes. In only a few moments we had found a rhythm, applied power, and had joined the momentum of the river current. The nuisance effects of weathercocking had been nullified.

Wow, I thought to myself. *I haven't said a word, and he is really moving the boat.*

This was very unusual. I had taken out countless athletic friends, clients, and associates. I had always had to make some adjustment.

I told Tony: "You seemed to have picked up my stroke very fast."

"I just keep a part of your shoulder in the corner of my eye and follow it. It's a lot like rowing."

I remembered from our first meeting at the bar that Tony had mentioned something about rowing at university. But because of the Tequila the details were a bit sketchy.

In rowing, two to eight men face backward in a slender shallow boat with their feet lashed on to small wooden boards and their butts plonked on tiny sliding seats, knees pulled tightly up against the chest. They coordinate the uncoiling of all their bodies onto the blades at the end of their oars, searching for the perfect *catch*. The catch is where the blade grabs the water and levers the boat forward like a catapult searching for a long, smooth glide. Ideally the catch is the same for each rower so that the exact same amount of pressure is exerted all along the boat. Rowing is the epitome of controlled fury.

"What did you row?"

"I won the Australia schoolboy championships in an eight and only lost once in two years at university."

The "eight" is the king of rowing. Eight men to a boat with one oar. The fastest of all blade-propelled boats in flatwater.

As we paddled, I thought to myself, *So he's got the paddle catch, timing, power, and the boat balance. Does he have long-term rhythm and perseverance?*

Competitive rowing races last about six minutes. A typical sea kayak expedition day is at least six hours. The normal stroke rate is sixty strokes per minute, like a heartbeat. Two people have to coordinate their heartbeats all day long.

We covered the twelve-mile half-Manhattan paddle in less than two hours. There was still plenty of daylight left. It was the fastest sustained paddle I had ever had. We had found that point where the boat feels like it is levitating, moving twice as fast with half the energy. This is when a double kayak is superior to a single. Where the whole is greater than the sum of its parts. It is rare when two good paddlers combine well in the same boat. Tony was a natural.

But what was his partner going to be like?

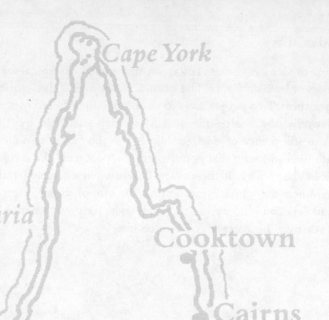

The Prodigal Son

Four months later and I had not heard a word from Tony. The shop was starting to hum with phone calls and walk-in traffic. Plenty of natural light poured into the showroom throughout the day. Spring was in the air and a new, trendy restaurant called the Coffee Shop had opened up a block away. It was owned by three models and was staffed by the same, with an emphasis on exotic racial diversity that coalesced in a Brazilian theme. I had found a new place to spend my lunchtimes and—before too long—many of my evenings. A different type of expeditioning was afoot. I had applied Tony training method number one: I got to know the bartender. Then I added one of my own: Get to know the doorman.

I was coming back from a lunchtime exploration and did a double take looking into the store window. A tall, broad-shouldered guy was standing over a two-seater. I hurried into the store and yelled "Tony!" The strong-jawed stranger turned to face me.

Déjà vu vaporized into reality and the man quizzically looked at me.

"Excuse me, I thought you were someone else."

"Did you say 'Tony'?"

"Yes, a guy about your size came in last fall wanting to—"

"Go around Australia!" he finished. "Yeah, I'm thinking of going with him."

I smiled broadly. "You must be Sam."

"No, I'm Kevin. You must be Epic."

I learned that Tony had given me a nickname and that Kevin had met Tony on the modeling circuit and then joined him for camper-vanning in southern Europe. Kevin didn't have a shred of kayaking experience but had been a competitive swimmer in his college days. Which, from the look of him, had not been too long ago.

"Tony said you could train me."

"Yes. Absolutely. Where's Tony?"

"I'm not sure. But he said something about coming back to New York for the summer."

What is it with these guys? I thought. *Are they part of some tribe of exceedingly good-looking nomads who wander the globe dreaming up big ideas and who throw people together into a kind of blender and see how it all works out?*

I immediately introduced Kevin to my father, who is always in a better mood after the selling season has arrived.

"Ahhh," he said, "another one for the Olympic team."

"Actually," I said, "this is the guy who wants to paddle with Tony. He wants me to train him."

"Ja," Dieter worried aloud, "the one who has gone AWOL."

"He's coming back soon, Mr. Stiller," Kevin promised.

That assurance bought us some training time. But I would have to wait until Sunday to start. I had no intention of pressing my luck. Leaving the shop during the day in season—and this season in particular—was verboten and I knew that. At the Klepper shop we were literally selling for our lives.

I started Kevin off with a ten-mile round trip from South Street to the Statue of Liberty. Right off the bat I realized that things were not going to be the same as they had been with Tony. Kevin's background in swimming meant he had a lot of upper body power, but he applied it in a more stop-and-go routine. He would paddle hard for a few hundred yards and stop. The he would start up again. Lurch and rest. Lurch and rest. His enthusiasm for the tour was undeniable. But he alternated his pauses with audible farts and accompanying stories. After one particularly explosive episode, he reported with unabashed pride, "They rolled down the windows in the camper van when it was snowing outside and they had to keep them down all the way to Innsbruck!"

In theory there was about a year to go before the trip. Kevin—in terms of skill—was going to have to train to be either as good as Tony or better. I worked with Kevin for a couple of weeks and then he went back to Germany. He had made decent progress but was in no way competent to paddle upward of twelve thousand miles with a partner. Unless Tony and Kevin could find a way to convert methane into a supplemental fuel source for paddling, going all the way around Australia was a dream.

A couple of weeks later Tony came breezing into the store brandishing a contraption under his arm. He acted as if no time had passed at all. He heartily greeted my father and gleefully presented his new toy.

"What do you think of it?"

"What is it?" I asked.

He put the machine down and unfolded a slender silver T-shaped steering post. He was grinning like a kid on Christmas morning. "It's a motorized skateboard to help me get around to my 'go sees.' This model can go thirty-five miles per hour. I can get a new engine for it so I can go forty."

"So, I take it you're back for a while?"

"That's right. I just moved into a flat on Twenty-third and I've got a roommate we have to get out in the kayak. How about this weekend?"

My God, I thought with exasperation. *Another one? Is this movie ever going to be cast or will it go on forever?* I had done some basic research. It was now the middle of May. I concluded that Tony & Company would have to leave just after cyclone season ended and head north out of Sydney. That would be the following March.

Then, as if reading my mind, Tony asked, "How did that ole fart Kevey-boy do? Big shoulders on that one."

"Not too bad."

Should I tell him the truth? There was still a chance that if the two of them trained together seriously for the rest of the year something could materialize. I did not want to rain on Tony's parade. I added: "It will be great when Kevin comes back and I can get you in the same boat!"

"Well, Sammy's still interested as well. I figured I will go back to Oz this winter and be ready to go by my birthday."

"When's that?"

"March eleventh."

Tony reached into his backpack and retrieved a thick manual with a light blue cover. He handed it to me. It was titled *The Coast Pilot to Australia.* "I've been reading over this, and that time seems about right."

No way! Tony did the research, too. Fantastic! He's serious. He's trying to find a way to make this work.

He gave me the book to keep.

"Thank you."

"I thought you would like it, Epic."

We took Tony's roommate on a number of excursions, including a paddle off Coney Island into the Atlantic. There was no one on the famous boardwalk and it was hard to believe that millions of people would carpet every inch of the beach in a couple of months.

Tony enjoyed taunting his friend as he donned layers of fleece and then struggled into the dreaded dry suit—a piece of equipment that makes being a contortionist practically a prerequisite. Early spring is a dangerous time. The water temperature is at its coldest, about thirty-five degrees. Falling in was not an option and yet we had to dress for that possibility. Hypothermia is the kayaker's silent killer.

We saw a seal lounging on a bell buoy about a mile offshore.

This was more like it! I was getting flashbacks to when Howard and I would go out from my apartment on Bleecker Street—which we had named the Vladivostok Training Center—for our obligatory two-hour morning paddle. Afterward we would hang up our sweat-drenched "skins" all over the apartment to dry. Your basic drysuit is a like a solid piece of skin. Nothing gets in. But nothing gets out, either.

The seal began to bark noisily at our approach. It may have been getting ancestral flashbacks to a bygone era when bizarre hooded creatures with long slender flanks skimmed toward them with a spear in one fin. The origins of kayaking had nothing to do with recreation or winning gold medals. Kayaks were built for hunting and trading and fishing. The boats were fashioned from skin and frame. Not for the sake of speed or convenience, but to emulate the sleek design of the animal they were hunting.

There are two basic categories of Eskimo kayak design. The Greenland style is very slender (less than twenty inches wide) and quite long (over seventeen feet) and shallow (less than a foot deep). It was used primarily in coastal plains, large river mouths, and the lagoons formed inside receding ice packs. It was used for day-long hunting trips and built for speed, ease of handling, and stealth. The paddler was his kayak. If capsized he rolled himself back up as easily as a fighter pilot peeling off for a dive.

Klepper boats were more akin to the Aleut Baidarka hunting and trading kayaks. They were born on the rugged coasts of Alaska where the seas were big and rough. They came in single, tandem, and even triple designs. They were fast but strong and extremely seaworthy. Current high-speed sea kayaks borrow more from Aleut shapes. Triples were popular with the Russian fur traders, who were less interested in paddling than in peddling. The Russians also invented a kayak rudder system.

The Baidarkas traveled in hundred-boat fleets for thousands of miles as far south as California and all the way to Siberia. Some were used to hunt whales. They were the long-range bombers of the kayak world.

For two months Tony's "training" consisted mainly of weekend outings with friends and colleagues from overseas. Being possessed of a slightly sadistic sense of humor, his favorite pastime became baiting them by suggesting a kayak trip "as a lark" and then reveling in the grueling fatigue that would overtake them halfway through an average paddle.

The weather warmed and we started going out on weekday evenings. It was becoming more clear with each outing that the "larks" he was having with his friends were very different from the talkless, sustained sprints he and I would have. Our communicating was done by feel—the feel of the boat moving efficiently through the water. For the first time I was beginning to think that Tony & Company might actually have a shot at the goal.

One afternoon Tony came to me in a dismal mood.

"Sam's going to law school," he announced somberly. "He can't go on the trip."

"And Kevin?"

Tony shrugged and his shoulders drooped. "I haven't heard from him, have you?"

"No. But he'll probably saunter in any day now."

Tony nodded. Then he asked: "Would you like to go?"

My mind went blank. I had been verbally knocked out by the weight of the question. As my brain rebooted, frivolous thoughts of a long vacation were replaced by a much more sobering equation: Logic said, *I* fill in *his* blanks. I add elements of practicality (P) and experience (E) to his innate confidence (C), daring (D), and naïveté (N).

$$P + E + C + D + N = ?$$

The question lingered in my mind. Was that enough? What if this is not simple arithmetic but more like algebra or calculus?

There was not a lot of time to solve the equation. I felt like I was being asked to volunteer to be drafted.

"I'll have to think about that one, Tony."

"Take your time, mate. I'll be back in two weeks. I've got work in London."

He took another book out of his pack. Hermann Hess's *Narcissus and Goldmund*. He handed it to me.

"Here's a read to keep you busy."

Tony vanished out the door. He left me with a question of a lifetime and only the back of a book to read as a clue: "Hesse's novel of two medieval men, one quietly content with his religion and monastic life, the other in fervent search for more worldly salvation. The conflict between flesh and spirit, between emotional and contemplative man, was a life study for Hess. It is a theme that transcends all time."

Was I the monk? Is that what he was suggesting. Is that how I came across to him? And worse: Is he right?!

The inner jacket describes Narcissus: An ascetic monk: a rigorous intellectual, remains in the monastery to become an abbot: the epitome of the masculine, analytical mind. That sounded more like my father. Life is learned through books, through study, through exchange of story and teaching. Dieter had helped a lot of others live their lives of adventure and then absorbed *their* stories. Dieter had stamped a lot of passports. But never his own. Was it age, circumstance, the business, having a wife and kid? Had he always been like that?

I glanced over to the five-foot-high triangular easel that my father meticulously constructed thirty years ago for boat shows and the New York World's Fair. On it was the July 24, 1957, issue of *Life* magazine. There was a sun-drenched, beaming thirty-five-year-old Dr. Hans Lindemann sitting in his Klepper Aerius II with a paddle in his hands. He had just landed in St. Thomas, nearly four thousand miles from where he had begun in Portugal. He had just crossed the Atlantic Ocean solo.

My father had filled with pride when he described how he had assembled Lindemann's boat for the Deutsche Engineering Museum in Munich and how many passersby at the World's Fair asked if he was the guy on the easel.

"Are *you* Dr. Lindemann?"

In 1964 that question would have still made sense. My father would have been thirty-two years old.

I had just turned thirty, and now customers and clients were asking me the same question. Therein lay my answer. By God! *This* Stiller was going to use the passport!

Tony and the memory of Hans Lindemann had ignited my spirit, but my mind rushed back to put out the fire. Over the next few days, I started learning all I could about what I was being asked to do. I queried an Australian outfitter named Al Bakker about the undertaking and received this fax response:

> If Tony is an Australian I presume he will have advised you of the serious-ness of your undertaking to paddle around Australia. Sailing the southeast-ern trades from Rockhampton north will be fun but the surf landings on thousands of miles of unprotected coastline won't be. We used our Klep-pers for a 7-day trip up the outside of Hinchinbrook Island in Queensland for a couple of years and often had 3–4 meter seas inside the reef which gives you a hell of a rough landing (so bring lots of rudders). I have only paddled sections of the coast and have taken Kleppers around the SW of tip of Tasmania in 5–6 meter swells but had an escape route there.

Surf . . . Surf . . . Surf . . . Surf. I wrote the word over and over on the black-board of my mind, hoping that sheer repetition might help ease my anxiety. My most thrilling but harrowing moments in a kayak have been in surf. I have always considered surf nature's hammer: brutal and powerful and unsentimental. The beach was the anvil and the kayak was in between. Time it right and you ride on the elephant's back galloping down Mt. Kilimanjaro. Time it wrong and you are crushed. It was that simple.

After Hawaii, Australia was arguably the most famous surfing location in the world. At the end of the movie *Point Break,* Patrick Swayze—playing the char-acter Bodi—commits a kind of surfer's hari-kari when he takes his life on the ultimate joyride on a storm wave on Bells Beach in southern Australia. As for-gettable as the movie was I had a hard time erasing from my mind the image of Swayze free-falling forty stories down the face of that murderous wave.

My anxiety went deeper than movie images.

I was afraid of the surf and I had been trying to come to terms with it for years. I frequently had nightmares about waves. I suspect a lot of my fear is based on an experience I had as a child. As a four-year-old, I had been put on the tall shoulders of a neighbor and walked out into the surf at Sandy Hook in New Jersey. Waves broke on his stomach. He laughed in frolic and defiance. It was fun until *it* came: the sledgehammer wave. I was knocked from his shoulders and tumbled through the surf and bludgeoned to shore. I was hacking and coughing and spitting, and my back was shredded, and crimson smears of blood were traced on the sand.

I have never forgotten the panic I felt.

Other anxieties preyed on my mind as well. Less than a year earlier a friend and client, Eric Konheim, had died in the surf off the coast of Oregon in a whitewater kayak I had sold him. His body was found with only half of his two-piece dry suit on. The cause of death was determined to be hypothermia. Eric was an experienced kayaker. In previous expeditions he had paddled the entire coasts of Belize and Venezuela in his Klepper. Like Tony, he would work for six months as a man-with-a-van moving service and quit to kayak the rest of the year. The Klepper Shop became a kind of home away from home for him. It was not unusual for Eric to ship his bedraggled Klepper bag to us out of the blue for storage, only to have him show up weeks later to pick it up en route to yet another impromptu expedition. My father came to tolerate the imposition with weary resignation.

"You could have put the bags in a strong box," my father would point out routinely.

"I know, Mr. Stiller," answered Eric. But the Klepper bags kept coming anyway.

I thought a lot about Eric. I returned to my mental calculations. From my experience (E) I knew that the Klepper Aerius II—as venerable a craft as it was—had not been designed for surf launching and landing. It had been designed in southern Germany for the purpose of paddling and sailing on big lakes, broad rivers, and sheltered seacoasts. Numerous expeditions on the open sea, however, had shown it capable way beyond the designer's original intentions. But most of those expeditions had been pretty much direct A-to-B affairs. Sailing a straight line across the Atlantic is a bit like an international flight: one takeoff and one landing and a whole bunch of airports to choose from.

On the other hand, landing a fully loaded Klepper onto exposed Australian coastline where the sea travels unimpeded for thousands of miles was more akin to gently dropping a lumbering 747 onto a short jungle airstrip known for its ferocious lateral wind shear. The Australian coastline is a nightmare of tightly coiled inlets and rocky coves and sheer rock cliff faces and bays as huge and forbidding as Saharan deserts. Knowing *where* to land the Klepper was going to be a more daunting challenge than knowing *how* to land. Prevention would be 90 percent of the cure. The ancient blacksmiths that hammered out the Australian coastline had been chipping and pounding away for countless millennia. We were going to try to dodge the hammer blows. I doubted we could avoid them all.

I had opened Pandora's box. It got worse.

I contacted a major in the Australian Special Boat Squadron, a specialized military service branch like our U.S. Navy Seals. (The Australians used more Kleppers for military service than anyone else.) I gave him the basic lowdown on the trip and asked for any details he thought might be relevant in terms of planning the expedition.

He confirmed that the total mileage of Australian coastline was thirty-six thousand kilometers, or about twenty thousand miles if one followed the coast literally. The perfect circle number was nearly ten thousand miles.

"Is that it?" I asked warily. "What about the winds or currents? Anything you can tell that I won't find in a book? Anything unusual?"

In his typically understated fashion the good major mentioned that he had "sent some of the boys out recently to spend some time with the Fremantle Doctor on the West Coast." Then he paused as if lost in thought. "Couldn't find 'em for a few days. That the kind of thing you mean?"

I thanked him. The Fremantle Doctor is a very persistent, strong local wind near Perth, Australia, that occasionally comes and blows things offshore *farther* offshore. Sometimes a whole lot farther. Forty knots of wind speed is normal. A kayak cannot make any progress against forty knots (strong gale) when paddling at full power, and drifts two knots in the wind's direction when idle. A fifteen-minute rest and you lose half mile. I took the major's tone to mean that the open sea was no place for a two-man kayak.

Maybe he was right.

On Howard Rice's expedition he had advanced within eyeshot of Cape Horn and decided to make a final run for it only to have fifty knots of wind blow him four miles backward.

The more I fed the accumulating data into the equation, the more ludicrous it got. It seemed like it would take a lifetime to get around Australia. But then I learned from John Dowd, the author of a sea-kayaking bible, and a Kiwi (a New Zealander), that countryman Paul Caffyn had actually completed a year-long solo circumnavigation a few years back.

Dowd reminded me of an article about the trip that had appeared in his magazine, *Sea Kayaker*. The article featured the picture of a man who appeared literally shriveled to the bone. He looked like a poor wretch you might expect to see on the streets of Bangladesh. Under the picture ran the following headline: "Australia: A Nice Place for a Holiday."

It was a very sobering read. The article was a laundry list of the disasters and unavoidable hazards that plagued the kayaker paddling around Australia. Caffyn had battled massive tides, whirlpools, enormous waves, monsoons, and packs of sharks who took nips at his rudder.

I had a dim memory of having read the article. But I remembered also—for some odd reason—having discounted its ominous and cautionary tone as probably exaggerated. Now I poured over the article like a Talmudic scholar, having to swallow and to digest its every word.

I wanted to throw up.

The truth is I was both inspired and appalled. Someone had actually circumnavigated Australia in a kayak—in less than a year! Suddenly we had our "realistic" benchmark. Bravado chimed in: *Hey! If some craggly Kiwi can do it in one of those skinny Greenland-style kayaks made of fiberglass then we can do it in less time in the Klepper! Yeah!*

But wait a minute. What's this??!

I discovered a loophole in his trip. Most of his expedition was done with a lightly laden boat with *direct land support* or *food drop-offs*. In my mind that was like a backpacker claiming to have "lived off the land" by hiking from one trailside diner to the next.

Klepper expeditions carry their support with them.

Arrogance harmonized with bravado and sang: *We will do it in less than a year, and fully self-contained! We will be Lewis and Clark but without a wagon train!*

The Klepper was designed to hold a lot of gear. Up to half a ton if necessary. Dowd considered its payload capacity a primary advantage over other craft. On his island-hopping expedition from Trinidad to Miami, Dowd fished, hunted, and made his own fresh water using only equipment that he carried with him in his Klepper.

An expedition mantra of Hans Lindemann was, Do not accept assistance. Lindemann was a member of the *autogenic* school of expedition training. Quite simply it means repeating something over and over again until you believe it. His mantra became my mantra.

No assistance. No assistance. No assistance.

Of course, even the most Spartan expedition must make certain allowances. On one expedition Hans had packed—among other provisions—sixty tins of condensed milk and *sixty tins of dark beer.*

We would use what we could carry and find along the way. I silently scoffed at Dowd's suggestion that we should try an average fifteen miles a day and expect to complete the trip in two years.

In my mind the virtues of practicality, respect, and a healthy fear—virtues that had been part of my personal pantheon—had been swept aside by the rush of the *challenge*. It was intoxicating. I had a purpose now. A goal. I could see it as clearly as a sprinter can see the tape at the finish line. There was something else bubbling and surging in my gut, too: *pride*. Honestly, it was a new sensation.

I visited one of my mentors, who—besides being one of the best personal trainers in the country—was an expert on pride. His name is Radu Teodorescu and he is known affectionately in New York as the "trainer of stars." He is a short man but has an enormously powerful build and a hulking, barrel chest. He emigrated to the United States from the University of Bucharest in Romania during the Cold War. One of his responsibilities in Romania was the physical training of promising young athletes. Olympic gymnast Nadia Comaneci was one of his peers.

After defecting he moved to New York City and drove a cab. He worked in a local gym run by Russian defectors until he earned enough money to quit driving a cab and open his own gym.

He earned his reputation as the "toughest trainer in town." Bianca Jagger came to him to rehabilitate after a car accident. Not only did she rehabilitate, she worked herself into the best shape of her life. Word leaked about this tyrannical Romanian who demanded hard work but worked miracles. Then they all came. Models like Cindy Crawford. And famous celebrities, including Calvin Klein.

One day Sandy Hill Pittmann—the ex-wife of MTV founder, Bob Pittmann—came to me and said she wanted to kayak around Manhattan. She asked me if she could bring her trainer.

I said sure.

Radu had been training Sandy for her quest to be the first woman to climb the highest mountain peaks on each continent. Unfortunately, Sandy would later earn a kind of infamy as a member of the ill-fated expedition up Everest that was the subject of Jon Krakauer's best-selling book, *Into Thin Air*.

After twenty-two miles of paddling, Radu confessed, "Airik, I'm a little tired. I do not get tired!"

Since then, I had become a regular at his gym, where I found an outlet for my office-squelched energy. Radu's regimen was based on a system of jumping, kicking, sprinting, calisthenics, weights, stair climbing, and boxing all blended together. The gym was a haven for me. I had run track and played soccer in high school and then learned to box. In college I added Tae Kwon Do to the mix. The Radu workout was continuous physical nostalgia for me.

I ran the idea past Tony of him and me training together at the gym. I learned that Tony had very different ideas about what constituted a fitness regimen. In fact, in the entire time we were training I only managed to haul Tony to one of the classes. He hated exercise classes. He was a natural athlete. For Tony it was not the repetition. It was the new experience, the new challenge.

Ever since that first trip around Manhattan, Radu had become an avid kayaker. One day I asked him what he thought about the idea of me accompanying Tony on the expedition. His answer was characteristically blunt and direct.

"Airik, you must go. Never will you find anyone who will do this again."

A short time later I called Howard. I needed a friend to push me over the edge.

"Howard, I think I'm going to do it. Some Kiwi did it years ago in a Nordkapp with land support."

"I know," he said. "Paul Caffyn had also paddled all the way around England and New Zealand before that."

Howard knew that the two most accomplished expedition kayak designs at the time were the British-designed Nordkapp and the German-made Klepper. Ironically, Howard had one-upped a young German kayak racer by beating him around Cape Horn in a Nordkapp.

Jorn Werkman had flown to southern Chile in a desperate last-minute attempt to catch Howard after learning that he was attempting the first solo rounding of the Horn. Days into his expedition he almost drowned after being tangled up in sea kelp. Jorn managed to catch up with Howard at the Glacier Hollandia on the western end of the Beagle Channel, but then fell dangerously far behind in steep *following* seas (surging waves coming from behind).

In a graciously sportsmanlike gesture, Howard—having rounded the Cape already—stopped and joined Jorn's boat to his and formed a catamaran. The two tandem-sailed the last fifty miles in six hours back to Puerto Williams, the Chilean naval base where it all began.

"I thought those (the Kleppers) boats were old and slow," Werkmann admitted afterward.

But Howard knew. There are few people alive who know more about the Klepper and what it can do than Howard Rice.

Howard also knew that the longest "expedition" I had ever completed was a one-week two-hundred-mile paddle in the Chesapeake Bay. He didn't try and talk me out of it.

"I understand it's a little windy down there. I'll make you some special sails."

The hell with the math! We're going around!

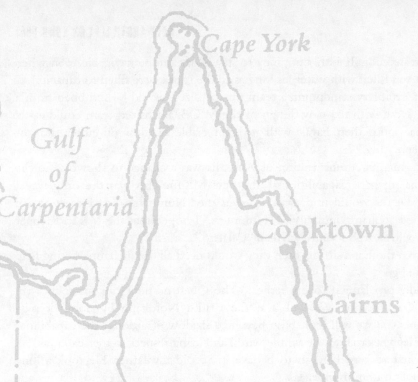

Berlin Wall

"What does your father think, mate?"

"He doesn't know yet."

Dieter Stiller was the final hurdle. Or was it a wall? This journey could only work with his and Klepper's support. We needed a boat. I knew we needed the latest military model of the Klepper MK13. Special Forces teams were routinely getting creamed in the surf until the new MK13 arrived.

The traditional Klepper was famous for its ease of assembly and its exceptional seaworthiness, provided by two internally mounted air sponsons (seventeen-foot-long air tubes with four-inch diameters) that were sewn into the hull just above the waterline. When deflated, they allowed the boat to be easily disassembled because there was no tension around the frame. When inflated, they provide a unique flare shape—like a Hershey's Kiss turned upside down. This gave the boat unparalleled lateral stability when the boat heeled on its side. Theoretically this addition made the boat unsinkable.

Surf zones are notorious for their unpredictability and rough surf. A boat in a surf zone can fill up with seawater almost instantly; the smack of a big wave can pop the spray skirt off and keep the water pouring in. A Klepper can hold over 150 gallons of water. That translates to 1,200 pounds.

The problem with the boats wasn't that they were sinking but that they were swamping (filling up to the coaming and becoming unnavigable).

The new design of MK13 added a second set of sponsons just below the first set to create enough extra buoyancy to stay afloat and be navigable even when the boat was filled with water (as long as all the tubes were filled to capacity).

From a military standpoint, a team that capsized would be scrubbed from a mission. Now, with the new design of the MK13, a capsized team could easily climb back into their kayak with no appreciable net loss of either time or equipment.

A two-man circumnavigation of Australia was a chance to showcase to the world the superior capabilities of the new MK13. This was the only way I thought Dieter would understand. Just as the "Hummvees" in Desert Storm would find civilian popularity as "Hummers," I hoped that the MK13 Klepper kayak would morph into the civilian "Quattro."

At seven thousand dollars each they would need all the niche marketing help they could get.

I boldly proclaimed to my father: "The Quattro and I can make the trip around Oz a reality! We will beat the British Nordkapp by doing it self-contained. *And* we will reestablish beyond a shadow of a doubt the capabilities of the Klepper kayak to the whole world and bring respect to the sea kayak."

I pitched so hard I began to believe it. So did my father. He took a long thoughtful pull on his pipe.

"We need to find a way to get you a boat, then."

I woke up the next morning light-headed with anticipation, but also with the burden of no longer having the familiar old excuses. On top of all that, I had added the additional weight of family honor.

My father grew up in Rosenheim, Germany, where the boats were hand-made. He had worked for the Klepper Kayak Company his whole life. He moved to the United States as a young man and opened his own Klepper shop. Almost single-handedly he spent the better part of his adult life popularizing a sport that to mainstream Americans was synonymous with canoeing.

"The kayak is more stable because you sit in it and have a lower center of gravity," he would explain. The myriad design intricacies and technical subtleties of the kayak and kayaking were music to Dieter's ears. "It is easier to paddle because you paddle evenly with two blades instead of one. It glides through the water better because of a superior hull shape that has a lower profile and is less affected by the wind."

Many of the largest canoe manufacturing outfits in the United States approached him with offers. He always firmly refused. He stood by his guns and watched the sea kayaking industry grow. He helped outfit John Dowd on his trans-Caribbean expedition.

Over time, however, the growing popularity of mass-produced fiberglass-hull kayaks—and then much cheaper plastic—had eroded into the Klepper business. Their expensive "made in Germany" price barred them from mainstream acceptance. Dieter didn't see the American-based wave of competition coming.

The price for decent day-trip kayaks has dropped to less than one thousand dollars. Who needed to go across the ocean for a boat that could cost four or five times that amount and required special handling and assembly? The new mass-produced plastic jobs were easy, fun, simple, and required absolutely no assembly or maintenance.

Paddles included.

Thirty-five years after gambling on a dream by opening up a Klepper shop in the heart of Manhattan, Dieter Stiller was very likely about to go under. He needed a home run. Tony and I were in the on-deck circle taking our swings.

Smack! Smack! Tony and I alternated sweaty hits on the seventy-pound Everest bag that hung in the basement of the Klepper shop. We were finishing our two-hour circuit training for the umpteenth time and hitting the heavy bag with our new wooden handmade shark clubs.

"Aim for the corner, mate!"

Smack!

After dozens of aborted attempts over a few months, I had finally found a way to "formalize" Tony's training in a way he *almost* liked. Howard and I had worked a more steady step-by-step weight program to build up his core strength. He had sailed and paddled for years, but had done little resistance training. Tony was strong from his years rowing and climbing, but traditional weightlifting bored him to death. Training had to be made relevant for him.

I moved some boxes around in the basement of the shop and constructed a makeshift gym. I rigged an Alden indoor rowing machine so it could be used to simulate alternating one-arm pulling actions and then reversed to work alternating pushing-muscle groups. I designed it so the torso was able to twist with the movement.

Then there was an original "total gym" machine station, which I had used to rehabilitate a severely separated shoulder. There we did cable flies, pullovers, more alternating pushing and pulling movements with stomach exercises.

We did pull-ups on the door jams and incline push-ups with feet raised on the kayak shipping cartons. We jumped from station to station, trying to repeat the circuit at least three times. We finished with the boxing duo. Heavy bag and jump rope.

But a routine is still a routine, and I was not surprised when one day Tony wandered in with an eight-foot-long piece of three-by-three wood. Without any explanation he promptly cut the wood in half.

"There you go, mate!" he said as he offered me his homemade nunchaku.

"Holy shit." Protruding from the head of the club was a very lethal seven-inch nail. Tony had improvised his first T shark club.

"No need for 'bang sticks' when you've got one of these!" He tapped the club in his palm like a riot cop.

In his excellent book on sea kayaking John Dowd is quite explicit about the utility of a "bang stick" to repel sharks. The average bang stick is a three-foot-long steel rod that holds a twelve-gauge shotgun shell at one end. The idea is that one waits for the sharks to roll close enough to impress the business end of the stick against his snout and then—*bang!*

Did Tony think he was going to repel an attacking shark with a stick and a nail? I wondered.

But the point was taken. There was no way getting around it. Sharks—shark attacks to be precise—and Australia were synonymous. Australia had the top two: the great white and the tiger shark. Australia had more documented shark attacks and fatalities than anywhere else in the world. Most scientists and experts insist that reports of unprovoked attacks by sharks have been greatly exaggerated. I really wanted to believe them.

As a commemorative gift of our upcoming adventure a client who designs for the Gap created a T-shirt with the words *Aussie Challenge* in script across the front. There is also a map of Australia with a great white shark covering it from coast to coast. We sold the shirts to help raise money for the trip.

"What are you going to do about the sharks?"

It was almost always the first question asked about the expedition.

Unlike surf and rough seas, I had had absolutely no direct experience with sharks. I didn't know what to fear. To me, worrying about sharks in Australian waters was like an astronaut in a space station worrying about meteors.

I was more concerned with the likelihood of more mundane catastrophes, like how we would make water if beached and marooned in the vast western desert sections of Australia.

In my wanderings I had found a source for a reverse-osmosis desalinator. It cost twelve hundred dollars wholesale.

Tony happily agreed that I would be in charge of outfitting the expedition. I would hunt up all the things we needed and Tony would foot the bill. The truth is he wanted no part of the preparation and packing. I had the feeling that if I had left things up to Tony we might be equipped with nothing more than a few granola bars and a tube of Chapstick.

In the truest sense of the term Tony and I were on an unsponsored expedition. No company or corporation would provide cash support. We agreed we did not want the burdens and obligations that inevitably come with corporate sponsorships. Plus it was far too late to court any potential suitors with a serious proposal. In an effort to cut costs, I began some serious marathon work on the phone. I pummeled and badgered every industry connection and contact I had to get equipment donated. If not donated, at least purchased at wholesale cost.

Klepper Germany came through big time with the donation of a Quattro.

My thanks were beyond belief, and I told them so.

"We usually don't do this kind of thing" was their grudging bon voyage.

The Voyager company sent us heavy-duty waterproof bags with a specially designed "air bleeding" valve that allowed us to fill them up and squeeze out excess air so we could fit more of them into the boat. Nike and Speedo agreed to send us an assortment of mismatched swim shorts and T-shirts.

The Power Bar company sent ten cases of their high-energy bars.

With each new piece of equipment I made a check mark on my list of expedition essentials. There were still many items—many expensive items—to go.

There are very few long expeditions in history that have gone unsponsored. In fact, most expeditions spend years trying to acquire sponsors. Finances are critical to the success of any expedition. Even a rather routine expedition can run up a tab in the hundred-thousand-dollar range. And higher. *Much* higher. I had worked out a cost based on being able to purchase what we needed and what I thought we could get donated and figured that something in the twenty-thousand-dollar range would be adequate.

But the simple truth is that the cost of the trip would come down to what we had at the time. No more and no less.

I was in no way financially prepared for the cost of the trip. Tony understood this. My only advantage was that I was single, I had no kids, and I didn't pay a mortgage. To save on rent I moved out of my apartment to "squat" in the vacated floor of the building over the Klepper shop.

Sales from T-shirts and commissions on boat sales were all I had to get my plane ticket and as much spending money as I could muster.

Adding to the problem, Tony's accountant had recently told him that he was going to have to come up with a lot more tax money for the following year. As a result Tony radically downsized his expectations about what was and was not necessary for outfitting the expedition. I had to lobby for almost every acquisition. Tony had become my de facto sponsor.

Meanwhile we also had to maintain a regular training regimen.

Paddles and workouts alternated daily and from week to week. In order to make more money Tony felt compelled to take on more modeling jobs, so that our "routine" would be broken as often as not. We did our ocean training off the Hamptons in eastern Long Island.

Radu had a second gym in East Hampton and graciously allowed us to crash there.

Every so often we would launch from Calvin Klein's spectacular oceanfront estate and paddle for one hour straight offshore until we could no longer see land, then make a left and paddle for another hour. Another left turn and we would head back toward shore. A last left and back to the beach.

That same summer Tony was hired for a Calvin Klein shoot for Bloomingdale's department store.

Six months until launch and the Quattro finally arrived.

My father ceremoniously opened the box. I wanted to tear it open like a Christmas present but I had to let Dieter go through the step-by-step. It was his contribution to us and it meant a lot. Tony stood by attentively. Half an hour later it was assembled and what a sight! I started to understand how our clients felt. Olive green canvas deck with four paddle pockets, four toggle handles, and a half-inch black lifeline around the perimeter. A black, keel-stripped, reinforced Perrelli-tire rubber hull. A freshly varnished mountain-ash frame with sparkling anodized aluminum fittings that hold the whole affair together.

Eighty years of Klepper design evolution at our feet and it was ours!

Spray cover and rudder included.

Tony had suggested naming the boat *Southern Cross* after the constellation by the same name, mainly visible in the Southern Hemisphere. It is also the sequence of stars found on the Australian national flag. I grinned in agreement. The Southern Cross expedition was officially born.

The acquisition of *Southern Cross*—with all of the accessories and including two specially made carbon fiber paddles that I acquired from the Werner Paddle company—helped ease Tony's resistance to the pricey acquisition of the desalinator and the handheld Global Positioning Satellite system (GPS).

Tony was aware of how much the boat had cost and he freed up some of his money for some of man's modern inventions that could give us a modern chance.

We were not ancient Polynesian Sea canoeists who traveled thousands of miles in open sea by the feel of the waves through the seat of their loincloths. We rode subways and ate at McDonald's. A GPS could tell us where we were within three hundred feet at the push of a button. It used over twenty satellites placed in orbit by the U.S. Defense Department to triangulate a position anywhere on earth. We were offered a chance to get a Magellan model GPS. The only one that was waterproof at the time. I knew we could have some long open-sea crossings and knowing where we were would be vital.

I also thought we needed an EPIRB (an emergency locator beacon). Litton Industries had just come up with a heavy-duty version that used two frequencies instead of just one. One for aircraft and one for satellites. I ordered one for seven hundred dollars.

Tony thought we were going too far.

I looked into some brand new Gore-Tex bivvy sacks that had a mini-tent-like arch built into the area around the head and shoulders. Gore-Tex is waterproof and breathes at the same time. They *are* more expensive than everyday bivvy sacks. But I was convinced the price difference was negligible considering the inherent advantages.

"We don't need tents!" argued Tony. "We just need a couple of regular bivvy sacks!"

Tony was referring to the body bag mountain climbers slip into when sleeping on rock ledges a thousand feet above ground. "The boats have plenty of room, and the beaches will, too. Besides, tents are too heavy and you're not going to want to pitch a tent every night, mate."

I tried to compromise. "Tony, I can get us some Gore-Tex bivvy sacks. Do you want me to order you one?"

"I'm happy with my own."

"Are you sure?"

"Yes."

It was around Thanksgiving when I took Tony to the airport for his trip back to Australia. I felt we had come a long way and were going to do just fine. I would be joining him in three months.

A few weeks later I sent a fax to Tony asking him to pick up the British admiralty charts for the first thousand miles of our trip. A contact I had, had fallen through, and I thought they would be cheaper in Sydney, anyway.

The fax I got back read: "We don't need charts, mate. I've been talking to people and they say we can potter up the coast and stay in the Surf clubhouses. They're everywhere here."

He must be joking, I thought. I showed the fax to my father and a couple of client friends and we all got a laugh out of it.

"Quite a sense of humor he has," Dieter chuckled.

I found out the specific chart numbers and even a place in Sydney that sells them. I faxed the information to Tony and received his response the next day.

"We don't need charts. We just keep Australia on our left!"

"They offered me a contract."

"Who did?"

"Donna Karan."

"That's great, right?"

"I could almost retire with it but I'm not going to take it; I wouldn't be able to go on the trip."

A modeling contract changes the variable, "go see" life of a model into highly paid steady work with a commitment to one designer for a set number of years. Donna Karan had recently started her men's line of clothing and really liked Tony. The designer usually needs to make a very substantial offer to override what a good working model can make. She had. The trip could have been over within a few scribbles of the pen. Tony would have been set for life financially.

Tony had turned down an opportunity of a lifetime for a *different*—maybe a more important—opportunity of a lifetime.

We were committed.

A client from New Zealand had heard about our trip, wanted to buy some T-shirts, and sent a quote that had been read at her wedding ceremony. It is a quote from H. W. Murray: "Until one is committed, there is some hesitancy, the chance to draw back, always ineffectiveness. Concerning all acts of initiative (and creation) there is one elementary truth, the ignorance of which calls countless ideas and splendid plans: that the moment one definitely commits oneself, providence moves too."

I had carte blanche to pick up whatever materials I saw fit to and I painstakingly weighed the options. Howard came into town around Christmas and delivered the specially built mast and sails for the trip. His lifelong passion was sailing. He assembled the new mast on *Southern Cross*.

"The mast is double-thick aluminum alloy. It's not going to bend."

Howard and I had spent an entire summer sailing regular Klepper sail rigs in high winds. We'd bent a number of the stock masts.

"The sails are extra-thick cloth," Howard reassured me.

Usually, Klepper sail rigs had a larger mainsail that the rear paddler controlled with a long boom and the mainsheet (line that controls the sail) attached to the end. The forward paddler controlled a smaller jib sail that was connected to a forestay on the top deck near the bow of the boat. This was the normal sport-sailing rig based on a sloop rig designed for recreational sailing.

"It looks like they are the same size."

"They are! So you can sail better wing to wing off the wind."

Howard explained that this configuration would keep the boat balanced bet-ter in high seas. He had shortened the mast and reduced the size of the mainsail. A fifty-five-square-foot rig had become less than forty.

"You can reef [make the sail smaller] it quickly; it has no shroud lines [lines that go from the top of the mast to the side of the boat to keep the mast from popping out] and you strike it all down with the pull of this one pin." Howard sat in the front seat and demonstrated.

"You can be paddling in less than a minute." He rolled up the sail and mast into a tight tube and attached it to the side deck of the boat.

"Wow," was about all I could say.

Howard had obviously thought long and hard about our expedition. A lot harder than I had—at least as far as sailing was concerned. Tony had emphatically said that this was a "paddling trip." Howard saw it the other way around.

Lindemann had primarily sailed across the Atlantic. "You'll be getting trade winds between twenty and twenty-five knots throughout the Great Barrier Reef. You'll be able to make up for any lost time."

He rubbed his chin thoughtfully. "I'm going to make you another mast just in case."

Howard and Dieter, two of the most detail-oriented people I knew, helped me sort out the two hundred square feet of gear that lay in back of the store. The booty included canisters and containers of every shape and size, stoves, bivvy sacks, sleeping bags, camping mattresses, GPS, rifle-length reverse-osmosis hand-pumped desalinator, spare parts, tools, clothes for all climates except arctic, shoes, compasses, night-lights, flashlights, batteries, battery rechargers, Power Bars, first-aid kit, flares, life jackets, ropes, cameras, Walkmans, sails, and on and on and on. Almost everything doubled up because of the "what if we lose one" syndrome.

My father spent hours gathering the materials and tools for my repair kit.

Howard systematically prioritized and laid out a LIFO (last in, first out) system of packing.

"Things you use every day should be easiest to get to."

On New Year's I received a fax from Tony: "Our place (in Bondi) is great, with the possibility of leaving the boat at the beach or at the lifeguard club. I am already up to 205 lbs. I've drunk, eaten, and exercised like a mad man since arriving. So weight is no problem. All is well, can't wait to go. This is really a major adventure but I guess we'll go one day at a time and you never know. Have a Happy New Year!"

I had fattened up as well. I was almost 180 pounds and was sporting the makings of a double chin. An average paddling day can burn five thousand calories. It is very difficult to bring or eat that much food (four Big Macs a day). We would be running constant calorie deficits. We could expect to lose thirty pounds in three months. Tony and I had high metabolisms and we would need every pound we could add. When the body runs out of fat, it starts going "catabolic" and eats muscle tissue.

Howard went home to Michigan and I felt that everything was shipshape and *in Ordnung*—a German term for "neatness" that I was all too familiar with. Another Australian client friend of mine named Martin had found a deal and reserved two seats on Qantas Airlines for a February 20 departure. Martin was a slightly older working model and was flying back to Australia to see his sister who was having a baby.

I got my hair cut to a nearly bald #1.

Less than five weeks to go.

"When are you going, Eric?"

Nicole was the shapely black Canadian bartender at the Coffee Shop. I had stopped in after an evening kayak with rocker David Lee Roth. I knew her but I expected that her interest in me was primarily to get to Dave. I introduced her to Dave. Almost unimpressed, she turned to me and asked me about the trip.

"In about a month," I answered.

"Let's go out for some sushi sometime. My treat." She smiled at me sweetly. "I've got to go. Nice to meet you, Dave."

Dave grinned. "Well, well, well." I could tell from his expression that he fully expected me to take Nicole up on her offer.

I cursed my timing. Or lack thereof.

Dave made a donation to the Southern Cross expedition and I was able to purchase my plane ticket. I did take Nicole up on that sushi dinner. I didn't know when I would be in the company of women again. No matter how far into the crystal ball I looked, I didn't see any.

We went out a few times. In the back of my mind I kept thinking about the trip. *How could I get something started with Nicole if I am going to be leaving soon?*

Nicole came by on my last night and we watched *Apocalypse Now* on the shop video. Later I tentatively kissed her.

She said: "Don't start what you can't finish."

And so I started.

Martin came by the next morning in a limousine provided by his modeling agency. I was able to put all five green duffel bags containing the Southern Cross expedition in the trunk of the black Lincoln stretch. Friends and family wished tearful good-byes. The limousine pulled away and I looked back at the Klepper Kayak Shop on Union Square for the last time.

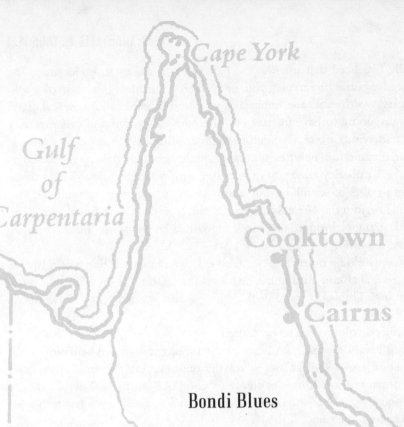

Bondi Blues

Nine thousand miles and two airlines and several movies and countless trays of plasticized food and endless bags of peanuts and half a world later . . .

Martin had fallen fast asleep with the aid of some concoction that zoo vets use to tranquilize rambunctious elephants. I hadn't been so lucky. The spell of Nicole's calming charm from the night before—*was it only last night? it felt like last year*—had broken. I was restless and fidgety with anxiety and spooked by countless misgivings.

The movie *Apocalypse Now* was respooling in my mind. I was going to try to circumnavigate Australia in a kayak with a person I barely knew who believed that you did not need nautical charts for such an undertaking. Tony was insane. I was paddling upriver in search of my Aussie Kurtz. I felt like I was in one of Robert Duvall's helicopters about to be dropped on a beach in Nam. We were going to try to paddle over ten thousand miles in a seventeen-foot-long wood and canvas kayak originally designed for holidays in Europe. The Australian coastline is a surfer's paradise but a kayaker's nightmare. We would have to maintain a daily average comparable to a paddle around Manhattan *plus* a side trip to the Statue of Liberty. We could not afford to start too slowly nor rest too much because the distance to make up would become too difficult.

The more I thought about it the more I expected an air sickness bag to drop from the overhead bin.

Actually, I realized that this was the part that was easiest to understand. The complicated logistics of carrying and/or acquiring our fuel (an estimated 3 million calories' worth) and our water (almost one thousand gallons) was staggering. We were going to have to steer clear of both monsoons and cyclones, race with the tradewinds, make a dangerous night crossing of the monstrous Gulf of Carpentaria, camp on beaches notorious for crocodiles, delicately maneuver through the Kimberley labyrinth of monster whirlpools, paddle at least a thousand miles parallel to scorching-hot uninhabited desert, meet up with the Fremantle Doctor, join the Great Southern Ocean, cross the Great Australian Bight, and travel straight through the most renowned great white shark breeding ground in the world.

Then we would be home free . . . almost. If we ran even a few weeks late we ran the very real risk of hitting the next cyclone season. All of this at the speed of a slow jog. Think of running the New York City marathon crawling on hands and knees.

I had indeed volunteered to be drafted.

I realized I was becoming *too* aware of the problems we would encounter. Yet the expedition had a shot at success for the one intangible I could never have prepared or packed for: Tony had plenty of good old-fashioned *luck*.

I will assume his luck tickets are interchangeable. It'll be fine. Tony is just pulling my leg. Of course we'll use maps.

This is going to be a great adventure!

"Are we there yet, mate?"

Martin was bleary from sleep.

"Almost. We have to fill out these customs forms."

I had already filled out the customs forms in a painfully honest fashion, declaring the ten thousand dollars in U.S. travelers checks and detailing some of the food products I'd brought along, like Power Bars.

Martin looked over my form and scoffed.

"Answer no to everything, mate. That way you don't get hassled."

I immediately crumpled the one form, put it in my shirt pocket and requested another.

After we landed, Martin and I exchanged our hasty good-byes and he hurried ahead to meet his family at the hospital where his sister was having a baby. The customs officer quickly stamped my passport and visa. I was glad that I had sheared off my ponytail a month ago, but I was still sweating my all-no answer sheet.

I lolled anxiously at the baggage claim, waiting for the five green duffel bags loaded with my portion of the Southern Cross expedition: boat, sail, carry bags, gear bags, bivvy sack, sleeping bag, camping roll, Power Bars, desalinator, global positioning system, flare guns with cartridges (illegal to take on a plane), flashlights, batteries, spare parts, tools, glues, epoxies, matches, and various other assorted essentials.

Finally, I plucked the last of the bags from the conveyer belt and lumped it onto one of those airport carts like a Black Plague victim onto the death buggy. Using the cart like a train cow-catcher I ploughed my way to the last checkpoint, where another customs official asked me for my "card."

The customs declaration card.

I could not find it. I searched all my pockets, once, twice, three times until my movements became jerky and spasmodic and sweat dripped from my brow and I was certain the official was on his walkie-talkie and that any second a SWAT team would explode into action with guns drawn. Images from the movie *Midnight Express* popped onto my screen.

I knew I looked suspicious when, at last, *Ahah!*

"Here it is, sir."

He sighed. "This one isn't signed. Do you have another?"

Here we go, I thought, *a fish out of water I am. The expedition isn't even going to get out of the airport. I have broken at least two airline regulations concerning flammables and projectiles and lied about food and currency on my person. Martin had pulled a practical joke. Let's have a lark with the Yank.*

He's just like Tony. They all must be.

The customs official patiently watched me fumble through my gear again until I found the card with the confirming check mark that reads, "He's okay. Let him through."

I steered my caravan out to the sidewalk with the joy of a convict through the prison gate to freedom.

It was a brilliantly sunny day in Sydney. I lowered my shades, wondering how forlorn I appeared sitting atop my mountain of duffels among the scattering ranks of international flight survivors. I checked my watch. I had been in customs for about forty-five minutes. Tony was nowhere to be found. I wasn't surprised.

If he's not fond of charts, calendars, and clocks, punctuality can't be high on the list, either.

An hour later, a small white car pulled to a stop at the curb. Tony and a friend jumped out and held up a large black sign that was nearly as wide as the car. They raised it over their heads like a protest sign at a political rally. It was a movie placard from a Steven Seagal movie: MARKED FOR DEATH!

They began hooting and grunting and shaking the sign.

I walked over dragging a few bags. We exchanged mock cordialities.

"Welcome to Australia, *Epic!*"

I recognized his friend as Michael, a photographer from England who had visited Tony in New York and had joined us for a couple of paddles.

"Hello! Septic Tank Yank."

"Hello gentlemen, got some room for an expedition in this . . . ?" I jutted my chin toward the tiny automobile behind them.

Tony purred. "A true beauuuuty, isn't she?"

I had seen coffee cups with more headroom. In what seemed a lifetime ago, a driver in an Armani suit had packed away the five duffel bags in the trunk of luxury car while I reclined against a plush leather seat that had more legroom than a chaise lounge.

Standing on the sidewalk I stared in horror at the Renault. Tony hefted a bag and half-kicked half-shoved it into the trunk. Then another. I watch with wonder and alarm as he improvisationally shoved, jammed, tied, and origamied one bag after another into and onto every available cubic centimeter of the ancient, rust-bottomed, compact sedan with half a steering wheel on the wrong side of the dash.

"In you go, Epic!"

I levered and wedged myself onto a patch of torn vinyl seat smaller than a kayak's that I shared with a number of beer bottles.

Tony and Michael climbed in and the car tore away. They grinned at one another like lunatics who have just escaped the asylum. Not surprisingly, Tony drove with fierce but reckless concentration. The Renault roared in and out of traffic. I could almost imagine him standing at the pinball machine, pounding the flippers and hipping the machine as he directed the balls through the maze.

"Whadya think, mate?!" asked Tony cheerily.

It was like riding a very crowded elevator sideways.

An Andy Scott cassette tape bellowed "Ghost Riders in the Sky," followed by "You're Much Too Young, Girl" and then "Rawhide"—over and over again. It seemed like forever before I saw a turnoff for Bondi.

The heavyweight title bout had begun. It was Queen's rules on the kangaroo's court.

The problem? I was a welterweight.

Baptism on the "Barbie."

Tony and Mike did not lose a step with my arrival. I entered their Bondi summer act in full swing. Part of the ritual involved endless recitation of sundry key lyrics from songs that were sung in the obligatory off-key harmony.

"Yar mauch tooooo yung gerllll!"

My neck ached from swinging back and forth trying to keep up with their chatter. The inside jokes shot back and forth faster than parallel processing.

Frequently Michael would lean far out the window to apprise a fellow driver of his automobile's aesthetic shortcomings.

"Lem, Lem, Lem-onnnn!" he hooted. I couldn't help but wonder about the irony of Michael commenting on the quality of *other* cars. In any case, his barbing was supplemented by Tony, who maintained a running commentary on his erratic driving.

"Ooohhhh," he quipped once as the car nearly steered off the road. "Dicey. Very *dicey*."

I felt like the stereotypical caricature of the uptight midwesterner who finds himself on a road trip with a couple of real-life fraternity boys from *Animal House*. They had the giddy demeanor of New Year's Eve revelers and I doubted if either one had slept a wink the night before.

Tony suddenly banged on the door as he chanted: "Tamarama! Tamarama! Tamarama!"

"What's Tamarama?" I asked Michael innocently.

They both grinned and smothered laughter like I was the butt of some incredibly hilarious joke. Finally they burst out laughing.

"You'll see, mate. Trust me." Tony's reassuring tone was anything but reassuring.

A short time later Tony yanked the Renault off the road and we jounced along a rutty road to a beach. Tony slammed on the brakes and the Renault skidded to a halt. Tony whistled and jumped out of the car. Through the window, I saw the beach and the waves rolling to shore, one giant set after another. As each wave reached the beach, it suddenly broke and peeled off in a cannonball left break that spit white water like a violent sideways volcano.

"Watch the undertow or you'll end up out on the Bondi Express," Michael offered matter-of-factly.

I remembered Martin back in New York talking about swimming the Bondi Express. The current was so strong it could sweep you for miles from one end of Bondi clear to the other. Paddling the Hudson River suddenly seemed rather tame by comparison.

Tony and Michael slung off their shirts. I realized that before we would head to the new apartment in Bondi we would be breaking the metaphorical ice with a bit of a "body bash." That would be body surfing, Aussie style. I didn't even have a chance to apply any sunblock.

My plan was simple: Do as little as possible to embarrass myself.

Tony and Michael plunged into the water and crawled effortlessly through the waves to the main break. I dived in behind them and matched their stroke. Out at the break I waited for what I thought would be a medium-sized wave. Anything too small and I knew I would be hooted mercilessly. Anything too big and they would need all five duffel bags to mail home my dislocated body parts.

I scoped a good wave and paddled. There was a moment of delicious exhilaration as my body was hung out over the curling wave. I angled left and dropped my shoulder. Suddenly I experienced a terrifying moment of weightlessness as the wave humped and spit me out like a grape seed. I plunged end over end as the wave crashed on top of me. I rolled over and over and washed up on the beach, hacking and coughing and spitting sand.

Standing on shore, Tony and Michael watched me stagger up the beach.

"A nice place for a floggin'!" said Tony.

"To help clear the noggin!" added Michael.

"After a biggg night out!" they both screamed.

I felt a bit wobbly and disoriented, like I had just been through one round with Mike Tyson. I didn't know how many more rounds I could take.

Later that day we pulled up to the Bondi penthouse on Curlewis Street. Milk crates supported an old black-and-white TV with one channel, while the phone was buried under heaps of papers and layer upon layer of scribbled messages and phone numbers.

Sleeping accommodations ranged from the relative privacy and luxury of Tony's single futon tucked inside a room with the one and only closed door, to the rustic extreme of something they referred to as Buffalo Bill. I gave Tony a confused glance.

Tony nodded and pointed to an old mattress in a corner. It was covered in plastic.

"Famous mattress, this one," Michael proudly declared.

"Oh really, why?"

"It was like this, mate. I was with a beauty of a sheila and we fell asleep. She woke up screaming in the middle of the night."

"What happened?"

"A warm golden tide had come in, you might say. Darn good thing the plastic was on."

"Oh yeah," Tony chimed in. "He had just a feewww too many."

"What happened to her?"

"Who?"

"Your sheila."

Michael shrugged. "Don't know. Must have scooted, I guess." He grinned proudly. "But I kept the mattress."

The kitchen cupboards were flung open haphazardly and the shelves were sparsely stocked with the barest of the bare essentials. A half-empty box of Weet-bix and an open container of skim milk sat on the counter. I presumed this was what remained from breakfast. More disturbing than their casual approach to refrigeration, I quickly discovered that Mike and Tony were sharing the apartment with a thriving colony of crawling friends who seemed to find the counter under the sink most appealing. I never saw so many little beauties come out of the drain of a sink. I wondered if they had their own "bodybashin' " beach down there.

Tony hopped up on the Buffalo Bill mattress and balanced one foot on a milk crate. Armed with a clip of nails in his mouth he hammered the MARKED FOR DEATH poster into the plaster above his door.

"How's it lookin', Mike?"

Mike hummed appreciatively. "Like the dog's ballocks, TB."

I cuffed some empty beer bottles and discarded food containers with my foot and unloaded my five duffels in the middle of the room.

This was the living definition of "flophousin'." It was less a penthouse than a playpen. It put all of my least spectacular living arrangements to shame. My hopeless fraternity room would be a model of balanced feng shui in comparison. The wildest wilderness campsite couldn't possibly have supported as many life forms. It was not possible and it was my *reality.*

The phone rang and Tony shuffle-shoved a pile of papers to the floor and found a clean notepad and pencil.

"Hello, Sammy. . . . Yes, Epic is here. . . . When's that? . . . No worries." He talked for a while longer, then hung up the phone.

I anxiously wondered if this was the infamous Sammy. The last thing I needed was to find out that his original partner had decided to throw in with the expedition after all. Tony and I were kayak partners. He and Sammy were mates. I knew the difference.

"That was Sammy, my booker," said Tony. "She just got me a job."

Tony and Michael showered, and I killed some time watching TV from the *dis*comfort of a beanbag chair just behind Buffalo Bill. I heard some shouting and Tony and Michael burst into the living room and faced off with tightly rolled towels like rival matadors.

Tony snapped his towel and caught Michael smartly.

"Ouch! Good one!" Michael tried to retaliate but Tony was quicker. "Ouch!

Two small welts formed on Michael's hip. The two gladiators scuttled after one another through the household clutter like scorpions on desert sand. Michael flayed at Tony, but Tony was just too fast and would beat Michael to the hit every time. The quest for one single hit drove Michael into fits. In an attempt to keep from being trampled I maneuvered around them like a referee in a hockey game after the players have thrown off their gloves.

"Had enough?" Tony demanded gleefully.

Definitely, I thought to myself.

Michael conceded.

Tony lifted his arms in triumph and roared. Rocky Balboa with a wet towel. Apparently the pecking order had been reestablished.

I excused myself and took a shower.

"Where to?" I asked.

"A couple of spots for a bit of refreshment."

"The thing is, Tony, I'm kind of beat. It was a long trip and all."

"Not to worry, mate. We won't be long. *Trust me.*"

Our first stop was Watson's Bay for some afternoon pints at an outdoor table in the sun. Still no sunblock. A "winterfied" New Yorker, my skin already had taken on the sweaty overcooked hue of a boiled lobster. Several pints and casual conversation in spectacular surroundings had primed us for yet another round of late afternoon pints at the Bondi Icebergs Club on the south side of Bondi. The club was tucked up on a cliff with a concrete-fortified outdoor swimming pool at its base. Waves crashing on shore occasionally exploded high into the air, nearly reaching the window where we were sitting.

The walls of the club were smothered with photographs and newspaper clippings of famous Bondi Icebergs swim teams. The club was crowded with seasoned, muscular, gray-haired men—men no longer in their prime—men who were a testament to the brevity of youth. One dusty news clip from the 1960s reported a story about a lifeguard who had battled raging twenty-foot surf during a cyclone to rescue an overmatched bodybasher. Both nearly died in the process.

From my prime-view perch window, the sun lowering on the horizon, I watched dozens of neoprene-clad young surfers bobbing up and down, waiting for the last big wave of this fading day.

After all the pints and the long flight, my brain was taking on a fuzzy glow.

" 'Ere we go, mate!" cheered Tony.

"Oy!" roared Michael. Tony and Michael had hardly warmed up.

Our next stop was the Bondi Diggers Returned Servicemen's Club. Red patent leather seats and walls plastered with military memorabilia like a post office with wanted posters. The Aussies love a good "blue."

The most crowded section of Diggers is the game room. The walls are hung with dartboards and there are pool tables arranged like dominoes, but what grabs your attention is the jangling clatter and buzzing of the slot machines. Men and women of all ages sit transfixed, yanking on the one-armed bandit and waiting mesmerized by the twirling lemons or full houses popping up onto the screens in front of them.

We put one more pint in the tank then headed off to The Cross.

Downtown Sydney. Evening. Lights come on everywhere like badly hung stars. Hip restaurants and cool clubs are everywhere. From my increasingly blurry perspective, downtown Sydney reminds me of a combination of Times Square and Greenwich Village with a very active club life spilling onto the streets.

We stroll up to a popular club with a line of stylish club-kids that snakes all the way down the street. Tony directs us to the front of the line. The velvet rope is already rising like a drawbridge. The doorman recognizes Tony and we sail inside.

New city. Same excesses and cultish pretensions: smoking, drinking, style, fashion, flirting, heat, music, staircases, more roped-off areas, short dresses, low-cut shirts, lips aglow, more heat, more drinking. All is awhirl. Tony and Mike are on a first-name basis with the who's who of fashionable Sydney. It seems just like Manhattan—except because of Tony I am more of an insider here than there.

Australian beer is much stronger than its tamer and watered-down American cousin. Tony and Michael are gliding through the crowd and air kissing the beautiful women and shouting at me but I cannot understand a word. A few more rounds of pints and we decamp like ghosts to a smaller, darker, but no less exclusive club where the full effect of all the pints finally begins to assert itself on mind and body.

Night becomes morning and the first sliver of pink is visible in the sky as we stumble back to the penthouse where I throw hygiene to the wind and collapse in a drunken heap onto Buffalo Bill.

The next morning—*jeezuz, later the same day*—I awake and notice that miraculously the plastic has been spared. I—on the other hand—peel open one eye warily, worried that I may not be as lucky. But providence has smiled on me. I don't feel too bad. A bit of a kettledrum at the back of the brain. A tongue that tastes as if it has been used as a dustpan. But no need to call the paramedics.

A gorgeous sheila emerges from the bathroom dressed in nada but an oversized T-shirt. I blink stupidly and she smiles and dances quickly back into Tony's room and the door clicks shut.

"Hey, Mike," I ask hoarsely of the heap that is flopped on the floor next to me. "Wasn't that the girl I saw on the cover of the Australian *Cosmo*?"

"Sure is. That's the way we like it around here."

Okay. I admit it: *I'm impressed.*

I realize with a mixture of pride and dread that I have survived my first day Down Under. We set off to a place called Speedos for pots of tea and "brekky" on a patio that overlooks north Bondi. I conclude that Australia is a place of almost overpowering natural beauty. Brilliant white sand, emerald green water, blue sky, puffy clouds. One worries about sensory overload. As I attack my oatmeal and banana pancakes I watch a group of topless sunbathers strolling along the shore, and the surfers and surfskiers, and even a few Japanese tourists. I think I could get used to this.

Revived and refreshed, we bodybashed and then worked out outside at an adult "jungle gym" next to the surf club. There was an orderly array of pull-up bars, dip bars, ministaircases, stretching poles, incline sit-up boards. Each station had its own textbook excerpt on how to perform the exercise, basically saying more repetitions equal higher fitness. I tried to eclipse all the highest numbers.

Michael and Tony followed each other. Meanwhile, I sampled all the different apparatus like a kid let loose in a toy store. I reveled in the variety of exercises in such an exquisite setting. Michael and Tony had a system. Michael followed Tony's lead as he migrated from area to area. I did my own thing.

Tony barked, "Why don't you just do the set routine instead of just jumping around all over the place?!" His question stunned me.

What fucking arrogance! I thought. Back in New York I had busted my hump trying to get Tony to follow a routine—*any* routine. And here he was criticizing *my* training habits.

"I'm figuring out my own routine, Tony," I snapped.

"Ooooh, touchy, touchy."

Michael smiled in support. Tony had spent the last three months with an eager playmate who had a similar sense of humor, yet I knew the towel whip was more than just good fun. I felt like I was rushing to get into a two-man fraternity. As a former pledge trainer I could recognize a good hazing but that part of my life was over. I thought.

Later I met the rest of the housemates: Brent, Moz, and sisters Sam (Tony's booker) and Caroline. Brent looked familiar.

"How the hell are ya, Epic?" Brent said. "Last time I saw you we were having a laugh back in New York."

"That's right," was about all I could muster.

"You're looking rather plump and red these days." The group laughed.

"Good of you to notice." I felt as if I had just been backed into the ropes with no way of escape.

"We've heard all about you," Sam said.

"I assume it was all rave reviews." The group guffawed and I realized I had been the butt of the joke again. I felt the color coming up in my face and I tried to smother my anger. I kept thinking how much I would have liked to be back in New York and to have a chance to return the favor.

But more important, I wondered, *What the hell am I doing here? Don't they know what we are about to do very soon? Can they really believe we are prepared to go? Hasn't Tony filled them in?*

The rest of the week I busied myself taking long walks along the beach and gazing at the surf for hours on end. The whole time, the CLOSED sign never went up at Tony's "playhouse." I was beyond frustrated.

I thought about Nicole and our one night together and the hundred days of preparation and how committed Tony had been. *Seemed.* What had become of the Tony I had taken to the airport three months before?

Martin had known Tony on both continents. Besides modeling, he was running a location van business in Sydney. He loved fun, but he also had balance. Martin was an older Tony. Wiser and bit more mature. We met in an elegant Italian restaurant. He immediately sensed my anxiety.

"Can you believe it? Have you ever seen him like this?"

Martin's broadening grin told me I wouldn't hear the whole story. "Well, actually he's had a bit of the *larrikin* (i.e., hell-raiser) in him for quite a while," Martin chuckled.

"How long?"

He paused for a moment. "He was kind of shy when I first met him. He was sort of a country boy when he first came to the agency. He said something about wanting to be a veterinarian. That was about ten years ago."

"Yeah?"

"It didn't take him long to get the knack of it."

Martin summarized my situation with one poignant statement: "You can always get out of it."

Could I really get out of it? Wasn't there a point of no return? A point where the quest takes better judgment along for the ride? God, I've told so many people I'm going to circumnavigate Australia in a kayak.

"No, Martin, I can't. I would have to try to find another partner or go it on my own at this stage of the game. Would you like to go?" I half-kidded.

"I don't think so. Not this time. Try me for your next vacation."

"Would you like to join us for a paddle to Manly tomorrow?"

"Certainly."

The next morning Tony, Mike, and I met Martin at Roses Beach. Mike proposed a race to Manly and back. Tony and Michael had been paddling this course frequently in my absence. Tony and I got in the older Klepper that I had smuggled to Tony before he left for Oz.

It looked worse for the wear but was still going to be OK for spare parts or even as a replacement boat if need be. The parts were interchangeable with our new one. Mike got in Martin's better-groomed sister ship. Martin had followed all of Dieter's—aka "Q"—instructions on Klepper care and feeding.

Manly and back. A routine ten-mile sprint. We splashed off and it soon became painfully apparent that it had been awhile. The boat lunged and lurched instead of gliding. The Tony and Eric team was rusty. Tony had also adopted a different rhythm by adapting to Mike's stroke. Also, it had been over a week since I had been in a boat. The effects of aerobic conditioning can drop off dramatically after as little as five days and can set one back a month after less than two weeks of inactivity.

"Come *on*, mate," Tony groused angrily. "Let's *move* this boat!"

I boosted the paddle rate.

"That's it, that's it! Now we're moving the boat well," Tony said.

Whose boat is this, anyway? I thought to myself.

I discovered a tear in my new bivvy sack. The mini-arch had snapped in half upon my first assembly and punctured the material. *Why* did they use fiberglass?! A late night call caught me in the midst of my frustration.

"Hello, is TB there?" The voice was sultry and very female.

"No he's out and about."

"You must be Epic. My name is Anya."

"Actually, it's Eric."

"You're the guy going around Oz with TB," she said excitedly. "How's it all going with that?"

I told her the truth. "Tony seems to be way out there these days. I don't think he comprehends what we are about to do."

"Oh, he's just a bit nervous about it all. He'll come around, he always does."

She got off the phone. I wanted to unload more. I had to let it out. I could not pretend that I was not pissed off anymore. Here I am sewing a brand new bivvy sack and keeping the kitchen pets company while Tony is out on the town again. I would have loved to be out on the town but who would handle the details of the trip?

"Hello, Nicole!"

"Hello, handsome. I miss you."

"Yeah . . . me too . . ."

"What's wrong? You sound upset."

I unloaded. I sounded like the kid who just found out he won't be playing the lead in the Christmas play. "Tony and I hardly talk. There are always friends or some commotion going on. I am sick and tired of it!

"Have you tried?"

"What?!"

"To talk to him?"

"I haven't had the chance."

"Sounds like you have to make one."

Before I left the States, Tony and I had talked about obtaining basic medicines for our expedition first-aid kit. I knew his father was a prominent reconstructive trauma surgeon in Canberra. My survival course clearly stated the need for some basic broad-range antibiotics like tetracycline and sulfa drugs to cover potential external, respiratory and lower intestinal infections.

I asked Tony: "Tony, did you get those antibiotics and other medicines from your father yet?"

"No."

"Are they on the way?"

"No, I never asked."

"You never asked?!"

"If we get in trouble, I can always call him."

"Jesus, Tony! We're gonna be in bumfuck nowhere! Where are we going to find a phone?"

"Relax, mate. There are towns along the whole east coast. He can just call in the prescription. I'll get the medicines by the time we get to Brisbane."

I didn't want to escalate the tension. I truly wanted to believe Tony, but a nagging feeling led me to the phone book to find the location of the closest pharmacy.

At the Bondi Centre Pharmacy I browsed and stopped to examine a small dark bottle of pure tea tree oil. An employee introduced herself as Rebecca and filled me in on the wonders of tea tree oil, a product indigenous to Australia.

"A marvelous antiseptic, good for so many things."

"Can it act like an antibiotic?"

"For cuts and scratches it works fine. It is also very good for fungus as is."

"How about internally?"

"Well, that's a bit tricky. You would have to carefully dilute it into a tea. Just a few drops will do. What might you need it for?"

"A partner and I are going around Australia in a kayak."

"Aw . . . right."

I disclosed the plan and my misgivings. I noticed a sign in the store that read, "Feldenkrais Massage Deep Relaxation—Managed Stress—Easier Movement."

I pointed to the sign. "Do you think this Felden . . . stuff could help?"

"Yes," she said unequivocally. "I can set an appointment up for tomorrow."

"Sign me up."

"I will also have the things you need for your kit. Oh, by the way, you should try to think of an animal to identify with for your massage."

I arrived early the next day and received the bulk of the painkillers, dressings, ointments, tea tree oil, even some body-plugging agents in case Montezuma visits Australia. She said the condoms were on the house.

Cheeky. I had to laugh. *Condoms would be the last item we would need. Does she know something I don't?* Then I remembered you can use them for emergency water bottles. I walked back to the massage table with great anticipation. I just wanted all of this turmoil to go away.

She explained that the Feldenkrais method was designed to soften tense muscles through the power of touch, using gentle, precise movements of the body.

Almost an hour later the combination of mind/body imagery and physical manipulation had created soft clay out of concrete.

Amazingly, on my way out she ripped off a page from a notepad and handed it to me. Outside on the sidewalk I read the note. She had scribbled three questions: "What do you want from this journey? What are you afraid of? How can we make this work?"

My tension was an open book.

I felt like I could finally bring my concerns to Tony's attention. When I got home that evening, Michael was not around. Tony and I had our first significant time alone in the almost two weeks since I'd arrived. Tony actually initiated the conversation:

"I know its been a bit mad around here. I'm just trying to see all the old mates before we go. It could be long time before I see them again. I hope you're having a good time."

I smiled from ear to ear. Just the acknowledgment that he was aware of me and the trip was all that mattered. I slipped the questions back into my pocket.

Then he dropped the bomb. "People have wondered if you are antisocial but I tell them you're just shy."

My smile turned to an angry crimson flush. I felt like having it out with him right then and there. And no pissant little towel snapping contest either. But I restrained myself.

"I just haven't got the hang of their sense of humor yet."

Tony nodded like he understood. The crisis having diffused for the moment, we started sorting out the gear together.

"What's this, mate?!"

Tony was pointing the barrel of a black three-foot-long metal tube at me. He looked like John Wayne with a Remington pump action. He was aiming for the whites of my eyes.

"That's the desalinator I was talking about. I had a choice of this one, which can make freshwater from saltwater at a rate of four gallons an hour. The other model, which was much smaller, could make about four quarts with constant pumping."

"It's awfully *big*, isn't it?"

"I suppose."

"It's pretty heavy, too. It must weigh almost a stone [fourteen pounds]."

"It's going to save us a lot of time trying to search for water. I figured we could spend one long morning a week making enough water to last for the rest of the week."

"Does it work?"

"I haven't tried it yet."

One week to go and I receive a card from Nicole. It was short, sweet, and to the point. "A path lies before you which you are called to follow. The gods await you." A quote from Hermann Hesse's *Siddartha*.

I also get a call from my mom.

"Well, the bastards did it."

"Did what?"

"They're going to close the Union Square store for sure and move it to a minimall near our home in Jersey."

"What?!" My heart dropped into the soles of my feet.

"They want to move everything in the next month, before the season gets too busy. They told your father now he will have to work half-days on Sundays, too."

"You've got to be kidding," I stammered.

"I'm afraid not." Sensing my shock, she softened her tone. "Don't worry. We'll be fine. Mr. Hoyt and a bunch of MASK [Metropolitan Area Sea Kayak club] members are helping with the move."

"What about Tim?" He had been a very loyal and productive salesman.

She paused. "Germany told your father to let him go. The thing that really gets me is that now instead of the Green Market across the street there is a Burger King."

We talked for a while. About the move and my father and about the trip.

"Your father says that a spark is missing from the store, and we both wish you the best of luck. We love you."

"I love you, too. And don't worry about me. I'll be fine." My mother was on the verge of tears. We chatted a little bit longer and then managed our good-byes.

In this case no one was really *fine*. The move from Union Square was a death in my family. The Union Square Klepper shop *was* my father. It was also a touchstone of thirty-five years of clients, friends, adventures, and associations. For my father to be moved to a minimall in New Jersey was like the admiral of an aircraft carrier being assigned watch duty on a mothballed battle cruiser. Denial stepped in, and I called Martin and asked him to take a tour in his classic Klepper around Sydney Harbour.

We met at the Canoe (*canoe* means kayak in king's English) Specialists store on The Spit in Mosman in northern Sydney. I called a prospective Australian Klepper agent named Bruce Easton to come join us. In the meantime we chatted with Canoe Imports proprietor, Gary Burnham.

"Yeah, I've heard about these Kleppers forever," he purred appreciatively. "Just haven't had a chance to see one up close."

"They're actively used by Australia's Special Boat squadron."

"I know," he said. "The Zed forces used to use them in WWII." A Zed was an amphibious commando unit.

I corrected him. "They didn't *actually* use Kleppers. But they did use an English-made copy called a Folbot." I fell into a familiar groove. "In fact, the Australian Zed force used the boats to sneak into Singapore harbor under the cover of darkness, paddled right up to Japanese tanker ships, and applied limpet (magnetic) mines under the waterline with a special pole. Hours later, they set off the charge and sank thirty-five thousand tons of shipping. There is an Australian movie called *The Heroes* that was made showing all about it."

Bruce Easton arrived. He was about my size, and looking at another guy eye to eye was a new and satisfying sensation. Not only that, he was a regular guy. He was definitely not part of the tribe of *Übermenschen* that I had been recently running with. I felt an immediate kinship with Bruce. We assembled our Kleppers and I showed Bruce a few tips.

A curious Gary interrupted us and changed the subject. "Paul is not your run-of-the-mill paddler, you know." Gary was referring to Paul Caffyn, the New Zealander who had circumnavigated Australia.

"I can only imagine." *What was he getting at?*

"He was almost killed on the Zuytdorp cliffs on the west side. A hundred miles of 'em with no place to land. It was the same thing in the Bight."

"He was really good with his boat in the surf," I agreed. "But my boats are designed to ride the waves all day."

Gary eyed my Klepper warily.

•   •   •

"Follow me lads, I'd like to show you something." Gary led us to the back of the shop, where he introduced us to his son, who was smoothing the finish on a brand-new kayak.

Gary and his son showed us their unique designs, which seemed to borrow some from the hull shapes of surf skis (long, narrow, sit-on-top surf rescue boats paddled with kayak paddles) and the decks of British Canoe Union sea kayaks like Caffyn's Nordkapp. They blended together to form a boat called the Mirage. They were glistening, sleek and white. Kayak design was clearly evolving in the local waters, much as it had done two thousand years ago. *Our* boats looked like freighters in comparison. After minutes of perfunctory respect Bruce redirected me back to the beach.

Bruce launched his single-seat Aerius I (same boat as Howard's). "Let's get going! I'll take you across the harbor."

We paddled south from the Spit into Sydney Harbour National Park. Bruce guided us past Middle Head three miles due west from North Head and South Head, the entranceway to the twenty-two-square-mile harbor of Port Jackson.

Way back in the 1770s Captain Cook had marked this harbor on his charts. But it was Governor Arthur Philip who brought England's first cargo of seven hundred convicts to Australia. Sydney was established as a penal colony in 1788. It would not be incorporated as a municipality until 1842. Sydney is now Australia's largest city and proudly boasts one of the finest natural harbors in the world.

Bruce pointed at Middle Head. "See those fortifications over there . . . and there. They were gun batteries set up to watch the harbor for the Japanese invasion fleet."

I rose to the bait and quipped: "Thanks to us it never got here."

"No," Bruce grinned. Then he became serious. "But the bastards did sneak in a minisub. And don't forget who tried to help your sorry asses in Vietnam!"

I brandished my paddle in mock surrender. Then, as I squinted to see the bunkers, I saw a small, dark object with three-foot-high coaming tower skimming across the water. My imagination said minisub but I fixed my gaze and saw that it was a lone kayaker who was changing his course to meet us.

It was a beautiful warm day in Sydney Harbour. The wind was light and there was no hint of a chill. But the approaching kayaker looked like Nanook of the north, complete with hooded anorak. In addition, he had an outside pocket crammed full with an expedition PFD (personal floatation device), sealed spray cover, and gloves. The deck carried all safety essentials: bilge pump, paddle float, chart, and compass. He was paddling a very British-looking sea kayak.

We were dressed in T-shirts and bathing trunks.

"G'day," I said in my best pidgin Australian.

"Hello, Eric! It's me! Ron!"

"Ron . . . ?"

"Ron . . . Ron *Arias*. I helped Ralph Diaz and your father with that folding kayak demonstration at my house back in Connecticut."

Jeezus. Talk about a small world!

"I told your dad I wanted to catch up with you before you left. *Who Weekly* [Australia's *People*] wants to do a story on you guys. Some luck, huh?!"

I gave Ron our address and phone number. I did remember him helping my dad and I thought this would make the trip very real for Tony. It might be just what the expedition doctor ordered.

"We'll see you this week. It'll be me and a couple of cameramen."

"OK!"

"Must be going out to the heads today, huh?"

"No, just cruising the harbor."

We said our good-byes, and the rest of the paddle was spent discussing the price of Kleppers with Bruce and how they are too high for the Australian market after the extra duties get added on. I arranged to have Bruce hold on to our second boat and other supplies because he was a fellow industry colleague who knew how to recognize the right parts and properly fill out a shipping form. I promised him he could keep what we did not use.

The last order of business was purchasing a boat cart from Gary back at the store.

"Yep. My wife and I used this one on a double when we were up the coast on holiday. Works pretty well in the sand."

His cart had broad tires, not at all like the Klepper cart we used to run *Southern Cross* around the streets of New York. I thought it might save Tony and me a lot of backbreaking portaging somewhere down the line.

"I'll take it. And give me that good-looking compass, too." We talked a bit more business and I assured him that I would talk more about importing boats into the States when I got back. The truth was Dieter would probably rather have his spine yanked out his ears before he would import boats from Australia. I didn't tell Bruce that.

"Good on ya and Godspeed!"

Tony came home late that night from a cricket match, brandishing an Australian flag and yelling "Aussie, Aussie, Aussie!" He then proceeded to tear the Union Jack part of the flag out with his teeth and resume his chant. After he simmered down I looked at the flag and realized that if I made an equal cut on the side opposite from which Tony had shredded it, the flag would form a Christian-style cross while retaining the Southern Cross constellation inside it.

The next day I aqua-sealed it to the foredeck of our kayak. Once it was applied, *Southern Cross* looked like an elongated Crusader's shield.

We were going into battle.

The final week was a physical and emotional cyclone. Ron and his cameramen invaded the Bondi penthouse like a CBS newsteam dropping in on the

Unabomber. They snapped away at the Buffalo Bill, without any inkling of its sordid past. They waded through the immense pile of expedition gear strewn in, on, and throughout the room to get a better angle on the Steven Seagal MARKED FOR DEATH masterpiece. Tony initially seemed to almost enjoy having this tangy slice of life immortalized, and yet gradually appeared more bothered by it all.

I listened to a part of Tony's interview.

Ron: "Why do you want to do this, anyway?"

Tony: "I don't want to read and talk about adventure when I'm sixty and sitting around with my grandchildren. I want to say I kayaked around Oz. Or at least I gave it a go."

Ron: "What do you think the hardest part of this trip will be?"

Tony: "Sitting in the boat listening to Eric." (Ron and the camera crew laughed.)

The crew followed us to Speedos where we had been having most of our breakfasts and captured our morning "tea" ceremony.

The next day Michael, Brent, and crew had sussed (found) out that the musical icon Andy Scott was playing at a Returned Servicemen's League club in downtown Sydney. Thus it was the perfect place for the TB Birthday and Bon Voyage Party. It also offered me a chance to redeem my "antisocial" behavior with newfound higher spirits.

Tony, Mike, and I rummaged for our "finest" clothes. Tony took the show with his white pair of jeans, a broad black belt, and a brightly flowered Hawaiian shirt. Mike matched the shirt and then tossed me a spare. I put it on to rave reviews.

"Spiffy, Spiffy," Tony said.

"A regular Don Ho," Michael added.

The redoubtable Renault sputtered to one of its final missions. Tony had instructed Michael to sell it or junk it in his absence. It delivered us intact to the Paddington RSL, one of the largest in the country. We were greeted instantly by the equally colorful crew. The pitchers of beer and stories started to pour.

I noticed that the majority of patrons were paired-off couples. Michael had found one solo character with a massive tattoo on his arm that read RAN, which stood for Royal Australian Navy. He was the Australian Popeye. At one point he clenched his fists and pounded on the table, and in a gruff and gravelly voice boomed: "You're all the dog's ballocks, I tell ya!"

A huge cheer went up, and down went another round of pints. Michael leaned over and laid his hand on my arm. In a cautionary tone he whispered, "Don't tell him you're a Yank." I nodded. *Holy shit,* I thought. *These people are nuts!*

We all sat at a table as close to Andy Scott and his wife, Anne, as we could. A fixture of 1970s disco chic, Andy and Anne wore matching white polyester clothes. Andy wore a cheap toupee. In contrast, Anne's hair was toned, tousled, and teased into what must have been its zillionth performance. Two undersized electronic keyboards and a rhythm machine rounded out the band. Not surprisingly, one of the first songs they launched into was "Ghost Riders in the Sky."

By now I knew almost all the words. The crowd sang along. They needed no prompting but joined in with lusty and eager bravado. Tony and I were suddenly the center of attention. Smiles turned to hugs, and before long couples were offering us their special senior discount cards to keep the pints coming. We happily obliged.

Maybe it was the intense emotion of that night that got us to the next level—getting us back to basics. Tony seemed finally focused on the fact that we were going to kayak around Australia.

Tony's mom and sister came by to help us with final preparations. We wanted to leave early the next day. The expansive, colorful, and exuberant "mum" enveloped me like a momma grizzly.

"Welcome to Australia, Eric."

"Thank you, Ms. Lewes."

"Call me Jan. This trip is all Tony has been talking about for so long! I am very excited and proud of you two."

"Well, we still have a ways to go."

"I'm thinking of meeting you in Cairns in a couple of months. I've always wanted to see Daintree and Cape Trib."

"I hear that area is beautiful. It's one of the few places in the world where rainforest meets the—"

Tony stepped in and cut me off. "Epic will talk your ear off if you let 'im, Mum. We'll be there in a couple of months if all goes well." He turned to me. "Come on mate—let's get this stuff sorted out."

We had brought the gear out into a small courtyard in the back of the apartment complex. Tony was wondering aloud where to start first.

All the gear had been accumulated, and the packing became real. The newly laden storage bags took on new shapes and proportions that lightweight stuffing materials simply do not duplicate. I had done a mock packing and presentation for a number of clients in the Klepper shop a couple of weeks before I had left. Everything fit like pieces of a puzzle.

Our first "final" packing was not a success. Tony's theory of packing was grab and shove.

"No, Tony!" I yelled. "The sleeping bags go into the green caboose bags, not the blue ones."

Tony impatiently and sulkily undid a couple of minutes of his work in ten seconds and heaped the sleeping bag back on the ground.

"Why the green ones?!" he snapped. "There's a lot more room in the blue ones?!"

"The green ones are the perfect size to fit under your butt in the boat. Here, let me show you."

I stuffed the seven-foot sleeping bag into the 2' × 1' × 10'–deep Voyager caboose bag. I then sealed it like a Ziplock storage bag with a patented two-foot-long, center-split, black plastic wand. I took the black, hard foam, one-size-fits-all standard seat bottom out of the boat and replaced it with the bag. I ran two compression straps around the keel board that the seat attaches to and across the bloated mass. I opened the air-bleed valve, sat on it, and descended three inches deeper into the boat, accompanied by the characteristic hissing sound of an old iron radiator. I got up, closed the valve, tightened the compression straps, and said: "There you have it, a custom fit butt cushion that gives us a lot more useable storage space for our bulkiest soft goods—sleeping bags, air mattresses, and clothes."

"Very nice," he mumbled.

We had never paddled a loaded kayak before. We had never gone on one overnight camping trip together. Part of this was because of our busy summer and schedules, and the rest was my selfish effort to preserve Tony's naïveté. I figured the fewer "details" I bombarded him with, the better.

But what confronted us now was the Mount Everest of expedition packing. I had planned for us to be self-sufficient for up to a month at a time, burning five thousand calories a day and encountering wide climate changes. Not surprisingly, it was difficult to underpack and terribly easy to overpack.

Ideally, an oceangoing kayak should have as little deck load as possible, to minimize windage and wave-catching surfaces. This means that most of the gear—food, water, repair pieces, and the lot—goes inside in a prioritized system of retrieval. First in, last out. The basic system of bags was sound. Most of our individual camp needs, sleeping bags, air mattresses, bivvy sacks, and clothing were in six green Voyager caboose bags, three for each seat. One caboose was loaded with a sleeping bag as a seat, and the other two were wedged and compression-strapped into the sides of the boat, making for a comfortably snug hip support.

The extra height positioned the lower back in a more supportive position compared to the stock backrest and allowed for greater paddle leverage. The more angled leg positioning encouraged greater blood flow to the toes. All in all an excellent system. That was not the problem.

It's all those little things you think you're going to need sometime that end up being randomly stuffed into a bag. These were low-priority items having to do with shipwreck scenarios, characterized by an iron hand drill and the *SBS Survival Handbook,* among the spare batteries, battery rechargers, extra "torches" (flashlights), and all those other details that I kept thinking about for untold hours. They turned into what seemed a horrible knot to untie—and of course, there was the *Book of Knots.*

How do I prioritize when I really don't know what we're up against? The basic camp needs: tent, sleeping bag, clothing—that was easy. *What about the different repair materials and spare bits? How frequently was this going to come into play? Where and when will what go wrong?*

"Planning to build another boat along the way, are you?" Tony asked, while I gathered and bundled dozens of strips of lacquered plywood."

"Maybe."

I figured this would be a journey of equipment attrition: a function of too many miles, too much time, and too much punishment. I wanted the problem-solving machine installed just right, right away. I wanted to have tool C ready for problem number ten on day three right where it was supposed to be at that moment. I wanted all contingency plans and the means to carry them out nearby. If Tony had it his way, we would have had boat, swim trunks, shirt, hat, paddle, food, water, bivvy sacks, Swiss army knife, and a shark club. No more, no less.

I had brought two masts and two sails, feeling that we were eventually going to do a lot of sailing. Tony believed we were going to primarily paddle and rarely go to the sails. Part of me shared the paddle purity point of view, yet another was seeing the much bigger picture. We left one mast at home.

Tony lumbered toward me cradling what looked like a giant black bag of garden soil. The veins bulged from his neck.

"I just filled this with water and I'd say it's just a wee bit over the top."

He was referring to the ten-gallon extra-heavy-duty PVC sea sack capable of holding heavy fluids like oil, if necessary. You could practically shoot it with a bullet and it would not pop or puncture. But at eighty pounds it was useless to us. Out it went.

It was getting dark when Tony began unloading the grocery bags. From the local supermarket, he had purchased boxes of rice, pasta, dried potatos, sauces, soup mixes, candy bars, macaroni and cheese, large squeeze bottles of sweetened condensed milk, crackers, and more. It looked like a UN air drop.

"So Epic, where does all *this* go?"

Just unpackaging the packaging consumed time. We then repackaged it all in waterproof Nalgene jars and then packed those into waterproof bags. The formerly ethereal transparent jars became grain- and pasta-filled calorie bombs.

Twelve dozen Power Bars were divided in half with some packed in long-term storage in the deep ends of the boat next to the hand drill and many dispersed in bags that would be "reasonably" easy to reach. There was still more repacking to do.

We figured *maybe* it would be an afternoon launch.

The morning dragged on. The endless drama of packing was getting to be too much for Tony, and he looked on with barely restrained disdain at all the gear and provisions.

"We're never gonna leave at this rate!"

The next-door neighbor came over carrying a long painted pole.

"What the hell *now?*" I grumbled.

"Do you mind if I bless your boat with my didgeridoo?"

"Be my guest, mate," Tony sneered. "We need all the help we can get."

A deep resonating sound like the exhaust manifold of a wobbling flying saucer from a B-grade sci-fi flick bombarded the boat.

The didgeridoo is a four-to-five-foot-long Aboriginal Australian wooden wind instrument. It has hundreds of colorfully painted lines and dots forming ritual imagery. The neighbor said that they were made from select branches of eucalyptus hollowed out by termites. It clearly took specifically contorted lips pressed against the beeswax mouthpiece to set the mysterious tone, and an acrobatic diaphragm to coax the obscure melodies out of the somewhat wider horn-like end.

The blessing completed, I resumed packing. Was it me who was the irresponsible one having brought all this "stuff" to this expedition? Was I being typically American about this whole thing? The more the better? Was the didgeridoo some way of forgiving me? Were all the deal making, phone calls, faxes, research, fact finding, and money spending worth it?

I watched Tony scrutinize the compass and chart panel that was to fit between us. It was the control panel from which Tony was to calculate the course as he sat in the aft seat with foot-control steering. He picked it up like Tarzan would pick up a radio for the first time, acknowledging it as unique and interesting but of no real use to him in the jungle.

Business in a fixed location had given me perspective on sustaining a venture day to day, week to week and month to month. Things like running out of copy paper at an inopportune time can make one miss a deadline. Tony rarely had to worry about things like that. I felt like a pack mule laden with picks and axes, while Tony was the bareback mustang.

"Do we *really* need that, mate?!"

"Well, if we get to Broome and we don't have access to any villages then—"

"OK, OK, OK!"

We eventually managed to get most of the gear loaded that day, leaving only a few items to be loaded on the deck for the next day—the day we now hoped to finally leave. I resigned myself to the fact that we were already a day behind schedule. Worse, I realized that I was as much a novice for this level of endeavor as Tony. In some ways more of one.

Tony had been out more than I had. Talking the talk for so long is not walking the walk. I was taking my first awkward steps. I felt that in some way we were overstepping the capacity of even *his* book of luck tickets.

Later that evening I went down to the beach, looked out on the vast dark mass, listened to the crashing surf, and plea-bargained for leniency.

After a fitful night's sleep, I rose bright and early to finish the packing. Tony, his mum, and I sat down for our last Bondi sit-down breakfast and pot of tea. Brilliant sunshine and gentle surf blessed Bondi Beach that day. Tony was strangely silent, as was I. We could no longer afford to trade punches. We needed all of our energies for "liftoff."

It will be a good launch! It will be a good launch! I repeated to myself.

Houston, We Have a Problem

I maneuvered the stern of *Southern Cross* perpendicular to the boat cart. I squatted down, grabbed underneath with both hands, and pulled up. The rear half of the frame flexed under the stress and rose six inches off the ground, while the rest of the boat just sat there wallowing in a field of gravity.

Holy shit! I have never felt a Klepper this heavy before!

"Need a little help, mate?!" Tony asked.

We need a friggin' crane, I wanted to say.

"Yeah, I could use a hand!" I said.

We arranged ourselves on each side like two wanna-be Arthurs trying to pull the Excalibur sword from the sacred stone. We pulled with all our might and barely managed to slide the cart underneath, three feet in from the stern.

"God, she's bloody *heavy*!" Tony exclaimed.

The carriage body of the Australian boat cart was a bit narrower than the Klepper cart I had left at home. The overall width was the same but that was due to the extra width of the tires. *Southern Cross* listed awkwardly atop the carriage with its swollen belly resting on one of the wheels. I quickly ran to the front and pulled to see if it had rolled. I hoped that the obvious problem would somehow magically disappear, like a stranded motorist who wishfully thinks the mere act of opening the hood, looking at it, and closing it will make the car continue merrily on.

Chchshchchsshcchchsssss.

"*Stop* mate! *Stop!* The wheel is wearing through the hull!" Tony yelled. "I'll get some webbing and make a better sling system to give her some clearance."

We unpacked the rear half until we got to the repair materials and found some one-inch webbing cloth, and Tony promptly improvised a sling lattice-work across the top of the side of the carriage with a rapid succession of knot work.

"Thar ya go mate! That should do it!" he said proudly.

We repositioned *Southern Cross* onto the webbing and—sure enough—she sat more level. Tony's knots tightened and the webbing held on for dear life. The wheels had an inch of clearance and rolled, albeit with a different, more internal grating sound.

Now the negotiation of the two small staircases that we had thoughtlessly scampered over half a dozen times with the empty kayak was more than an issue. It took both of us to lift the bow onto the top of the staircase, and then both of us clamored to the stern and heaved the behemoth up one step at a time. Perspiration poured on this graceless waltz. I watched Tony's face strain, as this former lightweight dance partner became a clumsy lump of canvas and rubber.

Sweat and toil escorted us down the street with no indications they were leaving anytime soon. Memories of racing each other down cobblestone streets, across Seventh Avenue and the mile back to the Klepper shop were erased and replaced by the new experience of self-contained expedition physics.

The boat was still heavy on the boat cart though it was centered for the best possible mechanical advantage. The stern of the boat sagged and the metal rudder blade occasionally scraped the sidewalk. I stayed at the front end to pull and Tony went to the back to lift and push.

How was it going to paddle? When I paddled the Chesapeake Bay our boats were full but only to the limits of the bulky uncompressable waterproof bags. This was much heavier.

I kept mentally reviewing the stories of others with heavy loads. I thought of John Dowd, who said it would take two years to go around Australia. "You'll be lucky to manage fifteen miles a day." He carried loads like this before, didn't he? But *we* were paddling machines . . . *right?*

We finally got to the north end of Bondi, where we had hoped to launch. I had been watching surf skiiers launch there for weeks. Tony's friend Moz was there to chronicle the whole affair. We tried rolling *SC* on the sand to try out the extrawide tires, and watched them sink to the axle.

"So much for the special sand tires, mate. Call me old-fashioned, but it looks like we'll have to lift and drag it from here to the water."

Tony was right. The water was still over a hundred yards away.

Now I know how the slaves who built the pyramids felt.

No sooner had the now bulging-armed Tony gotten onto the boardwalk than a "too-cool-for-school" zinc-nosed lifeguard appeared. I'd seen pairs of Rottweilers instinctively square off over territory in NYC like this.

That's all we need, I thought.

The guard approached Tony with the purposeful gait of authority. "Where do you think you're going with that, mate?"

Tony's chest expanded, his intense green eyes aimed, and his mouth fired. "To launch our kayak over there." He pointed to the launch area.

"Not here, you're not."

Tony bent his arms ninety degrees at the elbows with his hands outstretched like he was trying to shake the seeds out of a large watermelon or perhaps to strangle the shadow of the lifeguard. This further incensed the guard, who only wanted Tony to beg and concede the turf.

"Mate, we have to launch our kayak over there. We're about to go around Australia and we want to get off to a good start."

"You can't launch here during the day because you might hit somebody swimming." I looked around and didn't see more than a few people. "You have to launch up the beach," he said, pointing.

The north side of Bondi is noted for its mild surf. Further up the beach the surf looked much rougher. The two Rottweilers began snapping and snarling.

Tony barked: "We need to launch where the surf is smallest."

"If you can't launch through that surf today, you have no business going around Australia, mate."

Touché.

Tony's friend Moz stepped in to referee. He had a couple of cameras around his neck and claimed to be a *National Geographic* photographer documenting our launch. He explained what we were attempting, along with a subtle message that the readership would not take too kindly to this kind of harassment. After a short powwow with a second lifeguard we got the thumbs-up.

"No worries," he said. We were on our way.

I turned to Moz in a quiet moment and asked how to handle Tony in situations like this. He answered: "Creatively."

Getting the boat to the water was a relief, as some buoyancy relieved the slogging of the wheels dragging through sand. A small farewell party of Tony's family and a few friends saw us off. A man with a German accent, unrelated to the party, cleaned the sand off our spray covers in the water. He wished us luck as he handed us the clean covers. It was exactly what my father would have done if he were there.

Tony finished the last of his hugs while I finished zippering my life jacket. I walked calf deep into the water to the front of the boat, turned my back to the sea, and grabbed the lifting handle with both hands. I tried pivoting *Southern Cross* so the bow lined up perpendicular to the oncoming waves. The stern half of the boat remained anchored in the sand. I pulled and yanked the stubborn front end like Jim wrestling an alligator in the television series *Wild Kingdom*.

Tony hurried over to help finish the job. I finally stepped into the front cock-pit of the now ultrastable kayak. The extra weight had brought the upper flare shape of the boat onto the waterline, minimizing any rocking motion. Tony held the boat steady as I reached behind myself to fasten the elastic of my spray skirt over the thirty-inch-long hard rubber, oval cockpit of the spray cover, which covered the rest of the ninety-six-inch-long cockpit. I worked the elastic around the rim with both my hands from back to front. It's one of those processes that simply does not work the other way around and requires precise attention. Just as I got the elastic all the way to apex of the cockpit—

Ssshhhhhsshshshhsshh—thump.

The elastic slingshotted off the rim as the boat was bumped on the left side by a foot of surf surge. I quickly started poling and paddling on my right to keep the boat from being broadsided back to the beach. Tony ran into the water and pulled on the port side to reestablish the angle. Fuck the spray cover.

Tony shoved the rest of the boat into the water with the force of a bobsled driver and hopped in the same way. We took our first strokes in the fully laden, 650-pound *Southern Cross*. We levered *SC* slowly forward, and the initial slug-gishness was soon replaced with a welcome inertia. We punched through a small set of breakers like a tank smashing through a haystack. I got a bucket full of water in my lap. I looked back and saw a small girl waving with one hand and holding a red plastic pail in the other. A minute later I reminded Tony: "Don't forget to deploy the rudder—"

"Plunk!" The rudder flipped into its engaged position as Tony finished pulling the quarter-inch black nylon rudder deployment line under his right elbow on the side of the boat.

"One step ahead of you, mate . . ."

"Don't forget to put your spray cover on."

"Don't think I need it today, seas seem pretty small."

"Well, you never know."

We were now showing off, paddling with more than the usual frenzy of whirling carbon fiber. The boat glided through the water with little if any extra-neous chatter. The clipper bow sliced through and rose over the swells, the frame undulating with the sea's rhythm. *Southern Cross* was in her element. We passed the north point of Bondi. Things quickly slowed down, now out of the gaze of the fan club.

"Mate, I can't wait till we get back," Tony exulted.

"Get back to where?"

"Back to Bondi, of course."

"Well, we better pick up the pace then, because at this rate it will take three years."

An hour later, we passed the famous Sydney Heads, now seen from the Pacific side.

"Whew, slow it down, mate. I forgot how tiring this was."

Instead, I paddled a little faster. I was eager to get Tony far enough from Sydney that there would be no chance he might casually decide to turn back. A little while later we heard a voice from a fifty-foot sailing vessel approaching off our starboard bow.

"Where's your boat?" the captain hollered to the accompanying chuckles from his crew.

"You're lookin' at it!" I shouted.

"Going all around Australia, are you?"

"That's right, we are!" Tony added cockily.

"Good luck then!"

"No worries!" I called back.

Five miles down. Only nine thousand nine hundred and ninety-five to go.

"Raise the rudder and give me ramming speed, Mr. Brown!"

Half hoping to hear "Aye aye, sir!" I hear instead, "You really want to run her straight on the beach?"

"Looks like all sand to me, no surf, no problem." I find myself in the odd situation of reassuring Tony.

"Are you sure?"

"The bottom is double keel-strip reinforced. It's built for it."

During the course of the day, Tony had bonded with *Southern Cross* like a rider with a new horse. I saw her as a war machine. We ran her ten feet up the beach and stumbled out with stiff legs. We pulled the boat up another twenty yards and tethered her to a large rock to keep her out of the clutches of tidal bandits sneaking up the beach in the course of the night.

"Where do you think we are?"

"Somewhere in northern Sydney," Tony answered.

My spirits dropped like a pair of honeymoon pajamas. Jeez, I thought, we paddle half a day and we still are in Sydney. A trim, tan, and toned middle-aged man came running down the beach with his golden retriever by his side. He was nonplussed by our arrival.

"Sir, do you know what beach this is?" I asked.

"You're on Long Point," he said, barely losing a stride while his dog gave *Southern Cross* a good nose-over.

The whole scene reminded me of the Hamptons on eastern Long Island back in the States. The last rays of the sun mingled with the bright lights of Sydney to the south and contrasted with the absolute darkness to the north. We weren't moving toward the light. We were leaving it.

"No sense in unpacking," Tony decided. "We should just potter into town and find some tucker."

"I couldn't agree with you more, but I still need to change into my street clothes."

I unsnapped the fastex buckles on the compression straps holding the green caboose bags. They had made for a very comfortable seat. Much more comfortable than the standard seating. Better than I expected! I unwedged the squished and molded rectangles. They unflattened like blades of grass after a recently passed footstep.

I wasn't sure which one had the electric blue lightweight fleece tops and bottoms, so I opened the most likely choice and it gasped for air, puffing up like a party balloon. I rummaged around and pulled the pants out like long rabbit ears out of a hat. Minutes later, I was dressed like Captain Kirk, with a shiny silver chest patch that read "Stohlquist" instead of "Enterprise." Tony was dressed the same but looked more like Spock without the pointy ears.

We walked down the west toward town and saw a neon sign glowing across a wide dark stretch of grass.

"Looks like an eatery across the way, mate."

"Sure does. Tallyho!"

We turned on our Maglites and followed their darting funnels across an irrigation ditch and onto a very smooth section of grass with a hole in the middle.

"It's a bloody golf course," Tony said.

I had an instant flashback to the movie *Caddyshack*.

"Look out fer de gophers," I said in my best Bill Murray voice. Tony stared blankly at me, the humor missed. We continued our navigation toward the gradually enlarging neon sign, which I could start to read:

"P . . . I . . . Z . . . Pizza!" I exclaimed. One of my favorite New York foods.

We broke into a trot, Tony whirled open the door, and I heard the welcoming tinkle of the doorbell. Then, the din of fluorescent lights accompanied by a discerning gaze from the smudgy white-smocked pizza maker behind the counter.

We scooted into the diner-style seating and tore open the menus.

"I'm famished mate, how does this Hawaiian number sound?"

"Hmmmm . . . ham, onion, pineapple. I don't know about the pineapple part."

Tony cut to the chase. "This isn't New York. This is a favorite in Oz."

"OK, I'll give it a shot."

Tony ordered the pizza and I walked over to the refrigerator loaded with soft drinks and beers. I asked Tony what kind of beer he wanted.

"Just get me a liter of lemon soda."

"You're sure you don't want a beer?!"

"That's right, mate."

We inhaled the pizza and sucked down a couple of liters of lemon soda. The pizza filled the belly, but was a far cry from Rays on Sixth Avenue in the Village.

We trekked back to the kayaks and plotted our first illegal campsite, behind a set of rocks on the far end of the point. I went about unraveling the light purple Therm-a-rest mattress, which was as thin as a frozen waffle. I opened the automatic inflation valve waiting for it to expand to the expected one-inch thickness of outdoor bedtime luxury but nothing was happening. I began the CPR.

Next, I threaded the fiberglass arch rod through the thumb-sized half-oval slot on the top end of my spanking new, extremely lightweight Gor-Tex bivvy sack. I bent the narrow ends of the rod into their respective grommets. And . . . voilà! A prefabricated A-frame shelter that resembled a red, oversized Christmas sock.

I slid the inflated Therm-a-Rest into the sock, but had to let a little air out and fold it lengthwise in half to get it all the way in. Next came the sweater-thick fleece sleeping bag. A wise choice, I concluded proudly, as the night air was cooling rapidly.

I'll be sleeping in my warm fleece clothes tonight, I thought to myself. I sealed it all off with the oval zipper on the mosquito netting inside the oval zipper to the mosquito netting cover. Now it looked like a junior-sized sarcophagus with the mummy already inside.

After standing back to admire my handiwork, I sat down to write my first candlelight diary entry. The ground was bumpy and I had no coffee table or milk crate to balance the flickering light. I eventually improvised a crude nightstand from a number of stones and began to write.

Tony had set up his camp twenty yards away, but wandered over to inspect mine. He pinched and wiggled the crooked A frame and frowned.

"It doesn't look quite the way it did in the pictures, Epic."

"Very funny."

"Well, good night, mate. It was a good day after all."

"Good night."

I struggled into my bivvy sack for the first time and wondered *why* Tony had insisted on this style of shelter? First of all, getting in had to be harder than Alan Shepard climbing into the *Mercury* space capsule. I did not want to stab myself with the repaired headroom wand and therefore had to hook my feet in first while balancing on the straight-armed palms of my hands like a gymnast on a pommel horse.

Once my feet found bottom, I scooched (butt-walked) my shoulders and head into position underneath the compromised canopy. I found that the tomb accepted my lying flat on my back or on my side. When I rolled from one side to the other I simply became a red licorice Twizzler stick. I could not achieve the full fetal tuck position, yet it didn't matter tonight. The anxiety of the morning boat-cart commute, four hours of paddling, and the gentle lap and hiss of the tiny surf put me right out. It was nine o'clock.

Snniffff . . . Snniffff . . . Snort . . . Sniffff.

"Come here, Elizabeth!"

I awoke with a start. One of Long Point's early morning dog walkers was reconnoitering our camp. I just prayed I was not mistaken for a fire hydrant.

The threat passed as soon as it arrived, and it was to time to get out of the capsule. My butt muscles did not initially respond to the first "scooch up" command with any productive movement. Instead, my lower back had become a parliament of aching complaints. I thought it was a little early in the trip for this kind of soreness, but it dawned on me that it had been over a month since I had paddled for more than three hours at a stretch and that had been in an empty boat. There is no such thing as being completely "in shape."

I wriggled around a bit and the blood flow broke up the debates. *Thank God it's just stiffness and not strained muscles,* I thought to myself. I was glad that I had trained my lower body and midsection as much as my upper body. Although we had not trained with a loaded boat I knew that suddenly getting out and manhandling the boat on sandy beaches, rocks, and a gnarly seacoast was going to ask a lot more from my body. "Radu training" had been a great start, as it concentrated on "plyometrics."

Plyometrics conditions fast-twitch muscle fibers to respond quickly and powerfully, like a basketball player going up for a rebound or a tennis player darting sideways to get to a quick passing shot. A basic plyometric exercise involves fast prestretching of a muscle followed by an equally quick contraction. A jumping jack is a beginner's plyometric. A clap pushup is an intermediate's. Rocky Balboa jump-squatting up a mountain with a tree on his back is advanced.

John Dowd's manual had suggested that the best way to get "in shape" for sea kayaking expeditions was to paddle a lot and keep the endurance up with related exercises or to slowly get in shape en route by starting with low mileage and gradually build up. He does not talk much about strength, stretching, or leg work.

I always assumed this was because he was an avid outdoorsman and that his day-to-day lifestyle kept everything else solid and functional.

Living in a city with an office job and regular visits to the gym is not the same as being outdoors in a constantly variable environment. Walking up ten flights of stairs with a mountain bike on your shoulder is a more appropriate exercise than an hour on the StairMaster machine or three sets on the Cybex machine.

"Rise and shine, mate!" Tone bellowed cheerfully.

I hand-walked out of my sack like a fallen paraplegic getting back onto a wheelchair. Tony had already untethered *Southern Cross,* pivoted her around so the bow faced seaward, packed his camp, and even laid out some bread, honey, salami, and something that looked like dark chocolate in a jar labeled Vegemite. I thought it was the same nutty-tasting chocolate spread I had pilfered at the penthouse from a jar that had no label.

"What's your flavor, Epic?"

"What's this Vegemite stuff?"

"Open it up and give it a try."

I took my Leatherman knife and scooped up a bladeful and spread it on the bread. I gulped it all the way down, anticipating a taste sweet and yummy. Instead I found myself gagging like a cat with a giant fur ball.

"Jeez-us," I spat.

"Lotsa good B vitamins in it. Great for a hangover," Tony tried to say with a straight face.

"What the hell is it made of?"

"It's a yeast extract. Very healthy. You'll get a taste for it soon enough."

"Don't bet your bottom dollar on that one, Tony. Pass me the honey."

An hour and a half later we were on our way, gliding smoothly, as our paddles did the talking. We were in a sea of big, soft, green pillows, with swells no larger than the hillocks on the golf course the night before. Muscles quickly loosened up with our even cadence and strong, steady pulls. We had covered yesterday's distance in an hour's less time when a sudden single paddle clash changed the screen like a remote control.

We were now doing the herky-jerky and *Southern Cross* was buffeted by a series of oscillating pyramid-shaped waves. It was like an enormous shower nozzle set on "pulse" shooting at us from below. I half-expected a FASTEN SEAT BELTS sign to go on someplace in my cockpit. We were just beginning to cross Broken Bay where the Hawkesury River exits into the Pacific. The tide was starting to go in and the wrestling match had begun. Luckily there was no wind to speak of.

The paddling became frustrating as solid strokes got harder to find. By mid-bay the waves were two to three feet high and the bouncing only got more chaotic. Someone was turning up the water pressure. Hands were getting doused with every stroke. Water-softened skin and friction do not mix.

We were two-thirds across when Tony screamed: "Why is it taking so long to only go five miles?!"

"The sea's trying to run upriver, but the river is pushing back. We're in the middle of their argument!"

"My hands are going raw."

"Try to loosen your grip on the paddle."

This giant washing machine was also abrading my lower back as it got jostled on and off the backrest. My hands were getting tender in spots as well. My advice was easier to preach than to practice. We struggled to maintain verticle equilibrium, but our bodies began paying the price. Soaked to the skin, our soggy asses picked up the wrinkles of the bags we were sitting on like a forensic scientist lifting fingerprints. Toward the end of the crossing I had a half a dozen hot spots, two full-blown blisters at the base of the thumbs, and a few dark blood blisters under age-old calluses.

"Spock? Damage report?"

"That was a hell ride, mate."

"If it makes you feel better, take a look at these!" I showed him the dark red dots on the palm side of my middle and ring fingers just below the middle knuckle.

"Yeah, we used to pumice our calluses every day when I rowed."

"This happened to me on the Chesapeake, too. I just wrapped 'em with this duct tape and moved on."

I wrapped my hands like a boxer wrapping his fists before putting the gloves on. I handed the roll to Tony and flexed my hands with somewhat more dexterity than a mummy.

"Make sure you leave enough room to move your fingers, Tony."

It had taken another three hours to go half the distance that morning. But we were rewarded a couple of hours later as we pulled into idyllic Maitland Bay. I thought to myself, *this had to be one of the tucked-away white sand beaches with lush tropical vegetation that you see in Australian travel brochures.*

The boat practically parked itself as we skimmed a half-boat length up the beach. There was not a soul around, just the rusty skeleton of a half-sunken wreck a hundred yards to the east.

When I pushed myself up and out of the cockpit every hot spot ignited. Pulling on the grab handles to bring *SC* up the rest of the way fanned the flames. Not only did the hands feel blistered, they felt bruised.

It was a beautiful late afternoon and we both promptly stripped and enjoyed a deliriously refreshing soak in the shallow tropical water of Broken Bay. After the initial stings, I floated chest up spread-eagle. While pelicans flew overhead, I kept my rib cage filled with deep breaths and allowed the salty buoyancy to stretch out my back. It had really taken a beating. The fish underneath me could now read MONROE SHOCK ABSORBERS tattooed on my back by Broken Bay.

Later, I explored the beach and vegetation on my own, climbing up to an overlook and taking a few snapshots. When I came back, Tony was fussing with various pieces of cooking gear. He was trying to figure out the MSR stove that had been so highly recommended stateside by many reputable outdoor magazines. It now looked like a childhood chemistry set that Tony was trying to put together without the instructions. I had previously boiled one cup of water with it back on the worktable in the Klepper shop many moons ago in a land far far away.

"Tony," I said, "give me a shot with it. I think the direction card is still in the sack." We shook it out and there it was. "OK, no worries, here it is."

"Mate, you should have got the Gaz stove with those pop-on gas cartridges I told you about. They've worked great for me in the mountains."

"I know, I know. But this will work in places where there are no special camping stores to get those cartridges."

"Mate, those cartridges are sold everywhere in Oz."

"Not where there aren't any stores. Anyway, I'll show you how great this is."

I followed the directions to the letter. I proceeded to unscrew the fuel bottle tab where I had some premium MSR fuel just to make sure. I screwed in the special pump valve system. I then inserted the stove section, which looked like an upside-down lunar-landing-module toy, to the fuel valve vis-à-vis a thin, slightly angled metal pipe—making sure (as the instructions clearly marked) that the fuel bottle was level with the stove. I pumped the recommended number of times for sea-level altitude, I opened the valve the correct distance, heard the slight hiss, inserted the match and—*presto*—a small flame that I was instructed to leave burning until it flamed steadily. Then I could turn the valve higher for a hotter flame. I looked over at Tony and said a bit smugly, "No problem."

"It went out, mate."

I repeated the entire process . . . once again by the book. Then again. After a few sputtering attempts and after nearly burning my face off, I had managed to amend the manual's approach by improvising a procedure that finally worked. I finally had a solid flame.

"There," I said. "No problem."

Tony grumbled. "We could have eaten by now."

Tony took out a big one-quart pot and filled it with noodles, Italian corn pasta, onion flakes, spicy soap-mix flavor packets, a few chunks of salami and then thickened it with some dried mashed potatoes. In twenty minutes we had Tony's first pasta casserole. We ate it all with two spoons while we sat side to side on a crooked log. In ten minutes it was continuing to expand in our stomachs.

"Sticks to the ribs, doesn't it, mate?"

"And then some. It was really good, though."

"Glad you liked it. Looks like I'm the cook around here."

"I think you're right."

"Sam would have had us a regular blue-plate special."

I changed the subject. "Tony, you could have had yourself quite a vet practice back in Long Point with all those purebreds sniffin' around. I hear they need a lot of attention. Are you thinking of going back to finish school?"

"I just might, except the type of veterinarian I was going to be was for the big animals."

"What, like kangaroos?"

"Nah, horses, cattle, sheep. Did you know that it takes higher test scores to get into a good vet school in Oz than medical school."

"No way."

"Absolutely. Think about it, mate. There are a lot more farm animals than there are people in Oz. They are very important to the economy, more so than in the States."

He went on describing farm life and biochemistry until it was time to put the Broken Bay bodies to rest. I bootlegged into my bag and zippered the mosquito netting half an arm's length from my face. My last thought was about Nicole and me eating sushi on a level surface.

The next morning early I awoke drenched in sweat. The heat and color of my capsule convinced me that I had been picked up and hurled at the sun in the course of the night. It was too uncomfortable to go back to sleep so I clawed myself out of the bag far stiffer than the day before. The placid lagoon nearby looked inviting, but immersing my scuffed and bruised limbs into the salty water did not. Instead, I did a few slow toe touches, hip circles, and arm swings to see, like the Tin Man, that I still worked and I secretly hoped that WD 40 could work on my joints. I heard a grunting sound, like a farm animal coming from Tony's camp.

"*Uhhhhhmmmhhooo,*" he groaned as he emerged from his blue cocoon.

"Not exactly dancing like a butterfly today, huh TB?"

"Just a wee bit stiff."

"How're the hands?"

He showed me his hands and it looked like someone had played scratch bingo on them with the flip tab of an aluminum can. I broke out the tea tree oil and the duct tape and began my Florence Nightingale act.

"Your mum told me she was a nurse in Vietnam."

"That's right, mate. That's where she met my father."

"Your dad was a surgeon in Vietnam? He was a real-life *M*A*S*H* doc?"

"Yep, but he doesn't laugh about it much. Pretty serious business with a hundred surgeries a week I suppose."

"At least he met your mum."

"Well, that's good, Epic. The hands feel as good as new. Let's get going and take advantage of this beaut' of a day."

Tony packed up, I patched up, while the combination of warm sunshine and a more familiar routine straightened me out. We launched with no exact idea where we would end up. With weather and water conditions like this, it really didn't seem to matter. Tony's "potter up the coast" plan was working to a T.

The tape-protected hands and calm seas took us over twelve miles to Upright Point by noon. I saw a hundred-yard-long beach with a lifeguard stand and a small hamburger joint. The sun was straining to spotlight the discovery through thickening clouds.

"I'm famished," Tony announced as we hastily ditched *Southern Cross* and assaulted the hamburger stand.

Patrons at picnic tables with canopied sun umbrellas were putting large purple circles onto their burgers before sealing them with the bun.

"What'll it be, mate?"

"What's with the purple disks?"

"Beetroot, mate. Try it. You'll like 'em."

Here we go again, I thought. I didn't remember being a big beet fan back home but it had been a while and I could always pull it off if I didn't like it.

"Two with the works then!" The works included beets, bacon, cheese, and pineapple.

"Anything to drink?"

"Two liters of cola and throw in the *Australian,* too, please."

Minutes later I had a heap of hamburger and liter of Coke in front of me. We sat down and divvied up the newspaper. I felt a slight chill, as my body had cooled and the sun had all but disappeared. I took the section with the national weather map to get some clue as to what might be going on.

There was a thumb-sized black ink spot in the upper right corner (northeast) of the map. A tight compressed spiral of pressure-gradient lines was bent and twisted into a cometlike shape. Next to it was the word *Fran*. It was a late-season cyclone. The power and fury are the same as that of a hurricane but the winds spin in a clockwise instead of a counterclockwise direction. Coincidentally it is the same direction as the water spins in the toilet bowels Down Under. Put a thumb-sized model of a kayak in the bowel, flush, and you get the picture.

"Tony, check this out, what you make of it?"

"It's over a thousand miles away, mate. I don't see that's much worrying about yet."

We went back to the boat and I slipped the chart case from under the shock cords on the compass panel. I approached the lifeguard stand and caught the guard as he was climbing down.

"Excuse me, mate. G'day."

"Tony McDermitt, mate. G'day. What can I do for you?"

"What's with the weather? Does it have something to do with Fran?"

"Not exactly. But there is a change [front] and a big wind due in late this afternoon."

"Do you think Fran will get down here?"

"They [cyclones] don't usually come this far. They usually make the turn at Bundy [Bundaberg] and deflect out to sea. Fran's a big one, though, and could make things interestin' on the coast for quite a while. Wadda ya up to?"

"We're trying to circumnavigate Oz in that kayak over there."

"Fantastic! How fast can you go in it?"

"About four to five knots." I rolled out the chart onto a nearby table.

McDermitt quickly oriented himself and said authoritatively, "Ya want to make it to Catherine Hill Bay today. She faces a bit more north and ya can duck into a sweetheart of a landing spot." He pointed to about the third discernible divot on the less-than-detailed chart.

"Ya don't want to go here: Frazer Beach." He jammed his finger emphatically as he pointed to the second divot on the chart. Neither one was named as McDermitt described.

"Mate, quit ear-bashing the good man. Let's get going!" Tony called.

"Gotta go. Thank you very much."

"No worries, good on ya."

I brought the chart to Tony and pointed out the divots on the chart.

"Tony, we want to land *here*, not *here*. Got that? The lifeguard was real clear about it. Catherine Hill Bay, not Frazer Beach."

"Yeah, yeah. Hey Epic, the wind's picking up. Maybe it's a good day to try the sails?"

I looked at my meat-hook hands. "I'll set up the mast so we can deploy the sails when we want."

"Super."

I took the blue canvas bag, which looked like half a pair of Wilt Chamberlain's newest pair of jeans with a leg still in it, off the foredeck and untied the end. I poured the glistening two-part alloy mast and the crisp, straight, red sails with all lines attached and tied with perfect Howard Rice sailors' knots onto *Southern Cross*'s semiflat spray-covered midsection. I shook the bag out to make sure the very important two-foot-long adapting post was out. I began to feel the reverence that I imagined a professional sniper feels when he is about to assemble his gun. All the metal parts glistened and were lightly lubricated with a Teflon spray.

First came the post. It was forged to barely fit through the 1.5-inch-diameter cast-metal mast holder on the front of the coaming. I then slid it sixteen inches down and matched a hard, square piece of rubber into the square-shaped wooden receiver plate that is screwed to the keel board. Click. A pinky-sized stainless steel cotter pin fit through a hole on the post just above the top of the metal masthead casting. It had a tiny self-locking hub built into it and allowed less than an eighth of inch of verticle play. Click.

I mated the two 4.5-foot mast halves of the mast. Click. Slid the hollowed luff of the sail onto the mast. I did the same with the half-inch-thick boom and slid it into the hollowed-out foot of the mainsail. I attached the 1.75-inch-wide U-shaped, unbreakable nylon boom to the mast connector a fist's width away from the post pin. Click. Secured and tugged on the main halyard, undid the mainsheet, and *pow* the mainsail snapped to attention on one of the ever more frequent gusts.

The boat lurched forward on the sand—all from the power of a sail smaller than a cot-sized bedsheet. I rigged the jib sail, which was cut slightly larger with a little more curve in it. Pow. The jib parachuted open on the other side. The boat was facing northwest, the winds were coming from behind (southeast).

I saw Tony's eyes widen and watch as if stupefied. Meanwhile I was standing with my legs straddled amidships with arms outstretched, holding the mainsheet in my left hand and the jib in the right like a charioteer from a Charlton Heston film.

"Let me have the reins, mate," Tony said and proceeded to sit in the rear cockpit to get a better feel for it. A sudden shift of wind from the south quickly snapped the boom to the other side just in front of Tony's nose, and the boat rolled to starboard.

"Good thing you weren't in your seat, mate, you would have got quite a haircut."

"OK, Tony, let's get going. I'll funnel-wrap the sail to the mast and have it ready to go when we feel like sailing."

I hand-rolled the boom from bottom to top, until the sail was tightly wound, and then I placed it vertically to the mast. I had to tilt the boat on its side to reach the mainsheet on the end of the boom, which was now sitting near the top of the mast. I used the mainsheet to snake-wrap the mast to the boom and make an easy-to-release knot and attached it to a third nylon cleat vertically placed on the aft side of the mast—a long arm's reach of my seat. I map-folded the jib and placed it into one of the legal paper–sized paddle pockets on the fore-deck. We were now fully armed and dangerous.

We launched and decided to paddle for a while as the winds were alternating between sudden gusts and nothing at all. The sea was dark and closer to gray than sun-drenched aquamarine. Like someone forgot to colorize these particular frames of *The Wizard of Oz*. Hell, the water looked like the slate gray Hudson back home, which was definitely not in Kansas. One-foot waves had formed and lapped at the rear starboard quarter of the boat just like when Tony and I had paddled for the very first time.

We moved well for an hour, passed the narrow inlet to Tuggerah Lake a quarter mile to port and were heading toward higher bluffs in front of us. Except for the six-mile crossing of Broken Bay, Tony's simplistic concept of "keeping Australia close to our left" was the rule. However, by midafternoon the skies had darkened dramatically. Another hour and we were getting bounced around by two-foot seas rebounding off the steep rocky shoreline on the southern end of Wyrrabalong National Park.

The hands remembered Broken Bay. We passed a large cove or small bay and I mentally noted it as divot number one on the map.

"I think that's the first of the three dents on the chart, Tony."

"Mate, the wind's building. Let's put up the sails!"

The wind was steady now and I figured a little trial run for a few miles was about right. I was happy that Tony had suggested it. I took silent joy that his body was feeling a little beat up, too, and that the formerly ostracized sails were getting their chance to show what they could do.

I untied my knot and realized that the easy-to-release snake wrap had morphed into an anaconda that had no intention of releasing its death grip. I had to get up and kneel in my seat to reach high enough up the mast to unravel the creature. I snapped in the U-hook and coaxed a little more sail away from the boom and handed Tony the mainsheet. I kept my paddle handy just in case. Tony nested his on the side of the boat, attached by elastic toggles.

"Mate, could you finish off toggling my paddle?"

It dawned on me that the last time Tony and I had sailed it had been on Georgica Pond in the Hamptons after a day with Calvin and that we had capsized after only ten minutes. Back then the seas were calm, no waves to speak of.

We were now in chaotic seas of three-foot swells that were building and playing with their own shadows.

We were sailing about two hundred yards from shore. Waves were rushing toward shore, smashing into the steeply banked rocks like a backstop, and rebounding back out to sea. Each wave was intersecting, combining, and colliding with the previous one. This sea condition is known as *clapotis,* and it was getting worse. *Southern Cross* was stuck in the middle.

The familiar splish-splash of the paddles was replaced by a much quieter hum, hiss, and swoosh. It was like a noisy diesel-powered railroad train switching to electric. *Southern Cross* was confidently pulling along with the mainsail angling between forty-five and sixty degrees to the port (left) side for optimal trim. We were on a broad reach with a wind coming from the backside of our right cars.

It is a common misunderstanding that a sailboat is primarily pushed through water by wind hitting the sailcloth. In reality, this is only half true. A billowed sail forms an angle that pushes *and* "sucks" the boat forward. Ideally, the windward side of the sail is curved so as to capture enough wind to generate pressure on that side to push it, while maintaining clean curve on the other side to allow air to slide off of it quickly, creating low pressure like a vacuum. High pressure on the windward side now travels even faster toward the low pressure on the leeward side.

This is the same principle as with an airplane wing. A sailboat is like an airplane turned on its side. Sailboats would sail mainly sideways most of the time if a combination of hull shape and hull appendages (rudder, keel, daggerboard) didn't convert the sideways power into primarily forward motion. *Southern Cross* had a rudder but we were not using any keel appendages. We thought that they would be too bulky and cumbersome to use. We also had no intention of sailing close to the wind (upwind) like a pure sailboat, where underwater appendages become essential. We only wanted to use the wind ranging from our sides (reaching) to our back (running). For this the hull of a heavy Klepper is fine.

Tony found the groove and was itching for more.

"Whaddaya think about raising the jib, Epic?"

"The winds are getting pretty strong, Tony, I—"

"Ahh, let's give it a go!"

It was too much sail and I knew it. But I also knew that Tony wouldn't believe me. He had to prove it for himself. I pulled the jib out of its paddle pocket and raised the halyard. *Pop* went the sail. One of the jib lines was flailing on deck and whipping around the mast. I quickly got control of it. The boat suddenly leaned to starboard and then accelerated.

Tony howled with delight.

My stomach tightened with concern.

Southern Cross just galloped forward.

I was stretching my arm awkwardly to the right and behind me trying to keep the most effective curve on the sail.

WOP! Hmmmm . . . WOP! The jib would spasmodically collapse and expand. I could not reach out far enough, so I wrapped the jib sheet around the throat of one end of my paddle and poled out to the side. I was holding it like the boom of a windsurfer and the boat went even faster.

"This is the life, mate!"

The skies got darker, the winds increased, the waves were well over five feet and it started to rain . . . *hard*. I had lost track of shore. Tony had the see-through plastic chart case on the compass control board in front of him. "Is this the third divot?" I asked him. "Is this Catherine Hill Bay?"

"I don't know, mate. It seems pretty big compared to the other ones."

Catherine Hill Bay had appeared like the largest of the coastal cutouts on our overscaled chart.

"This must be it. Conditions are getting bad. Let's take it in."

"OK!" Tony steered us ninety degrees to the left and I flipped the jib to the other side of the boat as the wind was almost directly behind us now. We were running with the wind, down the waves, wing on wing. *Southern Cross* partially surfed forward but held a solid perpendicular line.

"Steer a bit towards the left [south] side! That's where McDermitt said the 'sweetheart of a landing spot' would be."

Staring through the pelting rain I couldn't see where the landing spot was going to magically appear—especially with all the waves being funneled to the beach. I wanted to believe we were in the right spot. The sailing felt good and the waves appeared more orderly as we approached a sandy beach and no longer had to contend with the echo waves off the cliffs. Individual waves were now marching in ordered rows like soldiers falling in to a morning inspection line.

I was anxious to get out of the storm. I optimistically announced, "I think we can sail her right in—"

"Prepare yourself, mate."

I looked behind me and saw three escalating, boiling waves stacked one right behind the next. I felt like I was returning a punt, but had forgotten to signal "fair catch." There was a moment of calm before they hit.

A few chords of the opening of *Hawaii Five-O* played in my mind. This had been my way to convert the fear of surf into thrill back home. Like Lindemman, a type of autogenic training. The waves back home never *really* looked like the ones during the opening scenes of that TV series. Now they did.

The song bubble burst and *Southern Cross's* stern lifted up suddenly, and her nose angled down. One wave swept under us, but only as a setup for the next one. The boat was lifted higher and higher while all the water on the beach was sucked up into the belly of our levitator with a loud hiss. Her bow dropped forward over the newly formed one-story-high wave cliff. We were suddenly vertical and I felt weightless. In the next instant Tony and I were catapulted straight out of the boat toward the beach. *Southern Cross* continued to pitchpole end over end.

She completed her front flip with no one in her. I was mercilessly bulldozed ashore when I saw Tony stumbling against the invisible tentacles of the outrushing undertow.

"You OK, mate?!" he yelled.

"Get the shoe, Tony!"

Tony looked to his left.

"No, over there!" I said to him. One of the Nike all-terrain shoes was floating away. Meanwhile, I scrambled for other floating objects that the wave had punched out of our boat.

"Got your paddle!?"

"Yes!" Tony said.

We were still scavenging for stray objects—hip deep in the beach foam—plucking gear from the water like scavengers picking up dollars that have been tossed on the floor of a busy airport when—*BAAAMMMM!* Another monster wave came in and knocked us off balance. It filled *Southern Cross* with water as we tried to yank her out of the sea. She starting waddling out broadside.

"Let's turn her on her side to empty her out!" Tony got started, heading to the high (beach) side to get the best leverage.

"*No,* not on that side! You'll break your—!" A wave surge hurtled the half-ton boat toward Tony's shins and he barely back-pedalled out of the way.

Sea kayaking protocol calls for exiting your boat on the sea side if the boat is broadside because of the chance of the boat breaking your legs if you get out the other way. I hurried to the sea side but now had a kayak roller pin sliding toward me as the beach angle was more acute than expected.

"I've got it, mate!" With his whole body, Tony wedged himself between the half-turned boat and the onslaught, like Samson trying to push down one of the pillars at Gaza. I joined him in a similar position and held *Southern Cross* half upside down to let as much water drain out as possible. "Shit." The "indestructible" double-thick alloy mast was bent at least forty-five degrees in two places.

BAMMMMM! Another wave! The combined mast-and-human-wedge held firm. I grabbed one of the two-foot-long hand bilge pumps from the deck lines and started pumping the remainder of the water.

"Tony! Get the other pump!"

BAMMMM! Another wave surge, dumping more water and some sand into the boat.

Tony shook his head. "No use for that, mate! We gotta haul her up fast."

I grabbed the heavy-duty bow handle that I had fashioned for *Southern Cross* back in New York, thinking that I would have to lift past the capacity of the standard handles, which I had seen give way. I started my personal tug-of-war.

Tony went back to his bobsled pushing position, all too aware that the two-man sled felt like four. We pushed-pulled.

"Time it with the surge, mate. The *surge!*"

Finally, *Southern Cross* was out of the grasp of the waves and standing right side up with a very crooked mast.

"Did it come out of its step!?" Tony asked.

"Nope, but the mast itself is bent in two places." I pointed to an area eight inches above the post pin, and another area half way up the mast.

"Can we bend it back?!"

I pulled the pin, took the mast off the post, and could not separate the two remaining halves. Tony got on one end and we tried to twist and countertwist.

Pop!

It suddenly came apart and I was butt-bounced onto the sand.

"Nice landing, mate!" Tony grinned. He held his half of the mast like a Neanderthal amazed that he had just pulled a tusk off of a woolly mammoth. Unfortunately, the normally arrow-straight mast had adopted the same curve. Tony opted for the brute-strength method and tried to bend it back into line over his knee, but with no effect whatsoever.

"Son of a bitch!"

"Double-thick alloy walls. Very hard to bend. But once it's bent, it's not bending back."

"Can we hammer it out?"

"No," I said definitively, while inspecting the tangled mess.

"You sure, mate?"

"Yes!" The truth is I was more than a bit upset that so soon into the expedition what I considered an indispensable piece of equipment had been rendered utterly useless. *Damnit!*

I realized something else: The unusual strength of the mast probably saved the boat from being crushed. Nature's hammer.

Our problems weren't over by any means. The "change" that McDermitt had described to us half a day ago was now a full-blown gale. Rain was striking us at forty-five-degree angles and we still had to set up camp. I was still feeling the pump of *surviving* the assault and had energy to burn. We found a small ridge seventy-five yards inland that was further bordered by a fallen tree.

"Mate, get me that tent fly that we brought and I'll make us a shelter."

We went back to the boat and unclipped our boat-seat camp bags.

"Ahhh, shit!" Tony yelled.

"What's up, Tony?"

"The seat back is broken." Sure enough, the alloy seat back was bent in half. These were the ones specially designed for the Special Forces after they had broken endless wooden varieties. In all their service they had not broken any of the new ones. We just did.

Nature's hammer . . . again.

"No worries," I said. "I can turn one of the gear bags into a fine backrest for you." My cheerfulness belied my anxiety. Only a few days into the expedition and we were losing equipment at an alarming rate. *What next?* I couldn't help thinking.

We continued to move gear, including the water bags and the kitchen bag with stove, jars of food, pots and pans, just behind Tony's seat. I used the pump to get the last two inches of water (about a one hundred pounds' worth) from the bottom of the boat. Tony took the cart off the stern deck and we slid it off underneath to help ease it up the beach.

"She's rolling a lot better, isn't she?!" Tony said.

The combination of a lighter boat and rain-packed sand *did* make for a slightly better go of it. *Excess adrenaline didn't hurt either,* I thought.

We dug a seven-by-six-foot-deep foxhole with the two halves of the spare paddle.

"Makes a pretty good shovel, doesn't it?" I said.

Tony fashioned a low-silhouette bunker by tying two ends of the queen-bed-size green nylon tent fly to the tree with parachute cord. He was like a kid constructing a hideout in the backyard.

"Tie up the back end to the paddle halves," he said while driving half his paddle nearly two feet into the sand. He beamed. "Makes for a pretty good tent pole as well!"

He crowned his masterpiece by levering the crooked mast in the center of the sheet. This added a little headroom. He put a T-shirt between the metal end and the tarp to avoid a tear.

"Quite the palace, I think."

I thought of the penthouse back at Bondi for comparison. "Impressive."

Next came the individual bivvies, mattresses, and the lot. We changed into our fleece. In less than half an hour we had a cozy nest with a hot pot of pasta cooking in the middle of it all. Tony was unusually adroit in the midgetlike environment. The food smelled delicious. I backhoed the pasta into my mouth with the tablespoon.

Tony, fork held aloft, shot me a horrified look. "Slow down. It's not going anywhere, mate."

The dancing amber shadows cast by the candle-lantern flames lit by wind-and-waterproof matches put me temporarily at ease.

I yawned. "I think I'll clean the pots in the morning."

"No worries."

Tony went right to sleep and I drifted out for a while, but woke up anxious with the realization that come tomorrow we were going to have to launch straight into the snarling teeth of what we had just barely escaped. The relentless roaring wind and rain joined the thunderous surf and vibrated the ground we slept on.

"Surf's up!" was the cry of the morning. The wind had vanished and I saw a pair of legs with a surfboard jog past our crib. I bailed out of my shell to see what all the fuss was about. The sun was burning a hole through some puffy clouds. Another surfer was heading toward the beach.

"Where are we?"

"Frazer Beach."

"Good surfing today?"

"Almost three meters! Gotta go!"

Frazer Beach is a beautiful, U-shaped double point-break—a surfer's heaven. I looked out the half-mile from point to point, and as far as my eyes could see, there were waves and more waves.

I watched the surfers paddling out to the break, looking for the best point of entry for *Southern Cross.* To my consternation the surfers used a variety of approaches to get out to the biggest waves more than a quarter-mile offshore. The shore was very rocky all the way around. At the break offshore the waves stacked up one after another. Farther in the waves re-formed and crashed again in an erratic but dangerous manner over the rocks close to shore. We had our work cut out for us.

Tony walked up behind me. "What are you lookin' for, Epic?"

I pointed to the endless succession of giant waves.

Tony nodded.

Years of sea kayaking had trained me to look for *patterns.* Waves that have traveled long distances are complex in their makeup. Usually they are not just one wave, but the sum total of many different waves that have overlapped or *piggybacked* over long distances. Ideally, sets of waves tend to cluster—usually about four to seven waves per cluster. Smaller trailing waves will follow but are usually of far less intensity.

Breaking waves can dump extraordinary volumes of water, and all the water rushing toward shore turns around and has to find a way back out to sea. The bigger the waves, the more volume of water, the more dramatic the undertow and rip currents. The retreating water can funnel back through a narrow lane that literally creates an autobahn shooting clear out past—and away from—the breakers to the open sea.

I did not see any express.

Instead, the rip was concentrated along a dangerous rock jetty on the southern point. Far too dangerous a place to attempt a kayak exit, especially since the end of the point was ballistic. The largest waves crashed directly into it, spewing broken water thirty feet into the sky.

Protocol further dictates that a kayak time its launch just after the last wave of a large set, to ride the rip out into the smaller oncoming waves and into the open sea.

No rampway was available to us. The entire bay was a mass of stacked waves as far as the eye could see. Not only that, but the windy conditions were causing the waves to break in irregular patterns. The swells poured toward shore like commuters cramming into a rush-hour subway train.

More often than not, the surfers had to suddenly aim their noses down and "duck dive" under one bent boomer after the next. The rip wanted to run everything into the rocks. The entry from the end of the rocks required extremely keen reflexes. Speed was not our strong suit—especially when our dance partner was a temperamental and unwieldy half-ton, fully loaded Klepper two-man kayak.

"See a way out, mate?!"

"I think something will show up as the tide changes," I said. "Right now it must be coming in because there are no holes at all."

"Good time to clean the pot then, don't you think?"

"Absolutely."

"How about some of that oatmeal you like so much, today?" Tony said comfortingly.

"Sounds good."

Those thoughts calmed me for a while as we made preparations to break camp. A short time later I strolled back to the beach for a damage report.

Nothing had changed. The sea looked as impenetrable as before. My spirits sank. Just then an enthusiastic surf kayaker with a short sit-on-top-style boat ran over.

"Tell me when you're ready to go. I'll escort you past the breakers!"

I beamed! "Should only be about half an hour!"

I ran back to Tony to tell him the good news. We hastily finished packing. We rolled *Southern Cross* into position. We exchanged another round of greetings.

"All set!" he said cheerily.

His smile was our green light. A triumphant thumbs-up.

We launched and bashed through the first three sets of broken water. The last one nearly toppled us and pushed us back. My confidence ebbed as we paddled harder and harder but could make absolutely no headway.

"Left! Left! Left!" I yelled. We were losing the all-critical perpendicular angle. If we came broadside to a wave we would be finished. We had to punch through the waves, not push alongside the wave.

"Left!" I screamed. A row of breakers was roaring down on us.

"I'm bloody trying, mate!"

"Left! Left!"

At the last second we swung *Southern Cross* into alignment and knifed through the first six-foot wave face. We plunged through the crest and dropped and paddled madly toward the second wave—larger than the first. Maybe eight feet.

"Faster!" I shouted.

"Paddle, mate. *Paddle!*"

Our surf kayaker friend yelled encouragement from our starboard flank.

"You're going to make it!"

And I believed him.

We pierced and cleared the eight-footer. We sat suspended in midair as the wave raced under us. And then we dropped with a loud *thud* as the boat absorbed and dampened most of the energy of the fall. We had lost our momentum and were pulling hard to regain it.

We were one wave away and could momentarily see open sea beyond it. The last wave, the goaltender, had other ideas as it rose steeply in front of us. We dug in harder as Tony yelled, "Come on mate. *Come on!!!!*" with an urgency that said we still had a chance.

The twelve-foot wave was spectacular! Our angle of approach was good but we seemed glued into its face. The top of the wave had an eerie shadow on its lip, indicating it was going to break any second. I heard a crash to my right and saw a domino wave coming at a clean right angle to us. The runaway train broadsided us at the same time the giant goaltender kicked us backward.

We were capsized and pushed down. No instant ejection this time. Just ten seconds of scrambling gurgles. I eventually popped out on the port side and somehow had both paddles under one arm. Sea kayaking protocol after a capsize states: Stay with your boat.

I reached out with one arm to grab a now upright *Southern Cross.* I grabbed the perimeter line and felt a supernatural tug as a wave threw *SC* toward shore like a quarterback throwing a Hail Mary bomb. I felt my arm tearing from my shoulder socket and let go. I watched *Southern Cross* shoot fifty yards ahead in a heartbeat. I concentrated on holding onto the paddles.

Tony dove after *Southern Cross* and began surf swimming toward her. He refused to wear a PFD and his unencumbered body started to catch up a bit when *SC* wallowed in the troughs between waves. Meanwhile, I bobbed up and down like a cork and kicked toward shore like an infant with "swimmie floats" trying to reach Mommy. Quiet pauses ended with explosions on the back of my head. I was belching bubbles as I was hit by wave after wave. I vaguely remembered seeing a diagram from *Sea Kayaking* magazine about using the paddles to swim with and started doing it.

Tony's rescue was getting more complicated as *Southern Cross* was heading southward toward the jetty at increasing speed. My last look saw him trying to cut her off at the pass. I ponderously paddle-clawed my way back.

Tony, *Southern Cross,* and I got in about the same time. Tony and I body-pried the boat onto its side, emptied it, and pivoted her back to the waves. We pulled her back just out of the foam's last darting tongue. I looked *Southern Cross* over and saw no damage, everything in place. There was no mast up to break this time and extra tugs on the compression straps held their cargo in place.

Just as I finished my "now what?" thought, the surf kayaker said: "If you guys wait an hour I'll take you guys a couple K's up the road to Catherine Hill Bay in my Ute [flatbed truck]. You'll be able to get out there."

I smiled with relief. I thought we had found a guardian angel with exactly the tools we needed to continue on our way unscathed. It was a no-brainer solution. But before I could say anything, Tony abruptly stated "our" position.

"Thanks, but no thanks."

Shocked, I looked at him in disbelief as he continued to sermonize. "If we take assistance now, we compromise the whole integrity of the trip," he explained.

I was speechless as he continued.

"I think we have to do whatever it takes to get out of here on our own power."

I was dumbfounded for two reasons. Part of me regarded him as an ignorant zealot, and another part agreed with him. I couldn't argue the point. Mostly I felt we had to do whatever it took, even if that meant waiting for days on end like Paul Caffyn had till the surf became passable. If worse came to worst I thought we could portage our whole affair to Catherine Hill Bay. That is how I figured expeditions go.

"Are ya sure?" the surf kayaker asked.

"Yes."

"If ya change your mind, let me know."

We watched him walk away. I never did ask him his name.

"Might as well practice some surf technique and see if conditions change," I suggested.

We paddled out to the first breaking wave, turned around, and began. We practiced broaching and bracing, a procedure that involves catching a wave, angling the boat toward shore, turning the boat till we are broadside and leaning the hull of the boat toward the oncoming wave. Simultaneously, we place the curved power-side faces of the paddle blades into the oncoming wave. The idea is to hold it there like they are resting level on an imaginary coffee table. We then hold the braced position until the wave energy has died and the boat is almost on shore. We practiced for an hour until we were more successful than not. Conditions had not substantially improved.

"Well, mate. Ready for another try up the gut?" Tony said.

"No, Tony, I don't think we can make it."

"So you think we're just going to sit here?" he snapped.

"I think we have to look for another way out up the beach. It looks a little better there now."

"Where?!"

"Over there." I pointed north. "About three hundred yards away by the other point."

Tony snarled with disgust. "It'll take half the day to get the bloody boat over there!"

"Let's take a look first by that gap past the little streamlet."

He sighed. "Awright then."

We scouted the northern beach for a better opportunity to launch. We found exactly one option—very risky. It was a small patch of beach wedged between two mounds of sand and rocks. It looked like a dilapidated launch pen for a bucking bronco, except water surged violently in and out.

"If we get in the boat quickly when the slot fills up we can eject out and paddle past just two waves instead of all that fucking foam first."

Tony had had enough theory. "Let's do it then."

The problem with the plan, I discovered immediately, was that making it through the two waves was mandatory. The small patch of beach was surrounded everywhere by jagged rocks. A capsize would not be just an inconvenience and a little bit of shattered pride. It would mean shattered boat and shattered bodies. The chances of capsizing and magically landing back on the sand were zero. I could see the clear water past the second wave. Freedom seemed so close. I imagine inmates on Alcatraz may have felt the same way.

We portaged the boat and all the gear nearly a quarter mile to the small patch of beach. It took over an hour. Getting the boat into the slot was hard enough. Once it was in, it oscillated between running away and getting swept backward into the rocks. I luckily managed to jump in on my first attempt but Tony was bucked out before he could get his second long leg in.

"Hold her steady, mate!" Tony screamed.

Scraaaatchhhhhh went my paddle blades as I tried to wedge the paddle crossways between the sides of the slot. Once again I felt the shoulder sockets distend.

"Hurry up, I don't think I can hold it!"

"I'm in. Go, Go, Go!"

We didn't eject, we burped out and were already getting shoved sideways back toward the rocks.

"Right, right, *right!*" We pulled exclusively on the right side.

"More left rudder!" I yelled.

We were almost perpendicular as we rose through some surge. We straightened out and accelerated toward the oncoming wave.

"Come on . . . come on!!!"

We punched through the first wave only to see the larger, looming piggybacked twin wrapping around the point.

"We've got to beat the point break!" Freedom was a hundred meters away. *"Here comes the wave!"*

I got the closeup, being in the bow. Tony saw things from a deeper, darker position. The last time, he saw the whole boat fall back on top of him.

"Come *onnnn!*" Tony cried.

I was momentarily submerged but soon felt the release and the now familiar airborne leveling sensation followed by a sudden *thud.*

Holy shit . . . *We made it!!!!*

"Keep paddling, mate! There might be a rogue around the corner!"

After a couple of minutes it was clear that we were out. We had escaped Frazer Beach on our own power!

It was late in the afternoon and we did not have much time to celebrate. I felt that we had met Australia's A-team and had won, but how many more times were we going to meet? We didn't even know what our next landing was going to be like and it was getting late in the day. We had ten miles to go to the next town.

"That was all a bit dicey. Glad we're through it, though," Tony said.

"I couldn't agree with you more."

Swansea to Newcastle—
A Long Way to Go

Our attempt to circumnavigate Australia had really begun. The war lines had been drawn. We savored the partly sunny glow of the day, the wind was light and variable. Paddling felt good, which helped settle worn nerves. I was glad to see two concrete break walls and nothing but even, unbroken swells at the entrance of Lake Macquarie and the small holiday town of Swansea. We arrived just right. The tide was coming in with the swell. The channel between the break-wall must be regularly dredged to keep it deep and prevent a sandbar buildup that could cause waves to break unpredictably in front of it. We entered the welcoming funnel and landed on a small sandy beach . . . uneventfully.

"I don't know about you, but I'm famished!" Tony was preaching to the choir. "Let's potter into town and find a milkbar!" he added.

We secured *Southern Cross* à la tug and bobsled, higher up the beach, and tethered her to a tree. We slipped into our *Star Trek* uniforms, zippered the spray skirts shut over the cockpit, walked a few hundred yards into the small town, and immediately saw a milkbar that was open. Technically, a milkbar is a general store, but this one had a small chicken grill, served breakfast, had some ice cream like a U.S. soda shop of yesterday, and served pizza and burgers as well.

"Let's get a couple of chook halves and a half-gallon of lemon soda."

"What's a chook?"

"A chicken, mate."

We ate our birds, chugged the soda, and finished it off with a couple of ice cream sundaes. That just about filled the previously empty tanks. We went out and set up camp. Next morning it was back to the milkbar for my first spaghetti on toast and eggs breakfast. The spaghetti must have been from a can but I wasn't going to complain.

"I saw a small hardware store in town," said Tony suddenly. "I have an idea for the mast."

"What's up?"

"I'll show you."

At the hardware store, Tony refused to tell me what he was looking for. "Now that's the ticket!" he beamed suddenly, pulling a long garden hoe handle out of a bin. "Exactly what I was hoping for. What do you think, Epic?"

"What do I think about what?"

"A new mast!"

I looked from Tony to the garden hoe then back to Tony. My face must have screamed, *Are you out of your mind?* Our specially constructed double alloy aluminum mast had been turned into a pretzel, and here Tony was suggesting we could replace it with a common garden hoe. Total cost: a few dollars. I took hold of it and was surprised by its heft and its varnished integrity.

Could Tony improvise on modern technology by going back to basics? Could this actually work?

"This could make it into a Smith and Hawken catalog back home," I agreed. "Hmmm, looks like the diameter is pretty close. Might need a little shaving, though, to fit into the post."

Tony shot me his no-worries look.

I smiled. "I think it might just work."

We hurried back to *Southern Cross* hoping that the new wooden garden-hoe handle would fit into the post like a skeleton key. We discovered that it would have to be substantially whittled down to fit. It was also going to be a bit short. But at this point we didn't really have much choice. We packed up camp.

I went about checking the charts and Tony began whittling.

A few hours later and Tony was still hard at work. I had to admire his dogged concentration. He reminded me of the convict digging his way out of Alcatraz with a spoon. But it looked pretty hopeless. Plus we were falling dangerously behind schedule.

"Tony, Newcastle is almost twenty nautical miles away and we have to make sure to get there."

"I'm almost finished, mate."

"It's nearly noon and the newspaper shows Fran getting closer and I think we have to try to get there in daylight."

"Relax. See?" Tony had shaved the hoe into a perfect hand-in-glove, hoe-to-post fit. "Put the sail on her, mate, and see how it looks."

I fed the mainsail luff cuff over the mast and immediately realized we were missing the two halyard guides at the top of the mast and that the inseam on this sail was about half a foot long for the new wooden leg.

"It's a bit short—"

"Where's the hacksaw, Epic? I'll take care of it."

An hour later Tony had effectively sawed off the top section of the mast and put it on the garden hoe like an extra-large Christmas tree capping ornament. We had our sail back.

We had half a day to do an eighteen-mile paddle. I did the mental math. *Let's see: five hours of daylight times four knots equals twenty. OK, it's possible.*

"We can make it to Newcastle before dark if we really get out asses in gear."

"It's a fine day, mate, no problem."

We paddled east out the channel with the tide and made a left, and I could feel the wind blowing in my face. *Shit! A northeast wind. Feels like it's blowing about ten knots. Force 3. Maybe higher.*

Wind is the primary variable in a sea kayaker's life. Wind makes waves. Wind forces range from zero (calm) to twelve (hurricane). "Whitecaps" generally form with winds between eleven and sixteen knots. This is considered a "moderate breeze" and is designated Force 4.

Wind in the face is a more insidious menace, especially when it's not blowing very hard. At first it keeps the paddler cool and feels refreshing. The cooler paddler feels like he can paddle a little faster, which in turn increases the wind speed in the paddler's face. A ten-knot wind is added to the speed of a kayak and becomes fourteen knots. The sea state is still less than two feet but the resistance against the paddler is much stronger as wind is an exponential force and not linear. Fourteen knots puts twice the pressure against us. Twenty knots would put four times the pressure.

Soon, even a modest breeze generates its own surface current. A kayaker at rest is penalized by drifting backward. Plus, because of the "cooling" effect, the paddler is unaware that he is sweating profusely and dehydrating, particularly when there is the splash and spray.

Tony beams. "See, mate? A lovely day."

About two hours and 1,400 calories later, breakfast is long gone. The wind has picked up a bit and Tony says: "This wind is a bit of a bore, don't you think?"

A shoe in one of my side bags was putting a pressure point in my hip but I did not want to stop for the five minutes it would take to try to readjust it. I thought I could put it out of my mind. I couldn't.

After another hour I could hear Tony sighing every so often, and the pressure point was now a full-blown *pain in the ass*.

"Surely we're over halfway by now," he whined. "Where the bloody hell is Newcastle?!"

Three hours became four and I could just see the setting sun spotlight a faint outline of a tower and a cluster of buildings in the distance.

"There it is Tony!" I felt like the watchman on the *Pequod* who first spots Moby Dick.

"What do think mate? Another hour or so?" I thought Tony optimistic.

I remembered something from the book *Kayak Navigation* by David Burch that said a kayaker can first sight an object when it is 1.5 miles plus the square root of the object's height. If that is the lighthouse and it it is sitting on some-what higher ground on the point, it must be fifty or sixty feet high. Square root of forty-nine is seven. I'll call it $7.5 + 1.5 = 9$ nautical or about 10 regular miles away. That is, if we had perfect visibility. We didn't. Add a mile. Goddamnit! *No way. We can't be eleven miles away.*

"I think it might be more like two," I said, hoping my calculations were sim-ply wrong.

An hour and countless blisters and hot spots later the wind would not stop and we weren't there yet. Night descended. So did my spirits. Finally we snuck around a small point and saw lights in houses that extended all the way out to the now dark but flashing lighthouse tower.

"Must be Newcastle's suburbs, TB!" I shouted jubilantly.

"Thank God," sighed Tony.

A half hour later we lost our rhythm. The seas grew more chaotic as waves rebounded off a man-made break wall fronting the houses close to shore. By now we had burned well over 3,000 calories. Last night's dinner was long gone too. We hadn't stopped for any kind of lunch, we had barely drunk any water. Our mistake was that we both thought we were going to sprint this one out and be done with it. But we were running out of fuel.

Darkness took control and the paltry individual lights of Newcastle suburbs could not match the moonless night.

"It's getting a wee bit chilly, mate," said Tony.

"We're almost there. Let's pick up the pace and get it over with."

Night paddling is a beautiful experience when you are in calm, familiar waters. But I was tired and irritable, and completely at a loss to explain our poor progress. *Was there some current against us now?* We were traveling just as strongly as in the first hour, but the lighthouse had seemed closer then. Our strokes became less automatic.

Long-distance paddling without rhythm is a disaster. The mind breaks out of its comforting trance into the harshness of every bloody stroke. Tony and I had taken this paddling rhythm as a right and not a privilege. It was gone. Paddling in sync had been like breathing to us. Now we labored for every stroke.

When the hell are we going to get there!!!!!!!!????

The anger translated into new resolve, new concentration, refound rhythm. We seemed to skip a mile in the transition. *The lighthouse was so close, wasn't it?* We accelerated to get those last few minutes over with. Those last few minutes took an hour.

We entered on a large undulating swell between the two long jetties. Inside the narrow harbor the swells were squeezed into larger swells. We elevatored up and down. We paddled faster and found ourselves hurtling forward on the business end of a rushing wave face.

"*Woooowww!* Backpaddle! Backpaddle!" I yelled.

"*Why* mate?" Tony was enjoying the roller coaster.

"I think this one might just break."

We backpaddled, and the cresting wave passed underneath us. *SC*'s stern dropped back as we accelerated backward on the backside of the harbor rogue.

Occasionally waves that piggyback will line up in such a way that their size and power increase exponentially. Called "rogues," these monsters have been known to sink full-sized ships in minutes. In this "protected" harbor we just missed getting hit by one.

"Close one, mate."

"Yep."

Sea kayaking protocol would first say—don't be out in this situation in the first place, but once committed, try to come in on the backside of these waves and not in front of them.

We can't be surfing, I raged to myself. *We are in a protected harbor entrance. There isn't supposed to be surf here!*

What we couldn't see, couldn't hurt us was the hope. We surfed another kilometer and finally entered the relative calm of the protected harbor.

Now what? Two channels? Where do they go? It's 10:00 P.M. It's getting cold, we're wet, it's windy, it's dark. What's that!!??

A lone motorboat accelerating across the harbor was headed . . . *right at us.*

Where's the flashlight? The whistle? The horn? All those things we had for just this occasion.

"It's coming right for us! Shine the torch, shine the torch!!" Tony yelped.

Torch? Oh, flashlight, right. Oh, OK.

"Hurry up, Epic!"

Shit, where is it? Did I put it . . . ?! I fumbled and found the Maglite and shined it right at the motorboat. I waved it frantically. But the boat roared straight ahead.

"Paddle!" screamed Tony. "Paddle!"

I fumbled for my paddle and we veered hard left, pumping the paddles with everything we had. The boat—its engines throttled wide open—bore down on us relentlessly.

AHHHHH!

It roared past, missing *Southern Cross* by no more than a boat length. A harrowing moment. I cannot describe the feeling of utter helplessness at the exact moment I expected that motorboat to Cuisinart *Southern Cross* into chips. I do not believe it ever did see us. *Southern Cross* was a military "canoe" designed for stealth capabilities. An intriguing feature. Only this time it almost got us killed.

Interestingly, too, Tony zeroed in immediately on a major flaw in my plan to fully equip *Southern Cross* with all the latest safety technology.

"Why have all these precautions, if we can't use them when we really need them?"

Point taken. He was right.

The false security of having all the "stuff" unveiled itself that particular eve.

Fatigue, night, water, and shock really made me want to believe it was just a dream. It had to be. Dream or not, I knew we had to find a camp. We went left and found a beach in the middle of the harbor. The only beach. We landed on a pesky two-foot surf wave that almost knocked us over trying to get out.

I threw my paddle at the beach like a harpoon toward a whale's back and jumped out of the boat only to fall on leaden legs. *Bloody surf on a protected island in a protected harbor. Fucking great, just fucking great!!*

"Careful getting out, Tony, it's a lot of gravel and logs."

He spilled out of the boat, immediately heaved *Southern Cross* as far up the beach as possible before a wave could come and fill it with water. There were no gimme's. A line of seaweed and beach debris delineated the tide line at the limits of the beach over twenty-five yards away. The wind was really blowing and I figured Fran was going to kick things up even more.

"We've gotta move the boat as high as we can in case of a tide surge."

"Yesss, sir!!!" he said sarcastically.

We placed the kayak on top of a couple of fallen trees. After this last burst of heavy activity we were quickly windchilled and scrambled to our dry bags for pile and polypro. Only concern: warmth and dryness.

Sleep or feed? Feed or sleep! It's likely we burned six thousand calories that day. At this rate, all of our fattening-up poundage was going to burn away in no time. It was after 10:00 P.M. and we appeared to be on some island in the middle of the harbor with no obvious way off. There was nothing but a park field and no milkbars to be found. There were the lights of the main city and the spire of a church steeple a few hundred yards away but we were not going to use *SC* as a ferry after all this.

With all civilized expectations doused, it was time to fire up the burners and cook up some more pasta extraordinaire. I had a hard time letting go of a notion that we might find some real lodging.

"Damn it! This *sucks*!" I yelled.

"What's wrong, mate?" Tony sighed wearily. He sounded resigned to my periodic tantrums.

"All this effort to get to a town. No, a goddamned *city*! And we're stuck on an island near a ball field!"

My stating of the obvious bounced off Tony.

"Get your spoon, mate. Dinner is served."

The concoction warmed the belly. We made another wind shelter with the tent fly, and my bivvy sack was now a warm, safe womb protecting me from the tumultuousness of a pissed off Mother Nature all around me.

Just as I was falling asleep, a deep droning sound interrupted the regular wind sonata. I quickly opened my head flap and saw a massive shadow blocking the low din of the city's lights. It was as big as an island and passing close by. I got a momentary flashback to the opening credits of a *Star Wars* spoof, when the spaceship looms overhead. A huge freighter ship was sneaking past our camp, going out where we had just come in. Jeezus, I shuddered to myself. The vessel filled the entrance. *What if we had been in the neck of the harbor when that came through?!* I let Tony sleep but kept wondering why a freighter was leaving at eleven-thirty on a Sunday night.

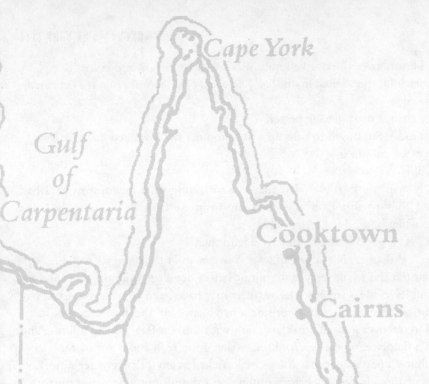

To Port Stephens

We awoke to howling wind and a white-capped harbor and rain. Our camp gave me an excellent view of the harbor entrance. It was like having the ability to watch one show on TV and have another playing in the corner. As convoluted as the inner harbor seas were on my "main" screen, the sea conditions past the jetty looked much worse even minimized on the smaller one.

Before I could generate any real fear about the day's conditions I had a pleasant realization that these conditions might be too severe to go out in. Childhood memories of a "snow day" emerged. Now I wondered what my newly inspired partner was going to think. Was he going to wake up with another "Let's get going, mate"?

"It's a regular maelstrom, mate," he said.

"I guess part of Fran is paying us a visit after all."

"Looks like we should get a cup of tea and let her simmer down."

"I saw a ferry coming from the mainland downbeach aways." I was actually quite relieved that Tony did not want to jump right into things. "I do want to find out what the weather's going to be like from the harbormaster."

Tony shot me a knowing smile. "I figured you would, Epic."

We secured camp and walked to the ferry dock. I found a pay phone and a spanking new phone book with all its pages. I found the harbormaster's number and gave him a ring.

"G'day, Newcastle harbormaster."

I asked about conditions.

"It's blowin' over thirty-five knots, seas are three meters and rising."

Hmmm. I did the mental math: *Full gale, about Force 8. Seas about ten feet already. And climbing.*

"Any chance of it getting better?"

"Not today. Supposed to ease up a little tomorrow." I walked back to Tony as the ferry was pulling in.

"Well?"

"It's blowin' a full gale all day, chance of it easing up a bit tomorrow." I half expected Tony to shrug off the news and insist we launch immediately. I was relieved when he nodded resignedly.

"Let's get a good brekky and have a read then."

Great, I thought. *He's picked up some discretion about these things.*

We shared the small ferry with about half a dozen people on this Monday morn in Newcastle. I suppose the weather may have been coaxing others to stay at home, because there was a conspicuous absence of the hustle and bustle. I wanted to discover a small breakfast nook with some soft, adequate lighting and perhaps a fireplace, where we could have that good read and a pot of tea.

We found a newsagent that was as well stocked as any NYC corner store. Lots and lots of models and celebrities smiling up through portable paper mirrors. I saw JFK Jr. on one, Cindy Crawford on a few others. Just like home. I actually knew these people in "real" life.

"One *Australian* and one *Herald,*" Tony said. "And these cards," he added.

"Do you want some postcards, mate?"

"Yes, but I'll need some time to sort it out. Thanks, anyway."

First came Nicole, then Mom and Dad. After a minute I realized how many people I wanted to reconnect with. A minute became several, and Tony saw the deck of cards I had collected, and put an end to it.

"We better get breakfast before they close, mate."

The only breakfast we found was in a mall. *A mall of all things!* We were relegated to a marquee menu and open cafeteria setting inundated with fast-food logos and harried women with screaming children. The suburban teenager in me felt temporarily comforted but the measly, mass-produced portions, synthetic serving containers, high prices, and brightly colored utensils they substituted for food quality proved distasteful. I longed for a cozy NYC diner, or at least a deli bagel.

Tony settled in and asked, "Which paper do you want first, Epic?"

I had read both in Sydney and had a hankering for the *Australian.* It had more interesting op-ed and world news. The *Sydney Morning Herald* seemed more provincial by comparison.

"The *Australian,* please."

After pouring through both papers I was warmed up for postcard and journal writing. After an hour punctuated by stiff fingers trying to scribe in tight places, I glanced over at Tony's production line and saw many cards with the same amount of writing, as well as one with a very dense load and one quite bare.

"Who's getting the novel?" I said, pointing to the microfilmlike card.

"That's Mum, she likes *allll* the gory details."

"Who gets the 'stick it' note?"

"That's Dad."

"Boy, you can really summarize medical terms for him. You must have a code or something," I said, referring to the medicines I had previously mentioned.

"What's that, mate?" asked Tony, oblivious to the inference.

"Nothing, I guess he's not a man for all the details then?"

"Only the important ones."

Tony and I got into a discussion about how he had to decide which parent to choose after the divorce. He was only twelve but the judge thought he was thirteen and therefore he was allowed to make the choice.

"I chose Mum."

Apparently, his mum had been a doctor's "widow" and rarely saw Tony's father, who was always at work or on call.

"She started to drink a bit too much."

Somewhere in it all his father had gotten involved and remarried a woman Tony wasn't terribly found of. The exact order of things wasn't clear.

"He met her in Vietnam also?"

"Yes, Mum didn't take that well. She knew her. There were many school nights that I would not get to bed till three in the morning. She would go a bit . . . off." He smiled. "I told her that if I can make it all around Australia in a kayak she could stop drinking."

"She seems so together and focused."

"She's got a *biggg* heart and is a great person. That's why I chose her."

Afterward my postcard writings stalled, and I hit the journal.

I took some time to use the light and table to write down a few notes. Under a page called "Health" I traced my hand and placed the blisters in all their respective places. The hand I traced had eight blisters, with a particularly nasty one between the bases of two fingers.

The next morning seemed slightly calmer but the seas were larger. A call to the coast pilot revealed twenty-eight-knot wind speeds and four-to-five-meter seas. Cyclone Fran had brushed us off with one temper tantrum from her outer spinning perimeter but was starting to head offshore. We would not have to wait out a cyclone after all.

There was not a lot of time to make a decision. The distance would be our longest to date, almost thirty-five miles. Moreover, it would be across open, exposed shoreline that was directly in the way of the huge waves churned up over the last few days. Landing there would not be an option. I believed that we had to become directly familiar with these types of conditions sooner rather than later.

"I think we have to give it a go," I said.

"It looks pretty *agro* (angry) out there, mate."

"The wind is basically going our way. It's coming from the southeast. Port Stephens is northeast. We'll be reaching the fastest point of sail."

"As good a time as any to try out the new rig, I suppose."

We packed up and took off. The relative protection of the inner harbor gave way to a fully developed fifteen-foot sea. We began paddling. Soon we put up just the mainsail and were already surging forward with the wind almost at our backs as we headed due north. The wind and wave conditions were way beyond anything we had been on before. The winds seemed gusty and fitful, not quite sure if they wanted to knock us down or help us along.

"Mate, let's hit the sticks (paddles) for a while. I just don't think we're moving too well."

I was a bit too overwhelmed to disagree and initiated a precarious kneel-to-the-front-of-my-cockpit move to fasten the boom vertically to the mast. I was rocked violently by the breaking crest of a wave and quickly sat back down while watching my half-done handiwork entangle itself.

We turned thirty-five degrees to starboard and started to head northeast along a vast sandy coast about two kilometers away. Another rusty ship skeleton gradually emerged to our port side. We were now getting hit broadside by the waves, and paddling became a struggle to keep a straight line. It felt like we were on a Home Depot–size hydraulic forklift that had a jammed switch. We were getting pressed up and down.

"Look at the size of that one!" Tony said, as we watched another giant green wall of water approach us.

"That has got to be over twenty feet," I said.

Oddly, I felt immune to it, as we were simply raised higher by the forklift. The waves were highly developed and did not appear to be in any hurry to break where we were. They were saving their best work for the coastline.

"Let's watch that one go in," I said excitedly.

THAABOOOOOMMMMMMMM!

"Can you imagine what it would have been like to be between that one and the beach?" No sooner had I said that then there was another *THABOOM!* And another. Each one louder than the first. And more frequent. We were getting pushed toward the anvil by an endless succession of large sledgehammers. I could see waves breaking in front of us and could hear them behind.

"Turn *right!*" shouted Tony.

"Paddle like *hell*! We've drifted in too far!!"

We were churning through surf almost a mile out from the beach, facing waves much bigger than the ones at Frazer Beach and spanned by enormous valleys between them. A full half-hour of sprinting got us out into slightly tamer but no less daunting versions of the same theme. *What was I thinking about, coming out into this?"*

Sea kayaking protocol would say we were truly mad to be out here. The chart had fine print just under the words Newcastle Bight that said, "In bad weather heavy rollers extend a long distance from the shore." The charts also show deep water gradating into a shelf of shallows, represented by white going into a light blue area. The distance of the gradation was relatively short. Waves will start to break when they reach 1.5 times their wave height. The bigger the waves, the sooner they break. That's where we were.

"Let's put up both sails, mate!" Tony suggested.

The winds felt calmer in the giant troughs but very strong on the peaks. We were on the peaks for just a few moments. It was a gamble to get more speed, but by going too slowly, we could risk running into darkness. That would make this whole show a living nightmare.

"OK. Keep the boat balanced with the paddle brace into the waves when they come."

Southern Cross was equipped with a custom-built control panel that had special cleats arrayed on two wooden boards—a longer one to span the full width of the cockpit in front of Tony, and a short one to fit the smaller, tapered area between my cockpit and the masthead. The idea was to be able to cleat off the main and jib halyards so the sails could be on "cruise control" to leave our hands free to paddle with. I felt that the boat was moving too unpredictably to go without a paddle ready to brace, and yet the boat did move consistently faster and on better lines than when paddling only. So we gave both a try.

Things went well for a while as both sails trimmed nicely in on the reaching angle and the long slopes of the waves gave us an even surface to travel on. This was a fully developed sea with large, fully formed waves with long wavelengths that actually help block the development of choppy waves.

We established a pattern of racing forward at a slight angle ten to twenty degrees toward shore, while manually controlling the sail lines. Then one or both of us would cleat off our control lines and steer *SC* forty-five degrees toward the wave crest. We paddle-braced on the crests while slicing through at that angle. Once on the downslope of the wave we would uncleat and sail again. We were preparing to uncleat, when suddenly—

"*Clunk. Cruooonch.*"

"What's that, mate?!"

"*Shit!* The mast is unstepped."

"Can you get it back in place?!"

The one thing Tony had not been able to fashion for the mast was a new hole through the garden hoe to put the special pin in to prevent the mast step from unstepping. We thought the hole might weaken the mast and that the pin was just for the convenience of demasting without having to take the post out as well.

I leaned forward and elongated my arms under the cockpit rim of the spray cover. I brailled for the bottom of the post and the wooden receiver plate.

"Hurry, mate, here comes a big one."

The wind tugged on the flapping sails. We were listing to port, and water was filling the sinking belly of the jib sail.

"No way, we have to derig."

"Okay. I'll keep paddling."

I started untangling lines, pulling in jibsail cloth like a lobster fisherman pulling up a trap. Minutes later I kneeled up and was tried to match the square peg into the very small square hole.

"Got it yet?!"

"Almost. Almost."

It took many attempts before it—

Click.

"It's in, it's in!"

"Can we put up a sail?"

"Maybe just the mainsail. The jib seemed to billow up and pull it out before."

We put up the main and I paddled with a very modified stroke. The boom was forty-five degrees toward port and I had to take a low-angle stroke so that I did not hit it every time. I now became paddler/bracer and Tony manned the mainsail full-time. The brace training at Frazer came in handy right away. I braced starboard into one crester and had the boom swing over and smack the top of my head.

"Sorry, mate."

"I'm glad the boom is still alloy," I said.

The winds calmed to fifteen to twenty knots by midafternoon, and we found a manageable groove. Sometimes the winds seemed to stop altogether and we had to hastily derig to go to paddles, thinking it was all over only to have them pick up again. Overall, we covered the distance nicely. I thought there must be a favorable current taking us upcoast. An angled ricochet or a guiding hand, perhaps?

By the end of the afternoon, we reached the end of the bight and started feeling the familiar bounce of an approaching point. The winds had died down a lot and I took the sail down and found some solace in a less modified form of paddling.

We landed at a sheltered spot on the south side of the beach at Port Stephens/Nelson Bay, where a restroom and overhang were located. The weather had improved, albeit rain came and went frequently. If a roof could be found, we were going to use it.

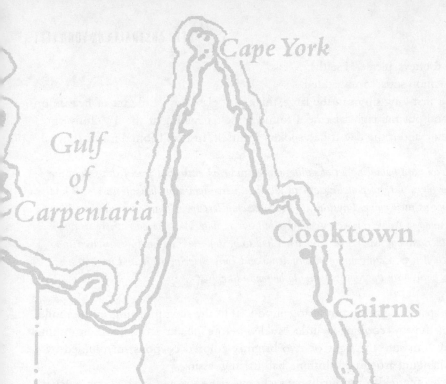

Port Stephens to Forster/Tuncurry

We landed on a sandy, inclined boat launch. There were a dozen small boats gathered together. They were wooden dories that had twenty-horsepower engines fastened to their sterns and plenty of nets and marker buoys inside. We pulled our boat out of the way, set up camp, and headed for the lights of town. I took the opportunity to hang many damp things under the tin roof over the barbecue grill, hoping the wind circulation would make them less wet. Dry was a pipe dream.

"You can finish your laundering later, mate. I'm pretty peckish and could use a good feed."

There had been no opportunity for any snacks in the course of the day and breakfast was a dim memory.

"Look, mate!" Tony said, as the last bits of daylight spotlit a couple of dorsal fins circling in the bay.

"Are they sharks?!"

"No, mate, they're dolphins."

After a short walk, we found a hotel bistro and looked in the windows. We heard the clanking of pint glasses and saw a rugby match on the TV over the bar. We walked in and Tony ordered for us. Numbers were called out loudly and ours eventually arrived. I was handed a giant plate filled with lamb chops, thick bacon strips, a piece of steak, a couple of sausages, and a few yams and other veggies to give it color.

"What to drink, mates?"

"A Tooheys, please," I said.

"A lemon soda," Tony added.

That first long sip from the large, thick pint glass was a little bit of heaven on earth and put me right at ease. I found myself gawking at the TV. Tony and I didn't talk about the day. It had spoken for itself. Instead I jotted in my journal:

The constant balancing act of sailing proved to be an entirely different stress than the sheer physicality of paddling. All in all more nerve-wracking, but the sails still had shown us their value. Physically, I feel somewhat less spent than on a pure paddling day and yet we've covered our longest mileage to date. We traveled entirely in rough weather and big seas. We've done what had to be done. We are finding ourselves up to the challenges. I am gaining in confidence and Tony is seeing more and more of what our "potter" up the coast is going to be really like.

The spattering of an outdoor grill roused us the next morning, as the mullet fishermen were cooking a little brekky before heading out to their fishing grounds. I'm sure the sight of two brightly colored cocoons surrounded by a dozen hanging articles of clothing had them guessing.

As we emerged from our bivvy sacks, we were greeted with classic "Ocker" banter.

"G'day, mates. Interestin' way to be doin' your laundry."

A bit dazed and a bit self-conscious with all the company, we stumbled into their circle and shook their hands.

"Reckon you'd be makin' us a feast this morning," Tony bantered back. "Those your boats?"

"Thaw's right."

"What are ya fishin' for?"

"Mullet."

A group gathered around *Southern Cross*. A bearded chap wanted to know what in the world we were doing.

"We're going around Australia."

The chanted "Ohhh yeah" seemed to imply we were crazy.

Helpful hints and a bevy of information about the next five miles ensued. Everyone had a special word about the waters from where we were to five miles "over there" but that was it. This was pure, unadulterated local knowledge.

"So what's it like by Crowdy Head?" It was a spot about sixty miles up the coast.

"Never been, but I hear . . ."

At that point I realized we may as well have asked them about Japan. We gave our best student faces to all of these Australian "good ole boys," gratefully partook of their breakfast, and helped them launch a few of their skiffs. Tony started making the hole for the pin so we could use both sails again without the mast popping out.

"There you have it, we'll be laughin' again."

"Excellent." We waved good-bye.

Shortly after launch, we passed a sixty-foot sailboat approaching from our starboard bow. One of the crewmen crowded to the railing and yelled: "They're callin' for high winds today. You might want to think twice about being out here today."

"What kind of winds?" I asked.

"Twenty knots or more."

"Thank you, mate," I said. *Twenty knots, beauty, fine sailing compared to yesterday,* I said to myself.

The weather improved and we were in and out of sun showers for most of the morning. The green and beige coastline glistened and the whole setting was refreshing compared to the stormy gray of the last three days. We paddled for a while in variable winds and then raised both sails. The mast held firm and we began a fine sail in Force 5 conditions with fifteen to twenty knots of steady breeze.

We were now heading north-northeast (NNE) compared with the east-northeast (ENE) of the day before. We had passed the acute angle of New South Wales's elbow. We were sailing on a broad reach to a run with the winds coming from the south-southwest (SSW) and were making excellent time. It was too windy to talk and too active to wander in thought. I was glad that we did not have giant waves and crashing surf all around us.

We sailed another thirty miles, made a turn to port, and headed west around Sugarloaf Point.

The wind slowly died as it was curved and eventually blocked by the landmass. We took the whole mast down, wrapped the sails around it, and secured it to the foredeck and side of *SC*. We then swell-surfed on wraparound waves.

Once again, it took an hour to cover a distance that "looked" like it would take ten minutes. We passed on a couple of dicey landing spots with the hope that the swell would dissipate as we went farther. It did. We landed in a perfect crescent-shaped nook of a beach completely protected from the swell. Another thirty-five-mile day in the bank.

"Ouch." Slap. "Goddamnit." Slap. *Slap!*

"What's up, Tony?"

"Bloody no-see-ums."

In moments my ankles were suffering the same deluge and a cluster of small red welts was concentrated on the knob of my ankle bone like it was an archery bull's-eye for midgets.

No-see-ums are biting, gnatlike creatures that, like flies, bite, suck some blood, and deposit saliva in the wound to mark the territory. The wet weather had inspired a mass hatching and they were hungry.

"You got the Rid, mate?" Tony asked.

I got the insect repellent and we hastily applied it everywhere we could. I wanted to believe it was working, but I kept hearing Tony swatting away as he set up the stove. About halfway into the pasta came the air assault.

Bzzzzzzzzzzzzzz!

"Bloody mossies, too?!"

The tops of the hands were the first targets and it was debatable how much the Rid was working. Tony seemed to have a thicker cluster around him than I did but I *did* opt to get the one item my father had picked out for me in a Campmors camping store back home.

"You'll need this," my father had said.

Now, I pulled on the mosquito hat, just as Dieter had sagely prophesied I'd need to do. I put extra Rid on my hands, neck, and ankles. Tony bounded off the log bench flailing away and said: "They're biting right through the fleece, mate!"

It was obvious that we had to set up our shelters as quickly as possible. We were outnumbered and needed to retreat. Camp was up in no time and we squirreled ourselves away for the night. It could not have been later than 8:30 P.M.

The calm conditions only highlighted the isolated buzzing sounds of the mosquitoes and the worry that a couple had stowed away in my bivvy sack waiting their chance for a dive-bomb raid on my flesh.

Slap.

"You're dead, you bastard," I crowed as I picked a plump, blood-filled mosquito off my forehead and rolled it between my thumb and forefinger.

It started to get warm and I debated whether to peel off a layer of fleece so as to cool down, or expose acres of target to the hidden Ninja assassins. I had heard Tony rolling around and sighing nearby. Then I heard some frustrated grumblings and thrashing noises followed by a drawn-out *zzzzipppppp.* Tony had opened his bag, I guessed in an effort to cool down. His bag was nylon and did not breathe. I imagined it must have been like trying to sleep wrapped up in cellophane. He had no ventilated mosquito-netting head area either. *He has to be slow roasting,* I thought.

A few minutes later I heard another *zzzzippp* and again followed by a sigh. This happened a few more times before I eventually nodded off.

I woke up after dreaming about Nicole to the sound of rustling nylon, and got out of my bag. Tony was getting out, too, and had a wild-eyed look on his face.

"Bloody hot last night," he grunted.

"Yeah, it was," I said.

"Barely slept a wink between the mossies and the heat. Ouch." he barked, slapping at his ankle.

The no-see-ums were having us for breakfast, too.

"How did you sleep?"

"Well, after killing a few sneaky mossies, I just took off my fleece top, put on a long-sleeve cotton T, and crashed. I think the Gore-Tex kept me a bit cooler because it breathes."

"Hmmmm," Tony shrugged.

I wanted to go into a full "I told you so" sermon, but Tony's condition was simply too feeble to attack any further.

We paddled, then sailed, and then paddled from Sugarloaf Point toward a hundred-meter-wide channel that enters Wallis Lake and has the townlets of Forster on the south head of the channel and Tuncurry on the north. We had made very good time to that point, averaging over five knots, with the aid of a fifteen-knot tail wind and good following seas. The boat's manners with both sails wing on wing were excellent. We managed to keep pace with a train of waves coming from astern. We surfed in front of many of them.

We reached the channel in the midafternoon, ahead of schedule, thinking that we had been given our first truly enjoyable ride. Then we followed the refraction curve around the point and were starting our final approach when things got bumpy. We turned *SC* into the mouth of the channel.

"Paddle a bit a harder, mate, we're not moving too well," Tony said.

I paddled harder as hard as I could, and we were barely making headway. A half hour later we had barely gotten into the channel and were hugging a jagged rock jetty to diminish the powerful ebbing current. A couple of large standing waves formed thirty meters to our right.

"Look, Tony!" I yelled.

A dozen dolphins were surfing standing waves. Leaping, lunging, gliding and angling in, on, over, and through the waves.

"Dolphins love to surf," Tony said.

Indeed it appeared they were not trying to go anyplace but were surfing for the sheer thrill of it. Meanwhile, we were not getting anywhere.

"You think we can use them like reindeer to pull this sled into the harbor?"

The joke wore thin fifteen minutes later when we had not moved at all and it was clear the ebb was getting stronger.

"Let's pull behind one of the larger rocks and stop!" I said.

"Why, mate?! We're almost in. Just paddle harder."

"It's not going to help. It is another half mile and we can't move against it. It must be going over five knots."

The entire contents of Wallis Lake were trying to exit out this tiny opening into the sea like a gallon milk jug turned upside down pouring into a lake. We were a toothpick trying to go back into the bottle. *Southern Cross* approached the rocks and I reached out to hold on.

"Ahhhhh, Jeezus!" I said as a razor-edged rock slashed two deep slivers on the tips of the fingers of my left hand. Many of the rocks were covered with oyster shells of different sizes. Bringing the boat out here would be folly. The hull would be gutted like Daniel Boone with a freshly killed buck.

"I'll get out and line the boat down the channel. You keep it straight and paddle as much as you can."

"What, that's not going to work!"

"We've got to give it a shot, otherwise we'll have to wait here out on the rocks until the tide turns, and I think it's just approaching full steam as is."

"All rigghhht."

I slipped and a point of a rock nearly went up my ass but hit my tail bone instead.

"That *reaaaalllly* hurt," I said.

The ebbing current hit the bow of *Southern Cross* and was forcing Tony into the channel.

"I can't hold it anymore, mate!!"

I pulled on the bowline and slipped again, scraping the palm of the hand that broke the fall. I got a better angle on the line from a seated tug-of-war position and then slowly stood up. I had to get close to the water's edge to keep *SC* from getting too close to phalanxed rocks and yet rein Tony and *SC* in when the current tugged.

An hour and many falls later we were clear of the channel and landed on a camper-van beach in Forster. Tony was sweating, irritated, and relieved at the same time.

"Now that was a real bore!"

I felt like I had played in the rugby match I had watched the night before. I had cuts and bruises on both hands and forearms, elbows, knees, and shins, as well as a nice sore spot on the tailbone.

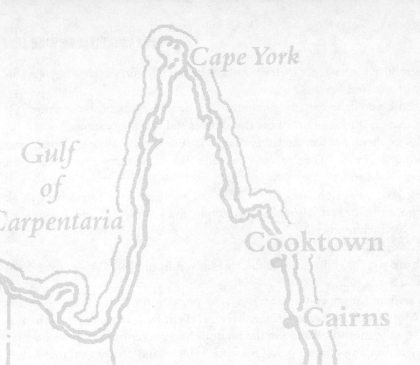

Forster/Tuncurry to Crowdy Head

We emptied *Southern Cross* of half her load and made a number of trips to a small vacant camper-van lot. I finished with three water bags in each hand and larger gear spilling from under my arms. We brought *Southern Cross* a hundred yards, halfway up a small hill on the boat cart and staked our claim. The lot was twenty-by-twenty feet and had an all-in-one electrical plug-in station and water-faucet station. We were flanked by two midsized camper vans, bigger than a VW microbus, smaller than a Winnebago, with roll-out canvas awning extensions and a settled-in appearance.

A middle-aged fellow with dark hair and a big belly was sitting on a simple straight-backed lounge chair under the canopy. He was staring out at a lone dolphin doing lazy circles in the orange-colored water reflecting the late afternoon sky. The water was calm. *How can that be? No standing waves, no surging current, all in the matter of an hour?*

A slim, tanned, and bushy-white-haired chap and his equally fit lady partner came by.

"That's quite a rig you've got there. Come far?"

"All the way from Sydney," I said proudly.

"You don't say?" he said.

"That's marvelous," she said.

"Are you an American?"

"Yes, but my partner is from Sydney," I said quickly, not quite sure how Yanks might be viewed in these parts. It seemed like Kansas to me but I knew it wasn't.

I introduced the couple to Tony and we began a friendly chat. They gave us the lay of the land.

"I think you'll be awright tonight. Most people check in before now. Of course there is the benefit of using the shower and washing stations."

"I'll get them our key and they won't have to worry about all that," the woman interjected. "They've come a long ways, let them save their dosh [money]."

"Yes, yes, you're right, of course. After you've all freshened up a bit I think we've got some dessert left over." Meanwhile, she got the key and a couple of clean, folded white towels.

"That should do you right."

"Thank you!" I said, staring at the clean towel in my hand like it was one of the Dead Sea Scrolls.

Caravanning (camper-vanning) is a very popular Australian form of recreation. Most towns and scenic villages have excellent facilities, but the emphasis is clearly on the motorized and not the random backpacker or rare sea kayaker.

Typical camping slots are gravel filled for vehicles and do not lend themselves to comfortable tenting. Overall, this network of caravanning parks seemed like a very economical and intimate way for city folk to see nature up close without severing the umbilical cord completely.

The Klepper kayak thrived in Europe in the 1950s, '60s, and '70s when it was part of the prime camper-vanning culture there. Many and perhaps most middle-class Europeans combined "faltboots" (folding kayaks) with motorized camper vans and would spend three to six weeks on their favorite lake, riverbank, or seacoast. That is what it was designed for. With good care it was also designed to last a generation for that lifestyle.

We had a key to the showers and washbasins and I didn't know what to do first. Wash myself, wash the clothes, wash the gear?! Except for the one dip in the ocean early in the trip, I could not remember bathing. My last shower had been in Bondi. We were in our second week of the trip.

"Let's get going, mate. We'll put the clothes in the washer and take a rinse."

The simple but exquisite joy of highly pressurized spray was an almost forgotten sensation.

"We're in the lap of luxury, Epic."

I had to agree. We both just stood and turned clockwise then counterclockwise for minutes on end. Layers of salt, sweat, oils, mosquito repellent, sunblock, blood, and more gradually dissolved.

Later we put on shorts, long sleeve T's, and held off on the Rid. Various antibug torches and blue-colored zapping grids set up by our neighbors had held the squadrons off for now. We were uphill and on dirt and grass instead of sand so the no-see-ums were out of range. We could almost relax. It was a Thursday night. I saw Tony looking at the chart.

"Do you think we can make it to Crowdy tomorrow?"

I looked carefully, did the measurement: twenty-five nautical miles as the crow flies, thirty or more as we paddle and sail.

"It'll be another long day but it can be done."

"Good. That's where I'll tell 'em to meet us."

"Who?!"

"Sammy, Carolyn, Brent, and Mike."

"Really?"

"I'm calling 'em right now."

I picked a few Power Bar and Milky Way wrappers out of *Southern Cross* and started to see that *Southern Cross* was feeling some wear and tear. The wooden longerons that form the boat's chines were looking splotchy instead of uniformly beige from being perpetually wet. I saw a couple of metal fittings bent and one rib knocked half out of place. A few wooden plates were peeling off the gunwales that form the sides of the boat. I set about taping them back on.

"*It's all set!* They're all driving up tomorrow!" Tony said ecstatically.

"Sammy says she's got a whole bunch of letters for you, including a number from Nicole," he said teasingly.

"Are you sure?!"

"Yep. And she's also got your precious EPIRB."

"I guess it finally cleared customs. Sounds like a regular bonanza then."

The next day we packed efficiently and with extra motivation to make the thirty miles to Crowdy Head National Park. We were almost well rested, spanking clean, and in good spirits. "Crowdy Head or Bust." We got on the water by 8:00 A.M. and fought a moderate current getting out. It took a half hour to go one mile.

We headed straight out the channel and directly into an unjust head wind. It was running into the current and creating a peaking and splashing wave pattern—antipattern. My dry cockpit was soon soaked because I had not bothered to fasten the spray cover. A new north-northeasterly breeze crisscrossed an uninterrupted south-southeasterly swell being spun toward us from Fran, now hundreds of miles offshore.

Pifffff, ahunh, ahunh, pehhhhh, pehhh!

Tony was spitting out spray that the wind was knocking off the top of the waves and blowing off my paddle blades. There wasn't much I could do.

"Any way we can use the sail, mate?" Tony said hopefully.

"Not at all. The wind is practically right in our face."

"Can we tack?"

"We won't get anywhere."

"Well that's the shits."

We put head down and paddled, and paddled some more. We didn't take a break for two hours. When we did, Tony tapped me on the shoulder and said: "Here, mate, put up your hand."

He put a piece of salami with a cracker in it.

We had a couple of chugs of water from the liter-size plastic Nalgene jars and I made sure to check that I had the one without the duct tape on it. That was the one I had been using as my pee bottle.

The boat had now half-broadsided itself to the wind and we were losing hard-earned distance fast. It was clear that rest breaks had to be brief.

Two hours turned to four. Four hours and we take a three-minute pitstop. No need to pee. This is the total amount of activity that my body would want to put out in a day. Against this type of wind, we burn nearly three thousand calories (five Big Macs) and a gallon of water and untold electrolytes. This is my personal paddler's wall: hours start to go by very slowly. I found myself looking at my watch every ten minutes, thinking a half-hour had gone by each and every time.

"Why do you keep looking at your watch, mate, it's not going to help you get there any faster!" Tony said with an exasperation that suggested he was going uphill as well.

"I just can't believe Crowdy Head isn't getting any closer."

Crowdy Head lighthouse is set on a 100-foot cliff. Add the height of the lighthouse itself and we can see it from almost twenty miles away. We were barely halfway there.

Hour six meandered into hour seven and I told myself I would not look up the whole time so that the next time I looked up we would at least appear closer. Tony just kept pounding away behind me.

The trick worked, and now I tried to steer us in for final approach, but to no avail. Instead my hands and forearms started to spasm, but I tried to paddle through it, telling myself: *Losing control of my hands is not going happen.*

Half an hour later, it got worse.

"Tony, I have to switch to the shorter spare paddle."

"*What,* we're almost there."

We were starting to get within recognition distance of the town of Harrington, about five miles south of Crowdy. We were just close enough to watch endless rows of giant, dark green, unbroken swells lump higher a half-mile off our port bow. These waves had been completely unfazed by the day's Force 2–3 winds from the north. They were coming from the east-southeast (ESE) and dominated the seascape around us. They were the fully grown children of Fran paying the town of Harrington a visit.

"No, I know myself, I have got to change to a paddle with less blade resistance and a different cadence so we don't have to stop, it'll only take a minute."

"Whatever you say."

I secured the 260-centimeter "war axe" to the side of the boat and slid out a 240-centimeter (7'6") number from the paddle pockets on the stern deck and clicked it together. I adjusted it for left-hand control to give my right wrist a break. I had done this during my Chesapeake Bay trip a decade earlier and it had kept tendonitis at bay for the rest of the trip.

Kayak paddles can be angled (feathered) in many ways. When the paddle blades are parallel to each other on the same plane it is called unfeathered. When the power-face (spooned) part, the left blade, is facing down and the right one is facing astern that is right-hand feathered at ninety degrees, and vice versa for the left. Paddles are feathered to allow one blade to cut through the air while the active side is in the water, thereby cutting down wind resistance. Some people feel that it adds greater "feel" for blade positioning when one's dominant hand is doing the fine-tuning.

When the paddle is right feathered, the right hand cocks back (like accelerating a motorcycle) to plant the left blade and straightens back to plant the right. The left hand stays in the same position, slightly agape to allow the shaft to rotate through it. Therefore, the right wrist/forearm gets more work throughout the day.

Unfeathered paddles can be an advantage for reducing fatigue on tendons and joints, except when going into a head wind. I believe the paddler should be familiar with all three positions and alternate accordingly.

Longer paddles and larger blades make for more leverage and require more force to keep moving. Normal sea-kayak paddle lengths are 220–240 centimeters for boats that are twenty to thirty inches wide. *Southern Cross* was thirty-four inches wide and Tony had really enjoyed the 260-centimeter (8'6") size back in NYC. This would seem short compared to the nearly ten-foot oar he used to swing once upon a time. The blade size we had was middling in surface area. When combined with the long shaft length, it was more like a mighty two-fisted Viking ax than a short Roman sword. Right now it had taken the starch (quite literally) out of my forearms.

The "wall," as it is known to endurance athletes, is often related to a severe drop in muscle glycogen (sugar) content that cannot be properly replenished consistent to the rate that it is being used up. Without the sugar (the fuel), the muscles start to "sputter" or spasm. This occurs when the body's fuel gauge is in the red. The muscles will painfully spasm and seize (not function) when the reserve tank (body eating muscle to get fuel) is used up. A well-timed candy bar, or a Power Bar, which provides longer-burning sugars, fats, and protein with sufficient water, can mollify the condition in the short run.

"Ready, mate?"

"Yep."

I started paddling furiously to make up for lost time. My stroke increased 20 percent, and the change in angle, slightly higher, and the slightly smaller blade size soon brought relief to my arms.

"Slow down, mate. I can't keep this up."

Tony could not match the faster cadence no matter how hard he tried. I knew his plight.

"Sorry about that. I'll slow it down."

I tried to slow it down but could not find that inbred catch tension that triggered the rest of my stroke. Our well-tuned engine started to knock and stutter.

"This is the shits."

"Would you like to try my paddle for a while?"

"No, mate, let's just keep going!"

The sun was setting and we were a mile away from the high, darkening cliffs of Crowdy Head. The tall, white lighthouse perched on top seemed bemused by our meager efforts. We had been traveling between three and four miles off the coast most of the day to stay in relatively clean (no rebounding waves, no surf break) water and now were getting into the bouncy, rebounding, chaotic shallows of the cliffy shoreline.

Plumes of waves reached up the cliff nearly grabbing the base of the lighthouse. I started to worry about the reach of these long green monsters bent around the north side of Crowdy on the refraction curve. *Not a nighttime Frazer Beach*, I dreaded to myself.

"Let me try that paddle," an exasperated Tony decided finally. It was hour ten on the water.

We switched, and now I tried to swing the longer axe. Tony was hopelessly out of step. He had worn a 260-centimeter-deep groove set in the gray matter of his brain that controls kinesthetic movement patterns. His muscle memory for paddling had become quite specific and this was not the time or the place to make changes.

"Give me back the war ax."

"No worries."

It got dark early under the shadows of the cliff and hills around Crowdy.

We gave Crowdy Point a wide berth, wary of any large fragment of rock that may have fallen into the sea in the last million years or so and now was hundreds of yards offshore waiting to trip giant waves early and create surf in one isolated place.

"We gotta watch the 'bombies,'" Tony said. "I think I saw a few about where we were, miles ago," he said.

That is what the Australians call them. They are also caused by isolated reef heads, sandbars, and sunken vessels. They may activate only during certain swell directions or tide cycles. They are unpredictable.

As our eyesight was lost we shifted to audio and tried to listen to noises. Any unusual *kaboom* or *thaboom* could not be taken lightly.

We rode the big swells and angled toward a small man-made harbor on the north-side armpit of Crowdy Head. The bigger waves kept going west and we ducked out of them by angling southwest toward the break-wall opening of the harbor.

Three quarters of an hour later we snuck in just to the left of the larger swells. It was immediately evident that this was not a resort harbor. It was a working harbor, and it pushed out a small procession of fishing trawlers that showed us the way in.

We paddled from one end of the harbor to the other, searching for the perfect out. Finally, we pulled *Southern Cross* up a corrugated concrete ramp next to a crane used for hauling incapacitated vessels out of the water. A thirty-foot fishing boat was being backed in off a trailer. "Goddamnit," I raged between clenched teeth. It was obvious we would have to move the boat *again*.

"Mate, we gotta get her outta the way. She's backin' in fast. I'll run up and tell them to hold on a minute!"

"*Oh, come on!? You've got to be kidding me?!*" I said accusingly.

"Pissy, pissy."

"Oh fuck off."

"You don't have to be so *shirty* with me. Quit whingeing and let's move the boat."

"Yeah, yeah, yeah," I said, throwing my hands high in the air. But Tony was right. Throwing a tantrum hadn't altered reality a bit.

We moved the boat to an empty mooring along a rickety wooden walkway, and tied her off to a pole like a horse to a hitching post outside a hotel saloon in the Wild West. Now, it was time to barge open the doors and libate.

A bone chill was in the air and a foggy haze was settling in. Our bodies had little internal fire left to use for warmth. My hands became even less dexterous. The combination of blisters, tape, after-spasms, and cold made it near impossible to pull off the black wand of my caboose bags. I felt like a cripple. Tony was not doing much better. A quarter-hour later we accomplished what five minutes used to do. Find and put on our fleece tops and bottoms.

Food!! Food!! Food!! rang my alarm, and it was time to find it. A sign for a restaurant was visible halfway up a large hill. We followed it up a winding road . . . and followed it . . . and followed it. After a trek that seemed to never end we reached a very dark restaurant/bed and breakfast with no hint that anyone was around. We banged on the doors but to no avail. Dogs barked. *It's only seven-thirty. How could the restaurant be closed?*

"That is a bit of disappointment," Tony said.

"A disappointment? *A disappointment, ahhhhhhhhhhh!*" I yelled at the sky.

We walked down the hill, peering left, scouring right, trying to find any kind of food. A loaf of stale bread and a jar of peanut butter were becoming my best hope. Nothing! It seemed like the *whole town* was closed. Few lights shone among the dozens of houses. There wasn't a soul on the streets.

We hiked back to the boat and found a few small ends of salami and a near empty jar of honey—the part that has collected all the bits and crumbs and looks more like a translucent near-petrified fossil. We took the salami ends and smeared them in the jar, toothing as much substance from the leathery rinds as we could. I continued cursing under my breath. I wanted food. Tony managed to find a quarter-can of Nestle's Quik which he quickly blended into a pint of chocolate-flavored water for us to split.

"It's not much, but it'll help wash it all down."

"Thank you, Tony. Sorry for being an asshole."

"No worries, I'm sure the mates will bring us a bite or two."

Tony had been the better man today, I said to myself.

Next came the task of setting up camp and positioning it in a place for our company to see in case they arrived. It started to rain. We set up fifteen feet away from a curve on the only road that came down to the shoreline. It was a clumpy, squishy, grass clearing that might prevent a lucky drunken driver from driving into the sea. A pair of lights pierced us as they sped toward us. I was part deer and part abductee simultaneously.

"Must be them, mate."

The car came and went, aggressively accelerating as it passed us by, perhaps wondering what we had crawled out of. It started raining harder and we made a paddle tepee totem near the bend to mark our turf.

"You think they'll find us, TB?"

"I have complete faith."

"Good night, then."

I had my doubts, but Tony knew his mates better than I did. I shimmied into my cocoon, exhausted and hopeful. I went out like a light. My body's road crews went to sleep as well; they had no more asphalt to pave my wornout roads.

"Thuonk, thuonk." The car doors shut.

Ha, ha, ha.

"Do ya think Epic is still in a coma?"

"I reckon."

I shook my head and wondered if it was true. I heard voices. Was I dreaming? My brain desperately tried to boot up to make sense of it all. There was a strong light and shadows dancing on my bivvy sack. Rain and wind jumbled the illusion. I scrambled out and squinted into the lights. *They're here! The nomad fraternity quartet.*

"Welcome back to life, Epic. We were wondering about you for a while," Michael said with a broad smile and a handshake.

"Hello, Epic," Carolyn said along with a hug. This was followed by similar greetings from Sammy and Brent. I was informed that they had all driven into Harrington for a few beers. It was now a couple of hours later.

"Almost had you for a goner," Brent said with broad grin.

"Here you go, Epic!" Sammy said, as she handed me a rugby-ball-sized box and a big manila envelope and a tin of cookies.

"Thank you! I . . ."

"Oh, be off and read your lovey letters," Tony finally added.

He had me pegged. I ran back to my cocoon, took out a torch, and pulled the clump of envelopes out of the big one. While I did see some letters from some good male friends, it was Nicole's letters I was looking for. Sam had done me the favor of numbering them in order of their arrival. One through five.

It started to pour. Lodging logistics interrupted the reunion. Brent and Sammy opted for the four-wheel drive and Caroline opted for Tony's bivvy sack, a seemingly improbable fit as far as I knew. I was solo with my letters and quite content. I fully zippered the outer flap and I was now alone with Nicole. A slight hint of perfume filled the tiny, Maglit bunker.

Dear Beautiful,

Thank you for all the cards and letters. I love them. I miss you. You are definitely my man! All the other guys here seem like boys. I feel like I am going through a transformation. I feel like you are my soulmate. Hey, would you like to get married on Sadie Hawkins day? I am saving some new lingerie for you.

Be strong. Be good. Just keep Oz on your left.

Love,
Nicole

I read the words over and over again and could feel my battery recharge. I didn't need solid food for now. I even think the flashlight started to get brighter. I could not have hoped for more. I went to sleep content.

Thuonk, thuonk.

"Ha, ha, ha."

Once again I was the last up by a mile. They had already driven into town and had breakfast, the stories and laughter were nonstop.

"Did ya have a little spankin' after all those lovey letters?" joked Michael.

"In fact I did," I said confidently, putting the taunt to rest, as the others laughed at both of us.

"Well, well, well, what have we got here," Brent said, holding the orange device that looked like a space capsule for GI Joe.

"That's the EPIRB."

"What's it for?"

"It is an emergency locator beacon that we set off in case we are lost at sea or injured!"

"Ahhhhhh, *no*, it's not. It is the hailing beacon for the planet Volgon," Michael announced. "It sends a signal out so they can find Tony to help repopulate their dying planet," he added.

"Actually, he's right and then this [the GPS] gives them specific landing instructions. I am just the middleman."

"No wonder it took so long to get through customs," Sammy added sternly and then laughed.

The tone was set and the sun was shining bright. Michael drove me back into town and dropped me off at milkbar for a big feed.

"One chook please with chips and this liter of juice."

"And one of those, too?"

"You mean a meat pie?" I said, pointing to something that reminded me of Swanson turkey pies with a golden crust from childhood.

"Yes, make it two."

"Ya want a whole chook, is that right?"

"Right."

"Where's the rest of the family?"

"You're lookin' at it."

"To go?"

"To stay."

I told Michael to pick me up in an hour.

"Are you sure?"

"Yeah, I need to be antisocial for a while, you know."

"I know, an hour it is then."

I laid everything out on a beauty of a picnic table overlooking the crashing and stumbling surf, glad not to be in it today. *This is going to be our first voluntary day and I'm going to enjoy it.*

I ate everything at the same time. A bite of chook with a bite of meat pie fresh out of the toaster oven, more chook, more meat pie, chips, and guzzled it down with orange juice.

Soon, I had a choir of black and white magpie birds singing for my attention. They thought they were going to make a killing. Not today. I ate everything. I chewed the cartilage off the ends of the bones, all the skin, heart, all of it. I went back in and said, "I would like a hot fudge vanilla sundae as well, please."

Michael came back, and I jumped in, and we drove back to the crew.

"You and TB have really picked it up in the last week, haven't you?"

"Yeah, we started sailing in some big winds."

"Took us over six hours to get up here from Sydney. Of course we did get a bit lost at the end."

"How far is it to Sydney?"

"About three hundred fifty kilometers, I would say?"

"So about two hundred twenty miles."

Let's see . . . 220 divided by 9 days on the water is about 24 miles a day. Just about a circumnavigation of Manhattan. Not a bad start, but not the pace we need in the long run, I thought. "Yeah, we'll have to keep up the pace of the last few days."

"You'll do it. You're just getting the hang of it, be my guess. Tony says it's been a bit over the top."

"He's right."

Upon return, the crew was gathered about Tony in shorts, short-sleeve shirts, sunglasses, and just the right hats for the occasion. They had well-worn personal styles that every Polo, Gap, Banana Republic, and Hilfiger design spy is trying to duplicate. I took off my fleecy top and joined the table. It felt good to have sunlight and not perpetually wet clothes reach my skin.

"You're lookin' pretty buff there, Epic," Brent said.

"A lot leaner," added Carolyn. "I like the new beard."

"Pretty hot," Sammy cooed and made me blush.

"I think I might actually be starting to like you guys," I said.

It was true: All the pretrip fat was gone. Muscle definition on both of us was high. Our bodies were adapting to the continuous work. I figured I had lost at least twelve pounds since Sydney. More than a pound a day. *Not a bad diet plan but a little early in the game to lose the reserve tanks?!* I thought.

I excused myself to the lone phone booth on the hill, where I dialed New York.

"Hello?"

"Hello, Nicole?"

"Eric, is it you? *Is it really you!?*" she said excitedly.

"In the flesh, sort of, well really not at all."

"Tell me everything! How are you, where are you, I miss you, did you get my letters?!"

I was smiling so hard it hurt. I went on and on about everything that had happened.

"How are you finally getting along with Tony?"

"Good, I mean this isn't what I would call fun, things can be pretty hairy, frustrating."

"I'm so glad. I was worried about that!"

"I'm even warming up to his mates. I think I even like them now."

An hour went by on her dime as I didn't have a calling card and nowhere near enough change to make even the initial call.

"Nicole, this is getting long, if there is any chance that you can come here and meet me someday, I don't want to have it blown because of phone bill expense."

"Don't worry, silly, I could listen to you all day. I'm just so glad you're on the other side of this line."

Another half-hour.

"Bye Nicole. I love, I miss."

"I love you, Eric." Five seconds, no hang up.

"Bye." Still no hang up.

"OK, we gotta hang up. I'll count to three and on three we'll hang up at the same time. OK?"

"Yes."

"Promise?" I asked.

"Yes."

One, two, three—

ClickClick.

I wandered back to the group in a daze.

"You look a little bewildered, mate," Tony said.

"Anything wrong?" Sammy asked.

"No, no, everything seems to be fine except . . ."

"What?"

"Nothing, really."

"I hope I get to meet her someday," Carolyn said.

"Nikky's a good ole bird," Tony added.

"And a real *minxxxx,* too," Michael said.

I spent the rest of the afternoon milling about through the gear and reading the instructions for the EPIRB. Tony was among his tribe and I could see him getting stronger every minute. The mutual love and admiration were palpable, yet these ultimately were his people. Mine could not drive here, mine were ten thousand miles away.

Around sunset we had our barbecue of mushroom omelets. Brent (aka Dr. Mushroom) made a mean and potent egg and fungus dish. Later we drove into Harrington and found a local pub with a jukebox and laughed the night away.

We drove back and spotted a particularly beautiful moonlit cove with small, spilling breakers. Everyone got naked and bodysurfed. The water was warm and soothing. The breakers were playful and the water was about chest deep. The euphoria, the camaraderie, and the ocean conspired in providing one of the most exquisite sensations of my life.

Tony, Mike, Sammy, Carolyn, Brent, and I were leaping, diving, gliding, and angling off the waves. *This must be what the dolphins feel like!*

The next morning we drove to Taree.

"See! There it is!" Carolyn said.

And there it was. *The Big Oyster*, welcoming us to town. It was a two-story-high oyster symbolizing the oyster-farming industry in the region. It looked like those oversized everythings along I-95 in the States when you get to the border of South Carolina.

We found the New Age eatery called Only Natural that had come highly recommended to Carolyn. When we got there, Mike made a few quips about the decor and some of the book titles, many of which implied visitors from "other" places.

"Epic, I think Carolyn might be helping you get TB to Volgon."

"Without a doubt, she's from there. It's almost time."

"Ohhhhhh, spooky, spooky," Brent said.

I liked the place. Carolyn had a bit of the sorceress look to her. She was statuesque. She had long, flowing auburn hair, a smattering of freckles, and an occasionally wicked grin. The food was organic, fresh and excellent. Banana and blueberry pancakes, heaps of eggs, and a couple of cups of the best coffee I had had since Speedo's back in Bondi.

I said to the table: "You guys should come by more often, ya hear!"

I picked out a few cards and we got into the car and headed back. The skies had turned gray. The ride back got quiet. The banter had lost some bounce. The weekend reunion was coming to an end.

Tony and I sorted out things to give back to the crew to take back to Sydney. There were extra clothes and shoes and repair supplies and an extra tent that I had stowed away onboard.

"We've been carrying that the whole way, mate?"

"I'm afraid so. I didn't know how the bivvy sack thing was going to work."

"Tsk, tsk."

It had been taking up a lot of room and was never used. We shed twenty pounds' worth. I added the five-pound EPIRB and fastened it to the deck with a special shock-resistant O-clip.

The weekend was over and the Sydney crew had a long drive and a work-week to concern themselves with. We had to quickly get our stride back for the long, long sea journey ahead. In a week we would be out of weekend-visit driving range. Our umbilical chord to our mates was being cut. Murmurings for flights and rendezvous were alluded to, but I think we all felt it would be the last day for quite a while. The 4WD pulled away.

Tony and I were alone again.

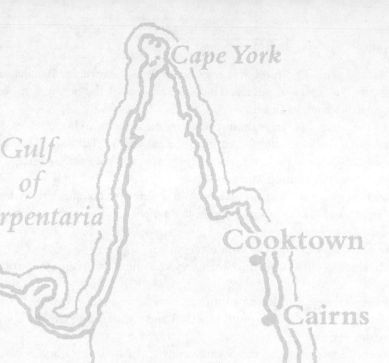

Crowdy On!

After final preparations and getting our water gear on we set off. There was no motivation to get someplace to meet somebody. The motivation was generated by something inexplicable.

The sea was agro that day. The waves nastily darted their tongues at us. All was gray, and rain clouds took turns dumping their full loads on us. I felt confident that the twelve-mile distance to Laurieton was just the right shakedown cruise before we prepared for "real" mileage again. I had looked at the chart and had measured and remeasured our first ten days of travel. We had gone 1.5 percent of the distance around Australia. No matter how many ways I compared the chart distance to the full-size Australian map could I make it more than it was.

The wind quickly picked up from the east, gusting over twenty knots and building seas up off our starboard side. Occasionally, they broke and spilled over our decks. We raised the sail, and *Southern Cross* heeled strongly to port on a gust and nearly capsized us.

"Ooooh, close one, mate!"

"I think we're a wee bit rusty TB, gotta stay concentrated."

We frenetically sailed on this fickle deluge until we were a few miles from Camden Head, and the seas close to it were already visibly chaotic. Swell smashed into the cliffs and bombies broke randomly in a necklace around it.

Thank God, it's only twelve miles, I thought. *At least the harbor should be like Crowdy and give us good protection when we're done.*

We took another wide berth but still felt the zigzagging of waves coming in and out around the point. Finally we rounded the corner and saw an east-facing harbor entrance and a massive buildup of surf in front of it. I could not believe it. My eyes scanned left and right, right and left.

"Ready to hit the sticks again, mate?"

"Yeaaaahh!" I said, reflexively wrapping up and striking the sail rig. I still did not believe my eyes. I secured the rig and I got elevatored on a high wave and saw the lagoon well beyond the breakers. It looked so inviting.

Hisssssssssssssssssssssssss.

THAAAAbooooooooomm . . . sssssssssssssssssss.

Southern Cross was side surfing on a broiling wave. I braced into the thick white foam. Then we popped out of that wave, Tony spat and heaved in a breath of air, another wave was bearing down on us from a different angle off our port bow. We quickly steered left and slightly surfed that wave in toward the river mouth. We had been volunteered to go in as if being drawn in by a tractor beam.

"Concentrate, concentrate," Tony said.

We sprinted and caught one long wave into the harbor. A strong tide attempted to spit us right back out into the surf, but we got caught in its throat. We paddled into a back eddy-pool section behind the entranceway and shook off our refresher course. Tony collected a shredded orange line dangling off the side of the boat.

"Mate, the EPIRB is gone!"

"What!!!??!!!"

He showed me the broken tether ring, and sure enough, the "find-us-anywhere-in-the-world" safety device that took weeks to get through customs and was hand delivered to us had been ripped from our deck. For a moment I thought that maybe Tony had sabotaged it, but that was ludicrous. He may not have liked all the "aids" but he did value money and effort. No, the emergency tether cord had snapped and it was gone.

We landed in two-foot re-formed surf and capsized. Two-foot surf! One moment of lost concentration and we're upside down. Only moments before we had "hanged ten" in a ten-foot wall of water, deftly avoiding being smashed into the rock jetty. *Where's the respect?*

After the indignity of being rolled, we set about to find the bright orange, seven-hundred-dollar EPIRB.

"We've got to find it!" I exclaimed.

Surely, luck will have it washed up on the beach. All we have to do is pay our dues and comb every nook and cranny of the immediate coast.

Tony combed one side of the entrance, I took the other. The tide was going out. An hour of searching was futile.

"The EPIRB's probably way out to sea by now, the current has been going out the whole time. That's what made those breakers."

"We've got to keep looking," Tony said.

"I've covered every inch of my side, TB."

"Let's go down over there." He pointed to a long stretch of sandy beach getting pummeled by the surf.

We searched for another hour but to no avail. Resigned to the loss, we got our gear and started the hike into the town of Laurieton. It was not visible from where we'd landed.

"How far is it, mate?"

"The map says about two miles," I said.

It was late afternoon when we stopped by a marina in town. We told them about our travails.

The proprietor said: "You're gonna have to report the loss in Coff's Harbor up the coast. If some boy gets his hands on the one you are describing, he'll have the bloody navy searching for him up and down the coast. I heard it can cost 'em a hundred thousand dollars to do a search. By the way, I do have another one here."

We walked around the corner and saw a stack of EPIRBs in boxes, like champagne bottles stacked in a wine shop during the holidays. I was excited and then I saw the price.

"Let's see here, it has frequencies for both aircraft and satellites, like the other one. It costs . . . a hundred fifty dollars [Australian—a hundred twenty U.S.]."

"Excuse me, sir. Is this the price?!"

"Yep."

"Why . . . well, why is it so reasonable?"

"It's Aussie law that every fishing boat has to have one. They're basically subsidized so everyone can afford one."

"Did you hear that Tony . . . Tony?"

"Look here, mate. Look what I found." He was holding a medium-sized plastic boat fender similar in size to what the lifeguards carry around them in *Baywatch*.

"I think this will work better than the boat cart did." We had sent the boat cart home with the crew.

"Do you boys have a good VHF radio?"

"Well, no, how much do they cost?"

"This one here is about four hundred U.S. dollars."

I looked at it and saw that it was made in the U.S.

"We don't need a radio," Tony said.

"Tony, I think it wouldn't hurt to have one."

"They have a short range and we haven't seen anyone we could talk to, anyway."

"Yeah but—"

"He's got a point," the proprietor interjected.

"The VHF works on line of sight. It's best for ship-to-ship."

We looked around a little more. Tony went to the counter and put the fender and a few odds and ends on the counter. I went to get the EPIRB box and put it on the counter as a matter of expectation.

"I'll take these things," Tony said, pointing to his original items.

"What about the EPIRB?"

Tony waved it away. "We don't need it yet. Not with all the towns and all."

I got my credit card out of my wallet. "We'll take it."

Tony shot me *the look*.

The walk back to the boat was a quiet one. It started to rain harder. We set up camp using *Southern Cross* turned on her side as a windbreak and built our tent-fly bunker.

I decided to break the tense silence. "Why didn't you want the EPIRB? You know how important it could be?"

"We've got to watch what we spend. I did some calculations in Crowdy and I've spent more than I thought."

More than he thought? Well, it's his money and it's not my position to tell him what to do with it, I suppose. I thought, *Thank God for plastic.*

I wrote in my journal:

Weather Flash

It has been a real shit. Cannot make up its mind. Good in that it has brought prevailing southerlies and blocked the sun. Bad because it is wet and humid and has incited mosquitoes to riot. I don't know if one can ever have it all.

I've studied the charts, and distances between "safe" harbors become greater than thirty nautical miles. There will be larger paddles ahead of us but we are pretty tough, I hope.

Nagging skin injuries (particularly on the back), hemorrhoids, red rashes are a bit of a "bore," as Tony would say.

Once again, we take this "port" thing as a real plus only to see a nice town sprawling behind endless phalanxes of surf.

Wish I had brought more dosh.

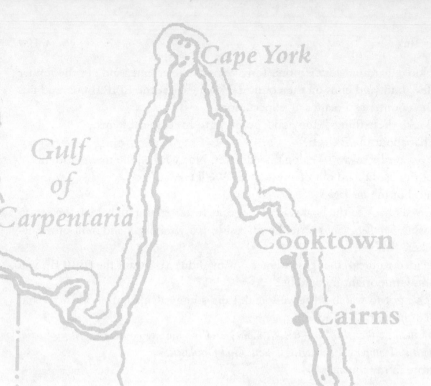

To Port Macquarie

The next day, the weather was brighter and I scouted a better line out of the Laurieton harbor.

"It looks like there is a gap to the north of those breakers, Tony."

We mounted up and went out at a near slack tide. This dramatically reduced the size and steepness of the breakers coming onto the river bar. The exit was almost perfect until the top of one wave smashed me in the chest and soaked me through.

Good morning Epic, I heard it say.

The way the coast laid itself out seemed to give us a choice of a twenty-mile, thirty-mile, or forty-mile day. The closest distance matched with the largest town, Port Macquarie, and a more surefire landing. The other distances matched with headlands on the chart that may or may not offer a proper landing. I believe we were both a little shell-shocked from ducking the hammers.

Port Stephens had been pretty good, Port Macquarie is even bigger, should be fine.

The somewhat finer weather brought the headwinds with it, and it was evident after a few hours that it was going to be the twenty-mile day, easy landing or not.

Not.

We rounded Port Macquarie's broad, potentially protective shoulder. It would block prevailing southerly swells. The SE winds of yesterday were now bent and turned by the NE headwinds and were running unencumbered into the east-facing entrance, generating a marvelous display of cresting rollers. I saw an exact replica of the *Hawaii Five-O* wave that had tormented me as a youth.

"Not too promising, mate."

"No kidding," I said.

There it was: a good-sized modern Australian town, right there, sunning on the hill, while we're cavorting with its enormous bouncers who are hell-bent to not let us in to the placid waters of the harbor mouth—and yet we kept going. *BOOOMMMM Spissssssshhhhhhhhhhhh.*

Our obstinacy had taken us in too far now. We could see the harbor entrance with its narrow exitway for the Hastings River completely blocked. We were in and among giant rollers that like their name did not suddenly break and dissipate but rather broke and rolled forward like an avalanche.

"Hold it steadyyyyyyy!" Tony said.

Ptttisshhhhhhhhhhhhhhhhhh. Bwwwwooooommmmmmmmmshhhhhhhh.

Southern Cross surfed the roller well for what seemed like an eternity.

"I should have had my diving tanks on for that one! We were underwater for quite a time."

I had been spared, as *Southern Cross* would level herself off into the meat of the wave and spurt forward. The four feet of distance between Tony's head and mine made the difference between him being underwater and me being just ahead of it.

"Over there, behind those rocks, there's a beauty of a beach. See it!"

"I'll turn her around."

"We'll have to angle in and sprint between waves."

"Let's *go*, let's *go*!"

We started sprinting, but I could see a big wave outracing us to the mark.

"Hold it, Tony!"

The wave exploded on and just past the rock we were heading for a hundred yards away.

"We have to watch a few sets come in to get the timing," I said.

At full sprinting speed it would take us at least forty-five seconds to get there. Plenty of time for a wave traveling twenty-five miles per hour to catch us from a quarter-mile out.

"We're almost there. One good sprint should do it. Let's go!" Tony said.

"Not yet, not yet."

I wanted to make sure we didn't get caught between a rock and a harder place, and yet other rollers were taking their bearings on us as well. We let the largest wave in the visible bunch go and sprinted in.

Booom Splssshhhhhhhh Boommmmmsssssshhhhhhh.

We were in. Our rock defender was slammed but it completely diverted the wave away from us. We had a one-kayak garage all to ourselves.

That was close.

It was late afternoon and we had plenty of time to get to a milkbar in town, eat massive quantities, and buy some Weet-bix for breakfast.

The next morning, Tony said, "Mate, we've got to get some distance in today. We're going too slow." His tone carried a hint of accusation.

"Well, we have a choice of Crescent Head about fifteen miles, or Hat Head, which is over thirty."

"Sounds like the haberdashery to me, mate."

We got an early start and were blessed with a good tide again. An hour into the paddle, we set sail and made good time. Three-and-a-half hours later Crescent Head was a mile abeam off our port side.

"Must be Crescent Head," I said.

"Wave good-bye," Tony added.

Spirits were high again as *Southern Cross* broad-reached and ran with a moderate SE wind and sea. Tony had cleated the mainsail and was almost getting bored with it all. He was offering me a host of morsels from salami to cookies that had been restocked in Macquarie. A conversation about modeling arose and he started to explain to me the difference between working and nonworking models.

"Most models don't make much dosh and don't stay with it too long. I've been lucky."

"Did you make a lot of money?" I asked.

"I had a few good years, you could say. It's a good thing my dad made me invest it, otherwise I might have just pissed it all away by now."

"What did he have you invest it in, stocks?"

"A couple of buildings in Bondi."

"Buildings?"

"Yes, some apartment buildings right on the beach."

"Not the penthouse."

"Nooo, mate, right on the main strip, on the beach."

"And why, pray tell, did you not live in it?"

"Awwh, I have from time to time but they do best as rentals. I don't need something so fancy."

The wind decreased.

Tony was now trying to coax as much wind into the mainsail as possible by grabbing the boom and waving it through the air. No luck. We could potter along at two miles per hour with this paltry Force 2 sneeze of a wind or go back to paddling.

We pottered for an hour but our safety cushion of daylight was deflating to nothing. We switched back to the sticks and aimed for a "fast hour" paddle to make up time.

After a couple of hours of "fast paddling" the wind had still not returned. I looked at the chart. We hadn't covered much distance at all. It became a hot day without a substantial head wind. Two miles to port I saw a sub-thirty-foot sailboat hugging the shoreline and gaining on us rapidly under sail. It was no racing boat, but it was obviously covering a much greater distance in a shorter time! In fifteen minutes it passed us and pulled gradually away. *What is going on? We've been able to outpaddle most sailboats like that on a straight line. The wind is light, I don't get it.*

"Why are we not moving the boat well?" Tony asked.

"They must be using an engine."

"I didn't hear one."

Just as frustration was getting the best of us, a fishing boat passed by and a fisherman asked: "Are you the guys going around Australia?"

"Yeah, we are!"

"Saw you in *People* magazine."

"Is there a safe landing on the other side of Port Korogoura (Hat Head)?" I asked, hopefully.

"Sure is." He gave us a thumbs-up.

Yes!! I thought to myself.

Enthusiasm restored, we rounded the seemingly endless point to find refuge—the finest protection we'd seen so far. About a mile deep was the silhouette of the sailboat that had passed us. We paddled toward her to find out her secret. On her stern was *Cinderella*.

As we arrived, a couple of Tooheys beers were being waved to us by the ship's captain, who introduced himself as Phil.

"We were wondering if you were going to come here?"

We tied off on *Cinderella*'s flank and boarded her in pirate fashion. We were just in time to sit in the steering well and watch the sunset. We were told we'd been catching eddy currents that run counter to the Great Southern Current that Tony and I had been running straight into all day.

A strong prevailing current running along a curving shoreline can create "back eddies" that can bend the current the other way.

"I thought that current lies about five miles offshore?!"

"Well, that's an average. Some years it's ten. Sometimes it's right where it was today. It's running particularly strong this year because of the cyclones."

I went on to explain all the surprises and shattered expectations, particularly the nastiness of the harbor entrances.

"Australia's east coast is notorious for these difficult river-bar entrances. The cyclones have also made them even less predictable because of the massive shift of sand underwater," Phil explained.

Phil went down into his cabin and came back with charts and a couple of books by Jeff Toghill. We were told that Toghill is *the* authority for yacht cruising the coast of Australia. I devoured the book like a famine victim.

Tony and the *Cinderella*'s crew kicked back into pleasant conversation. The books left me both delighted and disgruntled. Delighted, in that there was some disclosure of the nautical mysteries ahead. Disgruntled because it showed hundreds of miles of coast with more river-bar landings.

Somewhere in my planning, I had believed that all of these towns built on or near the sea would be safe houses protected from the relentless onslaught of the ocean. I wanted to believe civil engineers had built perfect fortresses with drawbridges for us to paddle in and out of. To hear that one late-season cyclone could erase most of those ideas was offensive to my citified sensibilities. To know that there was a lot more to come and that they still remained our best chance for refuge was mind opening. Another beer, some food, and the sunset closed the box of trouble.

Eventually, we left the yachtie's life and went to the beach, where we were greeted by the no-see-um and mossie land-and-air forces. A relatively still, muggy night in this protected area made us easy targets. I stripped off all clothing and was promptly bitten through the bivvy sack. Neither of us slept very well, the seven hours of paddling into the invisible current plus the relentless attacks was not adding up well. Tony got the worst of it again. He arose deflated. I had already gotten some oatmeal (porridge) started.

"Well, TB, we can go fourteen miles to South West Rocks or close to forty if we go for Nambucca Head."

"How's the wind?" he asked hopefully.

"Almost none."

"It looks like the Rocks, doesn't it?"

"I'm afraid so," I said, only half as dejected.

"Should be able to knock it off in half a day."

"This will have to be our 'easy' day for this week, then. Maybe we can work on the boat and all that when we get there?"

We gathered ourselves a bit more slowly knowing we would not have the get-there-before-dark pressure of the previous days.

The first hour off was glorious. We were back to our five-mile-an-hour clip, with no wind to speak of. We covered the first seven miles to the south side of Smoky Cape in good spirits. I basically knew that capes were usually bigger than points or heads. If you think of a point as the thick spoke of a wheel, and a head as half the wheel itself, a cape is the addition of an inner tube—the tire and possibly the studs as well. There was more.

Life on one side of a cape is not necessarily like life on the other side. As soon as we passed the first point we encountered wind and severe chop. We went from Act 1 to Act 2 without any intermission. Early-day optimism weathered the chop from Point 1 to Point 2. *It will change just after we get around it, and we should see our destination and be on the home stretch!?*

We crawled to Point 2. We passed between it and a nearby outlying islet only to have the chop intensity increase to a full rinse cycle. This had to have something to do with the cape sticking its oversized head out into the sea current that we'd fought the day before. Another point lay "just ahead."

The chop bucked us hard, up and down, pushed every which way. But it was still only an annoyance and I chose to enjoy the new experience for a while.

"She be a bit *shirty* with us, don't you think?" I said to Tony, trying to use some of his words in a sentence and ending up with Commonwealth hodgepodge.

We reached Point 3, only to see Point 4. More chop, more distance. Slow moving, no visible destination. I wanted to look at the chart to verify that it was only fourteen miles. Three hours had gone by. We should've been close, but all we were seeing was more cliff ahead.

"Tony, let me see the chart for a sec."

"Why do you need to do that?"

"I just want to make sure about exactly where our next destination is."

"Mate, we already know it's twelve to fourteen miles. It can't be much farther. Let's just keep paddling!" he yelled.

I conceded.

Point 4 turned into Points 5 and 6. No visible final destination. *Now this is getting ridiculous.*

"What the fuck is going on here?" I said in dismay.

"Mate, this is another hell ride!"

Point 6 turned into Point 7 and it was over—almost. Tony and I were shot. We'd been paddling as hard as we could to make it all go away—only to have more. *Two more miles to town.* We were facing southeast?!

South West Rocks greeted us with larger-than-expected surf that proved to be particularly aggressive just as we hit the beach, practically kicking us out of the boat like two unwelcome guests being "escorted" out the door of a club. Once onshore, we found a small strip of beach at low tide. It was obvious by the pervasive wet sand that part of the beach would be submerged later in the cycle, so we moved the boat forty yards farther using Tony's new fender method.

"OK, mate, now you hold the bow up and I'll get the roller."

We took the six-inch-diameter air-filled plastic fender and rolled *SC* across it, and the fender would pop out astern like the rugby ball after a scrum. Then one of us would hold the bow up until the fender was retrieved and placed under the bow and we would roll again in boat-length increments. Although lighter and more compact than the boat cart, it was not yet much of an advantage.

"I think this has great promise, TB, but we'll probably need two of them."

Tony was already gathering some driftwood pieces and placing them ahead. Now it almost worked like a little assembly line. Nevertheless, the wood had the tendency to dig in to the sand and cause a traffic jam.

More "easy" day consumed. We donned our poly street duds and stashed our camp bags in some bushes near a covered barbecue area. I took the chart and compared it to a local tourist map and saw what had happened. The town on the chart was not on the water. It was on top of the cape. We had gone almost in a complete circle to get to the low-lying neck of the cape. Elongate that neck a dozen miles and Smoky Cape could grow up to be a peninsula. More likely, the ocean will eventually sever the cape's neck and make an island of it. *Good riddance!*

It rained again. Then, rained harder. We found a milkbar and ate kebabs, pastry, milk shakes, tea, lemon mineral water, more tea, and ice cream. The downpour hadn't bothered us until we realized it wasn't going to stop.

"We're not going to get any work done on the boat!" Tony sulked.

"It looks like monsoon season has arrived."

We spent the rest of the evening at a hotel bistro watching televised cricket, which eventually morphed into a sing-a-along session with a number of retirees glued to a singing comedy revue. A truly bad one.

At one point an Aborigine, with dark skin, wavy hair, and bright eyes—but dressed in Western gear—strolled purposefully to our table to introduce himself. Tony pulled up a chair for him, and everyone in the bar looked at us and stared.

Coincidentaly, his name was Tony.

"You look like interesting chaps. Where have you been?" he said in the King's English.

"We're going around Australia in a kayak," I said.

"In a canoe, then?"

"Indeed, except it's enclosed and uses a double-bladed paddle."

"That's what I meant. You sound like you are from America."

"I am."

"Sounds like you are on quite a walkabout. It has been a pleasure to meet and converse with you. I wish you well."

After he walked away the whispering resumed. Shortly, we made our way back to camp, getting pelted by penny-sized raindrops.

Australian Aborigines are considered among the very oldest peoples on the planet, having been in Oz for more than forty thousand years. Indigenous to Australia, the entire Aborigine culture is based on living in accord with the environment.

Captain Cook talks about Aborigines in dug-out canoes virtually ignoring his boat, *The Endeavour,* and its crew.

> *The surf made it impossible to land. Next morning at daylight a bay was discovered sheltered in appearance, into which he resolved to take the ship. . . . He did so, anchoring off the south shore under the eyes of a few natives, some painted over with broad white stripes and armed with pikes and shorter weapons of wood. A few others, striking fish from canoes almost in the surf, seemed to take little notice of the ship.*

Like our Indians they had no concept of land ownership or any kind of organized government that the British could relate to. Therefore, Britain founded the colony of New South Wales based on the legal principle of *terra nullius* (a land belonging to no one). The Aborigine believed that the people belonged to the land.

This principle was defended by Australian courts until 1976 when the Aboriginal Land Rights Act was passed for the Northern Territory. This started the slow reclamation of some Aborigine land and rights. Progress has been slow. Certain things may never change.

We scrambled though the deluge to our metal-roof-covered barbecue pit and rigged up our cocoons. It sounded like someone was banging on the roof with pots and pans.

In the middle of the night I bounded out of sleep in a fright. I had dreamed that our boat was lost. I immediately started running back toward the boat, eyeing the formerly demure tidal brook. It looked like a white water river. I was convinced of the worst. The "high ground" where we had put the boat looked like "no ground" in the dark. I ran and ran trying to gain my bearings in the tempest.

There it is! Isn't it? Is it? Yes. Thank God!! There was still some beach left.

I double-checked the lines and added another to a tree. I came back to camp totally soaked. Tony was fast asleep. This was my personal nightmare.

Gulf
of
Carpentaria

Cape York

Cooktown

Cairns

QUEENSLAND

Brisbane

NEW SOUTH

LIA

To Nambucca Heads

Surge from the previous night's storm made for another difficult exit as wave after wave came cascading onto our small launching area. One wave tried to twist the boat upside down just as we were positioning for launch. It wrenched Tony's wrist, but we carried on. An early dose of adrenaline gave us a mile into less turbulent water.

"How's your wrist?" I asked.

"A bit crook'd, but I'll be all right."

It wasn't long before I could sense the change in his cadence by the sounds of the paddles hitting the water and the greater tension in one side of my back as my stroke automatically tried to compensate for the loss of one engine in this four-engine plane. Both pains started to get more than unpleasant by hour three. I opted to get the Nuprin out of the med kit for myself. Up to now Tony wouldn't touch the stuff.

"Pass me the bottle, mate," he said. "How many should I take?"

"Three for acute inflammation," I said. He took two.

A half-hour later Tony seemed OK. We paddled better and the wind was uncooperative, then it strengthened against us. We pushed on, and two hours later we saw the tumultuous river-bar entrance at Nambucca. An endless procession of surf was battling the exiting Nambucca River. It was like the Alamo. The sea had too many men.

"What do you think, Epic?"

"I can see a small spot just to the north of where the river is coming out. See it?!"

"It should be quite a ride but I'll kamikaze in if need be. Don't think the wrist is up for much more today."

"Hey, do you see that motorboat over there? It looks like it's coming right at us."

"That's all we need!" The boat was quickly cutting and jumping through the waves and Tony was the first to guess.

"I think it's that Ron Arias bloke," he said.

"What? How can than that be?"

"He said he was going to try to catch up with us after two weeks."

"How the hell did he find us?"

There were three people in the boat and one was already splayed out on the bow with a telephoto lens aimed at us. In moments, the twenty-foot red motorboat had passed us, circled us, and was coming at us from another direction. I felt like we were a lone slow American bomber being taunted by a Japanese Zero known for its maneuverability. The photographer was clicking away when we heard:

"Hello, Tony! Hello, Eric!"

"I told you, mate," Tony said.

"Ahhhh shittt," I said.

"My driver says there is a good place to the north of this point, you can get in ess . . . err . . . the . . ."

"What?!" I yelled, as I could not quite hear through the combined roar of the surf and the motor.

"Follow us, we'll guide you in!"

"Come on, mates! Follow me through betwain the two reef stacks and ya'll be right," the driver said with confidence.

It didn't *look* better from where I sat, but I decided to trust the local. We surfed into a calm pool of water—practically a lagoon—and landed *Southern Cross.*

Ron had aimed a little north of our estimated position and come south via the motorboat. Apparently they climbed a hill and saw us in the distance. The fisherman/boat driver turned out to be a relative of Fletcher Christian, the man who inspired *Mutiny on the Bounty.*

Pete Solness, the photographer, was already preparing his underwater camera as he announced his intentions to get a few more surf shots while the light was still good. *These people must think we're surf experts and go in and out as a matter of routine. Now he wants us to go in and out of these bombers like walking in and out of a door.*

We unloaded the kayak and put on our Speedos as per request. We had not been swimming much after the second day of the trip. There is no desire to *get* wet after *being* wet most of the day. But the sun was out and the water was warm. As soon as we paddled a few strokes, Peter said, "I need to straddle your boat to get the best shots."

This was the equivalent of balancing your grandfather on the handlebars of your mountain bike on a downhill course. The combination of Peter's positioning and the higher center of gravity of the unladen boat made for shaky paddling.

"OK, now paddle towards the surf."

Tony seemed to respond to these commands as if hypnotized by years of conditioning.

We played around for a while and inevitably capsized. I felt like an idiot. Peter clicked away at the two intrepid travelers with their pants down, bailing away and submerged to the coaming.

After surf follies, came speedo posing. Bringing the boat up the beach, stretching on the beach, walking together up and down the beach and all that. My normal get-on-stage persona felt somewhat violated by it all.

"That's it. That's . . . a little faster. No—look towards the ocean . . . chin higher, Eric . . ."

They're coming into our special world and dissecting it with formfit images. Ron clearly sensed our waning enthusiasm and suggested we get into town for some tucker "on the house." The thought of food perked us up and we continued to answer questions for our newfound provider.

"We're always in our own private houses of pain. It's all about pain management," Tony explained for Ron, who nodded obligingly. ". . . and the mossies are brutal."

While Tony narrated I modeled the blisters under blisters on the hands, the welts and bites on the ankles, and finished with two deep gnawing sores adjacent to my lower spine. I saw Ron's face blanch a bit.

"How did you get those?"

"I figure we average at least twenty thousand strokes per day. My back pivots on the backrest probably three or four times per hundred, so . . ."

"Have you seen any sharks?"

"Just a couple of nippers," Tony said with a sigh.

Ron could see we had had enough and said, "You must be hungry. Let me drive you into town and treat you to dinner."

"Now you're talkin'," I said.

On the car ride I explained to Ron how food and water weren't compensating for energy lost from paddling over consecutive days. Anything over two solid hours of paddling and we felt it. Four hours is moderate-comfort-recovery zone. Five to six hours is the practical limit for paddling consecutive days on end at this stage.

"You may think we'd been eating up a storm, yet we've lost at least fifteen pounds apiece in just over two weeks," I said.

All in all, I believe Ron found it difficult to get a lot of sensation from us. It all had been more humbling than sensational. We had only just begun and we were in no position to brag or boast. We were walking a thin line. There was no reason to make it thinner. It was easy to feel superstitious. Words we said could be used against us in the court of Neptune. Surely, he has spies on the beach.

The next day was our first bona fide "maintenance day." Over the first three hours, we completely unpacked, disassembled, dried out, and started to repair the boat. Tony picked up one of the 1.5-meter-long foldup wooden gunwhales (internal side panel), and two wooden plates fell off an area that had developed a very pronounced S-curve.

"Is this supposed to look like this, mate?" Tony asked, holding the piece fully extended to its nine-foot length.

Each half of the Klepper Acrius II design has three primary wooden "girder beams." There is the keel board. It is the widest and sits on the bottom of the boat. A couple of 20-cm-wide, 5–7-ply-thick (10 mm) pieces of laminated birch plating spans over most of the boat. Two 1.5 × 1.5-cm beveled rectangular rails for nearly three meters. The whole thing folds in half.

The gunwales (side panels) have the same 1.5 × 1.5-cm rails but are spanned by six to seven smaller plates (10 cm wide, 15 cm long and 10 mm thick) each. They are fastened to the rails via a special, heated glue-press process. Some are secured with "soft" rivets. Unlike hard rivets, these are malleable enough to give and take with the flexing of the boat and are easier to remove and repair. Older Kleppers had all the plates on all the primary panels glued and screwed. "It should always be done that way," my father would say. The total length of a gunwale is also about three meters and folds in half. The gunwales are expected to take on a modest symmetrical curve. This gunwale looked like a snake.

"No, no it's not." I had never seen a piece look like this; moreover, it was not just the two plates that had fallen off but a closer inspection showed that almost all of them were loose.

"And look at this rib?!" Tony continued. One of the ribs close to the bow had been dislodged and one side of it was bent.

Judging by the gunwales, the rib had probably been dislodged early in the trip when we'd tried to take gear out from the front of the boat. With normal wear and tear one rib means little to the whole structure. The boat can function well without two or three of its seven ribs. Not in our case. The entire design was being maxed out. Every part counted.

We spent the rest of the day adding screws to most of the plates, bending back the ribs by soaking them and putting stones on them to counterlever the curve. I wiped and waxed parts, aqua-sealed some tears in the deck canvas. I added lashes and duct tape to all the rib-to-beam attachments. All Eskimo kayaks were fastened together with gut lashings. I am sure they tied better knots than I had.

The day evaporated. We ate well again and said good-bye to our interviewers (planes to catch, people to see, stories to write). A reinvigorated Tony reiterated to Ron his desire to go on.

"We're going all the way around!"

At this rate it will take almost twenty months, I thought to myself. The last five days had been almost all paddling. We'd been out for almost two-and-a-half weeks. Our daily average had dropped to twenty-one miles per day. Water-time average was twenty-five miles but the three days off were clearly too many.

My journal that night read:

I teeter-totter on the total program mentality. I think I'll give myself to Brisbane to pace it. Then we've got to do more. It appears I will have to settle for singles and doubles before our run rate has to go up and we need to swing for the fences more. It's hard to mentally pace for this kind of distance and duration. I do not want to be doing this for two years or even eighteen months. I want to finish in twelve months. So, Eric, get your ass in gear and start thinking about putting the pedal to the metal, chap. We're going to have to do earlier and later cruising. More time on the water. We need to stay fueled and rested somehow. It's 9:00 P.M., time to hit the hay.

That night was muggy, and a symphony of mosquitoes buzzed right outside our bivvy sacks. Now, any body part that was up against the sack was fair game. I'd become convinced that these mossies have "extension beaks" that can pierce through Gore-tex, polypro, and then skin. We woke up with more welts on our "bums," thighs, knees, shoulders, and elbows. The drilling crews had been out all night. Ron or one of his crew had mentioned that we had to watch for Ross River syndrome. It wasn't quite malaria but it was in the same league as Lyme disease. All the rain had caused an outbreak of cases.

The next day, we were off! I was refreshed, relaxed, reset in our goals, and glad that *Southern Cross* had been checked from A to Z. I suppose a little bravado had been instilled from all the attention we received. We started in gentle two-foot seas and modest Force 2–3 wind. Just enough to sail along at about three knots.

By early afternoon the wind was stronger and blowing from the south. By 2:00 P.M. we passed the first possible stop, Urunga, three miles off our port beam.

"Here's where I thought we might land," I said to Tony.

"We need more distance and there is plenty of daylight."

"The next stop is Coffs Harbour. It's the distance we've just done and then some."

"You know we've got to go farther."

We headed to Coffs Harbour. The wind was getting stronger and we were sailing wing on wing. The wind pulled hard on my paddle-extended jib and my forearms started to burn. I was holding onto it like it was the boom of a sail board. It seemed to have that much force. We averaged over five knots and made it to the Coffs Harbour entrance an hour before sunset. The good news was that Coffs Harbour was not a river bar! Moreover, its construction was a safe house from the southerly swell we had been running with.

We made a ninety-degree turn to port. *Woooppp!*

"Watch your head!" Tony shouted.

Wappppp pa pa pa pa pa.

The mainsail had swung over my head and pulled away from Tony's grasp for a second. He tightened it quickly and the boat heaved to starboard.

"Ease it up, Tony!"

We were now on a full reach, with the wind coming from abeam and heeling the boat hard to starboard. Hours of adapting to the balanced wing-on-wing sailing in a coddling four-to-five-foot running sea were pulverized by turning one right angle.

The wind was over twenty knots, but the waves were very small, as the harbor was a mile wide. All twenty knots were hitting all of *Southern Cross* without any dilution or deflection from other waves.

"We're flyin' now!" Tony said. "Can you get up on the boat and hike out?"

I got up out of my seat, sat up on the deck, and leaned hard to port. My toes were wedged under the deck and I was holding myself up with the jib sail like it was a parachute.

"Yeeee haaaaa!" I screamed.

Less than one hundred meters to port were blocks of black-rock break wall that divided a private marina from the main harbor. Our destination was a small beach straight ahead. Our boat had no leeboards. There was a good chance that we would get blown into the break wall as the boat was losing almost five meters to starboard for every fifty we went forward. We had almost two miles to go.

"We're sailing her all the way in mate," Tony said confidently.

Ten minutes later we were fifty meters from the break wall and a mile away from the beach. The wind was now even stronger. We tried to turn into the wind.

"It's getting close, Tony," I said cautiously.

"We're almost there . . . almost there" Tony said.

"Hold on, I'm taking her all the way in!"

We skidded *Southern Cross* almost her full length up the gently graded sandy beach. We were five meters from the wall. We hadn't used the paddles all day long!

We went into town, had a few Aussie grills (assortment of grilled meats with veggies for color), and watched some brilliant Aussie Rules "footie" (Carlton Blue v. Hawthorne). Carlton thrashed them. This was my first opportunity to see Tony's favorite game.

The Aussie Rules game involves two teams of tall, tough, and lean players who make spectacular jumps to "mark" a ball, then fist-pass, kick, drop-kick, or dribble (bounce three times) the ball downfield until it is drop-kicked through uprights or passed through them from closer range. The closer-range net shots guarded by a goalkeeper are worth more points than the kicks. The scores get quite high. The action is nonstop.

"Moz and I played at Melbourne Grammar. I got knocked out something vicious once."

"Was Melbourne Grammar a prep school?"

"You could say that. I was first sent to an experiential-style school, with a lot of outdoor activity, flexible curriculum, and the like . . . well . . . I floundered a bit. Grammar set me straight, gave me a chance to play organized sports and the like."

The rain was back in force again as we headed back to the boat. We got our gear and waited out the downpour under a small awning in front of a local marine shop. We were homeless in Coffs Harbour. Soon we heard sirens and two police cars pulled up right in front of us. Two officers in full rain slickers approached us with two bright flashlights spotlighting us. We stood up slowly.

"Gedday, what's your business being here?"

Tony explained our plight and told them specifically where our boat was.

"Well, somebody called about a couple of suspicious characters being down here. Get in. We'll take ya over to a picnic area with a roof over it. You should be awright there."

We pitched our bivvies on top of the picnic tables.

GRRRRRRRRRRRRRRRRRRRRRRRRRRR followed by *Sshhshshshsh-shshsshshsh-honk honk honk—boooop booooop—clankty clank clank clankty clannkkk.*

Coffs Harbour was the biggest town between Newcastle and the "Gold Coast" and an important regional center. It had become a tourist town but the substantial jetty and harbor were built in 1892 to load cedar and other logs for export. Then it was bananas that became the cash crop once a railroad was built in 1918. You can see the banana plantations on the hills all around Coffs.

To us the early morning train was a most unwelcome guest. The tin roof reverberated. Next was the garbage truck loading up the picnic site's trash containers. Finally, it was the sound and smell of the buses and cars. These were the ghosts of Western society past, present, and future. It was Monday.

Enough already.

We scrambled into this invasion and headed back to *Southern Cross.* On the way we checked in with a chemist (pharmacist) and asked about Ross River syndrome, which had gotten a front-page headline in the morning paper.

His advice: "Keep long clothes on and use repellent!"

He obviously wasn't familiar with the new model of mosquito, with those fancy extension beaks, that had been drilling so successfully through all of our

defenses. It was clear that our choice of travel had put us out of the technolog-
ical bubble and into the food chain. Who ever thought that mosquitoes would
be above humans on the food chain? Sharks, crocs, yeah—mosquitoes??!?

When we checked in with the Australian coastal patrol about our lost
EPIRB, the gentleman told us he'd report it to the head office in Canberra
immediately. He was fascinated by our trip and asked us to keep checking in
with local authorities when possible. He wished us luck and Godspeed.

We were about to shove off on the chilly, overcast day, when a writer and a
photographer showed up. Apparently Ron had tipped them off and they found
us. This time we were more "shirty" (short curse) with them because we wanted
to leave Monday behind, but the blokes were nice enough so we spewed out
some of the details again. Finally we were away. Monday was left on land.

Tony had a "bee up his bum." The town had been noisy, we had been interrupted by the media again. We launched and paddled hard. We put up sail for a
while but the winds were Force 2–3 and we were only getting 2.5–3 knots
from it.

"We've got to hit the sticks, we're not moving well," Tony said. He was not in
the mood for reading.

We started paddling hard and the wind freshened in the afternoon. We raised
both sails. Late in the afternoon the wind got spotty and we went back to paddling to keep up the speed. Whatever it took to average over four knots. Finally
we approached Woolgoolga Beach, about twenty miles up the coast with about
two hours of daylight left.

"This looks like it could be a decent landing," I suggested. "At least we can
still see where we're going."

"We've still got daylight. We've got to keep going."

An hour later we were paddling hard and the sun was racing to the horizon.
We came to Arrawarra Point.

"When we round this point there should be a spot. That will give us nearly
thirty nautical miles for the day." This would be the equivalent of thirty-five
statute miles and almost sixty kilometers. *I'll fudge five over so he'll come to his
senses,* I thought.

"OK, that's sufficient. If it works we'll have just enough daylight to make the
landing."

We came around the point and immediately were lifted high by a swell. I
could see the river bar around a mile away. We started our approach and another
big swell rolled under us.

Why are these way out here all of sudden, I wondered. *They've got to be too far out
to start breaking.*

We paddled another hundred yards and rose to the very peak of a swell.

THABBBOOOM!SSSSSsssssssss.

"Back paddle! Back paddle!" I yelled.

I looked over my shoulder and saw a thick, dark green face with a wisping top that looked like a fuse ready to detonate the mass underneath.

Pummmpishhhhhhhhh.

We pierced through it backward and as we were sliding down its steep backside I looked back and saw another one with another fuse and something else crossing right beneath and glowing orange.

"It's a hammerhead! And a big one!" Tony yelled.

"What?!" I thought. *Gotta keep backpaddling through that wave.*

Same explosion, the glowing object was gone. We turned *Southern Cross* upcoast and hightailed out of this laced hydraulic minefield.

"Did you say *hammerhead*?"

"There was a three-to-four-meter hammie in that wave face. You can tell by the shape of the head and the belly. They usually travel in bunches."

Like everything in Australia, the type of hammerhead that swims its waters, the great hammerhead (*Sphyrna mokarran*), grows to six meters (almost twenty feet) and is known to be aggressive toward surfers and divers.

"We gotta try for Red Rock. If we sprint we might get in on some twilight."

We sprinted for an hour. As we got closer it was evident that it was closed off by surf as well.

"The tide must be going out of the rivers."

"Now what?!" Tony said.

"There's one more tiny point about two miles up."

I saw a spit of beach in the distance. We sprinted for another half an hour. This was the last shot for the day. *If this isn't it, we're out for our first all-nighter,* I thought.

"It's no worries, look at that bewdy of a spot," Tony said.

It *was* beautiful! No river bar, no swell machine making mountains out of molehills. Just a nice tucked-away beach behind a very modest strip of land. I was relieved.

I wanted to quickly set up camp, as I anticipated more rain.

Tony sneered, "It's not going to rain. Haven't you ever heard: Red sky at night, sailor's delight?"

"That means it will probably be fine tomorrow but we could still get rained on tonight," I clarified.

"Worry a bit more, why don't you?"

On to Yamba

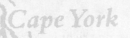 The next morning I went to find a tree to take care of business and nearly stepped on a four-foot brown viper crossing in front of me without an inkling of fear. The snake's nonchalant demeanor rubbed off on me. I was rather unfazed by its crossing although this type of snake was among the deadliest in the world. One bite would have put me in a very precarious position. No one else was around. Australia has some excellent antitoxin clinics and air rescue teams, but I would not have had a chance to use either, if I had been two feet farther up the path.

Past the trees, I found a clearing. It looked like an abandoned meadow once used for farming but I did not see any trace of domesticated beasts. Instead, I had crashed a private track meet for kangaroos. It was magnificent! Two dozen, four-to-six-foot jumping superstars. I secretly hoped I would see some type of goalpost or scoreboard somewhere.

The chart showed me that this wonderful refuge was called Hook Nose Point. It seemed to offer shelter for small boats in south-to-southeasterly swells. We had to paddle wide past the point and then make a sharp V-turn to come back to it.

What the viper could not summon, the concern for our day's travel plans did. I knew that the next chance for a landing that fell into the thirty-mile distance requirement was the town of Yamba. The Clarence River flowed into the sea there and that spelled river bar. The tides seemed to be running out in the late afternoon. We could be heading right into the same mess as we had today. There did not appear to be any Hook Nose Point halfway houses nearby. The next stop was Evans Head, almost thirty miles farther.

Launch went well except for the perfunctory splash in the chest that was the front seat's answer to the backseat's submarinelike behavior when coming into shore.

"Better than a splash of Old Spice, huh, mate?" Tony said, grinning.

"Yeah, well the Yamba River bar has a submarine base waiting for you there."

We had a little bit of everything in the course of the day. A couple of hours of high-speed paddling in a light head wind and modest seas. Followed by a couple of hours of monotonous paddling in a windless lull. In the early afternoon, a nice "sea breeze" had been generated as the land heated up creating a low pressure area over it. The denser, cooler air from the sea rushes in to fill the void. We got a wind to ride most of the way. The cliffs of Yamba started to grow in the late afternoon, as did the knot in my stomach.

"Time to drop the sail, mate," Tony said soberly.

"I know."

As we got closer, swell was crashing into the cliffs, sending booming echoes out to us like a war party banging their biggest bass drums. We passed the little red Surf clubhouse that we could see best on top of the swell coming from our starboard quarter and not see at all in troughs.

Luckily, the Yamba River bar widened as it entered the sea, so when we made our hard left we were gliding in on long unbroken waves, yet I knew the farther we went toward a narrower section ahead the more things were going to change.

"There's a spot!" Tony said.

There was a broad 150-meter deep indentation in the cliffs on our port beam that only siphoned off some of the swell as we entered it. The noise grew but it lacked the bass and the bang.

Piissssss shshshsshhshshshssssss ptshhs sshhhhhhhh . . .

The depth and shape of this gap had reduced what was left of the swell to row upon row of two-foot-high broken surf, which we rode all the way up to a pebble beach.

There was even some daylight left, so we climbed up a path to the fishing and growing resort town of Yamba, which is perched nicely on a cliff with beautiful views. As we got to the top, we passed a particularly romantic white-roofed collection of cottages.

"Mate," Tony said, "if you ever come back to Oz you have got to bring a girl to this place. It's quite fantastic."

"It sounds like you speak from experience?"

"I've been up here a number of times in the Kombi van."

This little village impressed me. It was clearly built for getting away and not for getting to business like Coffs was. The houses ranged from cute to quaint.

Low, angled roofs, awnings, shutters, picket fences, pretty flowers, and palm trees. The whole area, basking under the golden light of sunset, simply felt cozy.

"I really like this place and the way the houses fit into the whole lay of the land!"

"They've done a nice job here," Tony said.

I was starting to half hope that Tony might be thinking of staying in one of numerous inns that had vacancy signs up for all to see. It didn't happen. I wasn't a sheila.

The views to the east and west were stunning. It was so clear I was convinced I could see Cape Byron in the distance.

"No way. Byron is still a long way off," Tony said.

To Evans Head and Ballina and
Through Cape Byron and Surfers Paradise

Launch the next day was more rigorous. Much more "cologne" for my face, chest, and lap. Even Tony got a splash. We were off to Evans Head. We blasted through many waves and in turn were blasted by them. We exited our pen and were greeted by fair winds and fair seas. *Will the wonders never cease?* I thought.

It seemed like our first "gimme" day. We sailed in modest breezes and read a book called *The Restaurant at the End of the Universe*. The protagonist was Zaphod Beeblbrox. He in turn was surrounded by a cast of other bizarre characters, ideas, images, motifs, and hilarious wording. It made me laugh to the point of tears. Tony was stone-faced.

"You don't think that was funny?"

"Actually, I found it a bit tedious."

"You're kidding?"

"No."

When the wind suddenly died we realized we wouldn't be able to sail all the way. We weren't going fast enough to make it to Evans Head before sunset. We paddled hard for five straight hours and rounded the head expecting to see our landing. It wasn't there. *Evans Head must be bucking for a promotion to cape status*, I thought. The last few miles went on and on. A last bit of surging swell squirted us into the tiny river mouth and parklike atmosphere, swing sets and a seesaw included. It was a quiet place to set up camp so of course the mossies made the most of it.

We woke up a little later than usual. We had upped the pace and were feeling it. We packed a little slower and prepared to launch more casually than usual. I noticed that the incoming current had recently stopped. It was just going to slack and would begin to flow out. I wasn't terribly concerned because there hadn't been any surf break at the harbor entrance the night before. It seemed like a deep channel, and surf there didn't make sense.

Moreover, ever since day three we had been taking down the mast before landing and putting it up after we made sure to get out through the surf. We did not see any rough surf, and "cat's paws" on the surface of the lagoon indicated a favorable wind from the south. I had become fairly adept at guiding the whole mast through the spray-cover funnel into the masthead and slotting it into its square block near my feet, but it took a coordinated and patient interplay with all four of my extremities. I was starting to feel like a chimpanzee hanging from a tree and peeling a banana at the same time.

"TB, I think we can go out with the mast up and ready to go, the wind is already up and it looks like we'll be laughin' right away."

"Whatever you think, mate."

Upon launch we accelerated quickly with the tide out of the flats. *Hmmm, this current turns fast*, I thought. As we approached the harbor entrance, we saw our first whitecaps, indicating a stronger more favorable wind than I wished to believe. I was hoping to sail a lot. Days of intensive paddling were adding up.

The whitecaps were not just wind waves. They were surf waves, formed and magnified by the outgoing current. We had seen worse, much worse. No panic buttons were going to be pushed.

"Prepare for your morning spanking," Tony said kiddingly.

We quickened our stroke. *A little more wind will be enjoyable*, I thought. I watched the horizon start to disappear from view as we pierced through the first wave and I spat out its remains. I shook my head, cleared my eyes with one hand, and—

It came.

It was hard to believe at first sight. *It* didn't make sense! There really wasn't supposed to be a big swell there with the prevailing southerly winds we'd been having. The rest of the waves were three-to-four-footers. *It* was double that and then some—

Not a rogue, not now, come-on?! I said.

It was one of those three-times-larger-than-usual waves. We were not prepared, the adrenaline was kicking in a little slow. Tony and I were acting like we were casually playing on the seesaw back at the park we'd just left. Suddenly Tony snapped me to attention.

"Come on!! *Come on!!*" He steered *Southern Cross* into a good perpendicular angle. We accelerated to our best possible speed. The wave face rose steeper and steeper. I watched the green and white hammer come straight down and explode on my chest. I heard a loud *crack,* quickly drowned by the breaking wave.

The next second, we're rushing eight knots *backward.*

Upright and surfing backward! It was fun for a few seconds. *Are we OK, somehow?* I wondered. Then, a sad technical realization entered my mind. I *knew* the rudder blade was going to be pushed hard one way or the other and that it would possibly trip the boat like someone on the sidelines sticking their foot out in front of an unsuspecting wide receiver dashing down the sidelines trying to catch a pass. At that instant, we were pitch-poled upside down backward. Upon capsize, a number of waves broke over us just as we surfaced. I tried to hold the boat.

We'd been here before, but this time we still had our boat. The broken mast and sail were wandering, half-submerged under the boat. A few small items drifted about. We were a half-mile from shore and the tide was taking us out. We would not be allowed to go back to Go and start again from the beach. We had to rescue ourselves on the water for the very first time. On the horizon, I saw more and more white water. We had to get back into the boat and keep going. Tony and I had never gotten back into the boat as a team in water we could not stand in.

"Now what do we do, mate?!"

Another wave hammered us. They were coming more frequently. We didn't have a lot of time.

"We have to position the bow towards the oncoming waves."

I swam to the bow and started swimming it into place as Tony went to the stern to counterlever it. And then another wave came.

BOOMMMMMMMShshshshshsshissssssssssssss.

We shook our heads to get the water out of our eyes and ears.

"Then what?"

"You swim to the middle, reach over to the other side, and pull back as hard as you can!"

Tony positioned himself, reached for the other side, and pulled, and the boat slowly came upright with the dangling sailing apparatus entangled on its port side.

"Jump in fast!" I said, and like a circus lion he did, right into the hoop of his cockpit.

"Take the paddle, lean and brace to your right. I'm going to jump in now."

Sea kayaking protocol for reentering a Klepper kayak is: (1) Align your body perpendicular to the cockpit. (2) Reach one hand across the boat to the opposite side of the cockpit. (3) Bring the other hand to the near side). (Beginners often try to pull up at this point and only succeed in pulling the boat upside down.) (4) Before the pull, you must swim your legs to the surface of the water. (5) Then, with one or two strong swim-kicks and a simultaneous pull from the far hand and push from the near hand, the body is propelled diagonally on a level plane atop the boat with hips lined up above the cockpit hole. (6) At that point, you can rest and take a breather if conditions dictate. You must stay low. (7) Then you roll your hips 180 degrees until your butt is facing the seat. (8) Drop your butt and pivot your legs in and under the cockpit decking. (9) Start bailing the boat of excess water.

That's what I did. Until—

BOOOOMMMMMMMSHSHSHSHSHSHissssssssssss!

Another wave made other plans. Oops. Step 10: Get out of harm's way first.

"Come on!! Come on!! We gotta get out of here. We're sitting ducks."

We tried paddling but something felt very wrong.

"She's not steering!" Tony said.

I quickly checked the pedals and the cables inside the boat by reaching behind my back and guiding my hands over the foot control apparatus fastened to the keel board near the back of my butt. I felt for the chain link connection of the rudder cables to the hooks on the tips of the foot pedals.

"The pedals and cables are fine!"

"Can you see the blade?"

"*No!* Hold her steady. I'm going to climb back and see."

Tony climbed out of his cockpit, turned around, put his chest on the stern deck, and slithered to the rudder like a snake or caterpillar. This was an incredible move for a man who is 6'4". Tony's many years spent climbing vertical faces were now applying to this unstable horizontal one.

"Mate, it's totally bent!"

"Can you bend it back?" I said, wanting the problem to just go away.

"I'll try!"

The boat had become a seesaw and Tony had me trying to balance my light end while he and the rudder bobbed and sunk, bobbed and sunk. He tried to wrestle the blade, but to no avail.

"It's useless mate."

"I've got another rudder."

I had packed another rudder blade for this kind of situation. After reading about Lindemann losing his rudder at sea in a storm and steering downwind with a paddle for hours on end, I felt that in thousands and thousands of miles of paddling and sailing we would eventually reenact that scenario.

I thought I had put the blade in a handy position. I hadn't. Instead, it was under the bag I was sitting on, secured by two compression straps to the keel board. I tried to just yank it out.

BOOOOOMMMMMMSHHSHSHSHSHsssssssssss.

The boat filled with more water, Tony's weight at the end of the boat plus the water rushing to fill that side put us in a very precarious position. I took a deep breath and realized that what cannot be accomplished in a sudden jerk must be done in a deliberate, calm, and efficient manner.

"Don't you have it yet!"

"Almost!"

Do not rush, it won't help. Unsnap the other compression snap. Click. Good . . . Now, press up and get your butt off the bag and reach under it with your other hand and slide out . . . good, I advised myself.

"Got it!"

I now had to get out of my seat, turn around, and slither toward Tony so I could hand it to him. I made the hand-off. Now came the real Mission Impossible. Tony had to take a six-inch-long, quarter-inch-thick pin out of its slot to detach the three-ring-binder-size, three-pound rudder blade and separate eight-inch-long, quarter-inch-thick alloy rudder yoke without allowing any of the parts to drop out of his hands and sink to the bottom of the sea. If he could manage that then he would have to somehow realign and reinsert it all. A task sometimes difficult to do in the showroom if there are any tolerance glitches whatsoever.

BOOOOOOMMMMMMMMMSSHSHSHSHSHSSSSSSsssssssss.

Another wave surges through us.

"I can't get it. The blade is bent so badly it's jamming the whole bloody thing!"

He fiddled more. I could feel the wrestling match between man and aluminum alloy through the hull of the boat. I paddle-braced on one side and then the other. The tidal current was slowly taking us past the worst of the breakers but we were not home free.

Southern Cross sat very low in the water. In fact, Tony's butt and my head and shoulder were about the only things significantly above the waterline. Normally, I would say fuck it, I'd just detach the rudder cables and let the rudder swing free but the rudder was bent sideways, bending back almost onto itself. The only other option would be to take her all the way back to the beach against the ever strengthening current through lines and lines of now fully developed surf.

"Got it!

"You got it off?"

"I got it all back on!"

How the hell did he do all that so quickly? He must have activated a dormant surgeon's gene he got from his father, I thought.

"Here's your rudder, mate."

He handed me the special, military-issue, reinforced, extra-thick blade that looked like a beer can that had been crushed and mangled by a rugby player.

In reality, all those years of climbing and putting in and taking out "pro" (protection)—the various metal wedges, clamps, screws—to run climbing lines through had given him the full body dexterity to accomplish the task. When climbing, losing your pro ranges from a bad kick in the pocketbook to accidents and possibly death. Tony also had been a diver. Somehow all that muscle memory had become a specific and necessary skill for a procedure he had done once or twice on land. I am not sure I could have done the same thing even though I was far more familiar with the equipment.

We paddled out past the last of the breakers and we started licking our wounds. I finished pulling the wrapping up the broken mast, sails, and associated lines while Tony vigorously hand-bilged the fifty to sixty gallons of water in the boat. Pushing, pulling, pushing, pulling the plastic handle in one-foot strokes up and down, up and down. The whole process took over half an hour.

Things started to become darker. The early morning sun was being clouded over. The winds were now blowing due east and much harder. The shape of the Evans Head landmass, tall and thick, and the location of our campsite nestled in its arms had disguised what must have been going on for a while. The sea was rough.

The wind built to Force 5, blowing a solid twenty knots, with stronger gusts. The whitecaps were everywhere and got progressively worse as the day went on. The previous days' southeasterly swell pattern was being reshuffled by the easterlies. The day turned into a brawl. It was similar to the ride to Port Stephens from Newcastle but without any option to sail. There was no talking until Hour 4.

"We're just not moving the boat well!"

I took the comment personally, trying to figure out if it was something I was or wasn't doing. Actually, we were not moving slowly. It just was a rough day and it showed no signs of letting up. It only got worse as the wind roared in our ears. *Whoooowhhooooouuuuuuouuuuwhouuuuuuu.*

After a while, a long rock jetty presented the entrance to Ballina Harbour. We saw the jetty for hours and hours before it seemed truly close. *Will we ever get this time-distance relationship down?* The day was coming to a close and my worries about landing reignited; only time would tell. Once again, because of the way the coast was shaped, the next landing would have to be Cape Byron more than twenty miles farther on. I mentally kept my fingers crossed.

As we got closer, five fishing trawlers emerged from the harbor at funeral-procession speed. After they were out, we swung wide of the south break wall, and joined a nonbreaking swell closely following the line they had come out from. The current was going in. Swell and current were together and we went through the narrows and into the deep belly of Ballina. Before I knew it, we were all the way in. Painless?!

The paddling turned effortless with the wind at our back. A small beach tucked in the corner of the harbor looked like a landing. The beach was directly adjacent to a caravan park. *Do we check in, or don't we?* We were already on the beach, but not in a caravan slot. Nevertheless, we checked in and got the key to the facilities. We made a strong bunker on the beach near a particularly thick berm of sand, using the Frazer dig-and-cover method. We found a milkbar, came back, and retired. Lots of wind, some rain, no mossies.

The wind howled the next morning, turning even the "sheltered harbor" into a pool of swell littered with whitecaps. Windsurfers were already out, streaking across like rocket-powered drag racers on the Utah salt flats. This had to be pushing Force 7 or 8, galeforce conditions. Throughout the morning it showed no sign of letting up.

"It looks like we're stuck for the day."

"Sure does," I said.

"We probably should suss out a way to fix the mast."

"Yeah, and we got a lot of laundry to do."

On an expedition it becomes a matter of infection prevention and not vanity enhancement. The aesthetics of wearing the same clothes for days on end is meaningless to expeditioneers. Sir Shackleton's Antarctic survivors were in the same unwashed clothes for almost two years straight; however, the temperatures were rarely above freezing. The risk of fungus and bacterial infections was less than in humid subtropical conditions. We had more limits regarding sanitary fundamentals. We had come to that limit.

"They'll certainly dry fast if they don't blow all the way to Perth first," I said.

After laundry, we put on our street clothes and headed to town three miles away. We took our broken mast. We tried hitchhiking, but no one would pick us up. In fact, they didn't even look at us. Beards had grown in, clothes had that city homeless shape to them, and we were carrying a couple of four-foot sticks. The citizenry of Ballina was not amused. An hour later, someone picked us up a quarter-mile from our destination, which saved us from the brunt of a late-morning downpour.

We made it to the Ballina/Quay marina and bought a couple more plastic fenders to augment our beach-rolling performance. More important, we found the resident mechanic to help us take the broken wooden garden hoe out of the remaining aluminum parts of the old mast.

"I've got the tools right here. It'll be out in a jiff," he said.

It turned out to be a much more difficult project.

First he tried: (1) Gentle coercion—normal hammer and punch—tapping all around and finally finishing with some solid taps.

No reaction.

Then came: (2) Moderate force—sledgehammer and punch—starting with solid blows and ending with Paul Bunyan efforts. Sweat was dripping from his brow.

No reaction.

This was followed by (3) manipulation and force—industrial drill with long bit drilling numerous holes in wood—*then* sledgehammered. Forearm muscles strained, veins were sticking out of his neck, and a worried expression was now nestled in his brow.

No reaction.

(4) Heated manipulation and force—acetylene blow torching the wood in the aluminum—followed by the sledgehammer. Worry was replaced by a crazed, deeply focused, almost psychotic expression.

Slight reaction.

(5) Heated manipulation plus direct incineration plus force—burning the wood from the inside, heating the aluminum tube from the outside—and, finally, smashing with the hammer.

"Hah! It's out!" he yelled.

We offered him twenty dollars.

"Just ten dollars will be fine," he said.

Next came shaving, filing, and sanding the new garden hoe to fit the essential aluminum bits, for which we borrowed a host of tools that saved us hours of time.

On the walk back to the center of town, we decided Thursdays with the digit 2 in them (March 12 and April 2, e.g.) were bad days for our masts and agreed to be particularly careful on those days in the future. It's easy to understand the origins of superstitions after a few bouts with Big Momma.

In town we had a read and a good chat with Dave, the milkbar proprietor, over our feast. Dave enlightened us with the news that Ballina is a very windy place. Hard to debate that point. When we asked if the winds were usually this incessant, he replied, "Can be."

From there we went back to the boat, finished the last of the laundry, and started to feel a slight tingle of anticipation for a Saturday night on the town. Tony confessed to feeling a little "randy" after three weeks off the stud farm. We tried to primp a little more, increasing our town image from homeless to boat people. We were actually a little of both. Crusty tie-up sneakers were switched to flipflops.

It was not hard for our party senses to reactivate and find the active pub in town. A full mix was present with an "Ocker" bachelor party dominating and a rugby game between Easts and Balmain coming in a close second. Behind the bar were some barmaids clad in swimsuits strung together from dental floss. Tony perked up immediately, and four or five beers later we were part of it all.

The bachelor party had become a cross between a funeral and a roast with the bridegroom catching the "end of life and fun as you know it" philosophy from all those involved. This was done in a tribal circle of sorts, each mate passing on his condolences. I suppose it was a test of resolve. Inevitably, black humor pointed a finger to an already married bloke who appeared ever the more listless among his single peers, hence saying to the bridegroom, "*This* could happen to you."

None of us got lucky that night. Tony's usually reliable powers of magnetism had deserted him. The scraggly beard hid much of the chiseled face and perfectly formed lips, highlighting the intense green eyes (which by themselves prompt as much wariness as attraction). We stumbled back to camp and almost got swept up by some very strong gusts of wind on top of the low bridge.

"God, mate, that had to be forty knots or more."

"At least."

A sudden sobriety overcame us at the realization that we were to launch the next morning, and whatever idle chatter and joking there had been soon dissipated. A solemnness changed the polarity of our inebriation from light to dark.

We fell asleep to wind and woke up to it.

W H O O O O O O O O O O O O O O O O w h o o o u u u u u u u u u w W H O O-O O O O O O O O O!

The wind moaned and then shrieked, *Heeeeeeeeeeeeeeeeeeeeeeeeeeeee aiiiiiiiiiiiiiiiii-iiiiiii Heeeeeeeeeeeeeee!*

There were only a few windsurfers out. They were going faster with much smaller sails, leaping and flying off the tops of three-foot pyramid waves getting their peaks blown off in the harbor.

I looked forward to a real day of plain rest. A day of no physical or social obligations. The first such a day in three weeks. It soon became apparent that that was going to be a problem. The momentum we had built was slowing down and the relatively idle pursuits of reading the paper, writing in the journal, and no more excuses for not catching up on writing letters affected us in different ways.

Tony, more familiar with brevity, finished off his cards and letters in the course of the morning. I got caught in the now-you-have-a-chance-to-tell-the-whole-story syndrome, which developed into the now-I-have-the-chance-to-tell-the-whole-story-to-Dave, Nicole, Dierdre, Howard, etc., etc., affliction, and finally to the now-I-have-a-chance-to-send-a-card-to-all-those-that-I-have-not-sent-a-card-to-yet disease. A week would not be enough time to get it all down.

Tony was tapping his pen, rereading the newpaper for one more shred of novelty, and tapping his pen and steadily bouncing one foot up and down under his chair. Tony was developing a severe case of "itchy feet." Unused energy to burn.

"Why don't you write the pope and Santa Claus while you're at it, mate."

Then came the staring and general restlessness. I started to feel rushed. A true *need* for individual space and time arose. My few moments of peaceful joy in writing were dashed. The two minds were short-circuiting out of the boat. *Southern Cross* was our grounding cable to two over-amped batteries.

The conditions dictated we not leave that day. Yet, I started to feel responsible for our stranding. Tony's body language was practically mime. It was not just prudent but our only real choice. We had repaired our mast but easterly winds had been blowing for over seventy-two hours straight without a letup. The harbor entrance had to be a mess and the seas beyond large and fully developed. There are days that you just don't go. I remembered Howard Rice sitting in his tent for five straight days waiting for the winds to die down at Cape Horn.

Many mountaineers have had to wait weeks at a time for a "window" to summit. We were in a confinement more disturbing to Tony than a snow cave. We were in a tourist town. I enjoyed the chance to think, write, observe, and elaborate. He did not find the same solace.

The wind continued to blow all day and all night.

The third morning in Ballina, we woke to less wind. Instead of the usual twenty-five to thirty knots, it was down to fifteen or twenty. A favorable change, yes. A full green light to go? Hardly, yet Tony had a look that said, We're going. We were greeted by a small group of older people, two of whom, we found out, were former coast guard volunteers.

"You wouldn't be thinking of going today would you now?"

"Actually . . ." Tony started.

"The bar is known to be pretty bad after winds like this."

"I think we . . ."

"Perhaps you would like to take a little walk with us to the point and see how it's doing today before you decide."

Tony looked at me with that why-me expression, but I was glad that they were saying it and not me. Moreover, these people were like our grandparents and were showing sincere concern.

I was also starting to get antsy. It had been too many days now. The running average we had worked up so nicely in the last week was falling apart. If we did get out there, the wind could be nice. The "son of garden hoe" mast looked even stronger than the first, but what the hell would the seas be like?

To Byron

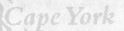 "So, now whattya think," one of the elderly volunteers asked.

I looked at Tony, not sure what I wanted to hear. I had powered through a lot of written material and cleaned my slate to get going, yet nothing had really changed. The original reasons for not leaving were basically the same. The only thing different was our attitudes toward the involuntary confinement. However, I still didn't think it would be wise to go. The one thing in our favor was that the tide fell slack for a while.

"Let's pack up, mate. We're going." Tony was adamant.

This threw the volunteers off guard. I think they thought he knew better now and their questioning was almost a joke.

"Seriously, how does it look?" I asked.

"It looks OK."

"Are you sure?"

"Yes" (like "yes, of course").

I joined in the packing, to the dismay of our visitors. I *wanted* to believe that Tony saw a clear launch through the harbor. Surely Tony knew that getting upended in huge surf wasn't a real laugh and would put us through something too iffy. We were getting tourist-town fever but it could not have clouded his basic judgment. Not after what we'd been through in the prior three weeks. The respect had to have been instilled in Tony by then. I'd seen it in his eyes and heard it in his voice. He *knew* what we were dealing with. Of course he did. If he said, "It looks OK," it looked OK. The rationalization helped.

Soon we were off and paddling with fully charged batteries. *Ahhh, we're finally on our way!* The buoyancy of the boat eased the tensions.

The exhilaration and buoyancy lasted for five minutes. First came the inner harbor swell, then I saw the walls of green and foam smashing each jetty. As we got closer, the sights were joined by the sound of waves breaking on rock. The intense sound. *Would lightning be so terrifying without the thunder?* I wondered. Waves were boiling, breaking, booming, rising, steaming, hissing all around. The dolphins were nowhere to be found today.

The bizarre truth was that we were traveling through the middle of it all as if on a magic carpet or more like it was the parting of the Red Sea. *How can this be? How long can it last?* I wondered.

"Told ya mate. There is the nice little channel taking us out."

Little was the word. Waves were breaking two boatlengths on either side. There was still a field of chaos as far as the eye could see. Divine intervention was going to have to last at least ten more minutes.

With no time to waste, we followed Moses and paddled with the fear of God. Huge walls of water continued to crash on either side of us. We focused on our path, which still had unbroken swell—fifteen-to-twenty-foot swell.

My front seat position let me see it coming first. I wanted to say, Prepare yourself, mate, but I couldn't. I just stared with an almost detached amazement. Of course the wave that would start breaking in this deeper channel that was preventing the other waves from breaking would have to be very, very big. It was, and the fuse had already been lit. There was nowhere to go and Tony finally got a glimpse.

"Come on!! Come on!! Come onnnnn!!!!!!" Tony yelled.

We paddled as if possessed. We had to. The wave steepened. We were in the trough. The perspective would have sickened us if there had been any real time to think about it. The bow of our boat went up and up and up. The angle of the water treadmill was easily forty-five degrees.

"Come *onnnnnnnn*!!" Tony yelled one more time.

I became perfectly calm in the face of the monstrous confrontation. It seemed so unreal. *This only happens from the comfort of my armchair at home watching a Discovery channel special on tsunamis,* I thought. *I must be in that armchair, but where is the remote?*

Southern Cross angled another ten degrees higher. Any higher and we were getting thrown backward. Just then, the bow started to pierce and enter into the top three feet of the wave. I became blind and deaf, not in the foam of the wave but in the wave itself. *Was this the hood that it puts on me before the execution?*

A moment later I could feel the angle of the boat changing. My end of the seesaw was dropping.

PUWHAPP!

I was back in the light and all I could see was a long deep valley in front of me. It was as if I had entered a parallel universe and was positioned a little out of frame. *Southern Cross* started free-falling into the valley. *Am I still alive? Is this really happening? The last time I felt this way I was having hallucinations as a child with a high fever and an ear infection.*

We landed hard on the wave's backside.

KAAABOOOOOOOOOOOMMMMMMMMMMMMMMMMMMMM!

The wave thundered behind us.

"Keep paddling hard, hard!" Tony shouted.

We paddled like madmen. A half-hour later we were out of the hammers and into surging fifteen-foot sea. The winds were ESE and alternated between screaming and muffling as we levitated up and down.

"What do you think about giving the new mast a try, Epic!" Tony said with a newly found composure.

He's got to be mad. First, he takes us into the valley of the shadow of death, but he's not finished. He must think Neptune is a just a larrikin—a jokester—and not the controller of the most massive force on earth. Yet, I was eager to try the new mast and sail again. *Is madness contagious?*

"All right" I said, half out of relief and half out of a desire to get this day over with. *We did it in Newcastle. We can do it here. I hoped.*

We audaciously hoisted a sail, thinking that the worst was over. The wind picked up again. The seas were gigantic.

It wasn't until fifteen minutes later, as I held my paddle across my cockpit, that I realized that we had just used up another dozen "luck tickets" on that launch. *How far were we from disaster?* Ten feet, three feet, one foot, one inch, one second? *Probably three feet and one second.* Once Tony became more comfortable with the sea conditions.

Tony confessed: "I thought we were dead back there, mate!"

An interesting place for the confession, I thought—somewhat insanely—*because it was almost twenty miles to Byron and no way were we out of harm's way.* We had to constantly shift and countershift to keep the boat on its precious line. We were running before the sea. I hoped, as long as we stayed a little ahead, we'd be OK.

Twenty minutes later, an orange helicopter circled above.

Wop, wop, wop wop, wop, wop, wop, wop.

It circled a number of times and we waved. After a few more circles it became annoying and dangerous. The downdraft threatened to knock us down when the sea had not. We had enough wind to deal with. We didn't need any man-made winds.

"What does he bloody want?" Tony said.

We had no radio and just wanted the helicopter to go away. There wasn't a thing we could do but continue on. Five minutes later he flew off.

An hour later I saw a small motorboat streaking toward us. It was the only boat we had seen all day. It couldn't have been a fishing boat. No small boat would be out if it didn't have to be. The Jacques Cousteau–style inflatable boat had two people in it. They were yelling something from a megaphone as they came alongside. *"Do you know what has been going on for the last hour and half?!?!"*

"No. What's going on?!"

"Your canoe was reported as capsized by the harbor tower. Every water rescue unit available has been combing the area looking for you. Just last year a canoe vanished on the bar. It's a very treacherous place!!!"

"Well, we're here and heading for Byron. We're sorry!?"

The two surf rescue chaps relaxed a little, and the confrontation de-escalated as they paralleled us for a few minutes and saw that we were moving nicely in the large seas. We told them more about our journey, and they left us with one last thought.

"The police will be waiting for you in Byron when you get there. They will have questions for you. Cheers! Good Luck!"

Well, now I get to look forward to police interrogation or worse if we make it to Byron, and I'm sure the surf is going to be licking its chops waiting for us to arrive.

My mood turned decidedly worse. I resented Tony for directing one too many action scenes this early in the day. There was no banter, let alone laughter. Eyes were focused on the walls of water coming from the east. Periods of downpours temporarily flattened the sea like a sudden gush of water on a very hot fire.

I put up the jib sail to quicken our speed and give me something to control.

Southern Cross moved in many different directions simultaneously. Meanwhile our bodies were doing everything they could to maintain vertical positions. The lower back is the shock absorber, and the pelvis is the wheel. There was not a second of relaxation as we tried to remain under full sail in order to make it to Byron with some daylight left.

The boat moved better with both sails and full concentration. The speed took some of the bumps out. The fully laden *Southern Cross* had excellent sea manners and maintained a strong momentum that rose and cut through the confused sea.

Paddling in this would be brutal to the hands and lower back. Sailing delivers more consistent speed in and through rough seas. However, one second of botched concentration and we'd be upside down. There were no easy ways out.

Cape Byron is the granddaddy of capes on the east coast and looms ominously on a stormy day, gloriously on a clear one.

We got ominous.

A large, white tower lighthouse sits on top of the steep cliffs. It's the first point of Australian land that a wave in the Pacific hits after thousands of miles of free travel. As we got closer I could see waves exploding hundreds of feet in the air. There were also some errant "boomers" (waves breaking over barely submerged rocks, reefs, etc., etc.) on the perimeter of the cape.

There were rebound-effect waves a mile back toward the Pacific, and we soon entered a large zone of clapotis. A large swell passed by us toward the cliff. An equally large swell came back from the cliffs. Every now and then the wavelengths would align themselves and create great plumes of water going straight up in the air. We didn't want to be on one of those plumes. *What is this! The midterm exam?! Is this (E) All of the above?*

My spirits sagged further as I watched the swell wrap all the way around the cape. *Goddamned Refraction Curve Principle!* With a pure southeast swell the wrap-around would've been less complete, with more clearings available on the north side of the cape. This swell was ESE and could wrap around farther and fill in all the nooks and crannies with bombers. The *only* chance was to go almost to the middle of the bay and head in, keeping our eyes peeled for clearings. The surf rescue guys had told us there would be one small place to land.

We paddled in slowly. The large swell lifted us up and down. The whole bay was filled with long lines of large swell. The town beach was pummeled. We finally spotted a pair of strong lights off our port beam.

"Well, there's the police!" I said acidly.

"How do you know?!" Tony said.

"Who the hell else would be out here?"

I just wanted to get it over with. After watching three or four gargantuan waves, I initiated a rapid stroke rate.

"Let's just go!" I yelled.

"Not yet, mate!" Tony said. "I think I see some more coming."

"We've just gotta sprint it in and handle it as it comes!"

"Let's just watch one more set," Tony said.

We watched a couple more sets and saw there was only a short gap of time between one and the next. It was only fifty meters—five seconds for the fastest human—about half a minute of exposure for us. OK.

"Go!! Go!! Go-o-o-o-o!!!" I yelled.

We sprinted, made it to the broken wave zone and surfed in on a modest surge. We spear-threw the paddles at the beach, jumped out of the boat, landing on wobbly knees, and started emptying some gear out. It was pouring. The tide was low and we were going to have to move the boat a couple hundred feet. It was getting dark. Along with the police were a couple of local surfers, all watching our approach. They were the first to say, "G'day."

"Good paddlin', mates. Good show. It's pretty mean today and this is the only place on this part of the coast you could have put her."

The welcome was heartening and converted smiles from frowns. Beyond our sense of accomplishment, there was also a sense that we got away with that last one by the skin of our teeth. A clean-cut, blue-uniformed man came up to us. He did not have rain gear on and acted as if it was not raining at all.

"Are you having fun today?" he asked rhetorically. "I don't think so." He sounded a bit irritated. Then he said, "When you're done moving the gear come back to the car."

After a brief summary of why he was there, he went into the, Who are we, where do our parents live, does anyone know about our plans, where have we come from, what kind of boat is that, how much experience do we have, do we have the proper safety equipment, do we have any idea of what we're doing? rap.

Both of us answered honestly. Thankfully, Tony had not gone into ram-butting mode.

The truth is, I felt chastened and almost relieved at being grilled. We both knew we had overstepped our bounds that day. By a long way. This was just a very tangible reminder of that fact. It was also the last straw for me. I was more than a little angry and pissed off. I felt I had to answer for someone else's mess, a mess that I didn't think I would have made if left alone. That is not how a tandem kayak expedition seems to work. *I must have signed a blanket "for better or for worse" clause someplace.*

Right then, I wanted a divorce for a day—or at least a trial separation. Tony didn't say much. Maybe he felt the same way. We secured the boat, put on some dry clothes and rain gear, and walked a long strip of wet sandy beach toward Byron. I had my head down. Tony started some friendly chatter. "That was bit dicey, wasn't it?"

I stopped, half turned, raised my head, looked straight into his eyes, and said: "Tony, we're not going tomorrow. I've had enough. I want to have a day alone in Byron."

"Mate, we haven't—"

"No, Tony, I have wanted to see Byron Bay for a while and I want to have some time to check it out. You have that friend that Brent told you about, Kala or Killee or something. We don't you look her up?"

I was shell-shocked—a few too many fifteen-foot green cannonballs had been shot our way. I wanted a bagel, a cappuccino and an outdoor café with an umbrella on a sunny day. I was determined the next day would consist of just that, even if it cost another luck ticket.

A Day in Byron

A sunny day. *Now to find the café and cappuccino.* I bid Tony farewell and said I would try to meet him for a beer at Paul Hogan's—Crocodile Dundee's—place around sundown. What freedom! To walk to town, on my own, with my little bum bag of Australian dollars to spend. I had forgotten how much I liked to be on my own, going where I want, when I want, doing what *I* want. Is this the "only child" thing, or an overload of a kayak marriage?

The town felt warmly familiar. Cape Byron was glorious that day. Images of Boulder, Colorado, and Bolinas, California, came to mind. There was that blend of art, health, and active mellowness mixed with sophistication. Surf and sauvignon. It was going to be a good day!

A long walk through town on the main drag revealed a couple of cappuccino stands with umbrellas. I read the menus and decided on the place with the best carrot cake. After all, I only had one day.

Later, I stopped at a newsstand. The headline in the local paper read: "Canoeists Found Safe After All," and went on to describe the incident further, interviewing the coast guard reservists who had called in the disappearance, the camper-van park manager who had told them of a previous capsize we'd had implying that we were not fully competent, and on and on. It was eerie. It had that premonition or obituary-like quality to it. The carrot cake started to taste better with the relief that I was still alive.

I wrote to Nicole, bellyaching a bit about the situation.

Dear Nicole,

I miss you very much! Things have gotten rough out here. Just when I think we have caught our stride something else happens. The sea and wind have been brutal. Yesterday Tony rashly decided that we should go out through a dangerous river bar. A giant wave nearly wiped us out. Later the police were waiting for us because someone thought we were lost at sea. Rescue boats, helicopters, the works! Just when I thought Tony understood what the wind and sea can do!

Love, Eric

I sent an "I'm here, you're not" card with surfers and bikinis to the Coffee Shop and Live Bait staffs. It was late afternoon. I walked back toward the bay to catch the sunset and see if Tony was around. Saw the sunset, didn't see Tony. I went back into town to a pizza shop.

I was greeted by an attractive woman named Holly, from Gainesville, Florida. We started chatting. She asked me about the trip. I let it fly: "He has no respect for the sea. He is so impatient. I never know what kind of brash thought he'll have next!" I ranted on . . . and on.

She sat and listened patiently, then said: "Remember, he's doing the best he can."

A short time later Tony walked in.

"There you are, Epic."

"Hello, TB. This is Holly."

Oddly, I had almost started to miss him by the time he arrived.

"Glad to see you're feeling better," he said with a smile. "I found Kiva and they've got a party tonight."

"Sounds good to me."

"I think we better get back to camp, TB. We've got to put in a long day tomorrow."

Kiva offered to drive us. It was 1:30 A.M. Both Tony and I had had a "good" day in our different ways.

The late night made for a late start and automatically jeopardized the chances of making it thirty miles to Tweed Heads harbor before nightfall. The seas had calmed a bit and exiting in daylight was fairly easy, yet there was little wind and quite a bit of sun. We were paddling and the seas were slowly undulating, not quite sure what to do. They were a beautiful aquamarine color. Tony was also a little "green." It had been almost a month since he had had his last "Big Night Out." I didn't feel too good, either. Two hours and eight miles into the day, we approached Brunswick Heads.

"What do you think about pulling in here, mate?"

"Hah, hah, hah, hah. Yeah, right, Tony. Good one."

"Seriously."

"It's only been eight miles. We've never done less than twelve once we're on the water."

"OK, but if we find a place later that looks good . . ."

"I'd like to make it to Tweeds if we can, but if it starts getting dark and we find a place, then no worries."

I knew there was a possibility we would have to spend our first full night out on the water if we bypassed Brunswick and got to Tweed Heads too late. This part of the coast is fully exposed and Tweeds is known to be a very dangerous river bar. I was reenergized and I was also counting on more wind.

Sea conditions were Force 2–3. We did much more paddling than sailing. There was a large underlying swell. Big mounds of water lifted us up and down. We paddled through Tony's seasickness, but were making poor time. A midafternoon sea breeze developed. It revived us but was too little too late. The sun was going down and it appeared that the north side of Henderson Rock had a possible landing spot. We saw cars at the end of the point. As we rounded the point and started a landing approach to get a better look, the boat's stern lifted dramatically. One wave passed and broke just in front of us, nearly a half-kilometer from shore. *Not this again? Look how close those 4WD's are, coming to watch the sunset.*

"Come on mate, we can make it in!" he said with a touch of knowing trepidation.

I knew he wanted to get in early today. We had covered over twenty miles. It would have to be fine. I wanted to go in, too.

"Let's take it slow. Remember Red Rocks?"

BOOOOOMMMMTHSSSSHSHSSHSHHISSSSssssss.

A breaker exploded fifty yards in front of us, still six hundred yards from the beach.

"We can't go in!" I sadly announced.

Tony steered the boat 150 degrees and we went back out. He hit the water with his paddle strokes. I could feel the boat lunge forward.

A mile or two farther, I found another possible landing. Again, we brought ourselves perpendicular to the shore, started paddling in and again, got the same treatment, and backpaddled vigorously to avoid an offshore breaker. The chance of a daytime or even twilight landing was over! There would be no Hook Nose Point halfway house for tired and forlorn sea kayakers. All I could hear was paddle splash and sighing behind me.

"Tweed is a good size harbor. There's a lighthouse nearby and a break wall," I said encouragingly. Tony did not respond.

It took a few hours for the moonless dark to take over daylight. The city glowed in the distance. Sensory deprivation and eye shifts from rods to cones made balance a seat-of-the-pants endeavor. Back to space travel. *We will get in at Tweed Heads. There will be plenty of light,* I thought.

A couple of hours later, we saw the sprawling lights of the beginning of the "Gold Coast," Australia's most popular resort area. While people were eating, drinking, dancing, and skinny-dipping, we were straining our eyes to make sense of it all.

Southern Cross started bouncing around more. Things felt different. I could swear I heard rollers to our right.

"Did you hear that, mate?" Tony said nervously.

"Yes."

"Hold on for a second while I look at the chart," he said.

Tony took out a torch, took out the chart, quietly studied it, folded it up, and put it back in the case.

"That's what I thought! We have to be *very* careful around here. There are reefs and shallows everywhere."

Tony was deeply concerned with the "bombies" breaking over the shallow reefs that dominate the area. We'd seen what they looked like by day and had no designs on meeting up with them at night. Every few minutes I was implored to stop and listen.

"Do you hear anything, mate?!"

"I don't think so."

Fully warned, the senses expanded to detect changes in wave size and direction as well as the sound of breaking water. *I felt like we were in a hydraulic minefield. I did hear hissing and echoes from many different directions. This is not good.* Over two hundred years earlier this is what Captain Cook saw:

> *At sunset on the 15th breakers were seen ahead on the starboard bow, though the ship was five miles from land and in twenty fathoms. . . . Passed breakers, which stretched two leagues over a shoal running from Point Danger.*

We were in those shoals approaching the point of land called Point Danger, which Cook had named and now has a fifty-foot-high statue of him on top of it that was watching us.

"We've to paddle due east and get out of here," Tony said.

"But Tweeds is only three miles farther north and west."

"There is reef nearby and I want to make sure we are clear of it."

We could barely detect an agitated horizon, as distant lights made it visible one second and not the next. It was ahead of us and a bit to starboard. We paddled a little farther and stopped. We looked, listened, and then saw the broken outlines of surf . . . again.

"There it is! And its a big one!"

Tony looked at the chart again. "This is reef, I'm sure of it. We can go by on this side and go around and come back in on the other side."

We paddled out for half an hour.

"I think we've come out far enough. We're starting to head to New Zealand."

"Just a little farther and that should be sufficient."

A little farther was another half an hour.

Eventually we turned north and did a wide arc back toward Tweeds. We could barely make out the red and green harbor entrance lights among the galaxy of others. It took an hour to get back in. There was no wind and the swell felt modest, but without visual perspective, it was hard to say.

We saw no apparent obstacles to the entrance. *It's clear, thank God!!*

We were within fifty yards when we saw the silhouette of mist and broken water on the crests of the swell. We approached the east-northeast facing entrance from the southeast. As we got a little closer we could see buildings in the distance through telescopes of spraying funnels. At least two or three sets of them closed off the narrow harbor entrance. They looked like perfect surfing tubes. They spelled *no* to landing. Tony instinctively turned north; he didn't feel a need to discuss it. The silence bothered me.

"A man in Byron had suggested a landing spot in Coolangatta," I said. "It's a few miles north of Tweed Heads. He had said something about hooking around the point, and it being a very nice spot."

We paddled on past the statue of Cook toward the lighthouse. The sea was turning to breakers. Tony steered us out to sea again because of the extended shallowness of the point. After another half-hour arc, we rounded the Coolangatta lighthouse and headed in to the large bay north of it.

We saw the cars and illuminated walkways of a large apartment complex. The swell grew and gave us, first, an expanded view of the city and, then, a contracted view from one wave crest to the next. The lights of the complex illuminated the size of the break, yet drew us like insects toward it.

KABOOOOOMMMMMMMMMSHSHSHSHiissssssssss.

A wave exploded right next to us. Another was right behind it, in the spotlight. We had drifted too close!

"Hard right! Paddle!! Paddle!!"

My dulling mind was sparked to life by another adrenal outburst. There was just no making heads or tails of it all. *Here comes the artillery again, back comes that shell-shocked feeling.*

Jesus!!!

This sucks!!

A vast expanse of resort and beach a few hundred yards away and we couldn't land. Off in the distance across the bay loomed Surfers Paradise, looking just like the "restaurant at the end of the universe" from my book. It was 1:30 A.M., it wasn't funny, and it didn't do take-out.

"Well, it's less than six hours till daybreak," I said.

"Yeah, and then what?"

We had now been on the water for almost seventeen hours. The next landing possibility was the Nerang River bar leading to Southport. The Nerang bar was another dubious situation. If nothing else because it was named Nerang, which might as well have been Da Nang. There were no real options after that except to kamikaze on a beach.

The night went very slowly, we tried to sail and sleep by cleating off the mainsail. I could hear Tony snoring and used my head to adjust the boom. We were on a close reach and the sail was only angled twenty degrees off the mid-line of the boat. The winds were coming from the northeast veering north. Suddenly, the boat jolted.

"What's that?!" Tony said.

"I don't know, but could you steer us back to port? We keep going right. Did you hear me?"

"It's not working," he said. "It feels like there's nothing there."

"What? You mean the cables are detached?"

"Maybe."

Tony caterpillared to the back with a flashlight and said,

"It's not there."

"It's not there?"

"The blade is gone."

Tony had hammered the original rudder back into shape and we were using it as the primary rudder again. Now it had broken completely off. Replacing it, on the water while it was dark, with our only good blade was not going to happen. Tony is not a wizard and he was not happy about this day. In a way, we had each exchanged personal hells. He gave me Ballistic Ballina and I gave him Gold Coast Horror.

I wished I had had fitful sleep. At least that would have been sleep. The night took forever. Daytime and the GPS showed us the truth of our night's "progress." Four miles in six hours. Surfers Paradise (aka End of Universe) was still a solid five miles away.

"Back to the sticks!" Tony warmly announced.

The swell was huge and as we got closer to Surfers Paradise, it started to look a lot more like Miami Beach, an endless glistening strip of high-rise hotels and condominiums. The glare hurt. No landing.

"Looks like Nerang," I said.

"I'll kamikaze in if I have to!" Tony said.

Nerang was a couple of hours away if we could keep paddling. We had had nothing to eat in twenty hours. Most of those twenty hours had been paddling, much of it at sprinting speeds, thinking one last effort would get us to landfall, only to sprint out to sea again. A dot drawing of our course would look like a ECG for an anxiety attack.

I felt like an outcast from society, civilization, life as I knew it. This endless strip of high-rises, which was completely out of sync with the coast up until then, represented all the glitter and the glamour we had *chosen* to give up. Here was New York, Miami, and Las Vegas all rolled into one place. In Australia they call it Surfers Paradise. It silently mocked us as we moved on. The overall view was impressive but disturbing. I doubt any surfer worth the sand in his Billabongs would call it "paradise."

As we moved farther north and could make out the end of the strip of high-rises and the tops of another pocket of them, we deduced that Nerang cut at the southern base of south Stradbroke Island. We saw a fishing boat making its rounds to various buoys and paddled toward it, waving our hands. This was the first boat we had seen since the inflatable rescue boat outside of Ballina.

As the noisy diesel-propelled vessel approached, I asked: "How's the Nerang Bar today?"

First, the older gentleman of the apparent father/son team discouraged us with, "You might make it through if you make the tide."

"It was no problem this morning, only a little bumpy," said the son, lifting our hopes.

Neither asked what we were doing or where we had come from. We had just crossed over the border to Queensland. *I wondered if that had anything to do with it?*

If we took both these comments and filtered out the best and worst of them, we were no better off than not knowing at all, yet it felt better to see other people just going about their daily affairs like nothing had ever happened. *Didn't they know what we had just done!! Didn't they care?!*

We were volunteers, not victims. Why did it feel like the latter? I felt victimized by my volunteering.

An hour later, we could see the bar. There was some significant surf on the north side of it but the south side looked passable although not flat. I added a boost of confidence, "Well, we are here at slack tide so this is as good a chance as any."

Getting closer showed a more chaotic entrance.

Tony added, "We're going in here, mate. *Prepare to kamikaze.*" Why he didn't *just say prepare to* FRAZER, *I didn't know.*

I prepared for the worst, but it wasn't so bad. I took down the sail gear. The entrance was messy, and there was the occasional large breaking set, but the sun was up and the worst that could happen would be an early morning bath and a ride into the bar upside down, like falling out of a raft in a white-water river. The swell surge would move us toward Southport and not out to sea. We found a path, paddled hard, surfed a long wave, enjoyed the thrill, and were in. A couple more miles to Southport.

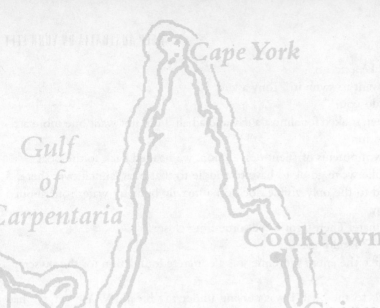

Southport

"Just another mile to landfall, just another mile."

The high-rises of Southport were clearly visible and we homed in on them. We came to a spit of land that seemed unpopulated except for a jet-ski beehive down the beach, launching one buzzing piece of machinery after the next. High-risers and jet skis. Hand in hand. We were now the strangers, in a strange land. Finally we hit landfall, nearly thirty hours after leaving Byron. It was sunny and we were on land.

There were very few congratulatory remarks. Instead we automatically pulled up the boat, unloaded our camp essentials, and set up the bivvy sack cocoons not yet knowing whether hunger or sleep was going to win out.

After changing into dry clothes, walking around and setting up camp, a last wave of energy entered me. Hunger was back! We were near a big town. That meant big tucker—images of milkshakes, chooks, ice cream, and cookies danced in my mind. We walked down the beach with a sense of purpose. Tony had even broken out his special Hawaiian print shirt for the event.

Just as our salivary glands were getting primed, we saw what I hoped was an illusion. There were one hundred years of water between us and the high-rises.

"It looks like we're on an island, mate."

"Do you see a bridge, a ferry, anything?" I said in disbelief.

"It looks like we'll have to wade across."

We forged ahead, thinking it was just a shallow pool and that we could walk through it. After a few steps I was already getting my shorts wet.

"It looks like a no go."

"Do you want to swim it?" Tony asked.

"No way, do you?!"

We had been soaked for almost a day and a half. I did not want one more arti-cle of wet clothing.

After a few moments of silent desperation, we headed back to the boat.

"It looks like we're going to have to paddle to that boat launch over there," I said. I pointed to the only visible dock on a heavily built-up waterfront about a half-mile away.

"No way, mate. There's got to be something closer."

" 'Fraid not," I sadly stated.

It looked like the entire shoreline was a concrete foundation for the skyscrap-ers.

It was back to the boat. I was cursing under my breath. Worse yet, we had completely dismantled our comfy gear seats. *Ah, how bad could it be for just half a mile?* I thought. We threw in some life jackets to sit on, jumped in, and paddled in our only dry clothes, thinking this was just a tiny distance to paddle.

Both of us were in awkward seating positions, and our normal rhythms were out of sync. It was one of the very few times we hit paddles trying to time our strokes. I was sitting almost ten inches lower in the boat. The cockpit rim was nearly up to my armpits. The lifejacket slid around and did not nestle me like my gear seat. We had emptied over half the boat and the boat sat higher on the water. It rocked more from side to side. All in all it was like stepping into your favorite car after a seven-foot valet driver had readjusted the seat.

About a quarter-mile later I exclaimed, "This sucks."

On top of that, the sunny morning had quickly turned overcast, threatening a downpour. As we paddled we searched for the type of milkbar we had grown accustomed to, to no avail. After ditching *Southern Cross* we found a residential section in a town with a totally different layout than what we were used to. *Where is that nice little main street with chemists and banks and milkbars?!*

We were not in New South Wales anymore. We were on Queensland's Gold Coast, a different province with a different mood. We asked for directions and found a very sterile food dispensary where everything was in packages. We cleaned out the place and they cleaned us out of cash. The last thing we bought were prewrapped ice cream bars. No chocolate ice cream sundae with heaps of hot fudge. It wasn't our day.

The first drops of rain started to fall, the wind became gusty, and the need for sleep was clearly starting to overtake hunger. We had dry clothes on. Our only dry clothes. *Do we try to dash the mile to the boat to paddle the half-mile back to the camp so we can go to sleep or try to wait out the storm under a covered picnic table?*

"What do you want to do, mate?"

"I need to crash, this picnic table looks fine to me."

The wind got stronger, blowing the rain horizontal, rendering the little roofs of the picnic tables impotent. We were getting soaked. I tried to ignore it and let fatigue rule, but it was cold and a chill set in.

"It's pretty hopeless here, TB."

"Back to the boat, then?" Tony said testily.

We paddled a half-mile back into a gale force wind that had already created whitecaps on a completely sheltered lagoon. I could not have been more wet as drops of water dripped from beard and brow. That half-mile took nearly half an hour.

"Good night, Tony."

"Good night, mate."

At five-thirty the next morning, Tony did the unspeakable. He woke me up.

"C'mon mate, let's go!"

Nightmare or waking nightmare? I wondered, half asleep.

"You've been asleep for almost fifteen hours. I've been up for a while already."

"No fucking way! Not a chance. Try again in two hours."

"Come on, we've been getting started too late these past days. The wind is good and we should go. We can make it to Brisbane."

"No, Tony, I'm not going now. Two hours and that's it."

"What a wanker," I heard Tony say as he walked away.

He successfully ignited my guilt trip, but I didn't think a couple of hours would make or break our chances for getting to Brisbane (not counting the unspoken goal of getting to Brisbane in a month). Brisbane was still over forty miles away. We hadn't done forty miles in daytime hours on the trip, and there was no way I was going to try another all-nighter on for size. Nevertheless, I could hear some wind, so I got up in an hour-and-a-half.

Tony wasn't pleased. He was obviously thinking that Brisbane was possible if we started early enough. He was right in that regard. It was *possible*. It just was not likely. I got the feeling something else had put the bee up his bum.

We packed quickly and sailed off. A strong breeze at our backs pushed us up a channel that would soon lead to the labyrinth called South Moreton Bay. It's a maze of islands, islets weaving channels, many leading to tidal dead ends. Our chart was not detailed enough to find an absolutely clear path.

After sailing briskly up the only well-marked channel we came to the fork in the road. Actually, it was more of a T. We stopped at the south side of Kangaroo Island to decide which way to go. My feeling from the charts, showing a wider channel and Brisbane located to the northwest plus the fact that I saw a few boats to the left, made me think left. Tony was clearly steering right.

"Which way are you going?"

"To the right, mate!"

"I think we should go left."

"Whhhhyyyyy?"

"I believe that's the right way."

"You just see some boats there and want to ask for directions so you know where we are. If we go that way we will have to sail miles upwind."

I couldn't understand that logic. A wrong turn could mean hours of wasted time, and the loss of a chance of making it to Brisbane. In the meantime, the boat was getting blown into the mangroves and rocky shore ahead. We would only have to paddle slightly against the wind for a mile and then we would be going almost due north. The wind was coming from the southwest today.

Soon we were beached, and Tony exploded.

"We always go where you want to go and do what you want to do!! OK, let's do it yooouuurrr way again," he roared.

Tony would have preferred to travel like Matthew Flinders, the chap who helped find and map most of the Australian coastline two hundred years ago. We were supposed to be exploring and discovering new places, not visiting towns and getting more maps to "know" where we were.

Before I left NYC, I had visualized the trip over and over again. I had imagined potential scenarios and outcomes. I foresaw our trip as a village tour for the first month, to build up our endurance and routine. Then a nirvanic express ride in the Great Barrier Reef, where we would sail the trade winds happily for a thousand miles, then inevitably get to remote areas where there would be a "town" every five hundred miles for the rest of the trip. Admittedly the "village tour" had been more like a series of village ruses. However, aiming for "towns," something I was familiar with, had given me hope along the way.

While I admired and even envied Tony's "go for it" attitude and his ability to act it out, Tony begrudged my pragmatism. Take it as it comes versus plan ahead. I would have loved to take it as it comes. But my experience wouldn't allow it.

"Look at the chart and you will see . . ."

"There *is* another path to the right!"

"Yeah, but if the tide goes out we might not make it . . ."

"All right, all right, we'll have it *your* way!"

We went left and found a mini—yacht club where I went to find out where we were. Indeed, the fishing shop had a detailed map and a man who knew the area. "We" had made the right decision. This was the last channel to get us to Moreton Bay and Brisbane. Moreover, I learned that we had a chance to make the tidal turnaround—a point where we could take the flood tide of South Moreton to its end and catch the beginning of the ebb tide in Moreton Bay. Ideal. We had no time to spare. Back to the boat. *We could make it to Brisbane today after all!*

No words about the previous exchange were mentioned but I had the silent satisfaction and relief that this was the way to go.

The wind was strong and we surged up the narrow channels switching off of one onto another like a high-speed train being changed over to another track.

The wind was strong and the narrow channels could only muster small waves. The jib sail tried to pull away from me like a German shepherd on a short leash chasing a cat.

We made the turn! Now, we had the tide and the wind!

Green lights down Moreton. Brisbane next stop.

I thought about how we'd survived our first overnight and the threat of the invisible rogue. We broke the rudder and broke the mast twice but Tony and I remained unbroken for better or for worse . . . barely.

We might even make it to Brisbane with some daylight left, I thought.

"My uncle lives in Brisbane. You might have a soft bed with clean sheets to sleep on tonight, mate," Tony said.

"Don't be a tease, TB."

Brisbane and Hervey Bay

The maze widened into Moreton Bay. We were approaching the southern outskirts of Brisbane and saw the industrial outline of East Brisbane ahead. I saw a number of jetliners flying in and flying out. It was the first bona fide *city* we had seen since Sydney. Tony seemed perkier about Brisbane than any other town before. It was good to feel Tony happy again, *yet I had to wonder what else was going on in Brisbane.*

We spotted a marina, made a hard left, and had a full-on beam reach in solid twenty- to twenty-five-knot winds for the last three miles. Just like Coffs Harbour but without the break wall to run into. We landed on a nearby beach and got out, only to find that there was no way to leave the boat there. Back in the boat, we paddled to the marina entrance and were greeted by many signs of officialdom—CAN'T GO HERE, CAN'T STAY THERE, etc., etc. A stern-faced, gray-haired, and bespeckled marina official greeted us.

"This is a private marina." As he got a closer look at *Southern Cross,* his facial expression changed to one of curiosity.

"Where have you come from?" he asked.

"Sydney."

"Fair dinkum, I think I can find a spot for you."

"What part of Brisbane is this?" Tony asked.

"Manly."

The sun set before we figured out that we had to find a place to stay. It was a city, not a sleepy coast town, and the locals weren't keen on vagrants. It was time to call some contacts. Tony started with his uncle from his father's side. A few minutes later, he came back to the boat to get another number.

"Any luck?"

"He's not home. There's one more chance, and I think she might be very close to here."

Score! Jenny Lee Lewes, a relative from Tony's mum's side, was only a few blocks up the hill from the yacht club. Her husband had gone to Melbourne and there were beds galore. A bed at last!

"He's moving!" the kids at the foot of my bed hollered excitedly. "He's moving!"

I opened my eyes to their wide eyes of wonder and excitement. Adventurers had come to their house, their mother had told them. There were three kids, in escalating ages from four to nine. They were damn cute, too. I had an urge to cry. Such wonder, such enthusiasm, unpredictable and completely legitimate. They don't wear social masks. All at once questions came. So many that I cannot recall exactly what they asked.

Tony got up and booked a flight back to Sydney to see Michael's (penthouse partner) departure back to England. Phone calls to mates back in Sydney got him fired up for some R&R. I knew he needed this and happily encouraged his travels. Later we quibbled over the weather, after which Tony remarked:

"I'm tired of arguing."

So was I.

We hit that one-month wall that seems the norm in kayak and mountain climbing expeditions. The honeymoon was long over, yet I knew Tony would be back and the trip would go on.

Tony found out through Sammy, back at Chadwicks (modeling agency), that Ron Arias wanted us to call him for updates on our trip. I was elected to give it first crack.

"Hello Ron, Eric Stiller from the Southern Cross Expedition."

"Hello Eric, how's it going?"

"We're in Brisbane."

"Fantastic, you really picked it up since we last saw you."

"Yeah, we sure have. Brisbane is about seven hundred kilometers as the crow flies, which means we covered about that many nautical miles as the kayak paddles."

We went on to discuss the various exciting events in the river bars, including the Ballina rescue scare. A journalist wants drama and "interesting" events for the readership. Ron knew better than to ask if we were "having any fun." The physical and mental mechanics of the trip itself were not "fun" by any traditional definition. Cricket in the backyard that afternoon with the kids was "fun." Talking about "highlights" to interested parties was "fun." My talk-to-journalist mask was on again and the entertainer turned snippets into sagas with the manipulation of octaves, and it started to feel wrong.

Why should I pretend? This journey is what it is. If people are not interested in it for what it is . . . so what? We're living it. It is our reality.

I thought it best to summon Tony for the rest of the details.

I heard Tony say, "Well Ron, it's monotony with underlying terror."

After Tony finished the conversation, I called Nicole. It was her birthday.

"Hello, Beautiful, Happy Birthday."

"Hello, Eric. It's been awhile. I'm glad to hear from you."

"How are ya doing? You sound a bit down?"

"I've been sick a lot, and I'm tired of all the crap in this city."

"What kind of sickness? Are are you OK?!"

"Yeah, I'm all right. I just can't get out of bed. I've had a cold, the flu, you name it. But I'm really sick of all the men and their leering at me at the Coffee Shop. The celebrities think they can say anything and get away with it."

"Have you thought about another job?"

"Well, it looks like the modeling is going to pick up, I just got some new pictures taken. They look pretty good. I've sent you one in the mail. I keep your picture near my bed and look at it before I go to sleep, and that helps. My friend Peter has been coming over with soup and stuff. He remembers seeing you and said you looked like a good guy."

"Peter?"

"Yeah. Works in the Coffee Shop. You probably don't remember him."

"No, I can't say I do."

"I miss you and love you, Eric."

"I've sent you a bunch of cards, have you got any of them?"

"I got one. . . ."

"Bye Nicole. I love you."

"Bye Eric."

Click.

The next day, I enjoyed the freedom of having the time to walk to the places I needed to to replace the casualties of the sea. I inspected the waterproof, shockproof camera and found sand in the O-rings, not allowing a complete seal to engage when film was put in, resulting in minuscule but potent ingress of saltwater that had ravaged the camera cell from the inside out. It had to be sent back to Sydney. That left us with one camera. Electronics, saltwater, and biweekly maintenance was not working.

All maintenance-intensive gear was showing signs of decline in this first telling month. Saltwater-"proof" binoculars were binding at the hinges, stainless steel "multi-tools" were jamming at their joints. Spriggets and sprockets to water bags were Heimlich-maneuver patients, hopelessly choked. The battery recharg-

ers were corroded, zippers failed, and the omnipotent Klepper kayak was showing more fatigue. *Southern Cross* had been brutalized. I had seen and serviced
many Klepper boats from various backgrounds and expeditions. *Southern Cross*
was showing its expedition scars.

Toggle handles had been torn away, rubber reinforcement pieces were peeling
away from the bottom, a lifting handle was tearing out, more wooden plates had
detached. The deck was fading from a dark olive to a greenish beige. To many, a
seven-hundred-mile, month-long sea kayak trip would be a complete expedition in its own right. *Things wearing out, and we're still just beginning.*

I returned to the house with time enough to read a book in peace, in a comfy
chair, with good lighting. *What a luxury.* I was tempted to read a short novel but
then the expedition pushed me into the bookshelf and guided my hand to the
Alan Lucas book *Cruising the Coral Coast.* The book jacket sealed my fate by
revealing to me that Mr. Lucas had circumnavigated Australia by small yacht and
by touting the book as the most detailed "yachting" guide of its kind.

Peace and naive wanderings were completely shattered by newfound "practical" knowledge of our trip to come. I immersed myself in the information, flip-
ping back and forth from chart to description to photograph. *Why me! Why can't
I remain innocent and unknowing?!* I had to keep looking.

The book had top-notch descriptions of the rest of the east coast and made
reference to other volumes, about the rest of Australia. Jenny's husband only had
one volume.

I got some satisfaction out of reading about where we'd been and about how
"dangerous," "treacherous," and "difficult" most of the places we had been were
described. Reading about the breaking surf and chaotic seas was entertaining.
The author talked about how many small boats had been lost at Ballina. Thank
God, we had done that; it was over. Then came the reminder that there was
more to come, and a lot more at that. I then looked further into the crystal ball.

I learned that although the bulk of our treacherous river-bar days was over
for a while, we were still scheduled for the granddaddy of them all. About eighty
miles up the coast sat Wide Bay bar between Inskip Point and the southern
point of Fraser Island.

The entrance was given a whole page of explanation, showing that there was
one specific narrow route and one specific window of time that this entrance
could be negotiated. The angle was from the northeast, and prospective vessels
were supposed to line up markers on the coast to guide them in. One was supposed to begin at the fourth hour of flood tide. Any later than that put the
approach in jeopardy. The associated charts showed an extensive bar that looked
more like a delta. Breakers existed in nearly every part of it starting up to five
kilometers offshore. This was an extremely specific set of instructions for tackling a diabolical hydraulic phenomenon.

In general, the small anchors on the charts representing "safe anchorages" meant safe landing for us, *if* a beach existed, which was not always the case. A yacht wants to be out of wind and swell in order to anchor but does not worry if its protected space has a beach, as long as there is a place to secure an anchor. I tried to make a list of where all the matching safe anchorages with beaches were in the upcoming portion of the trip.

Sometimes what might not be a safe or "comfortable" anchorage for a yacht can be a decent landing for a kayak, depending on surf. Information was limited in this regard. Since there were not that many anchorages, I could only hope. In theory, we had to make it through Wide Bay bar to get on the west side of giant Fraser Island and be in the swell shadow of the island and then north to the Great Barrier Reef.

The latter I imagined as like the tourist flyers, a kayaking heaven of sorts. To get there would require 125 more miles of open water, running in conditions like we had been in so far. That was depressing. Once again I was volunteering for ambush duty with an 80 percent chance of running into some serious action.

I redirected my attention to getting the locations of the post offices in the towns ahead to find out where mail could be sent and received. I wanted to find out exactly where the post office was in respect to where our landing might be. I had already missed some mail that we had overrun, and I hadn't sent some letters in as timely a fashion as overseas romances require. This was important information for me.

"*There he is. He's here, see, see!*"

A multi-octave chatter of kids and mom burst into the door followed by the welcoming and attention-demanding assault. There is no warmup or psyche-up for these transitions. *Kids are here. Change now,* I said to myself. It is not worth bruising such open enthusiasm with a solemn mood or by requesting silence and to be left alone. This would seem like too much of an about-face from the Peter Pan–like Uncle Eric of earlier.

I made the conversion and bounded about with the lads until Jenny said to the brood, "That's enough, time to wash your hands and get ready for dinner."

How did she do it? Where do you draw the line on open love and necessary authority without damaging the former? Open love is glorious but often chaotic and not "useful" to the "affairs" of the household, where cleaning up the room, doing the dishes, and making the bed are more important than play and open affection. Authority is pragmatic and trains discipline to the "necessary" things. Who decided what is necessary? When was making the bed given the nod over a few more minutes of giggling and gesturing?

Later that evening, the kids were put to bed, and Jenny had a glass of wine and said, "I had such a wonderful vacation last year."

"How long was it?"

"Eight glorious days with some of my girlfriends. We planned it for three years."

"You've been going for three years?"

"No, we planned it for three years and we had such a grand time, I'll never forget it."

They came back that night. Tony and the quest at hand. Tony was in excellent spirits but he was very nackered from having more than a few quiet ones. He felt time-warped, and the alcohol and the lack of any real sleep kept the entire experience in the surreal.

"Saw Andy and Anne again and had a riiipppper of a good time."

"How's Michael?"

"He had a big night, I think the ole boy became very fond of Oz."

"Why's he going back?"

"He can get more work there. Mate, I tell you, you would have loved it. There were minxes everywhere."

It was clear that the first and only thing Tony needed was sleep. We were scheduled to go the next day. I, for one, was getting too comfortable with beds, bathrooms, and affection. The next day.

It was time.

Jenny and the kids took us back to *Southern Cross,* which was still there patiently enduring our human vulnerabilities alone. It was back to sorting, packing, securing, double-checking, and getting adorned for Month 2 on the water. Shorts, long-sleeve shirts, hats, sunglasses, sneakers, life jackets, sunblock, and the rest.

It was time not for philosophies so earnestly and eloquently prescribed.

Jenny took a number of pictures of me and the kids and said: "I'll send one to your mum and one to Nicole if you'd like."

I thought it would be good, heart-string-tapping PR, giving Nick a booster shot in relationship actualization. Eric with kids, getting along, and all that.

Southern Cross was loaded and ready to go. The kids yelled in unison.

"Bye Eric! Bye Tony! Bye, byeeeeee!"

We had an uneventful, steady trip with enough wind and chop to keep us interested. Tony and I were chatty and covered the events of the past couple of days. The conversation took a serious, life-assessing turn when we talked about Jenny, kids, and family.

"It took her three years to work out her 'schedule' with a couple of other girlfriends with families before they could get eight days off for a vacation that did not include spouse and kids!" I said.

"It is part of being the perfect mother, mate."

"Yeah, but what about her life."

"The kids *are* her life. Her husband is an airplane pilot. He lives in south Oz and has to go where they station him. He's good man I hear but he's gone a lot."

"What do you think about the whole thing?" I asked.

"What thing?"

"Marriage, kids, and all?"

"Marriage and kids are for life, you have to be bloody sure about who you're going to be with. I've had a few birds ask me to marry them, but it wasn't my time."

This triggered our respective long-term-relationship files. All of our respective relationships had ended or were in a tenuous limbo. I was over thirty and Tony was a step away. We had many mates who were married, some with children.

"What about you, mate?"

"I agree about the mate and kids for life thing. I don't think marriage is supposed to be a training camp to get better for the next one."

"It makes you grow up faster than your time if you're a kid in that experiment," Tony added.

"Money is a big deal, too," I said.

"For love?"

"For marriage and kids. All my friends who seem to have 'successful' marriages with kids definitely were given the same rulebook sompelace. (A) Make a lot of money. (B) Get a nest. (C) Get a wife. (D) Have the kid. (E) Don't forget the nannies. (F) Make more money to pay for it all.

My relationships had ended after the "potential" status had worn thin and had not actualized to provider status in a "reasonable" period of time. There is an unspoken rule that assumes a white, single, educated male from a suburban background and major university is eligible and able for proper marriage and support after the age of thirty. There is a grace period in the midtwenties, allowing for a few more years of sorting things out than a generation ago.

I had gone the other way, starting off on the prescribed flight pattern and finding out I was not comfortable there. I was breaking out of society's preprogrammed flight paths, even questioning the act of flying altogether, questioning the institutions. A dangerous journey. There are very few charts these days for this kind of trip.

The city life had made a strong play for my soul again. It showed me that kids were fun but required a house, a wife, food, school, sports, activities, medical care, and concern, if not pure worry. *We're here to have kids, right? Shouldn't I be back home planning for the business, for my future. What am I doing here kayak-married to this guy, trying to go around a continent?*

Tony snapped me out of my daze, switching to politics and economics and describing himself as left of center.

"I think capitalism may have run its course, mate."

"Well, I've had my doubts about a system that believes in the principle of infinite growth in a finite world," I said. "Every country is going to want the same as we have—a car, a TV, and a PC."

"Here in Oz we have a giant hole in the ozone. People get skin cancer left and right."

"That's related to global warming, isn't it?"

"I don't know but I've been to Venice and it's going to be underwater any day now.

"Can you imagine if *China* wants a car in every garage?" I said.

"I think people are losing their respect for nature," Tony said. "If we use up this planet, we just get another one, right?" he added sarcastically.

"We can just jump on the Starship *Enterprise* and live with the Volgons," I said. "They want you there, anyway.

The day went fast and our landing was pleasant. We were still in the swell-sheltered shadow of Moreton Island and were setting ourselves up to scoot up the west side of Bribie Island the next day. In Brisbane I had learned about the strong low pressure systems that had been traveling south along the east coast for the past month, accounting for the big swell and all the squalls we had had. The last of the series was heading out to sea and we wanted to stay in sheltered waters before venturing out to the exposed coast again. We stayed in the village of Bongaree, got to the milkbar before it closed, got some chooks, fries, lemon soda, and ice cream. We sat outside and listened to some town gossip at the picnic table next door.

No worries today.

At least as far as the sea was concerned.

We woke up early, got some bread for the road, and launched for a more trying day of paddling and sailing in intermittent winds. Tony was still a little green in the gills from the Sydney affair, and the paddling started to sweat out the toxins in its uncompromising way through hard yakka.

Then a half an hour later, he said, "Slow it down, mate."

Then two hours later.

"It feels like we're fighting a bloody current, mate. We've got to move the boat better."

Just as the paddling and the heat were brewing up a real unpleasant disposition, a few cat paws of breeze appeared.

"Let's put up the sails!" Tony said.

The day had been a niggling, undecided, frustrating one ending with one last discouragement. Upon reaching the town of Caloundra we'd come to a "dead end." We found a campsite directly opposite the passage we'd have to take to get out into the open ocean again. We'd been ducking the surf for two days by staying on the sheltered side of Bribie Island. Once again the party was over. Caloundra bar had not been mentioned in the Lucas book so I had not given it much thought. This was a classic example of a false security based on "expert" knowledge.

In this case, Caloundra bar was not even listed as a bar. In fact, it wasn't listed as anything at all. Still, I should have known better. The chart told the story: a narrow opening between a large island and the mainland with nothing but shoals and shallows in front of it.

Caloundra is simply a nonoption altogether for ships and sailboats. That would explain its nonlisting. Something so rudimentary, it required no special notation. From our one-mile distance, we saw nothing but surging whitecaps endlessly flooding into the shallow body of water.

A local fisherman didn't help matters much by telling us, "No one goes through there except a few crazies in big-motored shallow-draft fishing boats."

They weren't the words of optimism I was hoping to hear. I knew we were not going to paddle twenty-five miles south and then twenty-five miles north to end up in the same place. We don't portage, as you may remember from the doctrine of Frazer Beach.

"It looks like yet another kamikaze," Tony said.

The journey was leading us again.

The lack of choice had me jot down these few bellyaches in my journal:

Tedium, fear, cramped quarters, constant concern about partner's temperament and desires, pressure to keep moving long distances and challenge the unknown otherwise days are considered wasted, great concern about rest of trip . . . Crocs, Kimberley whirlpools, west coast surf, SW coast exposure, the Great Southern Ocean and the 1,000 mile crossing. SIGH . . .

Sleep now. Big day tomorrow.

GOOD MORNING VIETNAM! Predawn wake-up under the self-assumed myth that the water was calmer then. Few words were spoken. I had no idea what we were going to see on the other side of the dune that had been obscuring most of the turmoil.

"I guess it's paddle in and find out?" Tony suggested.

"Fuck it, let's kick it."

We launched quietly in quiet, protected waters. Fear isn't invited on these missions but it likes to come anyway. There is no room for it once the action has begun. It is effective action's worst enemy. It is best to replace fear with anger. I, for one, had no problem making the switch. I was tired of being worried about the next hammer.

Paddling a kayak is a great place to use anger, as the paddles tear away at the flesh of the sea with prejudice. I was pissed off that we had been hoodwinked by a lack of information that led to not "seeing" the obvious from the charts. The charts showed the shallows and the large body of water trying to funnel into a much smaller body of water. I knew what that meant.

We paddled closer and closer to the white water and soon entered the channel. It was slack tide. That gave us a chance. As we turned the corner, we saw the golden orange glow of the horizon silhouetting the endless array of waves. This was not the succession of unbroken lines of swell like at Frazer. This was chaos. The only solution was to aim at the waves, paddle like hell, react as it came, and hope for the best.

We attacked this meringue hard, we went through, up, over, sideways, and around. Anger felt good.

Give us your best shot!

The water was glowing orange as if we were in aqua hell. That seemed appropriate for the mood. This was war.

It took over half an hour of sprinting at maximum effort to get out of the bombing zone. This was not one of those days we'd be out through the surf and then get some relief. We had won Round 1 and succeeded in really pissing off someone else on Neptune's board of directors. The sea past the surf was convulsing in peaks, bouncing off a rocky coast and a confused bottom.

Now it was the sea's turn to be angry. As angry as we had been. We had used up our anger. We were coping. Anger is not going to work for hours and hours on end. That is what we had ahead of us. It had suddenly darkened and we were getting doused. Payback is a bitch!

After ten miles, things settled down to moderate chaos, which felt like a full reprieve. A large motorboat came bearing down off our port bow. The word PILOT was painted on a deep navy blue hull. Standing on the foredeck was a blue-knickered, high-socked, straight-collared, middle-aged, getting-heavy official. The boat maneuvered closer, and in a pleasant manner, he said:

"Gedday, are ya awright?"

"Yessir."

"What ya being doing way out here?"

"We're paddling up the coast," Tony said.

"I was wondering if Noosa is a good spot to land today?" I asked.

"No . . . not . . . yes, yes . . . Noosa would be fine," he said, with knotted anticipation.

"Thank you very much."

"Good on ya, lads!"

We let the coast pilot's good words and blessing refuel us. The day stayed dark and rainy till the last few hours, when the sun came out. What a difference sunlight can make on a disposition. The Wagnerian day was giving way to easy listening. It took an hour to round Noosa Head, and a series of small points took turns tripping the wave refraction curve, turning the swells into a series of rolling point breaks. I approached Noosa with cautious anticipation. I saw a bespeckled white-sand beach surrounded by tall trees.

As we got closer, we saw our first omen. Surfers, human ones. *We're going in anyway, timing the sets, getting in and that's that,* I thought. Tony didn't break stride for a second. I watched the surfers jump from slivers on top of the waves' horizon line, to tenuously vertical, black paper cutouts that fell down out of view like insects being sucked in by a giant vacuum cleaner.

Southern Cross just kept plowing along toward the vacuum. We rode in smoothly on the back of a wave.

Sea kayaking protocol suggests that the best way to enter a surf zone is on the back of the last wave in a big set. As the wave breaks in front, the kayak lands on a cushion of bubbles.

This is what we did, but no sooner had we come through the wave when I saw a swimmer's head ten feet dead ahead, along with other swimmers randomly clustered all about. *Southern Cross* was traveling at least five knots. The physics was bad for the man ahead. Six hundred and fifty pounds times seven miles per hour concentrated on a narrow point equals hospital.

"Steer left, Tony! *Left!*" I yelled.

"Hoooo," whistled Tony as *SC* skimmed past the startled swimmer, "almost had ourselves a *Southern Cross* shish kebab, mate."

We continued S-curving the human obstacle course and beached among dozens of late-day beachgoers enjoying the last days of the season. Noosa was a bustling but restrained resort-town beach à la the Hamptons or Malibu. It was not the in-your-face entertainment complex of Surfers Paradise. To most, I'm sure, we appeared like just another beach toy coming in from a final ride.

Southern Cross's khaki olive form attracted a couple of surfers and others who wanted to know how far we had come, perhaps sensing that we were not just strolling about. Others started to inspect the vessel and saw pumps, our makeshift mast, weathered sails, black graphite paddles, rollers, sea anchor, and the lot.

"What's this for?" one young boy asked.

"Bailing the boat."

"How many k's have you come so far?" an older man asked.

"Well over a thousand."

"How do you piss?" a teenager asked, wide-eyed with wonder.

"Just throw the hose over the side," Tony said.

At that moment a tidal surge caught *Southern Cross* broadside and surged her violently up the beach nearly tackling all of the onlookers.

"Step *back!*" I yelled futilely.

Instead, a number of people helped pull her up. Twelve additional hands made easy work of it.

"We should hire them for our roadcrew, TB."

After *Southern Cross* was secure we chatted amicably with the most interested of the beach gatherers.

"There's a band playing at the Reefclub tonight," one of them volunteered. "You should come by. It's on Hastings Street."

"Sounds great," I said.

"We'll see, mate," Tony added.

The man left and I looked at Tony and said earnestly: "Sounds good, doesn't it?"

"We've got to find a place to stay and make sure the boat is OK."

We walked to the nearby Surf Club but the decision-maker was at ironman practice. The roving receptionist seemed positive so we waited awhile.

After ten minutes Tony said: "I'm going back to the boat to keep an eye on her."

Meanwhile, I had new-town explorationitis. I hung around for five minutes and then got post-office fever as well. I snuck a peak at Tony with *Southern Cross* from about twenty yards and out of his sight. I watched him inspect, adjust, caress, and sit with her.

I pottered into town by passing through a long, narrow pass adjacent to a resort complex. Noosa seemed to be the place that Brisbainites and others went if the Atlantic City–style, gambling-focused tackiness of the Gold Coast was not their style. Noosa was nice.

I got the paper and some overpriced sandwiches. I dropped a letter to a Nicole at the post and returned to TB.

"I hope you found your little town agreeable." His tone was taunting.

I shot him a dose of countertaunt. "Indeed, it was quite pleasant."

As darkness comes, we go to town, see the band, and see what clothes and a tan can do for otherwise bland, shapeless physiques. How different the same people who were just on the beach look, proving the theory that simulated beauty *can* be bought. After all, this was what Tony's profession up to now had been based on. Put Armani on Tony and you get Bond. Put the same Armani on Mr. 5'6" 200 pounds and you get a guy who thinks he's Bond as long as he's in the suit. Tony did not own a suit. He didn't need one.

The granddaddy of all river bars loomed less than two days away. We were on an oceaneering adventure. These people were on holiday. The life or death dilemma was not in the forefront of many of their minds. Death is a blown deal or a share devaluation. Life is a made deal and stock options gone right. They were out in "nature" in Noosa. Nature *looked* nice. Nature was another asset, something to add to the till. Something to see from a bay window or from the freshwater pool set meters from the ocean itself.

Noosa was a necessary stop to an uncertain future for us. We unraveled our cocoons under the mixture of engineered lighting and shadow. Tony stayed on the beach. I found a hidden area behind some shrubbery. *Exposed coast tomorrow, river bar next. Pleasant dreams.*

I was lulled to sleep by the sound of mirth and merriment blocks away as the band began. Tony's night was different. Besides the humid heat and mosquito attacks, Tony was awakened to the sound of droplets and giggling. This was not typical male sword play but rather a couple of girls marking "their" territory after a skinny-dip. Tony arose and had to smile. The girls were clearly "happy" and stayed for conversation. TB moved them along and waited for the next show.

The next show came with the deep voices and mustached faces of Noosa's finest.

"Get up, get up. There is not camping here!"

Tony arose to the two officers' flashlights shining in his face. He quickly described what he was doing there.

"Mates, my partner and I are on a sea kayaking expedition. Our boat is over by the rocks and we have come from Sydney. We'll be out of here at sunrise."

The officers were taken aback and responded with the utmost courtesy. "Sorry, mate, get some sleep and good on ya."

Tony did not have a restful sleep and we had some work cut out for us.

We were up and gone before the earliest of Noosa's beach worshipers. The swell was dropping and we did not want to use more luck tickets. If we made it to Double Island Point, it would put us within shooting distance to make it through the bar, in the early morning, with the proper tide. This was a precarious window dependent on weather.

Moreover, *if* we made it through the bar I wanted to believe that we would not have to deal with the large ocean surf for thousands of miles, until the west coast of Australia. We would finally be in the protection of the Great Barrier Reef and among countless island paradises. Two more determined days and we were home free for a while was my personal mantra.

We methodically paddled and sailed to Double Island Point. A shipwreck marked the spot. As usual, the sun was dipping into the horizon and we needed more distance to give us a real chance for the entrance. We dropped the mast and paddled all the way around the point and cut into a protected notch, surfing a succession of gentle shoal breaks into a desolate cliff-outlined beach. A couple of larger fishing vessels were a few miles away working the area of Wide Bay where cliff met water.

We landed *Southern Cross* on the shallow gradient of beach and searched for the high tide mark.

"Looks like there's a salt marsh behind the beach. The whole area looks pretty flat," Tony said.

"I think I find some dry sand here. This must be the high spot."

Tony and I systematically emptied *Southern Cross,* bringing armfuls of gear to our outpost. When half-emptied we took the plastic fender rollers and brought her up to. The wind had picked up and the beach offered no trees or dunes to deflect it. We set up *Southern Cross* on her side, facing the wind. We wrapped out tarp around her and held the corners down with some rocks. We rolled out the rest of the tarp and supported the corners with halves of paddles dug deeply into the sand.

After a while we had shelter suitable for cooking and eating. The wind was also keeping the mosquitoes away, including the special turbo-charged variety that have been known to windsurf into camp. Just as all the cooking gear was laid out, a sudden splash sent a few rivulets into our now "secure" enclave. I crawled out of the tarp igloo to find the surf breaking much farther up the beach.

Tony's mate Michael Penn:
"Did you say keep her
on the left, or the right?"

The Klepper Shop on Union Square.

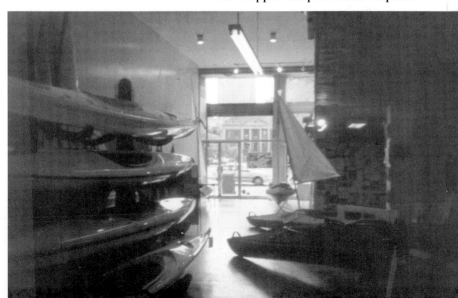

A day in the life of the urban kayaker.

Shades of Christmas morning as
Dieter "assembles" new toy.

The expedition pose: way too cocky!

Subdued "subway" Tony.

"Revved up" Tony and mate on
Gansevoort Street in Manhattan.

Backyard at the Bondi "penthouse."

No way it's all going to fit.

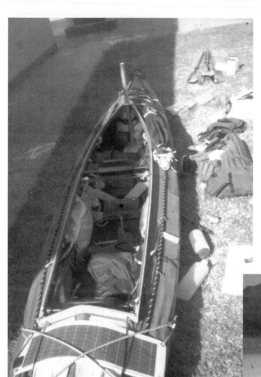

Our new home for the next year.

You can't take the model out of the man.

Feeling confident.

Twenty miles down. Only ten thousand to go.

"No worries, mate!"

Less than glamorous accommodations at Crowdy Head.

A reunion with Tony's mates Brent, Carolyn, Mike, and Sammy.

undaberg farewell: "Blackie" and Rosary and Ian Gibson.

Chez Eric: as commodious as the Ritz at half the price.

Local fishermen who insisted we share their catch.

A slice and a newspaper. All that's missing is a cappuccino

Sheer misery: a gloomy day of rough seas and rain.

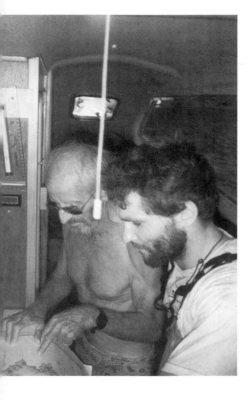

Dez and me.
"I thought I was the crazy one around here!"

Tony and friends
Carl and
Paunch Svendesen.

Phinny—the Dean of Decadence—was the first human we saw in five days.

Tony and a new mate compare notes in MacKay Harbor.

Feeling very feral today.

Tony and his mum at Cairns.

ome days it's like climbing into a soggy coffin.

Still a long way to go.

A complete dismantling and cleaning at Cooktow

...ue and the "Hut" on Portland Roads.

Not exactly a stretch limousine.

Tony, looking very "Robinson Crusoe," as he improvises a new mast.

Pulling *Southern Cross*
into Cape York.

Tony morphs into a twelve-gauge version of Crocodile Dundee.

Fort Crocodile.

Almost five months and the strain begins to show.

Launching *Southern Cross* for the last time.

Good-bye to a land of unspeakable beauty . . .

. . . and welcome back

"TB, the tide's coming in farther than I thought."

Tony angled his way out of the low-slung camp and witnessed the scene.

The wind had developed larger waves for which the larger sets shoved millions of foam bubbles toward us like eager sperm toward an egg.

"One more problem."

"What is it this time?"

"It's a full moon tonight and the tide is going to be higher than usual."

Sea kayaking and nautical protocol says that tidal heights are significantly higher during full and new moon cycles. A new moon is the one you don't see. The tides at this time are traditionally called "spring" tides. In between these times the tides and corresponding currents are at their monthly weakest. Moreover, less frequently the moon's orbit is closer to the earth and is called perigee. The tides and resultant currents will be even stronger then.

Tony handed me a paddle. "We're gonna have to build a drainage ditch."

The ditch started as one four-inch-wide-by-three-inch-deep trench about ten feet long. This temporarily diverted the farthest-swimming bubbles. Soon, we were being outflanked, so the trench became a half circle. More water came, and we built an inner-perimeter moat with drainage ditches to divert the water away. It started to look like a Roman aqueduct system.

We worked quietly and fastidiously. It was our precious camp. No pesky little bay was going to run us off. In an hour, most of our beach was covered by a shimmering of water that backlit our whole engineering endeavor.

"I need a wall here, mate!" Tony said.

H_2O storm troopers had breached our moats, so we built foot-high berms. No sooner had we fortified the perimeter than one side was eroding under the onslaught. We worked another hour nonstop and it finally appeared the water had stopped rising.

"That should do it," Tony said.

"We should go into the dam-building business, TB."

Sea kayaking protocol speaks of the "rule of twelfths." A basic tidal cycle runs approximately twelve hours. For approximately half of that time the tide rises, and vice versa. Tides will rise slowly at first, then accelerate, and finally taper off. More often than not they follow the rule of twelfths. Given a basic six-hour flood cycle (tide rising) the tide will rise one twelfth its potential height in the first and sixth hour, two twelfths in the second and fifth hours and three twelfths in the third and fourth hours.

We were on the highest patch of land and the perpetually maintained moats did their job. An hour later, even the largest waves' greedy paws were slipping back into the sea, as the moon tugged the tide away at the same rate it had brought it in.

The camp-saving effort had used up a lot of time and energy. We had to leave our camp toward the end of this ebbing tide cycle and come into the wide bay bar in the fourth hour of the flood tide. Absolutely no later than slack tide. Every hour afterward radically increased a shut-out. Lucas's book was quite specific that this bar was an open-and-shut case in the best of weather. The full moon was starting to create a second daylight and yet we had to get some sleep. We were fifteen miles away from the entrance.

ONHHHHHHHHHHHHHHHHHH!!!!!

The drone of the alarm bliztkrieged me to consciousness. The moon was at its apex and silverscreened the bay.

"What time is it, Epic?"

"Three-thirty, we got to get going," I said groggily.

Slack tide was at eight-thirty, if my rough calculations were correct that high tide had occurred only hours earlier.

When camp was silently and efficiently broken down we had to carry the boat back to the water's edge over a hundred yards away. *We must have come in the middle of the flood cycle last night*, I thought. A mild wind reminded me to put on a spray jacket. We were on the water by four-fifteen.

Our first strokes were magic. The moonlit water was alive!

"Mate, your blades are on fire!" Tony yelled excitedly.

I looked down and saw my own personal green fireworks display trailing my every stroke. I had seen this a few times before.

"It's phosphorescence—very cool—isn't it?"

"Look to your right!" Tony implored.

"Holy shit!" A dorsal fin was slowly paralleling our boat close to starboard.

"Don't worry mate, it's a dolphin. A bloody big one."

Chills ran up and down my spine.

We paddled the top speed we knew we could sustain with a mild breeze in our face. *Five knots an hour . . . times three . . . equals fifteen nautical miles. The exact right amount to get where we had to go with zero errors*, I thought to myself.

We were moving well. It felt good. After an hour I had a gnawing suspicion that we were veering from our target.

"Tony, which way are you heading?"

"Over there, mate, toward that light."

"Tony, I think the opening is farther to the left. I think we must turn in now before we overrun it."

After some reluctance, Tony agreed, but after another half-hour of additional paddling, Tony said, "I don't think this is right. I think we are going too far left."

"I think we're dead on."

"Let's look at the GPS, then."

We dialed in the satellites. The couple-minute pause wore on me, knowing that we had no margin for error. Just as patience waned, we got the reading—25 degrees, 50 minutes latitude, 153 degrees, 10 minutes longitude.

Exactly due east of where we were supposed to be and yet a disturbing five miles from it. Our direction was right but we were behind schedule. The sun was just starting to pull off its covers, preparing to get out of bed. It was six-thirty. We paddled hard in a sloppy following sea, killing *Southern Cross*'s momentum. *It feels like we are going against the current. How is that possible. I thought. What if my tide calculations are all wrong? What if there is some anomaly I'm not aware of?*

"We are not moving the boat sufficiently!" Tony said.

It felt like we were paddling in molasses. Sea conditions can rob half the speed of a boat. If that were to happen to us, we'd be out of luck for sure.

Paddling harder did not seem to help. Sweat was dripping. The still ambiguous destination cloaked itself behind a morning haze. We followed the "E" on our compass. The brightening sky erased and replaced the magic night light. We were supposed to be at the bar shortly after sunrise.

I saw glimpses of a gap between one prominent bluff to the north and a sliver of land to the south. I saw two gossamer forms working their way around the bluff from the northeast.

"Follow the line of the sailboats," I said.

"Why?" Tony asked.

"The Lucas book tells yachts to take one specific route in."

"It looks like we can go in anywhere."

"There it is, see!?"

I saw the first of the line-up markers on the northern landmass. *Must be Fraser Island. It better be, otherwise we're not even close. Southern Cross* sped up. We aimed for the sailboats. *They know the way. They have to. If they don't work this right they are run aground, battered senseless, or both. We won't be run aground but we have been battered.*

Seven-thirty A.M.

The layout of the entrance soon matched my visualization of Lucas's description. Whitecaps now topped three quarters of the area. It was very turbulent off our port bow, south of the entrance. Fifteen minutes later and the water was bubbling on both sides. Wide Gap finally looked like a wide gap, as we approached the second line-up marker that was visible on the other side. It was a yellow/orange color with a parallax pattern. Come on the right line and it looks like one numeral, otherwise you see double. Our ENE approach appeared to be working.

Seven-fifty-five.

There was no huge breaking surf, the wind was modest, the tide seemed OK.

"I think we may have done it, I just hope we get in there before the tidal current starts racing out."

In the last mile our concern switched from just making it through the gap to making it far *enough*, so as not to hit too much resistance before finding a decent stop. Damage control pragmatism replaced terror energy. The gap is known to generate almost five knots of current at full moon. Tony picked up the pace. Two miles in front of us, the sailing boats turned to starboard and headed north.

Our next clue on what to do came from a bright orange ferry that crosses the gap to get people to and from Fraser Island. We took chase to keep it in our vision. *The ferry landing must have a milkbar*, I hoped. A long line of ant-sized cars waited from where the ferry had just left.

Eight-thirty-five A.M.

We're all the way in! Mission accomplished! We rounded the southern tip of Fraser Island. Another mile of paddling was rewarded with a totally surfless tropical gem of a beach. On the opposite side were thick mangroves as far as I could see. Thick foliage was outlining our stakeless claim. I felt we were in a completely different climate zone. It was like Wide Bay bar was a doorway to a terrarium. It was already getting hot. In fact we had gained almost ten degrees of latitude since we had started from a temperate thirty-five degrees in Sydney to almost twenty-five degrees. We were nearing the Tropic of Capricorn.

Sea kayaking protocol states—each degree of latitude equals sixty nautical miles.

Moreover we were now heading more sharply to the northwest after the previous month of NE travel.

Once inside the protective shoulders of Fraser Island, where my personal surf nightmares could take a rest, Tony said, "Funny thing we saw that dorsal fin last night."

"Funny?" I asked.

"I thought the dolphin was spectacular. And sooo close! Just before we saw it I had one of my dreams."

"About what?"

"Well, it's the same every time; I'm in a boat with another person and I look over the left side and I lose my arm to a shark."

"What?! You have a recurring dream about a shark biting off your arm? How frequently?"

"A few times a year."

"You've got to be kidding me? What the hell are you doing on a kayak trip around Australia when you have the same dream about a shark?"

"Just a dream, that's all."

It reminded me that a few years back I had confronted a good-size black dorsal fin a mile off the coast of East Hampton, Long Island. The feeling of helplessness was replaced by a resolve to stay calm and paddle evenly back to shore, while my body prepared for impact. I thought that upon further inspection the shark would see that the kayak wasn't good eatin' and would leave me alone. Then I realized my boat was made of skin on a frame. So are seals—one of their favorite foods. It followed me for about two hundred yards and disappeared. I went in for the day. But going in was not always an option for me and Tony.

We stopped, got out of the boat, and laid our bodies down on the inviting sand. Moments later, I was scratching furiously and so was Tony. I thought I could hear the sandflies saying, "Where have *you* been all my life!"

If it's not one thing it's another.

My attempt to ignore the assault was hopeless.

"Get up, Eric. Get your bags out of the boat, set up your bivvy sack, and get some real sleep."

"No! I don't *wannnnt to*!!" I whined. I wanted to sprawl out and lounge on this formerly perfect picture postcard of a spot.

"Eric, you've got to. A little work now will make you sleep a lot better."

"OK. OK."

I spotted some people down the beach. "Make them go away, please," I said to myself in a continued personal fit of crankiness.

Out here, they don't go away.

Their names were Val and Barry, and they took us back to their jungle compound. One of those compounds combining the best of the Swiss Family Robinson and the Mosquito Coast. Generators, gardens, heavy tarps covering most of the area like a circus tent, wooden stakes and all. Nearby was the Toyota Land Cruiser and fishing boat. All of this interspersed with thick foliage and invisible from the beach. They had no neighbors.

We learned what this was all about. The robust-looking Barry was diagnosed with cancer years ago and took it as a sign to completely change his lifestyle from nine-to-five city stressing to the outdoors. Eating organic homemade vegetables, catching and eating fresh fish, living in the jungle near a desolate beach, and occasionally having friends and family come to visit. So far, it had worked. He appeared to be in remission and, more important, living a lifestyle that he had always dreamed of.

"The missus and I would like to take you for a tour of the island."

"Actually . . ." I was about to plead sleep when—

"We know a perfect spot to get an ice cream."

"Sounds great."

We loaded into the Land Cruiser for a tour of Fraser Island. There were few roads to speak of and therefore the beach became the roadway.

We drove south and around the southern point of Fraser Island, where we got a great view of the whitewash covering the wide gap entrance we had safely entered a couple of hours beforehand. The tide was ebbing with velocity, colliding with the sea and closing the entrance. *The Lucas book was not playing it safe. It was telling it like it is*, I thought.

When we got to the east side, the beach got very wide and Barry accelerated to nearly 50 kph and was soon passing on the left and the right. I thought I heard a tint of mumbled road rage.

"One of the busiest weekends of the year," he said tensely.

"What's the occasion?" I asked, obliviously.

"Easter." He added, "We've had some bad accidents on the beach in recent years. They're all in a hurry to stock up before the stores close and before the tide cuts them off from getting around the island."

"Check out the entrance *now*, Tony!"

"Ah, it's a pussycat today," Barry said.

As we sped along, we passed a lone "dingo" watching the caravan of 4WD's on one of the longest stretches of unbroken beaches on the continent. In fact, we learned that it is the largest all-sand island in the world.

The island's name comes from a certain Captain Fraser who got wrecked there in 1836 and with the help of the Aborigines survived until he was rescued two months later. The local Aborigines call the island K'gari, which translates as "Paradise." Eventually the island's thick forests attracted the timber industry. Industry representatives moved the Aborigines onto missions.

"Yeah, they're trying to get it all back now," Barry said. He sounded a trifle resentful.

"I suppose they have a right to it," he continued, softening. "But I hear some of their English-trained lawyers are as greedy as the guy who monopolizes the ferry system here. They don't want anyone else to be able to use it."

"You mean kick everybody off?" I asked.

"Everyone but them. I heard something about a casino."

"See that area over there," Barry said, pointing to a large area that looked like a meteorite had hit it.

"Big fire almost burned down the island a few years ago."

As we drove closer I saw thick, vivid green new growth filling in miles and miles of burned trees that looked like the remnants of blown-out birthday cake for the Jolly Green Giant.

We returned to the boat early in the afternoon.

"You're welcome to stay the night, or longer, if you like."

"Thank you," I said, "but I'm afraid we have to push on. I figure we can get through the Great Sandy Strait tomorrow if we get a head start with today's flood tide."

We packed up and slid off the waveless beach into the Great Sandy Strait that passes between the mainland and Fraser Island. It was a tidally dominated, sheltered shortcut, that passage through the gap had given us access to. Fraser Island's east side was nothing but a large open anvil that the ocean used to test out its newest sledgehammers. A number of ships had gotten wrecked along its shores.

The toll for the shortcut was going with the tide and not against it. The strait was shaped like a funnel with the wide-mouthed Hervey Bay to the north and the narrow spout we had just passed through to the south. Changes in depth and a maze of islets added to the intricacies of the vortex. Like at Moreton we wanted to use today's flood tide on the strait's south end till dusk and then, tomorrow try to use the flood/ebb combo trick that had gotten us to Brisbane in one fifty-mile day.

We landed at a small fishing launch and were greeted by a couple of locals who offered to take us to the one and only milkbar associated with the caravan park on the other side of town. They told us we were in the hamlet of Buna-roo. We never had succeeded in getting those ice-cream bars on Fraser. They were all out.

We waited patiently for the proprietor of the milkbar to end his phone call. We stocked up on cereal, milk, and Coca Cola. The proprietor recognized us from *People* magazine as the crazy kayakers trying to go around Australia.

"Hey, you're the blokes that . . ."

"That's us, mate. Thanks. Cheers."

"Good on ya."

Our ride dropped us at our boat. We shared food and thoughts at the nearby picnic table by the light of a couple of candle lanterns.

That night I made a few quick notes about the New South Wales coast's legions of river bars and surf assaults, realizing with a combination of relief and regret that I would not see them again.

The NSW coast is comprised of long open stretches marked by rocky headlands. Points, capes, and bluffs. In any weather they are imposing. In the dark—intimidating. Area around Coffs Harbour was lush and marked with banana plantations. The Gold Coast was like Miami Beach except the waves inundating it are much larger. The threat of surf was constant and town harbors that I thought would be safe were often more dangerous than beach landings.

The next morning, I noticed that Tony was already off and about. I was relieved. I had a few minutes to quietly sort things out and be packed and ready to go before him this time. Tony had made a point of being the first one packed up nearly every day. I started to slowly bleed the air out of my air mattress, when I heard: "Mate! Let's go! Breakfast is being served!" The patronizing tone struck an early morning nerve.

"Excuse me, Tony???"

He glowered back. "They're serving pancakes and they're getting cold."

The obligatory breakfast became tense and I felt a need to explain to Barry.

"I'm concerned about getting the tides right today. I'm trying to figure out where the turnaround might be."

"Ahhh, I can show you where that is right from the launch site. Come on let me show you," he obliged. He pointed to a cluster of islands on the horizon of our vision. "The turn should be just after there."

"It looks like fifteen kilometers?" I guessed.

"Sounds 'bout right." He shrugged.

Another waveless launch with no wind. In less than fifteen minutes we were sweating and still being badgered by sand flies quite happy to be going on a morning cruise. Tony was not in the mood to paddle. I could hear it in his breathing. His sigh-to-breath ratio was running high. The sun only got higher and warmer. The paddling seemed idiotic. Why would anyone choose to do something that made hot *hotter? A wind would be really nice right now,* I thought.

We paddled and sweated. I took my canvas hat and dunked it in the water and poured it over myself. It was the first time I had to *self*-wet. I did it another half-dozen times before we got near the cluster of islands that had been pointed out to us, only to find that we were on a treadmill.

"What's going on?" Tony exclaimed.

"As soon as we get through this we're free," I said appeasingly.

I was wrong. We fought an ever-increasing ebbing tide for almost two hours until we passed through a large section of water. Water was rushing, trampolining, and falling over itself. Dozens of miniwhirlpools surrounded *Southern Cross* like we were in the paddle wash of a invisible war canoe. *This is the turning point,* I thought. It still wasn't clear if we were getting any assistance, but there was less resistance.

Still no wind.

Tony's sigh-to-breath ratio got worse. I started to wonder if he had done this before and I had never heard it before.

I continued my periodic hat baths and made a point of doing it without losing my stroke in order not to agitate Tony further.

We wound ourselves through curve after curve of the Great Sandy Strait. *They could make a movie of Conrad's* Heart of Darkness *here,* I thought. *Southern Cross* searched for the open water of Hervey Bay. Three hours later, a dark blue channel emerged in the distance, accompanied by a slight wind. We put up our sails and sailed slowly through the last of the labyrinth.

"It's about bloody time," Tony said, relieved.

The wind was too light and a half-hour later I realized we were moving too slowly. Time was running out. I was concerned that Tony had not already said something, so I did.

"We have to hit the sticks again."

"I know, I know," he sighed resignedly.

Paddling hours were adding up again. My hands were getting raw, my back was sore, and my butt was terminal. Both Tony and I had to take butt breaks where we raised ourselves a few inches off our seats and held them there for a minute or so. The release of pressure felt great and lasted about five minutes before it would get even worse.

We had sailed very little during the five days prior and had logged nearly 150 miles at full power. *Too much fucking sprinting,* I thought, yet the other option was missing windows and waiting. Sleep had been sparse, food less than adequate, and there was no expressway just waiting to speed us along as I had imagined.

Hervey Bay was not the vast, open stretch of blue that I had expected, either. In fact, the deep blue channel we had seen was now far to the east, near Fraser Island, which angles northeast toward the Pacific. We were going northwest, near the mainland. Our fork in the road was leading into murky channels that soon became a series of dead ends.

"It's nothing but a mudflat, mate."

Hervey Bay was disappearing.

A fully loaded double kayak drafts eight to ten inches. When water depth drops to six feet, you feel a noticeable drag on the hull. When it is three feet, it is a tremendous drag but still not more difficult than lining the boat in waist-deep water.

We paddled until we hit yet another dead end. We lifted the boat over the sandbar, paddled, lifted, paddled, lifted, getting nowhere fast. We frantically tried to change our state of affairs thinking that speed was the answer.

"It's no use, mate, look up ahead," Tony said.

Flat-bottomed fishing skiffs sat dead in the water about a quarter-mile away. The crews were walking around. Their engines were pulled up. That was it. Low tide in the middle of south Hervey Bay, at least five miles from any point of land. Now, the only option was to wait for the tide to come in.

"This wouldn't have happened if you could only get up earlier!" Tony grumbled.

"I wasn't the one who arranged for breakfast." I snapped back. "I just wanted to pack and go!"

"That would have been rude!" He shot me a withering glance. "They had breakfast ready for almost *an hour.*"

We waited in the boat, nursing a tense and brittle silence. I hoped the tide would lift us soon. A half-hour later. *Shit,* I thought. *No lift.*

We decided to call a truce and went exploring.

"Mate, come over here. Look at this!" Tony yelled.

He had found a giant sea turtle shell on the mudflat. It wasn't moving, and Tony crept toward it. "I think it's dead, mate."

He bent over for closer inspection. "Jeezus. It's as big as a Volkswagen." He ran his hand over the humped shell.

"Ahhhhhhhh!!!!! Tony yelled, as the sea turtle lurched at him with viciously snapping jaws. *"Ahhhhhhh!!"* He continued backpedalling as the turtle kept charging. I had never seen a Volkswagen move so fast.

Before the frightened turtle could do any real damage it began furiously burying itself in a shallow channel of mud and water.

Tony was grinning like a foolish kid. So was I. The tension between us had lifted.

And so had the tide! Tiny rivulets were widening and panning out, spawning new ones. It was about three-thirty, and there was still a chance that we might make it to Urangua, the only town in the area, before nightfall. All we needed was six more inches within the hour.

We kept a keen eye out for a channel deep enough to float us out. An hour later we made a futile attempt to push *Southern Cross* out the channel. No go. *More waiting.* I sighed. Time was running out.

"Look, mate!" Tony was pointing to a group of fishermen who had appeared down the beach. "They're getting back into their boats!"

The fishermen waded to their boats in shin-deep water. A good sign, a very good sign. The increasingly flooded mud basin was looking more and more like a time-lapse film. The tide was coming in and dispersing water ever faster in the pattern.

"It won't be long now," I called to Tony. But it was another half-hour before we could scrape the boat along by the Lewis and Clark "line and trudge" method. Thick, gooey, stinky mud sucked on our lower legs threatening to rip off our shoes. Tony took off his precious Blundstones and disgustedly threw them on the boat. I was more concerned with what I might step on if I took mine off as well. I could see deeper blue a hundred yards away. I tried to rub the mirage from eyes but it was still there.

Come on tide! Come on!

Waiting for a rising tide is only marginally faster than watching the grass grow. Or paint dry.

We paddled by the fishermen, who were just dropping their outboards into the water. They would need at least another six inches of clearance for the props.

Hasta la vista, I thought mercilessly, enjoying their continued plight.

The sun hunted for the horizon. The lights of Urangua were starting to dot the distant shore. The sunset was spectacular and I knew we didn't have to worry about big surf.

An hour later I saw a string of lights stretching out from the harbor in a long, clean uninterrupted line, like a space station. Light is both a blessing and a bane to the nighttime kayaker. A blessing for the obvious reason that it is a beacon to shore. However, the human eye can see a candle from more than sixty miles away on a clear, moonless night. More often than not a kayaker underestimates the distance to shore, which can make for weary and frustrating paddling.

My mind started calculating an optimistic ETA (estimated time of arrival). But without a reliable reference to the source of the lights, they simply appeared like a string of Christmas bulbs on the next-door-neighbor's walkway. They could just as easily have been a hundred yards or ten miles.

It took us awhile to finally see the dim green-and-red running lights of craft approaching land on the water runway. The silhouettes of the boats were specks. We still had a long way to go.

"It's got to be more than ten miles away!" Tony guessed.

"It can't be. It wasn't that far away to begin with, when we were stuck with the turtle." At that moment the motorboats we had seen stuck in the mud sped rapidly by and reached the distant space station at warp speed.

An hour later we reached the six-foot-high pylons that the lights had been sitting on. The sea kayaker's square-distance formula applies to night distance as well. One-point-five plus the square root of 6 (approx. 2.5) = 4 nautical miles. OK.

Once we were on the landing strip, it felt like what I imagine a Cessna pilot experiences when he taxis a lumbering 747 at La Guardia. The pylon lights were obviously set up to guide larger boats in from the ocean. Not freighters or ocean liners, just your normal fifty-foot-long, twenty-foot-high deep-sea sport-fishing boat. We chose to get off the landing strip, knowing that we would be the last thing get-me-home recreational fishermen would be thinking of. The procession of lights to the marina was impressive.

Once in the harbor, we saw a long, steep, concrete ramp and pulled up onto it, only to be advised by two exiting fishermen that a number of boats would be coming up the ramp that night. We got back in and tied off *Southern Cross* among some dinghies, where marina muck was waiting along with broken bits, fishing line, and the reflective sheen of oil rebounding from some lampposts.

"We've got to tie her with enough line to handle the tidal variation," I said.

"Mate, if we give her too much slack she's going to bang around."

Our verbal tug-of-war broke off when I noticed an elderly couple climb out of their car and walk toward us. We exchanged greetings, and the gentleman pointed knowingly at *Southern Cross*.

"Hmmm, the Navy ZED forces used to use boats like yours all around here in their training exercises. Their base was supposedly on Fraser Island." He smiled mischievously. "One of their favorite missions was to steal full kegs from the pubs one night and return them empty the next. They were instructed to put 'thank-you' notes on them."

Hunger and a certain madness were etched on Tony's face. We were close to raiding a nearby pub.

"Get in lads, we'll take you to the Esplanade. Something should still be open for your there."

Fifteen minutes later, the dark and the sleepy fishing town became a mile strip of lights, arcades, and car cruising.

We gorged our troubles away at an overly lit milkbar. The usual—chooks, chips, and ice cream—were washed down with lemon soda. All of it instantly incinerated and devoured by our cells like fresh kill to a pride of lions. Once satiated, it was time to go back and set up camp in a town park across from the marina.

"Sweet dreams, Tony."

"You too, mate."

●   ●   ●

I thought, *No surf, free ride for the next thousand miles or more because we are in a swell shield set up by Fraser Island and then the Great Barrier Reef.* We set off with confidence and the intent to log as many miles as possible. The goal was a little town on the Elliot River. After a couple of hours of paddling, a strong wind developed on Hervey Bay and we were moving well.

"Raise the sails, Epic!"

"Happily, TB!"

The bumpy ride made the procedure harder than I remembered. Lining the mast into the post and step took many restarts. *How long has it been since we used the sail in choppy seas,* I thought to myself. *Almost a week and half. How quickly I forgot.*

The wind picked up. "Sheltered" Hervey Bay became a froth of four-foot whitecaps. The ride got very wet and bouncy.

Hours later, I noticed much larger swells intersecting and then underlying the frothing, whipped-up surface waves. We were sailing out of Fraser Island's north shoulder of protection and back to an exposed coast. Heat, boredom, and sand flies were now the distant memory. The jib sail tugged impetuously on my hands. My forearms started to burn while holding the paddle that acted as my boom. Unlike paddling, both my hands were clenched tightly instead of staying relaxed and tensing only hard enough to guide the paddle to the next stroke. The winds increased to near gale proportions.

"*Yeaaaahaahahhhahaha!*" Tony screamed primally.

As the elements combined their forces on us, I wanted to believe we were somehow "protected," and none of this was real, like it had been before Wide Gap.

By late afternoon, I could see a tower representing Elliot River and we both had had just about enough of this wind-and-sea reunion party.

"*Careful, mate, lean right!*" Tony ordered.

Pisshshshshshshshshsssssss. A wave broadsided and nearly capsized us, followed by an apparently endless series of new, improved, supercharged waves.

"Where the hell did these come from?"

We had a succession of very close calls as the larger sea swell lifted us up and another wave ran over the top in a well-practiced high-low tackle pattern.

Southern Cross was zigzagging and seesawing, unable to get a clean line anymore. All of our attention was focused to seaward to starboard. Tony was "submarining" a lot today as *Southern Cross* did everything she could to level herself in the tempest. I heard Tony spitting out white water after a succession of deeper waves and troughs. It was a sailing kayak rodeo ride. We felt we had stayed on our steed too long. *Where's the entrance? I don't see the tower anymore,* I thought, about to inspire panic.

"*Where's the tower?*" I said, hoping Tony could simply make it reappear right where we wanted it.

"It's behind us already, mate, way behind us," he said hammering the last nail in the coffin of my hopes.

All we saw to port was a twenty-foot-high, black-rock, man-made break wall. I sickeningly remembered reading about it in the Lucas book. A twenty-mile section of coast in the vicinity consists of man-made breakwater walls, with little, if any, breaks. On top of the walls small ranch-style houses welcomed head-lit cars back from church on this Easter Sunday. We were close enough to hear the doors shut. It started to rain.

We were no closer to getting in those houses than the satellite that was beaming images into their TV sets. The wind and sea were rapidly taking us past the last northern fringes of the town. There was no way to backtrack to the Elliot River entrance now three miles to the south.

"I think there might be some kind of landing on the north side of town," I said.

Another strong wind gust and wave combo nearly knocked us down again and I had had enough of riding the edge.

"I'm taking the jib down, Tony."

"Why?"

"It's getting too hard to handle."

I hadn't felt the need to do that in weeks. *I thought this is supposed to be the easier part?* I was now paddling and bracing while the mainsail continued to speed us along. We sailed past the northern edge of town.

No entrance!!?

We had missed it. The tower was the only entrance after all.

"Where's that beach of yours?" Tony asked.

The sun was long gone and the wind and rain showed no signs of easing up. As night dug in, I saw the soft glow of light well in the distance.

"I guess we'll have to head for the lights. I think it is Bundaberg."

"That's got to be another twenty miles, mate?!"

"I know."

"Oh *bloody hell,* we'll just beach it the first chance we get!"

"It's all break wall, Tony."

"How the hell do you know?"

The sails were going to have to come down. Time to hit the sticks and try to find a landing spot. Once again we followed imaginary light carrots just ahead. Always just ahead.

We came upon another community where houses were just beyond reach. We could see softly lit cozy living rooms with the strobelike flashing of changing images on the television screen. I saw a man sit in a lounge chair and open up a newspaper. Tony thought he saw a town beach.

"Mate, I think there's a beach up there. What do you think?!"

"I don't think there are any beaches on this part of the coast. The Lucas books said—"

"*Mate,* I've never heard of an Australian town on the coast without a beach! I think that's one right there."

Tony steered *Southern Cross* in the direction of a less dark area of coast, holding up a hundred meters away, where we both strained our eyes to make out more detail, more confirmation that this was a beach and not a break wall. The *difference* was important.

We eased in a little closer and all of sudden heard breakers booming. *Why are there breakers? This is a sheltered bay.* I still erroneously clung to this belief. Up we went, knocked to the side by a powerful wave. Tony and I instinctively leaned and braced into the wave to counteract the impending capsize.

A closer look didn't more clearly reveal anything. A committed run at an uncertain, wave-ridden beach in the dark would've been unwise.

"Let's get outta here, Tony, I don't think that's a beach."

"Mate, it's got to be a beach. I can see sand."

My gut said, and I forcefully reiterated, "I don't think so, lets get outta here."

"Ohhhhhhkkkaaayyyy," Tony grudgingly yielded.

We went back out to sea a few hundred yards. We continued up the coast a number of miles and the distinct possibility of another night at sea started to creep into my thinking. It wasn't looking good. *What if Tony was right? What if that was a beach? Have I doomed us to another miserable night, an even more miserable night than at Surfers Paradise?*

Hours later, another larger, grayish patch became visible in the break wall. Somehow, it looked more inviting. The moon provided intermittent light, playing hide-and-seek with the fast-moving clouds. We got strobelike glimpses of our potential rest stop. We slowed down and eased in. Once again we found ourselves at the fringe of breaking surf with some large waves passing under us. *How is this possible?* We were hit, but not nearly as hard as before.

"Mate, what do you think?"

"It looks possible, Tony. I just don't think there are many breaks in this break wall until Bundaberg, and we're not there yet."

I didn't want to encourage or discourage too much. It was clear in his voice that he wanted to get off the water, as did I. Unfortunately, I was cursed with the memory of information that I had logged in Brisbane. It was my call.

"Let's give it a shot, Tony."

"That's what I wanted to hear!"

We let another set of waves slip past us and sprinted behind them. After one initial rise and fall we cleared all the waves. We were in some type of shallows and had to paddle hard to make headway but there were no more large waves. The shoreline was looking more and more like a beach.

It was!! We landed with gusto dead center on a fifty-meter stretch of beach between two black-rock break walls. We hastily jumped out of the boat and hugged each other.

"I've had enough. Wow! What a day this was!"

"Mate, lets find some tucker," Tony said gleefully.

We secured *Southern Cross* up the beach, put on our *Star Trek* suits, and climbed over a dune and through some trees to come upon a strange all-blue house, with blue lights. The homes around it made it look like the introductory scene to the *X-Files*. A pizza car pulled up to one of the houses. No movie cameras. *It must be real!!*

We ran out of the forested dunes atop the breakwall, past a movie-sized project-development sign and flagged down the pizza man. He stopped. I don't think *I* would have stopped if *I* had seen us. Two blue-suited, half-bearded, laser-eyed maniacs running out of the woods.

He stopped. "What are you looking for?"

"You're exactly what we're looking for," I said. "I mean, the pizza."

He seemed very laid-back. Maybe a bit stoned, but who was I to tell. He was older, midthirties. He was not your typical teenage delivery boy.

We quickly described ourselves. He took it in stride. We asked to order a pizza and have it delivered to the street corner where we stood. He took the order and said he would be back in half an hour. Was it too good to be true or had we earned that pizza?

"Oh, and could we have two liters of Coke with that."

"Sure, mates."

The pizza car sped away.

"He's not coming back, mate," Tony said, and I was not going to dispute the call. The odds weren't high.

"Let's give him forty-five minutes and then see what we can stir up."

"All right."

And so we sat on the street corner, near an all-blue house by an overly large project sign, in a surreal outskirt of Bundaberg. We exchanged Hitchcock-style tales of the serial killer who obviously lived in the blue house with blue lights.

Thirty minutes. No pizza car. Expectations dimmed. Another twenty go by and we were going to plan B.

"Here he comes!"

"Are you sure, mate?"

"Yes, it's the same car!"

It *was* our pizza man. He came, he delivered, he collected.

The next day was calmer. The wind had come down but still provided good cruising speed. It was just a few hours before we passed the town of Bundaberg—the town that cyclone Fran had targeted a month ago. The same cyclone that had given us a month of big swell, rain, and storms. The same town that I knew possessed an important package from Nicole. It was a package that had had to be re-sent because it had missed us at one of our prior destinations. Sammy told me she had sent it to Bundaberg.

It was Easter weekend and the post office was closed on Monday. We were not going to stop for two extra days to get my package. The package would have to be returned to Sydney to be re-sent again.

"You seem a little sad, Epic."

"Remember that Sammy said she was sending Nicole's packages to Bundy?"

"I believe I do."

"Well, there it goes, two miles off our port beam."

"Sammy'll just repack and send 'em again, mate."

"Yep, I'll get 'em when I get 'em."

I'm not sure if Tony fell for my indifferent attitude. He didn't mention Nicole or the letters again.

The wind moved us along at a brisk but very manageable pace, not at all like the day before. We were cruising along a desolate stretch of coast of low-lying, sparsely vegetated hillocks. No trace of civilization. Until I thought I saw a shiny flash on the other side of a narrow spit of land.

"Something's over there, Tony, unless I'm just imagining it again."

Tony squinted toward where I pointed. "I don't see anything."

"Keep looking. You can only see it when we are on top of a wave."

"It looks like a tin roof."

"Exactly."

The day was closing and we headed toward it. The closer we got, the more it disappeared, as a short dune formation in the foreground blocked our lowest line of sight. We hadn't gotten a real look at the shininess but I hoped it was houses making up some kind of town. It then appeared there was some type of narrow waterway coming out from the area.

"There, see! Two people walking on the sand?!" I said

They stopped and peered out our way. *Did they see us?* We were still five hundred yards out. We took down the sails and started sprinting to shore to get a clue. The people started walking away.

The small inlet became obvious. We met some resistance as the tide ebbed into us. The people reappeared as we approached the entrance. He had his khakis rolled up to his knees and had a cultured, weathered face.

"Mate, he looks like Ralph Lauren. What the hell is Ralph Lauren doing way out here?"

"Hello, hello. Do you know if there is a town or a place to get some food inside this inlet?"

"No, there isn't. There is only a tiny vacation fishing community."

"Oh, really?"

"Yes, but if you would like a big steak, a shower, and a bed with clean sheets, just head for that shack with the yellow roof on it. That's our place. By the way, did you guys have a little red sail up before?"

"Yeah."

"We were watching it for a quite a time and could never make out exactly what it was. We thought it might be a model sailboat or something. Never seen such a small sail out there before. It just seemed to appear and disappear for the longest while. Then . . . vanished."

"We took it down . . . to paddle."

"Of course, we'll meet you over there, follow the deepest channel. The tide can empty this whole lagoon, so you better hurry."

"We only draft ten inches. We should be okay. See ya there."

The outgoing current increased along with the wind, and the water got shallower creating boat-in-concrete effect. The race to the yellow shack was no longer a race. It would take half an hour to go half a mile. We managed to stay in the channel, made the left by some anchored motorboats, and headed up a few meters past them, as they became grounded. We lined *Southern Cross* in thigh-deep mud till we got to the shack. It was almost dark.

Our hosts were Ian and Rosary Gibson, who made us right at home in Battle Creek. They had a son in New York City training to be a stockbroker. Ian himself was involved in investments in Bundaberg, but went to the shack as often as possible.

In short time the barbie was lit, a few 4X "stubbies" were passed around, and we met the expert mud crabber/neighbor nicknamed Blackie, who brought over some of the famous Bundaberg Blackened Rum special reserve. The rum was in different strengths and qualities. Upon seeing the bottle, Tony said nostalgically:

"I used to get plastered on this stuff at school."

"For me it was Tequila."

Another neighbor came by and joined us for some cool ones. My first real Australian barbie would be one I would not soon forget.

Blackie set back out to his crab pots to see if he could garner a few more mud crabs so as to make the surf-and-turf barbie that much finer. A few "real bewdies" were pulled from their cages. I was surprised at how large they were. I was told "muddies" are a real treat. Blackie looked keen on introducing me to them.

"They can get as big as a car tire."

Awhile later, and we are livin' large in Battle Creek. A perfect steak, some homemade chips, delicious mud crab (better than lobster), good company, and Bundaberg Special Reserve. Smooth, very smooth. We exchanged tales of the sea and drifted to sleep on fine cots with fresh sheets.

I dreamed of Nicole. She was getting dressed to go out on the town in NYC. She was in the bathroom doing some last touch-ups, obviously excited about the night's upcoming events. I was standing by the bathroom door and reaching out to her to make her see me. Then, I decided to leave. I kissed her on the forehead in spectral form and left. She was unaware and continued her primping.

I woke up depressed, like I'd seen the future through a crystal ball. That morning, I wrote her a card and asked Ian to drop it in the post for me.

Rosary whipped up a hearty breakfast and sent us off with some bread and fruit for the road. We gathered *Southern Cross* from her anchorage and prepared to leave. Photos snapped and addresses exchanged hands. It was time to go.

"Good-bye."

"Good on ya!"

"Fair dinkum!"

Well fueled, we hit the sea and sailed our little "model" boat to Round Head and the town of 1770 where the *Bounty* had paid a visit that year. It was the place Captain Cook had landed on his second visit. On the way, we saw some of the Brisbane-to-Gladstone racing yachts motoring their way back south.

The first one, which we passed closely, was the second-place finisher, called *Hammer,* an extremely sleek local favorite. I had read the results in one of Ian's newspapers.

"Youuuuwanna couple of bieeers, mates!" one crewman said.

"Looks like youz could use a few," another added.

The 4X's were flowing freely onboard and they tossed us a couple as we passed by. *What a machine it was,* I thought, *Kevlar this and Mylar that, with a touch of graphite here and spectra 2000 there.* A modern hi-tech sailor, with top speed approaching twenty knots in perfect conditions. Even so, it was faster to use the high-powered auxiliary motor to go south against the prevailing breezes and it saved valuable sailcloth for another battle.

The contrast of *Southern Cross* to *Hammer* was on a par with the contrast between New York City and Battle Creek. *Hammer* had come in second and that, in modern Western tradition, was losing. The crew were drowning their sorrows.

We followed another racer along the channel markers of Round Head into Round Head Bay. Wraparound swell pushed us along on small, well-formed, unbroken rolls of water. Upon reaching the harbor, another smaller yacht and celebrating crew hailed us.

"You lads move that canoe pretty fast."

The yacht was named *Fine Cotton.*

"How did the race go?" I asked

"Very well, we raced in the recreational class and I can speak for all aboard and say we had a ripper of a good time. Why don't you come onboard when we get to dock?"

We tossed back a few stubbies with the captain and crew, whereupon they got into their dinghy and we all paddled to shore. Both boats were pulled above the high-tide line and we regathered for the walk to town. The path was very dark and we all did our share of stumbling, and this was going *to* the pub.

Seventeen Seventy was clearly a one-stop town. The proprietor, Vladimir, and his family operated the pub, store, beer stand, and café. More sea stories were told, more beers were drunk, and eventually we headed back to the boats, with a few more stumbles than before. I could not help but time-warp to 1770 and imagine some of the *Bounty*'s crew sometimes celebrating on land, with some casks reserved for just such an event. I am sure some of our footprints crossed the memory of theirs. *Not much had really changed in two centuries in this town in Round Head Bay.*

Tony and I opted for our cocoons as the *Fine Cotton* crew headed for some final libations on their ship. The mossies were waiting with knife, fork, and extension beaks. While we were in the pub, some scout mossies had gotten the word out. We were exhausted and slept soundly despite the symphony of wings in A minor.

The next morning I got up early to call Nicole.

"Hello, Nicole."

"Hello Eric, how are you?"

"About the same, just putting the distance in each day."

I went on to tell a bit about the sea turtle, the stormy night, and the pizza man to a lot of "umhums" and "ah hahs."

"Have you gotten the packages yet, Eric?" she said impatiently.

"No, they were sent to Bundaberg but we passed it during a holiday."

"I can't believe it. It has been almost a month since I sent them."

"Have you received a bunch of cards, lately?" I asked.

"No, I haven't gotten anything. I hope I get something soon."

"I have sent something from every town I could. I guess Queensland doesn't get the mail stateside as quickly as NSW. You should be getting a bunch of cards soon!"

"I hope so," she said cynically.

"Well, we have to hit the water. I love you, Nicole."

"I love you, too, Eric."

"It will probably be about a week before I call again."

"OK. Good luck. Take care of yourself."

"I will."

"Bye."

"Bye."

Click.

Once again I began the day quietly and Tony picked up on it.

"How did it go?"

"I don't know."

"She was glad to hear from you, right?"

"Yeah, but . . ."

"That's all ya need."

Something was missing, I did not get to say.

We packed up leisurely. We only had to go about twenty miles to Richards Point. The next stop was Gladstone, another twenty miles. Tony was in no hurry to paddle all day and half the night to get to another town. There was little wind. *What's going on? This is supposed to be the beginning of the Great Barrier Reef. Where was it? Where are the glorious tradewinds?* I wondered.

The Great Barrier Reef is 2,000 kilometers in length. It is up to 80 kilometers wide. It is not one giant reef but rather 2,600 separate ones, and at the southern end these reefs start almost 300 kilometers offshore and gradually taper closer to shore as the coast goes on. It is the largest reef system in the world and the biggest structure made by living organisms.

Coral is formed by a small primitive animal, a marine polyp. Some polyps, known as hard corals, form a hard surface by excreting lime. When they die, their skeletons remain and these gradually build up the reef. New polyps grow on their dead predecessors. Coral needs warm, clear, relatively shallow water to grow. The area from Bundaberg to the Torres Straits provides these conditions in abundance.

It was a slow, uneventful day where we eventually got to sail on a light breeze with no exceptional challenge involved. The monotony let me dwell on Nicole.

I wanted to get to Gladstone for a big-town fix. It had been almost two weeks since Brisbane. I needed that personal wandering and pondering space again. I wanted the day's edition of the *Australian* for a good read. I wanted a cappuccino. I wanted to feel connected to more than Tony. I missed Nicole and I knew that wasn't fair to the expedition. I had been trying to avoid relationships like that the whole time before I left New York. I was not supposed to worry about women. Women had been the distraction, the blessing and the curse. The trip was too important to let a woman impede the goal, *wasn't it?*

That evening we camped on a beach near a point that looked just like a Dr. Seuss forest, laden with trees and vegetation that looked familiar from afar but was alien to me upon closer inspection. On the edge of the woods, there were dozens of cows and bulls walking about.

"Is this some special type of Australian farm?"

"No, mate, those are feral animals."

"Feral?"

"Yeah, not indigenous, they are domesticated animals that have gone wild. They are doing a lot of damage in Oz, where they overwhelm other species. Some even blame them for the dust storms getting worse over the years."

"What? How's that?"

"They're eating vegetation like mad."

"What can be done?"

"They're trying to build long fences to keep them out of different parks and grazing lands."

That night we were the butt of a living Gary Larsen cartoon. Upon looking in the other direction or getting into our cocoons, I imagined the whole group of bovines standing on their hind legs and discussing who, what, and why we were there. The theories must have been outstanding, the plans to dishevel our camp, equally so.

"Are these animals going to trample us in the middle of the night?"

"Naw, your smell alone will keep them miles away."

Nevertheless, I thought of one hapless Metropolitan Area Sea Kayakers club member who woke up surrounded by cows within arm's reach on a trip from NYC to Montreal up the Hudson River. Trampled by buffalo is one thing. Stomped by cows is another. The epitaph would never read quite right.

Tony was right. The cows didn't like our smell, but the mossies did. They're not finicky, as far as we're concerned.

"You have more RID, mate?"

"Sure do, Tony. Wait a sec, while I get my ankles."

There I slept, in the land of the cows, with a male icon, surrounded by a RID/sweat/salt musk, in a large Gore-tex sock, with thousands of mosquitoes setting up their blood-drilling rigs on any body part that was available. We had been out forty-two days. Three hundred twenty more nights to go . . . if all went *right*.

I woke up to the sound of cows mooing. The closest one was a mere ten meters away. No time to waste. I wanted to get to Gladstone with plenty of daylight left. I needed to get a letter off to Nicole ASAP.

Gladstone was taking forever to get to in my mind, yet only three hours had elapsed before I saw the massive channel-marker system set up to guide in very large freighter ships coming from the world over. This had the same purpose as the pylons in Urangua but was roughly a hundred times bigger in all dimensions. Gladstone is one of the busiest ports in Australia. The wind died and we paddled some more. Sweat and sun, sweat and sun. I began my periodic hat baths.

I saw dozens of boats in single file coming out from some distant, yet unseen source. I saw some giant, horizon-blocking vessels heading in. These made the Princess Cunard Line megacruisers in New York harbor look like lifeboats.

Gladstone is a very protected harbor with a northern and southern approach. Wind and swell from the east were totally blocked by Curtis Island. In the distance we saw a number of buildings we thought were Gladstone and paddled in file toward them. The buildings were factories. More paddling. More paddling. *Surely those cranes in the distance can't be where we have to go?!*

"This is getting pretty tedious. Do you see any place to land?" Tony asked with a sigh, wiping sweat and salt from my paddle spray out of his eyes.

"There's supposed to be a park someplace but all I see are all these ugly factories, cranes, and whatnot."

The early morning hope of getting to Gladstone was quelled by the depressing antiscenery of industrialism performing its initially impressive but ultimately revolting waltz of megamachinery. Gladstone is a big iron ore distribution center. Massive ore loaders ground, rumbled, and beeped while they loaded. Ore makes steel, and steel still makes the world go round.

Australia uses massive machinery to extract ore from its core and ship it to

Japan, where the Japanese use massive machinery to turn it into steel, which it sells back to Australia as steel or as cars and trucks, making much more money on Australia in the process. If Japan had the ore and had mined as much of it as Australia has, there would be little left of the Japanese isles by now.

I suppose if you've never seen mile after mile of uncluttered open space and sky, you would be unbothered by the process. I don't think that way. I've seen the open prairies of Iowa, the plains of Colorado and Wyoming. I've seen the endless sky from the top of a Colorado mountain. I have driven endless miles in the grandeur of gold in Utah, Arizona, and Nevada. I have seen the mountains touch the sea in Alaska. I have seen millions of acres of red in the Adirondacks in late September. That's why I can't think that way.

Man had really done a number on Gladstone. I have also driven through Gary, Indiana, and Elizabeth, New Jersey, watching flames coming out of refinery vents, turning everything to smoke and fire. Hells on earth. That Gladstone did not seem that bad was the best I could come up with.

We found the beach near a park. A group of curious kids and equally curious moms and dads approached in the guise of nonchalance.

"Can I go in the boat? Can I? Can I???!!"

"Let the men be. They look like they've come a long way and they need to rest."

We rinsed hair, faces, bodies, and clothing in a faucet. We hung up the shorts, rain jackets, T-shirts, and shoes—all of which were salty, sandy, and sweaty. It was a really hot day in Gladstone.

A hundred meters away, we found a bathroom to finish the cleaning we had already started. An hour later, we asked one of the moms how to get to town.

"It's a couple of miles, across a bridge."

The hike felt great in the warm dry sun. We had ventured from a semigreen suburb to the outskirts of working Gladstone. Auto-part supply stores and endless concrete lined the street. Once over a hill, Gladstone congealed into main streets: chemists, milkbars, banks, RSL's, pubs, and the lot.

I found an *Australian* at the newsagent. Tony and I exchanged sections, feasting on the words and the connection to the rest of the world. I needed more personal space. We left, walked around, exchanged small talk, and then I arranged to go my way.

"I gotta take a little walk, Tony."

"Well, I'm going to do a little shopping myself. My wardrobe could use some refreshing."

I took a walk, found a small café and wrote a letter to Nicole.

I let the letter fly unedited, raw and anguished and angry. I felt a bit better as I watched it go into the belly of the mailbox. *The lowest moment of the trip to date.*

"What's up, mate? You don't seem to be too happy about things," Tony said to me later.

"Oh, I don't know Tony . . ."

"Mate, I have to know how you're doing, to see if I can help. After all, we *are* together."

"*I feel like a prisoner, Tony!*"

"What do you mean?"

"I feel like I *have* to do this trip, and I am not sure if I *want* to."

"You don't *have* to do anything."

"Maybe I'm just low today, but I feel like I volunteered for a prison sentence. I'm just not feeling very good about things right now. I feel damned if I do and damned if I don't. It feels like I just substituted one hardship for another."

"Mate, you have to let me know if you don't want to do this trip. I'm rather enjoying it right now and really want to make it all the way around."

In Gladstone it became clear that Tony and I were polar opposites. He had regained a lot of determination since Brisbane, and I had slowly leaked another quart of emotional oil. I suppose much of it had to do with the tribal booster shot he got in Sydney, where caring, loving friends reenergized him with their support.

Meanwhile, I felt very distant from my support group. I hadn't received mail in weeks. Phone calls had been few and far between and the last one had been lukewarm. I felt alone. I was feeling more of an obligation to continue than a desire to. I was going to have to pull out of the downward spiral. We slept restlessly in the park, interrupted throughout the night by town youth with a brick of beer.

More unsettling dreams: High winds blowing cars around my childhood hometown street. The neighbor's car flies toward the living room of my house and nearly hits my parents. I run to the room to warn them. It misses, but puts a car-sized hole in the house. My parents are rather casual about it. I'm the one who's afraid, my car and wallet having been stolen. A former fraternity mate seems like the culprit.

A mossie was in my tent and spurred me to slap myself awake.

Splat. He died.

Too late. I had dozens of mossie welts. *Busy little monster. Ross River syndrome . . . here we come. I am depleted, Tony is energized. I feel guilty and dishonorable. I do need a USA contact fix.* I hoped to talk Tony into staying in Yeppoon or Mackay during a weekday to get my mail, my nourishment, my boost. I saw Tony, at the time, as maniacally driven, when in fact he was simply inspired and enthusiastic about carrying on with the quest as planned. I vowed to shape up.

Come on, Eric, you're better than this, I say to myself, and I start to feel stronger, as if a fog has passed.

We were scheduled to do "the Narrows" on the west side of Curtis Island. I was glad that it was a flatwater day. Curtis Island completely blocked the ocean, the wind, everything, creating a twenty-five-mile estuary. It looked like a perfect crocodile-breeding area and I was half-hoping to see one. I also wanted to do some paddling.

"Come on, mate, slow it down," huffed Tony.

The pace felt great to me. Like the days training on the Hudson. Without wind and waves, I could only hear the *splash . . . splash . . . splash* of the synchronized paddling and feel the flow of *Southern Cross* moving faster and faster. It was my way of pulling out.

An old man with a long pipe leaned out of the cabin of a small wooden crab boat thirty feet to port. The pipe smoke drifted back and joined the bluish white engine smoke while a large, less than astute sidekick stood obediently on the flat, working deck, staring at the cab.

The boat approached and I could see a tattoo on the stub of what had once been an arm. He questioned us cordially with an old salt's grizzled voice.

"Are you blokes all right?! Do you need a tow or something?"

He thought we were completely out of place.

"We're fine, mate, but could you tell us where the tide turns up ahead?"

"About fourteen or fifteen miles up that way."

"Thanks, mate."

"No worries."

As pleasant as the exchange was, we were still glad to have the boat chug away up the narrows. The sidekick looked like he was plotting what to do to us.

The narrows were infamous for a closed society of crab men, not unlike the villages on the eastern shore of the Chesapeake Bay or the Jackson whites in the hills of Appalachia. They are eons away from society. There are stories of inbreeding, fierce territorialism, and suspicion and hostility toward outsiders.

I wonder where these stories get started?

These people were different and odd to us. What were we to them? Bearded, floppy-hatted, multicolored chaps practically attached to an olive green, canvas paddle boat with the equivalent of an Australian Confederate flag glued to the bow deck. Maybe this mutual oddity was the bond? People living on the very ragged fringe of society. The kayak does not offend the sensibilities of any particular group—rich or poor, king or peasant. Instead, it seems to fascinate and intrigue.

We made the turnaround on time, like our one-armed Popeye mate told us. Just before the turnaround a more common "tinny" with two crab men spotted, circled, and greeted us, smiling and wanting to have their picture taken. We obliged and then we had ours taken.

"Do ya like the muddies?"

"Sure do," I said after the Battle Creek barbie experience.

"We'll bring you a few for tea tonight."

And on that blanket statement they motored away at high speed, soon out of sight.

The rest of the day stalled. After twenty miles of pure paddling, my body started a series of prompts trying to get me to stop. A tweak here, a crick there, a hot spot on the back, a torn callous, a friction rash under the arm. All of that in an overheated, slow-headed, dehydrated malaise. All made more noticeable without the distraction of the overt terror we had become accustomed to. An hour later Tony announced.

"They're coming back, Epic!"

Our mutable mud crabbers dropped off five of their lot in a net that we had affixed to our stern deck just next to the kitchen sink. As quickly as they came, they were off to make it to the last couple of their pots before sunset. We kept thinking we could make it out of the narrows, only to round a bend and see more dark green mangrove-choked narrows that went on and on.

Finally, we could see the end, but no beach to land on. It was still all dense mangroves. At first we thought it was just a matter of a little searching. But when we reached the end of the west bank of the narrows, there was still no clearing. We were left with the choice of paddling a mile out to an island or a mile to the other side of the narrows. The sun was almost down.

We headed for the island and found a shoreline of oyster-covered rocks. A veritable D-Day phalanx of fortifications to pass through before getting to the beach of ground rock and shells. Billions of shell fragments. We took out *Southern Cross,* tied her off to a rock, and dredged a narrow channel to the beach by lifting one large stone after another, receiving one oyster cut after the next. We were able to clear most of the rocks, empty the boat as best we could, and carefully ease the kayak through—lifting, stumbling, submerging in mud till she was on land. That was not enough. We had to lift the boat above the high tide mark.

Then came the mossies. More than ever before. *How is that possible?* Tony was inundated.

"AhhhHH!" Slap, Slap.

"Bastards!" Tony added, while doing an impromptu jig.

I could not resist saying, "I'm really glad they seem to like you more."

"Must be the same . . . Slap . . . thing that attracts the sheilas, too, then?"

"Probably is," I reluctantly acknowledged.

We got our torches and scoured the islet for firewood to cook up the crabs. The idea was to make a bed of coals and place the crabs right on top of it so that they cooked in their shells. My torch light went out, but Tony's was bright as day. I replaced the batteries. No effect. *It's the bulb.* The bulbs were in the reserve bag buried deep in the bow of the boat, or was it the stern? I knew I'd brought them. I remembered making sure I got just the right serial number for the Pelican light and not the Maglite. I remembered calculating how many bulbs we would probably go through in the course of up to sixteen months. I had spare bulbs all right . . . just not readily available on a pitch black night during an invasion of mosquitoes.

We managed to start the fire and get the coals burning red hot. We detangled the crabs from their net. Tony knew exactly the spot to grab them to avoid being clawed. It was different from the perfectly served mud crab Blackie and Ian had cooked for us earlier in the trip. We threw one struggling crustacean after the next onto the fire, watching the limbs flinch and the shell change color. A hissing, and what had to be screaming, chimed in above the buzz of the mosquitoes. There were no rum, no chairs, no beer, and no sunset. There was a small ring of red-hot coals broiling mud crabs inside their shells.

The long day of paddling, dredging, gathering, and cooking had made me mud-crab crazy. After finishing the third out of five, I turned to Tony with a psychotic look, strands of crab and pieces of broken shells on my face and fingers.

"Are you sure you don't want any, Tony?"

"No, mate, I don't want any."

Tony was clearly revolted by the whole scene. I pondered briefly on my barbarism and finished off one more crab. *This is what this was supposed to be all about,* I thought. *Living off the sea and land. Eating with fingers, ignoring the dozen mossies on each hand. If this is how its going to be, so be it, bring it to me.*

Any time a situation occurs that is very difficult, dangerous, or unavoidable it often is best to let some of the innate wild person out to handle it. That's what he was there for out on that rock-shell beach, crudely tearing up crabs and eating them after cooking them alive with a gleam in his eye. This was my little way of getting through this journey of physical and psychological pain. *Go ahead— come and get me!* I thought Tony took a half-step back after seeing the gusto I showed in the execution of the mud crabs.

The encounters with the unbelievably wide variance in tides and high winds had taken a lot out of me. But my head was finally getting back into the rigors of our oceaneering trip and a little bit out of my head trip. At least for the moment. *Tomorrow is another day.*

Great Keppel Island to Mackay

I had long looked forward to making it to Great Keppel Island. In NYC, a client named Rufus Albermarle told me about a distant relative, Captain Keppel, who had found the island and the bay. Captain Keppel was a pirate of sorts. Moreover, there was a resort that I had been told not to miss upon getting there.

The morning launch began in hazy skies and with long streaks of breaking waves to our west. My eyes squinted to make out was happening. It took longer than expected to pass the Curtis Island lighthouse and get it lined up behind us to use as a bearing point on our way to an island we could not see. As long as we kept the lighthouse directly at our stern, we had a physical reference point for staying on course for Great Keppel. We lined up and viewed the compass reading. We needed to head almost due north. We had no idea how long the haze would last. If it lasted much longer, we would lose sight of the lighthouse and be in a fog. I didn't like fog much. Tony hadn't experienced it yet.

The lighthouse disappeared.

We were probably halfway between here and there. Fog wasn't normal for this area at this time of year. I had been glad to discover that fog and thunderstorms were not typical of the first two-thirds of the Australian circumnavigation. Thunderstorms became a possibility in southwest Australia and fog became more likely in southeast Australia. *It probably is just a temporary morning haze—it'll burn off,* I hoped.

Sea kayaking protocol says: There are two kinds of fog—sea fog and radiation fog. Radiation fog comes with no wind, and it burns off as the day heats; sea fog can come with strong winds and last for days. All fog is formed the same way: When the air temperature drops to the dew point, water vapor in the air condenses to fog.

I had been stuck in thick sea fog for two days off the coast of Maine with Howard. Few experiences are as initially captivating as life becomes a cloud. However, when the cloud did not lift and it thickened as the wind blew and night turned back into day, I was struck with a blind helplessness. When we chose to escape our captivity, trust of compass and course was paramount. Fear of being hit by every lobster boat, and doubts about where we were continually plagued me.

After intense concentration on the compass for an hour, the haze lifted. A few islets appeared in the foreground and a larger landmass was visible behind them.

"That must be Keppel Island!" I said, relieved.

"Hip, hip horray!" Tony answered, yet there was no wind and the continued paddling on top of weeks of paddling was debilitating. Islets that looked minutes away took an hour to get to. I almost wished the veil of fog had lasted a bit longer so that Keppel Island would have magically appeared right in front of us.

Another islet and another hour. Finally, the last islet and then Great Keppel Island beyond. Tony steered us toward the low-lying islets to the east side of the island, mainly because it was a little closer. No buildings and no ferries heading to or from the island were visible. I was trying to recall where the resort was. I remembered drawing it in a notebook back in Brisbane, but I wasn't getting a clear picture in my mind. I didn't think the island was very big. It doesn't matter when you're at the end of your day's paddle tolerance.

"So where is this resort of yours?" Tony asked skeptically.

"I'm not sure. I'm pretty sure it's on the north side. I have it written down someplace, give me a minute and I'll check."

"Don't bother! If it's on the north side, either direction will get us there at about the same time."

I wasn't going to start another Kangaroo Island tiff, because I didn't think we'd get lost. The resort *is* on the island. *We would eventually get there, yet I was getting a nagging sense it was on the other side.* Tony wanted to go around the east point, thinking that once past it, we could sail on a light northeasterly breeze as the island angled west.

As we crossed from the islet to the island, the wind increased in our faces. It got stronger and stronger. The waves around the point became more confused.

"We're not moving the boat well. We're just not moving the boat well!" Tony shouted.

Once around one point, we saw another point, then another, and another. We briefly tried the sails, but the angle of the wind was not right to move with any speed.

"It's no use, no use at all," Tony said.

Back to the paddles. The sun was going down. Another point, no resort, another point, no resort.

Incensed and fed up, Tony asked, *"Where is this bloody place?!"*

I saw a small roof reflecting this day's last rays of light.

"There's a house, doesn't look much like a resort, though."

"That's where we're going. There will be other resorts."

"I'm sure it can't be much farther."

"We're getting out!"

The sun disappeared as did the roof reflection. Our homing beacon was erased. We just kept paddling and paddling around yet another point. The house was not there. *It's got to be around that next point.* I thought. Tony just kept paddling without a word. We finally went around another point and saw a couple of sailboats moored about a mile in front of us. I looked over my left shoulder and saw the tucked-away, lone house.

"The house is right behind us."

"It's about bloody time!"

There was a quarter-mile section of beach and the house did not look particularly inviting. There was no welcoming committee and I was in no mood to get kicked off the beach. We opted to quietly set up camp. Tony made an extra-thick pasta stew to quell the frustration.

Before I retired I checked my drawing, copied from the Lucas book of Great Keppel. I had an anchor drawn on the largest bay on the northwest corner of the island, just where we were. However, I had drawn a small box representing the resort and it was on the southwest side of the island. We had gone almost seven miles out of the way. Yacht books put more emphasis on safe anchorages than island resorts unless they are one and the same. I remembered the anchorage more vividly than the resort. It cost us two hours of hard "yakka" and even more frayed nerves.

The next morning was taken with no rush. Great Keppel was a scheduled stop and our second overhaul maintenance day. However, I wanted to know where things were, so I volunteered to go to the house and "suss" things out. I didn't know what to expect. *Are these people going to have a shotgun?*

I could hear some chattering in one room right above the modest series of steps.

"Hello, hello, anybody there?" I shouted.

I got to the top of the stairs and saw some faces through the fly's eyes of a window screen. One of them got up and greeted me at the door.

"Good day, why don't you come in. My name is Carl and that is my father Paunch Svendsen."

He was medium height, with sharp features, a refined Australian accent. He seemed mildly surprised and amused by my appearance. I was invited inside, supplied an overview, and immediately shown a detailed map of the island.

"This is where you are."

"Svendsen's Beach. You have your very own beach?"

"Paunch got the land a long time ago."

"So, there is the resort after all."

"Yes, I can take you there by boat if you like. It's twenty minutes away."

"First we've got to overhaul our boat."

It was time for another stem-to-stern cleanup of *Southern Cross* and all the gear. Carl was great in providing water from his rain well. It was a minisilo nestled under the roof that was angled in a way to funnel every drip into it. *Southern Cross* was filled with sand, grit, Mars bar wrappers stuck under the frame, salt, and more. The deck had become a floating flea market of odd things arrayed haphazardly. Six weeks and over a thousand miles with less rest than ourselves. *SC* had been outside in the elements the whole time.

Southern Cross breathed a great sigh of relief when I let the four air nozzles open and let the usually drum-tight skin go limp. Another sigh was heralded when I unclamped the various snap locks and took the frame apart. Klepper kayaks have been on many a long expedition with nearly the same loads, yet this trip was already coming up to par with some of the more intense ones in history. A couple more of the wooden support plates dropped to the sand as I removed the rear half of the frame from its skin. Closer inspection showed a number of these plates loosening up, and I saw I had my work cut out for me this hot and sunny day.

Tony took most of the gear bags to a clearing and started emptying them and cleaning them from the inside out. Besides the heavy-duty Voyageur bags, the rest of our "waterproof" and water-resistant bags had been completely invaded. Mix sand, food, fuel, countless bits and pieces, strands and tangles, and the project looked ever more daunting.

Tony emptied, cleaned, dried, and sorted. I tinkered. First, I reinforced the support plates with a manual drill, stainless steel screws, and some wood epoxy. I also had to reapply a snap lock, which involved filing off the head of a couple of soft rivets with a Leatherman file, punching them out of their hole, using a rock as a hammer, and forming a new head with the same. It didn't take much time to have Paunch and Carl's beach looking like an old-fashioned garage sale with items virtually useless to anyone but ourselves.

Carl had a strained look, as if he were personally being assaulted by this chaos. Paunch busied himself by fixing an old fishing net. *Can these two really be related?* I wondered.

In the midst of all of this, the crews of a couple of sailboats anchored down the beach had paid us a visit. A gracious and curious Asian couple requested our presence for dinner on their boat. We had to put the request on a wait-and-see basis. Then came a gray-bearded, craggy, sinewy, leather-skinned man accompanied by a cheerful, rosy-cheeked, older woman in a billowy fuscia-colored sundress. The man came over. I rose to shake his hand with a modest grip and soon found my hand in a vise.

"Gidday. My name is Dez. This is my wife Dawn."

"That's *Valkyre* over there," he said, pointing to his boat proudly. "What are you mad bastards up to?"

Upon disclosing our travel, Dez added, "You mad bloody bastards. I thought I was the only crazy around here."

This was a wiry older man with a leathery tan from head to toe. He had a strong eagle nose and a fitting pair of shades. His torso and limbs looked like taut, coiled rope. Dez was a man of the sea, but it had not always been that way. He and his wife had owned and operated a large hardware store in the town of Rockhampton. A "big city" for folks up this way. By the time Dez had reached his early fifties, the city was getting the best of them.

"I was shitting blood and she was zapped twice."

This translated into colon cancer and two heart attacks in the span of a few years. The less than auspicious omens had made Dez's dream become reality. Dez sold the business and bought a beautiful thirty-four-foot catamaran to sail the Great Barrier Reef virtually year-round, which he had been doing for twenty years.

Dez was quick to explain the advantages of a multihull over a monohull, especially for the waters in the Barrier Reef. He cited speed, stability in chop, access to more anchorages, very shallow draft for making it over reef systems unpassable by monohulls without appreciable loss of amenities. He invited us onboard, but he understood our need to get our maintenance work finished first. Both couples went back to relax on their yachts.

"Bastards," Dez chuckled as he walked off. "You mad bloody bastards."

A solid six hours of constant work had done the job. Our first rest day was over and it was time to go to the fabled Great Keppel Island resort area and get that beer. There were two ways. A very hilly and windy land trail that would take a couple of hours, or a more direct water route that would take less than half an hour by motor skiff. We were running out of time and Dez took us over. Carl said he would meet us there in a couple of hours.

Dez took us to *Valkyre* first where he offered us some tea and showed us his ride. He was clearly proud of the boat and clearly glad he had made the decision to change his life.

"Yeah, sold the house, sold the business, got the boat. The wife and I keep a PO box for mail and make occasional visits to the doctor but that's it. The rest of the time is on the sea."

He imparted to us some of the wisdom he'd gained from years on the sea. We went to the charts and he lectured us on the next section to come, from Great Keppel to Mackay, two hundred-fifty miles away.

"She can be a real fucking cunt up there, big tides, hitting winds, yeah a real cunt. . . ."

We hadn't thought much about this next area. We'd thought it would be business as usual, but looking closer at the charts along with Dez's commentary showed that it was the most remote and tricky section to that point. There were two large crossings, Shoalwater Bay and Broad Sound, respectively. Moreover there was the Shoalwater Bay Military Training Center, which was off limits to outsiders. I felt confident we could commando land if necessary but it would be best not to have to use their property.

Tides were the second highest in the country in the region approaching Mackay and the velocity of the water coming in and out of these areas had to be calculated accurately, otherwise an entire day's worth of energy could be misspent. Moreover, there was no visible and accessible population to speak of, along with minimal boat traffic, because of the military moratorium. *Things did get shot at and blown up here.*

Dez reluctantly showed us a short cut called Strong Tide Passage or Canoe Passage depending on what was referenced.

"You gotta time that cunt perfectly. Not a minute too late to make it through. The current really flies through there. . . . You gotta go through at slack tide and try to catch the beginning of the ebb when you get into the bay."

Dez made it perfectly clear. Any illusions of an easy cruise were shattered. Expectation reared its dark side. Dez didn't seem like the type to exaggerate conditions to us, but I hoped he did not fully understand the capabilities of *Southern Cross* and the duo of "crazy bastards" at her helm.

We finally got to the resort we'd aimed for two days earlier. The motorized dinghy made it a breeze. Dez revved the engine and the bow rose high.

"Sit in the front. It'll level 'er off and we'll really fucking fly!"

Hey, this type of boat travel is fun, I caught myself thinking. *And fast too!* After rounding the point we saw the beautiful half-moon strip of beach with recreational craft of various shapes and sizes frolicking about or sunning. At the far end of the beach was the resort—a massive, layered, semi-pyramid–like structure with perfectly manicured pathways. Up the beach was the public "resort" for day visitors, yachtsmen with less extravagant, yet comfortable, lodging.

WAPPABURA HAVEN WELCOMES YOU, read the sign, held high and horizontal between two Polynesian totems. Dez let us off and told us to enjoy ourselves. He then winced and mentioned a sore and swollen testicle.

"Yeah, my ball sure is sore today. I suppose I better see the doctor again."

I felt a little deflated upon hearing this. Dez had represented such a "success" story to me. He'd left the city, changed his life, lived in his form of joy, yet some sinister vestige of darkness hadn't completely let go of him. I remember the sun reflecting on the water all around him as he stood in his dinghy preparing to cast off. I silently wished the best for him.

Past the sign was a beautiful complex with signs telling what, where, and how far away the various facilities were. No compass or map required. There was a well-stocked shop and adjacent indoor/outdoor pub and bistro. Upon learning of a live band performance that evening, I felt the tingling of social anticipation. *What would we hear, who would we meet?*

First things first. I had some shirts and shorts to clean and dry, letters to write, journal entries to catch up on, and the like, which easily consumed the rest of the afternoon. By the time we had a chance to hit the beach with the other visitors, it was cooling down and everyone was leaving. I checked to see if the slowest-drying long-sleeve tee was ready to fold.

Although I could appreciate a day or two of slothing it, I could not imagine a week or more of lying about being catered to. Fidgetiness would not allow it. Tony could not dream of it.

"It *is* a beautiful resort, isn't it?" I said.

"It's all a bit over the top, don't you think?"

"Yeah, but the architecture blends in with the landscape. I think they've blended it pretty well."

"Next thing you'll be sellin' time-shares for it, mate."

That night was more than music. It was a weekly bonding ritual with a high percentage of "locals," some yachtsmen, and a few intrepid resortees. Great island food in aluminum foil and big plastic bins. The smells of curry and other spices wafted through the balmy air. The locals were mainly workers for the resort. After a few beers we felt right at home.

Tiki torches lit up the main path of the private resort. The primary hotel structure became tactically lighted with various spotlight combinations. I was more impressed. Someone had thought this resort out very carefully and it did appear like a faceted jewel on the opposite side of the beach. The resort, technically at the same altitude in feet above sea level, had successfully put itself on another stratum. As we peasants and rogues cavorted together in unabashed merriment, the resortees sat at well-attended quiet dinners under the glow of inoffensive lighting and the controlled flame of the tiki torch. Carl was among us and was chatting with a few mates while eyeing and flirting with some of the ladies.

Tony and I treated ourselves to some seconds in the all-you-can-eat affair and added a few more beers to our agenda. Although there were some pleasant introductions and a fair amount of ogling, energy levels started to fall and all three bachelors went back to our encampment on Carl's glorified Honda motor tricycle with trailer. We went for a roller-coaster ride. The backwoods motorcycle trail was the same as the hiking trail. It was far more suitable for hiking—and rugged hiking at that. Carl was competent and knew the trail well, yet he had had his share of beers and something to prove to us.

After some ribbing from Tony about Carl's different girl interests, Carl chimed in some of his philosophy on society: "We are a society dependant on dead animals, fossil fuels, and the combustion engine."

He stated this with the intensity of an advocate for Greenpeace, as we chugged and churned about on his 250-cc motorbike. He elaborated on its relative gasoline efficiency. We labored in first gear up a steep hill till we ground to a halt. Tony and I got off and Carl finished the gradient as we walked just behind. Once on top, Tony resumed his Ben Hur position on the trailer. A certain regalness and odd familiarity accompanied the position.

"Look out for overhangs," Carl said, just before a series of decapitating opportunities arrived.

Seven winding kilometers later we birthed through the trees and saw the glassy reflection of a moonlit sea. We were back . . . alive. That was good. The trip would continue. We thanked Carl and bid him good night. We knew we were leaving the next day, but our goal was modest—Little Keppel Island—about ten miles away.

The next morning, I awoke with a revived enthusiasm and the prospect of a challenge soon ahead. I was beginning to see how I needed a certain level of challenge to sustain my motivation for this long, seemingly endless journey. Tony's words "monotony with underlying terror" played in my mind. One without the other is more devastating psychologically then when combined in a tenuous balance. We took our time to properly assemble and pack *Southern Cross*. It was a good feeling to know every bit and piece had been given the once-over.

Paunch and Carl came down and Dez came by to see the puzzle pieced together. We had met some special people in our short stay and I was now glad not to have found the resort on that first frustrating night. *Everything happens for a reason*, an age-old saying goes.

It took longer than expected to launch. It was midafternoon before we were ready go. Now the "easy" ten-miler had built up some time pressure. We launched, paddled awhile, and set our sails and our course for Little Keppel Island.

It felt good to be on the water knowing we would not be in the boat too long. I believed a short paddling run was important after a couple of days off the water. A short run would feel more like an excursion than a long-distance-defined travail—an expedition sleight-of-hand trick used to ease us back into the thick of things.

Little Keppel soon became visible and appeared close. Hours later we were there just as the sun started to color the earth in golds and oranges.

"There's another island a mile or so farther. I think we should go for it," Tony said.

"*Ohhhkayyy!*" I said, irritated by the change in plan. "I just hope it's got a place to land," I added.

"I can practically see a perfect little beach already," Tony prodded.

We still had some time and there appeared to be another small island just a couple of kilometers farther on so I wasn't going to belabor it. When we got closer to it, we could see a small boat on the far end of the short hundred-meter-long island. I assumed it was a fishing boat and it would be on its way. We landed on the opposite end of the island. To my surprise there was still a slice of daylight left and a nice hill to scramble. There was also a picnic table and a camp grill.

"What did I tell ya, mate, the purrrfeeect little beach!"

I ran up the hill, enjoying the sensation of fast-moving legs and then the reward—the view. The wind at the peak whistled through my eardrums. The view to the north was empty. Nothing but water and the dark silhouette of the shoreline miles away. Moreover, clear skies were giving way to curtains of clouds. The north appeared cold. There were no red carpet and no yellow-brick road. I took fifteen minutes to work out my legs with some plyometrics and some karate kicks. I previewed the next challenge. Tony would take it as it comes, as always.

When I returned to camp, Tony was busy sorting out dinner on the convenient picnic table. The wind was playing the poltergeist role very well, pushing over containers and blowing out the stove. We formed a wind block by arranging our gear bags around the stove.

The other boat and its crew had set up their own camp. A far more involved camp at that. I could see at least a couple of full-sized lanterns and could hear the din of a radio. A motorboat, kerosene lanterns, and radios were not our style.

Tony was a little more put out by it than I and said, "The next thing we're going to see is a bloody fireworks display!"

"I just hope they don't come to visit. I could use a night's sleep without the mossies."

"Yeah, at least the wind is keeping them away. Oh no," I said, as I saw a shadowy form approaching with a large torch. *Maybe he's just going to find a nice place to take a shit,* I hoped. The lantern grew larger and larger and soon was illuminating our whole camp from boat to bivvy sacks.

A cordial voice said, "G'day. I made some cookies and we were wondering if you would like some?"

Cookies? I thought, *from a fisherman?*

Then I got a better look at our benevolent neighbor. He was very clean, very white, very urbane without a smudge on his shirt or an extra wrinkle on his pants.

This is no fisherman.

"Sure, thank you very much."

"We also have a pot of tea and some cake at our camp. Would you like to come over for bit?"

I looked at Tony who looked at me with the head-down resignation of social duty. We were a little weary but not totally knackered. We had a long day in store tomorrow but this was an offer we could not refuse. This chap had been very friendly and might be interested in a little color and perhaps a yarn. We walked back to the camp, cookies rising from hand to mouth.

"The name's Phil and this is Wally."

"Good on ya!" Wally added enthusiastically.

Phil and Wally were from "Rockie" (Rockhampton), had been friends since high school, both had been married for nearly twenty years, with two kids apiece and steady jobs. Wally had more of the chat in him than Phil. He was a radio industry man and was intrigued about our communication "systems."

"You really should have a radio, you know?" Wally implored.

Tony explained the limitations of line-of-sight communications, and I said: "We have hardly seen any boats on the water and we do have an EPIRB."

"I still think you could rig an HF (high-frequency unit). You could communicate thousands of miles. It's what the Flying Doctor Service uses."

Before the late 1920s many people living in remote areas of Australia were dying of curable diseases and accidents but there was no way for them to get to qualified medical attention. In 1912 a Presbyterian reverend named John Flynn built an outback medical station in Oodnadatta. Through the years, advances in airplanes and then a long distance radio invented by Alfred Traeger made the Flying Doctor Service possible. In 1933 the Royal Flying Doctor Service was formed and now has twelve bases scattered throughout Australia to provide top-notch care to remote places. The key was the radio.

"Of course the power source could be a problem, you couldn't put a small generator in your boat, could you?"

"Not a chance."

"Maybe some car batteries connected together might just do it," he said inventively.

"We have problems just keeping our waterproof torches working in the kayak," I said. I went on to explain the attrition of electronics in intimate contact with saltwater.

"I see, I see. Boy, if you could have that kind of radio, though," he pondered.

We learned that landing on Pleasant Island required a permit secured six months in advance from the Australian park commission. We continued to explain our travels to astonished expressions. Wally lit up a pipe to listen to it all.

"That is amazing, I never had my big 'adventure.' Got married. Had two kids. You guys are heroes," Wally said forlornly. Phil nodded halfheartedly, seemingly more content with his draw in life.

"Wally, to me you're the 'heroes.' You are happily married, have healthy kids, have a home, and have maintained an obviously special long-term friendship," Tony said.

"What you have done is as unfathomable and heroic to us as our trip may seem to you guys," I added.

I think this caught them by surprise and it certainly set the stage for more discussions about marriage, family, and worldview philosophy. We all shared a great appreciation for nature, as many Australians do. Europe, America, and Japan were cited as having gone too far. Third World nations were cited for out-of-control population increases. All of which spelled trouble for the planet. I added a little bit about earth changes and how Mother Earth will start doing her spring cleaning if we don't. We felt safe for the time being on this speck of land.

Wally added: "Yes, nature does come with ways of combating these problems. Some say that AIDS is a way to warn us about population control."

I don't know if Phil and Wally would have touched on these questions if we weren't there. I think they were at that comfortably silent stage in their friendship where they validated each other's life choices through familiar actions and easier conversations. Offering us cookies and tea had opened a different can of worms.

Soon enough Phil and Wally would reengage their "normal" lives. Did they view marriage and children as seriously as Tony and I did? Were *we* supposed to? *Had I overcomplicated it all?* It seemed that they both married local sweethearts and had children without ever having peered into Pandora's box . . . figuratively and literally.

"Some people have to try to climb mountains, cross deserts, and circumnavigate continents in kayaks. That's what they're designed to do. Sometimes, that's all they can do," I said.

Phil poured some Bundaberg rum into some nice glasses for a nightcap and then it was back to our camp of relative desolation. We had more searching to do. It had become clear to me that I was a far cry from Phil and Wally and it seemed like ten thousand miles in a kayak was taking me even farther away.

We were off early the next morning under windy and overcast conditions. Our goal was Cape Manifold and with good wind we could make it. Showers pelted us. Twenty knots of wind added to six-foot seas and we galloped north, while keeping Australia steady to our left. By early afternoon, we could see the cape. By late afternoon, we landed in an unvisited cut on the cape's north side. We paddled in through modest surf with a small pod of porpoises and found the high-tide mark a hundred meters inland approaching the cliffs, which cathedraled over this particular fleck of beach.

The wind was not well blocked but rather funneled in and quickly helped the showers chill us down. We used beach debris, including a washed-up milk crate and sea-carved driftwood to create some wind blocks and a stove shelter. *No people tonight. Amen,* I praised. Thirty miles had embedded us in no-man's-land.

An identical day takes us to a much less exposed, much more hospitable-looking beach with a thick growth of vegetation marking its boundary. It was nearly high tide and the distance we had to move the boat was much less. The beach was no more than thirty meters wide and twenty-five meters deep to the vegetation, which was a cliff in its own right. It was downright cozy when the wind had died down. Ahhh . . . the solitude we were looking for. With no towns and no people in the foreseeable future, I happily resigned myself to the provisions we had and the chance to absorb the peace of isolation. It was on this kind of day that I believed our respective wavelengths were closest.

Then the mossies came. This chip of paradise in Pearl Bay sent squadron upon squadron of the thirsty demons our way not unlike the flying monkeys in the *Wizard of Oz*. Although it was a balmy eve, we wore a couple of layers of clothing and had to apply RID periodically. It was so bad I had to break out the mossie headset that my father had made me buy. I reserved this for the worst of times and felt a tinge of guilt when I put it on, akin to putting on a gas mask when your partner doesn't have one.

Tony would slap himself frequently even when no mosquito was around, like a horse perpetually flicking its tail to keep any number of biting nasties away from its private parts.

Tony became completely exasperated when he put one of the few remaining Gaz propane gas cartridges onto the stove. (We converted to this method after Brisbane.) His hands were gloved by mozzies. He started lining up the sharp bottom section of the stove spigot with a receiving indentation on the top of the canister. Tony had done it dozens of times, but the lack of light and the relentlessness of the mosquitoes caused a mishit and gas spewed everywhere.

Tony angrily tossed the can into the sand.

"Fuck it!!!"

We had very few cans left, and I scrambled for the can and tried to direct pressure on the receiver to prevent more gas from being lost. Tony then shook off his cumulative frustration and turned the can into the proper position, allowing for another meal or two to be cooked. It mattered.

That night Tony hopelessly tossed his hot-blooded body around in his ill-fitting bivvy sack and an occasional curse was blurted out as his quest for ventilation with mosquito prevention was thwarted time and again. Tony had tried to sew on his own mosquito netting and create his own head and shoulder foyer like my sack had built in. It had taken him hours. Now the mosquito netting would tangle on a limb and pull the foyer down with it. I would hear the momentary nylon avalanche and then: *"Shit!"*

I proceeded to have an unsettling dream.

I was watching a movie instead of a convoluted series of images. I was instantly ten thousand miles away, and the famous Klepper shop was in its last days of existence on Union Square West in New York.

In the dream, the Klepper shop is abandoned, the sign is gone, some life jackets and some stuffed animals lie on the floor inside the otherwise dark and empty hall. A few pictures cling angularly to the wall. All appears dark, shabby, abandoned, and sad. I have a key but I don't go inside. Instead I go to the park and start to sleep on one of the benches. Before I doze off, I see my Wall Street friend Algis walking on the opposite side of the park in his striking gray suit with smart well-proportioned tie. I don't hail him because in the dream/vision I'm only allowed a few moments on this side before I have to return. As I start to come back I keep thinking I need that life jacket.

I woke up feeling very sad, realizing it was not just a bad dream, but a glimpse of the truth.

Going farther on into real wilderness was bringing on more and more reflections about home and the life and times of NYC. There would be no Klepper shop on Union Square, where I had established many "communities" of people. There was the steady stream of Klepper fanatics that visited from far and wide, as well as very regular regulars. Sure, it got to be a bit much at times but all in all they were good people with many a slice of life to share. I started to miss home. I was also missing my own slice of life—a slice of New York–style pizza.

I felt less than alone. We woke up before the sun and launched by 6:15 A.M. We sprinted toward the mouth of Strong Tide Passage and entered the expected fray. Swirling water licked its chops as we approached. I had a good sense that we were timing it right by the estimations I'd calculated for the tide to be slack, but I could not be sure. There had not been any current tables available for this area. I longed for the Australian version of my *Eldridge* tide table book at home.

The picture that Dez had drawn in my mind was one of uncertainty, if not sea monsters. We paddled hard throughout the channel, not sure if we were going to meet a fate similar to that of the Egyptians in the Red Sea. Everything was going too well, which can be as unnerving as everything going very wrong. The sea is rarely this gracious. At about seven o'clock we saw the end of the tunnel and the beginning of Shoalwater Bay.

"We made it, TB!"

"Good job, mate."

"Chalk it up to Dez."

"You mean the mad bloody bastard back on Keppel?"

"He gave me all the clues."

Upon arriving in Shoalwater Bay, we turned *Southern Cross* north-by-north-west and continued paddling at a more relaxed pace that soon became tedious. Luckily the wind picked up just as a cluster of islands appeared in the distance. Sails were promptly deployed and we started to move out. The breeze was just strong enough, with the help of the ebbing tide, to move us at a "sufficient pace."

Frustration hit when the wind died down. In fact we traveled at a "subsufficient" speed for too long. As the ebbing tide started to slow down and we had not yet crossed Shoalwater Bay, I worried that a flood tide might come in. It was important to cross the bay and not worry too much about overall distance, or so I thought. Around four o'clock, I pointed out a beach due west and slightly farther north.

"It'll probably take forty-five minutes to get there and it will leave us with at least half an hour of daylight today."

I was mentally calculating the fact that the tide had taken us as far as we were going to go. We had gone farther than we expected, more than thirty miles, and although we both wanted to make it to Arthur Point, I figured a few miles short with a little daylight to cook by would do us good. However, Tony had that "point or bust" look on his face.

"I don't get you! We have nearly two hours of daylight to get around the point."

I sighed and shook my head.

"If you're fed up and want to go to the beach, that's fine. Just *tell* me. Don't you have the balls to tell me what you want? I always have to decipher some cryptic code with you! Are you trying to prove you are somebody that you're not?"

I was in no mood to escalate anything. *What was that last comment all about?* After an additional hour the progress slowed dramatically and we landed at a place equidistant between Point Arthur and where I had wanted to go. I wrote in my journal. "Don't talk to Tony much. Lot's of disagreement over things that are not worth it. I feel less than alone. What am I trying to prove by doing this?"

That night I dreamed that Tony had shaved off his Rasputin-like beard and was happy and smiling. This in turn made me happy. When I woke up, I saw he still had the beard. We had gotten a better rest than the night before and started the day with a good morning land breeze.

Denser, colder morning air over land charged toward the comparatively warmer and less dense air over the water. The greater the differentiation, the stronger the wind. It had been a very cool night and the morning breeze picked up strongly as we made it across a small bay west of Arthur Point. Wavelets quickly turned into very steep and choppy three-to-four-foot waves. Galelike gusts punched at our sails randomly, sometimes coming from an opposite direction, yet we sailed over our first five miles quickly.

The west end of Hart Island in Broadwater Sound was our target. We confidently headed across the passage, thinking the tide would be turning in our favor. To our dismay, the first efforts to cross over to Hart Island found us heading northeast. Halfway across the passage, we were facing practically due west and paddling as hard as we could to stand still.

"The current must be moving at over five knots . . . maybe six or more!"

"Come on, mate! *It's right there!*" Tony said.

The current was pushing us backward. We would be lucky to make it to the east side of Hart Island.

"It's no use, we'll never make it to the west side!" I said.

"We have to angle towards the island and ferry-glide over there."

Sea kayaking protocol suggests when confronted with a strong current that cannot be avoided, it is best to either not confront it or to in some way use it to reach a destination. Ferry-gliding is a technique where the bow of the kayak is angled toward a destination instead of directly at it. The kayaker paddles forward and a combination of current and angled boat-paddling glides the boat laterally toward its destination. The stronger the current, the smaller the angle and vice versa.

We pointed *Southern Cross* twenty-five degrees to starboard and paddled full speed forward. As we got much closer to the south shore of the island, we started to make headway, our angle went to forty-five degrees, and finally we were in shallows that cut the current to a negligible speed.

The water was very shallow. Paddling was excruciatingly slow. We were paddling too hard to be frustrated. It was not yet noon, but I knew we had to stop. We were using up too much energy, to no avail.

"We're gonna have to stop here and wait for the tide to switch."

"I know, mate."

Thank God this one is obvious. I am so glad he agrees!

It had been a long time since we had taken a break in the middle of a day. The quest for distance had outweighed pleasure since the Frazer Beach wipeout on Day 3 of the trip. What a treat it was to stop on one of Australia's many sandy beaches, take off all our clothes, and dive into the warm blue-green waters without even a hint of another soul anywhere around.

I broke out the Sea Suds, and we proceeded to clean off a week of sweat, insect repellent, and grime. We cleaned our boating garb in the water and then I just backfloated on the warm buoyancy of the sea. *Finally, the sea as a friend, instead of an antagonist or a fickle host.*

Tony seemed to be enjoying it even more than I, as he swam and dove all about. Once upon a time there was his plan of "pottering" up the coast, keeping Australia on the left, stopping for lunch and the like, instead of the all-day slogs that had become the norm.

"We go from endless point one to endless point two and three and four and five and on and on," he had said recently.

Now there was always a silent clock ticking. It would not be long before we could make headway again. I made some oatmeal, fueled up, and got ready to make more distance.

It took two and a half hours for slack tide to arrive. The chance of crossing the thirty miles across all of Broad Sound during daylight hours was practically nil, yet we had to try. We launched and paddled hard, very hard. Hours later I saw a cluster of islands in the distance. We passed them without missing a beat. Two mesa-shaped islands appeared about five more miles off. An afternoon sea breeze did not materialize.

"I think one of those flattop islands would be a good end point for today."

"We'll just keep paddling and see what happens."

We sprinted toward them. I knew the lights were going out soon and had no idea about the "landability" of the islands. As we got closer to "flattop island" I found *Southern Cross* veering south.

"The tide's coming in again, we've got to get to that island soon."

Tony silently acknowledged and steered toward it, angling some to adjust for our current drift.

We were paddling harder and still losing contact with the island of our choice. We were under the influence of a new moon, which acts to push and pull the oceans of the earth often with greater force than a full moon. On average, tide ranges are 20 percent larger at these times. Broadwater Sound has more than twenty-foot tide variation. That is a tremendous volume of water to be straining through islands. The effect on currents is profound. The faster the tidal current at a location, the shorter the slack period and the quicker the current will turn and accelerate in the opposite direction. The currents graced us the day before and confounded us today.

Flattop Island was a gem. It was a red-rock mesa that was eroding uniformly on its perimeter, producing a red sand beach all around. There was an eagle keeping watch over it all. We camped on what I imagined to be a starter colony for the planet Mars. We quickly set up camp, ate, and retired. Tony mumbled something about a "cunt of current out there." Today was really two days—BHI (before Hart Island) and AHI (after Hart Island). We paddled a total of eight hours but it felt like much more.

"Winds up, mate!"

That meant we had to pack up fast and get the hell out of there, finish the crossing, and try to get out of the grips of Broadwater Sound's hellish tides once and for all. *Even though the tide would be coming in soon, getting to the mainland would give us a chance to use eddy currents close to shore to aid our travels north,* I thought.

It was a bright and beautiful morn with whitecaps all around. We aimed for an islet a mile from the shore bank. The boat heeled hard to the right, and we both instantly arched our bodies left to stabilize it. Although the wind was coming from the south, we opted to sail on a reach straight across and ensure safety from the tide. *Get to shore!* Get to shore! I anagrammed.

A "reach" is generally the fastest point of sail, with the boat practically broadside to the full power of the wind. The reach can also be the most precarious position for kayak sailing, especially as wavelets become waves that dart, duck, dive, and collide with the boat like hungry pushing and pulling hands. It was an exhilarating morning, but I just wanted to get to shore. I had had enough of Nature shaking her giant Etch A Sketch set with us stuck inside.

An hour later *Southern Cross* turned to the north and we proceeded to make good time with the wind for a few more hours. The wind lulled in the early afternoon and we broke out the sticks again. All the paddling of the past few days had conditioned us nicely. The boat was moving well. I spotted a promontory in the distance and asked Tony, who had the chart in front of him.

"Is that Cape Palmerston up there?"

"I think it is indeed."

It looked reachable, barring any surprises.

Hours later we closed in and started to round what we thought was the end of Cape Palmerston, only to find a mile of broken rock necklacing to the east. The tide was very low and crossing through it was precarious. We worked farther and farther out on the chain until we found a small gap just wide and deep enough for *Southern Cross* to sneak through. We then redoubled our distance back toward the point, desperately trying to find deep enough water to keep paddling.

"Someone's on the point!" I yelled.

I saw another human being. The first in five days! He had a fishing rod. No one else was around. We tried to paddle closer. He didn't acknowledge us, so we didn't acknowledge him. *Truce based on mutual solitude*, I figured. We headed toward a beach a mile in the distance. About halfway there we ran out of water. We were stuck. We saw the outline of a "ute" (flatbed truck) on the beach.

We got out of the boat and lined it a couple hundred yards until we could move it no more. We had to wait for the tide. The fisherman continued fishing, seemingly oblivious to our condition. Eventually, the fisherman worked his way toward us, and Tony went to talk to him—Aussie to Aussie. It didn't look like this fellow would take kindly to a "septic-tank Yank" being the source of his broken peace. However, we were certainly weather-beaten enough to relate to any man who looks to the remote for solace.

Tony came back with, "Good news! His name is Phinny, he owns the truck on the beach, and he offered to share a few bricks of beer and some fresh fish and vegetables." Tony added, "He is a *higggg* boy!"

I was almost elated, except we were still stuck in the mud a quarter mile off shore and it was getting dark fast. Yet here was a chance to communicate with the outside world, a chance for some variety in our diet . . . fresh fish and veggies? A chance to have a few beers.

The first rivulets of the incoming tide were forming but it would be a couple of hours before we could float our boat again. Waiting is the worst, so we started carrying our gear to shore. After a couple more trips unloading gear, *Southern Cross* was tenuously buoyant. We still had to wait. Meanwhile Phinny was getting a start on the tucker.

We finally got the boat to the beach and were able to relax with a few beers. Phinny sported a strong stocky body with plenty of reserve calories in his belly. He had medium-long curly hair, a bushy red mustache/goatee combo, and some striking tattoos across his shoulders and back. He was pure Central Casting: the bad-ass biker with a heart of gold. At least as far as we were concerned. Boy, do angels come in different packages.

He described his sister as a green New Ager. I got a sense that he respected her very much and that some of her was rubbing off on him. He had a great laugh and did an outstanding John Belushi imitation. He loved Jimmy Buffet and reminisced about seeing the Beatles in Brisbane many years ago. Life stories come out fast and furious in the wilderness.

Phinny shifted the conversation to politics and drugs.

"I won't do hammer (heroin). I'm paranoid of 'shrooms. Acid is great stuff depending on the setting, attitude, and people you're with."

The beers kept coming and coming. Our original truce of solitude was becoming a détente of decadence, when I heard a voice reach through the crackly radio that had been playing nothing but background music for our party. *"Late breaking news—We have just gotten word that there has been an eruption of race riots in the United States. They are confirmed in Los Angeles, California, and expected in major Eastern cities as well! Details to come."*

"Goddamn it!" I yelled in grief, *"I thought we were over this kind of shit!"*

"Easy, mate," Tony said.

"Nothing has changed in over thirty years! That's bullshit."

"I've always liked the brothers!" Phinney said. "They always had deadly cool style," he added as he went on to explain his weekly encounters with some "brothers" at a common watering hole back in the late 1970s.

"Got to watch those Maoris, though! Big, tough, and mean! You don't want to fight any of them if you can help it."

He was talking about the indigenous peoples of New Zealand, and unlike the very slender Aborigines of Australia, the Maoris were often thick boned, thick necked. Their favorite barroom trick was the head butt, we were told.

"Yeah, that goes for the Torres Strait Islanders. You'll want to look out for them, too."

Nope, nothing has changed, I concluded.

An hour later I walked out to the beach to relieve myself and decided to lie down and watch the stars. In seconds I was sprawled out like a starfish. Tony and the coal miner had me outweighed and outgunned. Phinny took Tony night fishing. Phinny said he was our "mate." He talked about meeting us in Cooktown for some type of Captain Cook spectacle where the who's who show up in wigs of the age and dance like the Aborigines all night long. I knew we probably would never see Phinny again. He saw us off the next morn. The hangover was set for time delay and time release.

I could hear the ghosts of some old-school British mountaineers who viewed the hangover with esteem, feeling that it increased the difficulty of a climb and therefore climbs taken on with hangovers rose higher in the level of difficulty and corresponding accomplishment upon completion.

We left Phinny and Cape Palmerston on a melancholy note. We were heading into more populated areas for a while. The near week-long odyssey in this midcoast wilderness had been vexing but awe-inspiring. Our supplies were running low, our weight was down, and I believed we were both ready for a good read and a pot of tea.

That day we were reprieved by mild wind, which lazily took us the eighteen miles to Sarina, the first town on the coast that *Southern Cross* found in over two hundred fifty miles of travel. As usual, we saw Sarina well before we would have a chance to land.

Melancholy was morphing into impatience. I wanted to enjoy as much of the afternoon as possible. At the beaches of Sarina we were faced with a dilemma that we had not had to worry about for a long time.

"Where do you think we should put the boat, mate?" Tony said, concerned about the humans-en-masse variable again.

I scanned from one end to the other. It was a long beach and yet I could see structures going from one end to the next. There was a tremendous amount of activity on the west side, so I said, "I think we've got to put her at least half a mile away from that mess down there." So, we steered for a spot near a small creek that seemed the most "un-private."

The main beach closest to the heart of town was buzzing with activity, balloons, banners, and the lot. As we got closer we saw what the "buzz" was all about. It was a surf rescue competition without surf. Instead, red-capped blokes in high-powered inflatables zoomed around prepositioned orange cones. Sarina didn't get three-meter surf unless there was a cyclone nearby. It all reminded me of the dirt-track stock-car races in Eldora, Iowa, near my grandfather's farm. The teams had their various vans and trailers with logos and slogans.

At the landing Tony must have sensed a low ebb in my constitution. Could have been the blood starting to replace the alcohol.

"How ya doing, mate?" he said with concern. I had figured out what was gnawing at my core and I let it go. I just couldn't hold it in anymore.

"I am just thinking that we just covered a hell of a lot of mileage in relatively short time and it barely is a drop in the bucket compared with the distance left ahead. I compare the distance we've gone on the map of Australia and it's absurd. I'm also thinking that this is an all-or-nothing proposition. If we don't go all the way around, the trip will be considered a failure. I feel damned if I do and damned if I don't."

Tony put his chin in his hand, pulled the tip of the beard, and said with a penetrating poise, "Mate, you don't have to go on if you don't want to. You've done a tremendous amount already. None of these people back in New York have a clue of what we've done so far, none of them ever will. If there are people who consider you lesser for giving this God's honest try and not going all the way around then those are people you shouldn't have in your life, anyway. The trip is for *you*, Eric. *Not* for them."

"I suppose you're right," I said, but only half-believing.

It was the first time I had seen Tony openly convey that level of respect and admiration for my efforts in the campaign. It felt like sun on my face. Up to now I had no idea if I was accomplishing anything at all, and I often felt like I was alone with an indifferent maniacally driven stranger.

These were the stakes of a goal of this magnitude. I had talked up a big storm back home. I did it partly to inform an interested public, partly to sell more T-shirts, partly to psych myself up, partly to keep a candle burning for the Klepper company, partly for family honor, partly to feel like a big shot in a city full of them.

I had to be in the thick of things before I could realize why this kind of endeavor is universally considered a big deal, even among those who are involved with big deals all the time. New Yorkers are a fickle lot. It is a win-lose scenario. It didn't matter that only a handful of all the people in New York would be where we were now in the same situation. They hadn't said they were going *All the way around Australia in a kayak*! I had.

We put *Southern Cross* in a sparsely populated part of the beach and walked a mile into town. We found the milkbar. We had a number of hours left in the afternoon and the sun was coming through the clouds again. We got a copy of the *Australian*, split up the sections, and started on our first round of feasting.

Both of us made calls back home. He talked to Mum, Caroline, and Dad. I talked to my parents, which felt very good. Dad sounded almost adjusted to the move.

"She says it's bad. Burger King across the street is not the Green Market," he told me of my mother. Dad was keeping busy doing a lot of small things, but the new store was quiet.

"Howard has sent you two masts. You should be getting them soon."

Mom got on the phone and added exuberantly, "Your friend Jeptha is due to have a baby and so is your uncle Richard's wife."

I read someplace that people with babies are healthier. It gives a purpose and a focus to life. I believe it is especially true for moms.

"Radu is going to have another raffle at his gym to raise funds for your trip. He's got a big map of Australia in his gym and is marking your progress with pushpins."

The news sparked me a bit, and I started to look forward to moving on. *I am doing this for myself but there are many others who are vicariously living this through me and I do feel a responsibility to them.*

That night we saw a police car pass a couple of times. Finally it stopped and the officer asked us if we were the owners of a kayak that had been left on the beach.

"Yes. Why?"

"We thought it had washed ashore. Some of the locals have moved it."

Tony and I leaped from our seats and asked where the boat was moved to. The answer was less than clear. The policeman said he would take us to it. Tony jumped in the car; I paid the bill.

I started jogging down the dark street after them. The distance was not that far. We felt it important to waste no time. Plus I feared the worst. I figured those who lifted the boat would not know how to do it and might have broken *Southern Cross*'s back. I started running. The boat was fully loaded and had some water in it as well. It had to weigh in at close to three hundred pounds.

I wandered and darted aimlessly looking for the approximate place we had left the boat and some clue as to where it had been taken. It was very dark and I had no torch. I walked on the beach calling out Tony's name. No reply. I backtracked to the main beach and asked some fellows in the "surf rescue" repair room.

"No idea, mate."

I ran up the beach again and found an incensed Tony.

"They put her on a flatbed trailer and dragged her off the beach across the road. She got a bad tear, I hope you can fix it."

"How bad?!"

"Bad."

Tony hastily walked me to the house with a gait that I had seen in the play *West Side Story*. The driver and house owner came up to us and, under Tony's continued glare, said "Terribly sorry about this. You can camp on my property and I'll provide anything I can to help you with the repairs."

I got to see the wound. A seven-inch tear straight through the multilayered bow-protecting rubbing strake. Straight down to the metal reinforcement I had put on the wooden bow piece before leaving the States. *Sewing, Aquaseal, and patch should do it*, I thought. It would be the next day's project. I was glad to see it was a deep laceration rather than a broken spine, which would have left *Southern Cross* and our expedition paralyzed.

We were grounded the next day and spent the bulk of it repairing, cleaning, and sorting. I took my Speedy Stitcher with waxed linen thread and sewed the wound back together. It took approximately twenty-five stitches. I then turned the skin of *Southern Cross* inside out and Aquasealed and taped the inside.

Finally, a form-fit patch was placed over the area on the outside. Structurally the repair was solid. I was dubious as to how long the outside patch would last and I could see that a replacement of the entire rubber nose cone might have to be done someday. For the moment, we were in business again. I enjoyed doing the surgery on *Southern Cross*. After all, *SC* was nothing but flesh and bones, just like us.

That night we barbied with our temporary landlord and fortified ourselves for the next day's travel. All was forgiven. I thought only of the package from Nicole.

"Are you sure Sammy said it was in Mackay?"

"She sent it express mail and it is definitely there."

"Are you sure?!"

"*Yes!*"

Anticipation danced in my stomach setting it to grumble as I slept next to a slide and set of swings.

We carried the *Southern Cross* Expedition item by item to the launch. The destination was Mackay. Looking at the map, I thought it would be a resort city near the entry to the picture-postcard Whitsunday Island, lying only another fifty miles north.

The day's paddle was uneventful, monotonous, and did not end upon arriving at the point on the chart. As we got closer I saw a large marsh and a river entrance instead of a man-made harbor. Instead the town was set well back a mile or more.

Shhhhshshshshshshshshshshshshshhuuuttttt.

"Shit!" I said.

We ran aground on a river bar almost half a mile from the river entrance. *The tide was still going out! We weren't going to get any help for a very long time. We wouldn't get into town for another six to eight hours if we didn't get in now!*

"A fine jam we got ourselves into!" Tony narrated.

"Look! There's a motorboat going in to the north. There must be deeper water there!" I raised my voice to the gods of the sea: *"All we need is eight inches of water! Is that too much to ask for from an entire ocean?!"*

I had pumped up all four air sponsons to the max to create the flattest, most buoyant surface *Southern Cross* could offer. It had helped. We were able to haul the boat faster with Tony and me alternating between pushing and pulling in knee-to-hip-deep mud.

"Wait a minute, mate. I gotta find my shoe," I said, while groping into the gray/black ooze and finally hauling out a glistening mud cast of a Nike all-terrain shoe. I splooched my foot back in and was pulled backward into the mud by slimy invisible hands hell-bent or making the experience indelible. Tony was not amused as time was fleeting.

"Come on, mate, enough of the antics!"

"I was just trying to put the shoe on!"

We struggled to the river entrance and saw some channel markers. There was not a lot of water to spare. I hoped the tide had finished most of its ebbing. We coasted for a little while down the meandering river, making our way toward and then past the cluster of humanity in the obscure near-distance.

An impurity tainted the sunset—a little haze, a little construction, and the distant hum of rush hour. We aimed for the stream of headlights on a bridge. We stayed in the center of the river and paddled as fast as we could, trying to eye a clue as to where to land once we got under the bridge, but the cloak of night fell quickly.

"Dez had mentioned some camping opposite the town at the north side of the bridge," I said.

We paddled into industrial Mackay, passing one fishing-fleet boat after another docked so far below the high-water mark that tall ladders went up from the boats trying to reach the plankways. Mackay was two stories above us. It was near low tide. The man-made cliffs continued all the way to the bridge. A small park at the edge of town was still twenty feet above us. We had no Batman and Robin grappling hooks. I was tired, Tony was frustrated.

"Where is this alleged camp?!" I looked across the river and saw nothing but dense thickets and mangrove. I pointed toward it.

"Dez said that there was some good camping on the other side of the bridge. Let's go over and check it out."

"Are you sure?!"

"That's what he said."

"OK, whatever Dez says."

We paddled over to the other side of the bridge. It was very dark. We got out of the boats onto a bundle of cement blocks that represented the base of the bridge support. The mass of darkness was comprised of heavily vegetated wetland. *It could disappear during high tide. How far would we have to shuttle SC into this thicketed maze to be tide safe?*

"Mate, this a haven for crocodiles. No way I'm camping in here!"

Saltwater crocodiles (*Crocodylus porosus*) are always described as extremely dangerous. They grow to over twenty-two feet long and can approach a ton in weight. What is more unnerving is their seven-foot girth and enormous tail, capable of snapping small trees. They are very fast when moving in a straight line and like to crush victims in their jaws just enough to "half-kill, bewilder, and tenderize." Then they store you in a shallow mangrove cubbyhole for a later feed.

In Africa they have been known to bring down small rhinos and even challenge elephants. In Oz, they have a penchant for forty-horsepower engines, mangling them and befuddling their owners. Crocs are also stalkers. They will "pattern" the activity of their prey. You go wash your pots and pans at the same spot on the river every day in croc territory and you are asking for a surprise.

The area near Mackay is the start of the crocs' range, which would end some two thousand miles later in northwest Australia. There was a time when the crocs were nearly hunted to extinction but endangered-species legislation was passed and the estimated croc population is now up to seventy thousand.

"Salties" love estuarine environments like Mackay's Pioneer River, which we had passed through, but have been known to live much farther upriver where the saline content is minimal, and they can also be found up to fifty miles offshore in the ocean. It is no stretch to extract the Japanese monster Godzilla from a croc. At over 200 million years old with a seventy-plus-year lifespan we might have to give them the nod over the cockroach for sheer survivability.

"Let's backtrack to the fishing boats. I think I saw a space there," Tony suggested.

We paddled a mile back and came across an apparently active fishing boat. The lights were on and I thought I heard the din of a radio. *Some benevolent chap will invite us on board and ask us to have a great feed on some fresh catch,* I wished.

Southern Cross eased closer. The boat's size, immaculate upkeep, and modern technology surprised me. It was as big as a supertanker harbor tug, the decks were spotless without a hint of fish odor, the machinery was all shiny steel, and radar equipment and antennae rose from the roof. I softened the pirating with a loud shout.

"G'day, g'day, anybody home?!"

"Anybody there?!"

No response. We kayaked all the way around the vessel. *Surely, somebody was "home."* We tied up and boarded the vessel. We walked all around inside, hailing the ghost crew. Nobody was home. I climbed to the roof of the cabin and peered in, saw a tousled cot, heard and saw the radio. Still no one. We climbed two stories farther up to the deck of the compound and walked all around. No one, no one at all anywhere?

We couldn't tie up *Southern Cross* to a fishing boat that could leave at any moment. *What if we hiked to town for some tucker, came back and the* Flying Dutchman *was gone with* Southern Cross? The palpable eeriness made it all too likely. I started to feel unwelcome.

"I think it's time to get out of here," I said. Then I added, "I have a bad feeling about this one."

Next stop on the Mackay late-night harbor ghost tour was the rickety boat berths lying in the darkest shadows. The boats here were not large, immaculate, and high-tech. This was a ragtag fleet that was completely run aground. The keel of a sailboat was fully dug into the muck like a spoon in soft chocky-junky ice cream.

There was one boat berth available in the twenty-boat array. As we approached the dark uninviting slot, we saw the silhouettes of metal scraps, old tires, and odd junk in the berth. A foul stench à la the swamp lands in New Jersey predominated. I had no shoes on. I had opted to take them off so that the one I had dredged up earlier would not contaminate *SC*.

Soon I was going to have to get out in this thick, gooey, smelly, tetanus playground and pull *Southern Cross* up. My first step was more revolting than I thought it would be. The texture and suction of this tepid meringue was unsettling. I gagged.

We walked up a little farther and called out to a flickering light in one of our neighbors' vessels whose keel was the one embedded in this goo. A large, bearded, Viking-like character stuck his body half out the window of the twenty-five-foot wooden sailboat and sweetly bellowed. "Yar awright tonight. The boat that was here pulled out earlier and I don't expect it back."

"Do you think another boat will pull in tonight?" I asked.

"Be a bad bit of luck, wouldn't it?"

I confirmed that the tide rises nearly to the top of the crooked wooden dividers. That meant we had to be mindful of *Southern Cross* rising in a controlled fashion, at least fifteen feet, over the following five hours. We had to climb to the top of the berths, where equally rickety walking planks awaited us like a rope bridge in an old Tarzan film. We had to set up two long lines coming out of the bow and the stern with just the right tension so as not to allow *SC* to drift under something, yet not too tight that she ended up submerged. We finally agreed on a solution, took our bags out to the slanted grassy knoll, changed clothes, and headed toward town. It was ten o'clock on a work night. Prospects for food were looking bleak.

I was a little disturbed at the thought of just leaving *SC* and the gear. This part of town didn't present a sense of abundance but rather a sense of depression, survival, desperation. Our gear—which by then looked like glorified bag-person luggage—could be valuable to someone else.

We walked from the outskirts to the center of town, where we found a small crossroads of commerce and shops quietly asleep. It took a half-hour of earnest sleuthing to find the lone open milkbar and feed on hot-plate food half-wrapped in aluminum foil, amid poorly lit, lusterless surroundings.

"You've got to try the dim sims," Tony said. "They're not even that bad," he added. "Quite tasty," he said as the hard crackle of the fried shell gave way to a short gush of grease erupting from its innards.

I made some mental notes for the post office, bank, and outdoor shop for my next day's walkabout. I stared at the post office, where I was convinced my precious care packages from Nicole, David, and family were waiting. *Tomorrow, tomorrow, tomorrow they would be in my hands!* I could hardly calm myself.

We walked our way back to *SC* like a couple of hobos wandering the gravel shoulders of an old industrial center's railroad tracks to our tilted sleeping location. Tony opted to move his digs to the somewhat less tilted pier planks. I stayed angled on the gravel-and-grass knoll near the dirt access road. I just wanted tomorrow to be here.

I bounded up early the next morn, but it was only seven o'clock and the post didn't open till nine. *How could I possibly wait two more hours?* Tony had had a very poor night's sleep. I was surprised he hadn't rolled into the sea.

"I thought I was gonna go right over the side all night long. I kept waking up."

Tony chatted with our stuck-again neighbors—the tide had come and gone. The bearded giant also had a large tattoo on his shoulder. The man volunteered information on the upcoming events. He mollified some of our doubts about the area north of Cooktown—the place where the main road ends and where Captain Cook ran aground.

"Cape York is bewdy! My favorite part of the whole coast! You gotta make sure to go to Portland Roads."

I retrieved our chart so he could point it out. It was north of the Lockhart River and would save us a big detour to the Aboriginal village with the same name—the only place I saw in the whole five-hundred-mile stretch of coast that resembled a town.

"This way ya won't have to tangle with the Abos."

"Are they a problem? I asked.

"Depends, ya never know."

Nine A.M. was drawing near, and I was getting itchy to move. We hoboed back to town and were just coming out of a breakfast spot when we saw a rugged Toyota truck come to a screeching halt right in front of us. A large bearded fellow jumped out of the truck and headed toward us with prejudice.

"Phinny, how ya doing, mate?" I said, happily surprised.

I watched the stern look and pace of an angered grizzly subside as he got closer and TB reiterated the enthusiastic greeting.

"Phinny, ya ole lout." The look of a roar became a plea of distress.

"You guys haven't seen my wallet, have you?"

"No, Phinny, I haven't. What happened?" Tony said, surprised.

"Until I saw your faces just now, I thought you'd taken it."

We offered him some money, which he declined. He said he would sort it all out but he had to get to it.

"It must of fell out of the cab into the sand."

Phinny parted with us amicably but we felt the lack of total trust. I think he still had an inkling of doubt when he left. So form the scars of unsolved mysteries.

I was off to the post and told Tony I'd meet him at the milkbar.

"Good luck, mate," he said, sensing the importance of this to me.

I honed in on the previous night's coordinates, went in, waited briefly, and asked for parcels under my name. The postmaster rooted about a bit, then came back shaking his head.

Nothing. *Damn.*

How 'bout under Tony's name?

Nothing. I was getting desperate.

Southern Cross Expedition?

Zip. Nada. Nothing.

Not again, not again!?!

Utterly crushed, I limped out of the post office in a daze, like a child whose birthday balloon has just burst. I clung to the hope that the things would arrive in the afternoon delivery.

I returned to the assigned meeting spot hopelessly deflated.

"Call Sammy," said Tony.

"I just talked to her yesterday, Tony. She said she sent it express. It's supposed to be here today and it isn't," I grumbled.

"Call her, anyway. She doesn't make mistakes."

A few minutes later I returned, floating perceptively off the sidewalk.

"What's the good news?" Tony said cheerily.

"The packages were sent Express Courier not mail. They are at the airport for sure."

"Told ya it'd be fine!"

"Thanks! Gotta go!"

One letter from Nicole, one from David, and one from Mom and Dad. A regular grand slam!! I took the cab back to town and resisted tearing all the packages apart like a ten-year-old under the Christmas tree. I waited till I was out of the cab, on the sidewalk, under a modest overhang. It started to rain and I tore them open simultaneously.

There was more! There were extra letters that Sammy had inserted into a separate envelope. I was beside myself, grinning from ear to ear as I bounded from Nicole's letters to the twenty homemade tapes, Sony Walkman, and letter from my Chicago friend David, to the letters and new drytop from Mom and Dad. It was Christmas in May.

Nicole's letter, written a month previously, nourished my heart with the opening, "Hello beautiful . . ."

She would simultaneously explain how she would be getting truly sick from the propositions she would be getting from other men so that she would have an ironclad excuse not to go out with them. This would be followed by a hint of jealousy after meeting an attractive female friend of mine who met her in the laundry room of her apartment building after identifying the *Southern Cross* Expedition T-shirt that she was wearing. "I told her I had one, *too!*"

This diverged to unpleasant day-to-day New York downers like "homeless people who have been systematically burned in the subways and the injustices all around." There was mixed frustration and encouragement for the voyage we were on, hints about coming to Australia to see us, or "I may have to go to Africa to follow my own path." Peter was mentioned again. "He had been running out to get medicine for me when I was nursing a 103-degree fever and sore throat."

Along with a book, she sent me a charm necklace of malachite. Malachite is known for its abilities to calm and soothe the nerves when you encounter crisis situations. "I thought this would be most appropriate for you."

This was a lot of love and emotion to take, but my well was empty and I let it all flow in. Part of it was balanced by my longtime college friend David's more sarcastic humor, showing equal concern: "Don't fuck up this waterproof Walkman because I'm not sending you another one."

He also sent a tape from his and Jeff Martin's kayak voyage to Baja California—quite an adventure in its own right. It was good to hear the old banter and needling slights tossed back and forth.

As always—as was his style—my father's letter was short on emotion but long on facts. "Here is the dry jacket you asked for. Radu and Ralph Diaz are having another raffle to raise money for trip. Howard has sent two more masts. It is busy in shop again. Good luck."

I was numbed by the deluge of love and care. My long-drained battery was recharging. Since the beginning of the trip, I had never felt fully recharged, mentally or physically. I felt much like a deep-cycle battery that can be recharged many times over but can never get quite to the level of the initial power. In fact such batteries gradually start to lose overall power.

I had theorized back in NYC that the trip would add capabilities and generate the additional energy to feed them through experience and the efficiencies that go with that experience. What I was starting to deduce was that we were trying to use a rechargeable flashlight battery for a motorcycle.

I was at my highest charge in months. After a smiley and pleasant evening with Tony that night, I woke up promptly the next morning to call Nicole and tell her how much I loved her and appreciated all the things she'd sent. I felt downright blessed.

I dialed her number.

"Hello."

"Hello, Nicole—I love you!!!"

"Eric?! . . . Oh, hi, you got the package."

"Yes, yes, all of the letters, the charm, the book. Everything is great!!"

"Oh . . . that's great . . . I'm glad. It took long enough. . . ."

"Oh, Nicole, it was the best. It is just what I needed!"

I was as giddy as a child. I was talking a mile a minute.

"You know we really should spread out these phone calls; they are very expensive." Nicole had shifted tacks.

"Nicole . . . what's up?"

"What do you mean?"

"What's up, Nicole. Tell me."

"I knew you would know."

"What, Nicole?"

"Its not like I'm married or anything . . ." Silence. "Oh, now you're upset. That's not good. I did not want to make you upset," she added. "All right. So be it. I just figured we're really good friends and I want it to stay that way. I still love you like before."

"Yeah . . . right. Well, OK."

"Are you all right?!"

"Well, Nicole . . . it's just that I was as high as they come till now. I suppose what goes up must come down. I just didn't expect to come down this far this fast. Well, I've done it before. I just don't really like it that much."

"I knew you would know."

"I gotta go, Nicole."

"Good-bye."

"I love you, Eric."

Click.

I lost a lot of sleep that night.

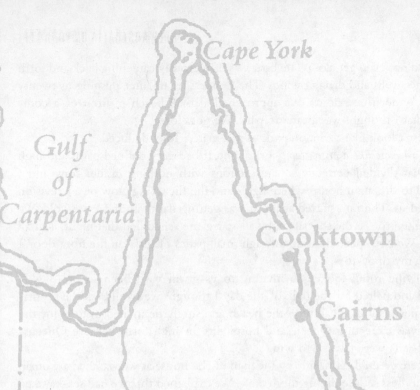

Whitsunday

The next morning we loaded up our boats under threatening skies that were turning into a tempest as we launched and headed out to sea. We paddled straight into the wind for an hour more in a windy fog, out through that maddening switchbacking snake of a river.

After an hour of purgatory, we exited and turned *SC* north, quickly setting sail in twenty-five knots of wind that was coming from the near perfect southeast for a fast sail north. I held on for dear life as *SC* and crew wind-skated across rain-flattened seas. There were sustained thirty-five-knot gusts, which committed us to the sails for as long as the wind blew. I did not have an instant to scratch my nose much less drop the sails.

It rained harder than I have ever imagined. It drummed *SC*'s canvas skin, and Tony's spanking-new, head-to-toe, bright yellow rain gear that he had just purchased in Mackay. I found myself surrounded by bongos, snares, and cymbals, with some mad maestro conducting it all from above.

"Lean right, lean!!!" Tony yelled.

I leaned as far over the right side as I could while holding my control lines just right. *This was what I need!* I thought. The power. This was raw, primal, and perfect for the "purging" of clingy attitudes. *I hoped.*

I saw another sailboat rocking, listing, sail-less, and in moderate distress, and this was more perverse fuel for my soul. She was making a final approach toward Mackay off our starboard bow and there was not a thing we could do for her.

We could not even get close. The boat was dangerously careening back and forth under the swells and driving winds. The tempest let up after pushing us twenty miles in under three hours. We approached a small beach in front of a compound that I thought was a caravan park. We got closer.

"Doesn't look like a caravan park to me, mate," Tony deduced.

It looked more like a prison camp, I thought. It had very defined paths and high fences that divided perfectly square sections with nothing inside. Tony and I marched to the main house, where lights and the flickering glow of a television beckoned us. The rain started again. It was getting dark fast and I was cold. We both wanted to see the special rugby all-star game scheduled that night, if at all possible. We both peered inside through small panes of glass on the front door. I stood on my tippy-toes.

The living room looked so inviting to us given we'd been so thoroughly thrashed and pelted for the bulk of the day. I thought we would ask the proprietor for permission to camp on the beach and surely be invited in to enjoy the game. I was expecting Queensland hospitality in high form because Queensland's all-stars were favored to win.

We were greeted cautiously by the man of the house as we watched a woman in a floral dress set the dining room table. We explained that we had sea-kayaked here from Mackay and needed a place to camp. He talked from the shield of a front door half-open.

"Aw right," he said, in a monotone not offering the camp.

"We thought this was the caravan park shown here on Cape Hillsborough."

"You're on the cape. The park is about a half-hour away by car. You could boat there in a couple hours, I imagine."

"Our boat is on the beach over there and we were wondering if we could camp the night there?" Tony asked while starting to stew in a cold soup of disinterest.

"Yeah, it's OK, but you'll wanna move yar boat. Crocs been known to be where it is now. Move it up to the clearing near the fence at the top of the stairs."

"Thanks."

We could hear the cheering of the crowd as the commentators for the game just came on the TV.

"You gonna watch the game tonight?!" I said hopefully. The man summoned a smirk of smile and said: "Sure am."

"Go Queensland," I said.

"Right," he said, while closing the door.

The door shut, extinguishing the glow and sound of the all-star game.

Tony and I both shared wide-mouthed expressions of rude surprise.

"I think we have just been dissed big time," I said.

My gloom deepened. That night I tortured myself with "our SEAL tape cassette," which I had given Nicole. She in turn had sent another copy to me. I read and reread the "good" letters, trying to decipher in her words signs of the early cracks.

An hour of masochism later, I switched to my friends' "live from Baja" tape of their recent sea-kayak adventure. Hearing Dave and Jeff's synopsis of events along with respective interviews was heartening. Dave's comment about "packing being an art form and I'm sure you must be a master by now" was perfectly on target. Like in college and while living together in NYC after school, he had always been there to take the edge off at just the right time. *I am a lucky man to have such a guide to help keep my head on straight.* I slept better realizing that.

I woke up remembering what a beautiful, long-legged femme fatale French woman had told me: "Eric, lovers cannot be friends." I wish this had all gone away overnight, but it was festering, simmering, and blowing into my consciousness every chance it could. *I am alone with it. I cannot hold the sail better or paddle harder to make the distance and pain that goes with it evaporate*, I realized.

The winds started early and had us actively manning our battle stations from the get-go. They steadily increased and built up as we set out to cross the Hillsborough Channel and Repulse Bay on the way toward Cape Conway over thirty-five miles away. If we reached Cape Conway today we could pass through the door to the legendary Whitsunday Islands tomorrow, the special piece of Australian coast I had mentioned to Tony on the first day we met. Somehow, that idea had lost some of its charm as an incessantly surging wind kept me counterbalancing and readjusting sail tension. *Have we finally gotten into the tradewinds?* I wondered.

The trade winds—a sailor's delight when they are with you. Twenty-five-knot winds for from many hours to days on end. They were certainly a blessing to a three-hundred-foot sailboat of yesteryear going back to Indonesia for a spice run. I was finding out firsthand that there's a significant difference for a seventeen-foot kayak.

These prevailing seasonal offshore winds that connect the dots from pressure system to pressure system amounted to water highway shortcuts for sailing mariners. They gradually became better charted and easier to predict. In some years they start earlier or later and can be found in wider or narrower bands, yet they inevitably occur in certain regions of the world in certain seasons. Trade winds are based on the tilt of the earth and its effects on land, sea, and air temperature, which in turn effect the lining up of pressure systems and the resultant wind through them.

There was no time to do anything but hold onto our sails, constantly tune the rudder, and lean our bodies toward the waves, while they buffeted our flanks in one instance and then tipped us over and onto the short but steep valleys on the other side. This bob and weave had been thrilling at first . . . then trying . . . and then tedious.

The sea started to change its patterns and started lumping parts of waves onto other parts of waves as if to purposely test our reflexes. Tedium switched back to excitement and then back to a more concerted tedium. Conditions were deteriorating, the winds were getting stronger.

The Hillsborough Channel was stacked with peaking, spitting, and drooling whitecaps. We were dead center in the middle of it and at least five miles from any point of land. The wind howled, and sailcloth, hat brims, and rain jackets reverberated like a sudden flat tire on the freeway. It was two o'clock and it felt like I had been tightrope walking for six hours. We had blown off breakfast to make the most of the wind, and there had been no time for water or snacks.

Capsize.

It all happened in the blink of an eye. Our total margin for error. The very first capsize way out at sea. The magic spell was over. *Southern Cross* had thrown us off after all. *Will the rejections never cease?* My hair was barely wet. Tony was next to me looking at me as if thinking, *I thought Kleppers don't capsize out here.*

"Mate, now what do we do?"

"Same as."

"Just gotta make sure we both pull back hard so the water spills off the sails underwater!"

It worked, and we easily jumped back in, but my sail was awry and I spent ten minutes trying to unravel it from its tenacious hold on the mast as thousands of windborne poltergeists worked in concert to keep it there.

Meanwhile, Tony pumped out the seventy-five gallons of water sloshing about in *Southern Cross* and regathered his errant sail from its own pranksters. Mercifully, the relatively short four-foot waves did not manage to refill *SC* like the surf did during the shoreline capsizes. This seemed to be our only saving grace for the moment.

Ten minutes later, we were alert and involuntarily refreshed. I was sailing by the skin of my teeth. I held my jib sheet in my mouth while keeping my paddle firmly gripped in both hands. I wanted to rewrap it to the throat of the paddle, where shaft meets blade, to re-form my paddle-boom configuration. Just as I thought there was a lull in which to complete the ten-second task, the wind would gust and the boat rock. It took a quarter-hour before I houdinied the knot.

The huge shoulders of Cape Conway finally got closer after three more hours of this humiliating sail-a-thon. We closed the gap and I saw a very steep shoreline with trees and rocks meeting the water's edge. The whole southern side was a large NO VACANCY sign. We proceeded to sail around the cape, buffeted by the associated turbulence of an irresistible force meeting an immovable object. I squinted my eyes to see some place to land. At this point, I would sleep on a rock.

A tiny gray break in an otherwise dark green canvas appeared as we rounded the cape's right shoulder. *Was it . . . ? Could it . . . ? It's got to be . . . ?!* We started our descent from a half-mile or so out and waited for some kind of optical confirmation. Meanwhile, the sun tugged its previously bright sheets toward the other end of the globe. The broad, steep cape finished it off. A gray clearing was now a dark gray clearing. We paddled harder with a hope we weren't ready to resign.

We got to the base of a steep incline of stones leading to a narrow, flat section of stones leading straight into dense forest. This dense forest rose and then was parted by a vast V-shaped gully. *Man does not frequent this place.* There was the *hissshhhhhhhh, tsssssssssss* sound of the sea meeting a multipebble sifter. The spaces between the stones swallowed half, then spit out the rest in hissing harmony.

"I guess this is our first bivouac, huh, Tony?"

"More like the Ritz, don't you think?"

The ten-foot-by-ten-foot pebble ledge would have to do. We half-emptied *SC* to make her light enough to pull up the incline. We made camp, rummaged at the edge of the forest for firewood, and ran into a tarantula imitating a Humm-Vee scrambling up the slope. We ate our one-pot concoction and slept away the rest of our leave on a speck of terra firma. We were just a few miles from one of the most popular sections of Australia's coast and had not seen a soul.

Next day, we "toured" the Whitsunday Passage in a fifteen-knot steady breeze. North of Cape Conway we saw many neatly tucked white-sand beaches punctuating a less imposing yet hilly and lush terrain. Captain Cook had passed through this region on June 3, 1770, which he thought was June 2 and "Whit Sunday" back in England, but his meticulous records had not addressed crossing the international date line.

His journal reads:

One long fair afternoon, that of 3 June, was spent steering through the Whitsunday Passage, between the Cumberland Islands and the main, in deep water, with pleasant bays and coves on either side, hills valleys woods and green levels. On a beach were seen two men with an out-rigger canoe, very different from the crude bark contrivances further south.

The white-sand pockets nestled at the base of the hilly islands were ideal for mooring and getting out of harm's way. The Whitsunday Islands are not technically part of the Barrier Reef, which is still sixty miles farther east. They are the tips of continental mountains now covered by the sea.

"There's all the sailboats you've been lookin' for, Epic. Brilliant," he said, as I pulled out the camera.

"Smile, TB." He did me one better and stuck out a high thumbs-up. "Now you see why I suggested the Whitsundays to you in the first place."

"What, mate?"

"Never mind."

To starboard we saw a dozen or more cruising yachts in various states of migration and anchorages in the coves. These were glorious cruising grounds that "yachties" could spend weeks or months exploring. We were doing the one-day fly-by in our self-imposed race with the clock and quest for distance. The day was drawing to a close. I assumed Tony had the same agenda as I did of getting to the popular vacation town of Airlie Beach. We started rounding Pioneer Point and I sensed we were not starting the left turn that would eventually get us to town.

"I know you're going to hate this, but I think we've got to take advantage of this wind and make more distance."

"*What?* Airlie Beach is supposed to be great. I've been lookin' forward to it," I said.

I also wanted to get a letter off to Nicole to magically save the relationship somehow before the post closed. I thought to myself: *You and your skinny little ass better get to a town.*

Snap!!!!

Our boat was hit by a freak wind that had originated from somewhere atop the heights of the point. The force was so strong and so quick that it had snapped our second wooden garden hoe mast cleanly in half without even shaking the boat.

These types of winds called williwaws are common in Patagonia but not in this part of Oz. They usually involve temperature-related air pressure changes atop colder peaks that convert into funneled streams of air and follow the contour of the elevation to the sea and then skim across the water's surface at unusual speed. The snapped mast was my answer to Tony's impending request to go farther.

"We're going to have to go in and fix the mast again." I said. "It broke in the middle. I think I can cuff it with a spare paddle sleeve I brought." Tony nodded his head front and back with disbelief.

To Airlie we went. *Thank you Merlin,* I thought.

We paddled the two miles out of our way, as Tony begrudgingly acquiesced to a higher power against a steady head wind. In an hour we were among dozens and dozens of masts. We neared the epicenter of pleasant activities ranging from sunset barbies to back-deck diving. A few heads turned to and watched the demasted *Southern Cross* lumber into town. We pulled up on the beach and I had that space alien feeling again.

I wanted to immediately run into town to take care of lost love business but a wave of expedition responsibility swept over me. We needed the mast to sail the continuing trade winds. Before we met landfall I had been thinking how I could do the fix without having to go to a third garden hoe or radically shorten the existing mast. The break was a diagonal severance rather than a straight cut. That was good!

If I could find a way of bracing the break we could have a workable mast by the next day. I had a gut feeling that I had what we needed in the spare parts bag.

I certainly hoped we did after all the time I'd spent preparing for troubleshooting this type of scenario.

I climbed into the boat looking like Winnie-the-Pooh caught in a honey tree. I pulled out the emergency spare parts, aka build-an-entire-boat-from-scratch repair kit. I opened it with zeal and *voilà!*—an eight-inch-long, tubular, chrome-plated brass paddle sleeve. This was used for old-style Klepper wooden paddles to join two halves. I thought it might instantly fit on the break, like a preformed whiplash neck brace, and I would soon be off to get a cappuccino. I told Tony I had the repair under control and to go and relax.

"Are you sure, mate?"

"Absolutely!"

I hadn't counted on a quarter-inch diameter difference. Close, but not a Cinderella fit by anyone's count. Pi tells us that small differences in diameter make big differences in circumference. I took out the now-less-than-new multitask-capable Leatherman tool. It was jammed.

"Tony," I yelled after him. "I need your Swiss army knife."

I used the thick screwdriver feature to open the Leatherman tool. I then used the Leatherman's more robust knife blade and carved, whittled, shaved, scraped, scratched, and tore the excess diameter away. I carved with John Henry vigor because—*goddamn it!*—I was going to see the town, send a letter, and have a cappuccino.

The process was more arduous, time-consuming, and precise than I had expected. The more time and effort I invested, the more important it became to me that the repair work be better than just a Band-Aid. I obsessed on the fix.

After an hour Tony came by and said.

"I think I can take it from here on in, Epic."

Tony's calmer, detached attitude made his carving more efficient. Ecstatic with a job well done and renewed in a sense of teamwork I set off and found the perfect little corner café. *First the letter. It's getting late!* The cappuccino livened my mind.

As I sat in my bar-stool-style seat, I watched all the young, blond, khakied, and sandaled wayfarers out the window. They had that tanned, over-rosy glow of youthful adventure. The world was still their oyster and I'm sure they thought they were immortal. I imagined what it would've been like if I'd been out there, postcollege, with a backpack, meandering from one youth hostel to the next, meeting countless other twenty-year-olds from around the world. A quick look at my clothes and a shake of my hair reminded me of our pact with the sea. Salt and sand shellacked me. The "bed" of a youth hostel was not my reality.

As the two hundred milligrams of caffeine finally coursed through the capillaries of my brain, I came to and wrote the "I'm there for you . . . save a date for me . . . when I come back, everything will be great . . ." denial letter. I sprinkled it with a few mutually familiar song lyrics and some type of fated-by-the-stars destiny stuff and thought these few minutes of scribe really would make it all "like it was." I used one of the prestamped Australian letter envelopes called aerogrammes—the kind that every American who gets one for the first time opens like a normal letter, ripping four or five key sentences apart.

After dropping the letter in the international slot at the post, I sidetracked through town scouting out a place where tucker, carousing, flirting, and nightlife coexisted.

Back at the boat, I barged in on Tony's conversation with a leggy girl to announce my find.

"Tucker. Beer. Sheilas. Music."

Tony was subdued, clearly enjoying the beautiful blonde paying attention to him. I told him we had twenty minutes. The young lady had to catch a yacht that was leaving in the next hour or so.

I retreated and let the two naturally disembark. Internally, I paced, wanting this down-to-the-minute day to work out just right once again.

Somewhere in all the eating and drinking, my hunting instincts perked up. With so many young women around, I wanted to boost my ego. Especially after my last dive off the pedestal. The beers and earlier accomplishments had me thinking that a nearby table of Englishwomen was keen on us. Then the only other facial-haired man in the place came up and boisterously joined us. He assumed a facial-hair bond and exclaimed at the top of his lungs:

"Party on feral men!!"

Tony found this hilarious as I sat dumbfounded, not making the immediate association between "feral" (untamed) and "men" (meaning us). *We* were the feral men. The chances of the table of Englishwomen associating with us were not calculable. My daydream of being fresh out of college and comingling safari babes was just that—a dream that I should have left at the café.

Tony and I were feral men. We were not tourists, or warm-up-team adventurers. We were becoming more and more creatures on the fringe. You could see it in us from head to foot. It's always the eyes that show where the soul is going. Our eyes had changed, our souls were changing. We were living ghosts among gregarious, fun-loving world hoppers. We did not appear squeaky clean. We weren't wearing Doc Martens or any other style symbol. I think Tony knew and wanted this while I was still kicking at imaginary bouncers who were kicking me out of the club.

The next morning, we picked up the newspaper at the most complete newsagent I had seen so far. Newsagents kept all the world hoppers in connection with the world while away from home. I was once again struck by the all-too-familiar faces on the covers of the magazines. JFK Jr., Cindy Crawford, Kelly and Calvin Klein. I think those reminders kept me more attached to civilization than Tony. He didn't browse much in the newsagent.

"Lets go, mate."

"One second, Tony."

We packed the boat. A group of fellows came to help us launch. There was a guy from England who had watched us land the night before and had the savvy not to approach us at that time, knowing the difference between an empty gas tank and a full one.

"Saw you chaps pull in last night. You looked knackered."

There was the water-sport manager, Malcolm, of the particular beach we had landed on, taking a look at a water craft he had never seen before. And Martin, a younger man, very excited, said that he had seen us launch from Laurieton two months earlier.

"I'm going around Oz on a motorbike," he added.

I felt pretty good that we were pacing a motorbike. However, I'm sure he was smelling the roses a bit more frequently than we were. Finally, there was a lanky sailor type attracted to the adventurous feel of it all. *Southern Cross* had long accepted its role as feral kayak, having not been ostentatious to begin with in its drab olive clothing. The four chaps helped us haul *Southern Cross* forty meters to the water and shove off.

We paddled an hour or so past Pioneer Point and soon had a modest breeze in our favor. We had recently been spoiled by the wind, and although it was light, neither one of us complained or suggested paddling. I took the opportunity to read a section of the *Australian* while the Lozano control panel held on to the breeze. I opened it up to the Ostrow column, written by a NYC ex-pat, a Jewish woman of insight who on that particular day conveyed her pity for men because of "the confusing roles they encountered, expected to be both sensitive-nurturing, yet manly and providing. Men can't seem to do anything right." *Yeah . . . I know.*

A bit later, Tony started a tiff about going into towns.

"What's with you and going into towns, mate? You know we've got distance to cover. We still had a few hours yesterday."

"The mast broke. We had to fix it."

"We didn't have to fix it in *town*."

"It looked like you were having a pretty good time in town. Listen, I wanted to get a letter off to Nicole to see if I could save the relationship thing. Unlike your women, who will seem to wait for you till hell freezes over, mine flew the coop in two months."

"Why didn't you say so?"

"I don't know. Anyway, my father says Howard sent two brand-new masts. I don't know if this repair can handle any big blows."

"Plus, real soon we're not going to be anywhere near any goddamned towns."

We were coming to our two-month expedition anniversary together. We were approaching the fifteen-hundred-mile mark. We were averaging a little over twenty-five miles a day. More than thirty a day if you took water time only, but it *does not work that way*! We were just starting to get into the trade winds. Hundreds of miles past "Rockie" (Rockhampton), where Al Bakker had said they would begin.

I then tried to focus the conversation on water supply and logistics for that more remote future. The conversation died and the rest of the day was spent in pensive silence. Such a shame, because nature was keeping its bargain with beautiful sights left and right. Boats sailed against mountain-to-water backdrops. Lush green vegetation blanketed the scene. Yes, there was a good reason I had been keenly awaiting the Whitsundays after all. Alas, we were sailing out of them, and turning the corner west-northwest at George Point, pushing us out of view once and for all.

I had looked at the chart that showed a place called Dingo Beach on the other side of George Point, a logical place to stop before slipping past Gloucester Island for another long crossing. However, just as we passed the point we saw a small island that was calling our name. A glance at the chart listed it as Manta Ray Island. Moreover, the wind and sea had calmed, and the setting sun was rolling out an orange carpet. We rolled up to the tiny, completely isolated beach.

"I like having my own island better than the towns, TB."

"I'm glad."

We pulled *SC* up past the line of washed-up vegetation. It was evident high tide had just been there and was slowly receding, as the biggest wavelets barely touched the still-wet vegetation. *Southern Cross* crackled into the dead coral and shell beach. We pulled her up another ten yards or so for good measure, as the highest tides had been in the evenings. Without a cloud in the sky, a mere wisp of a wind, and our camp twenty yards from the boat, we couldn't have felt more secure about our situation. As night enveloped us, we could see a half-dome of diffused light through the gap between the southern end of Gloucester Island and the mainland.

"Those must be the lights of Bowen," I said.

"Another town, Eric?"

"Don't worry, Tony, it's not on the coast."

As the last little spatter of attitude fizzled in the eve, we both turned to enjoying the magnificent solitude of our very own little island.

I awoke by the earliest morning light to check out our handiwork and appreciate a morning without launch anxiety. I had done a niggling repair on a loose rubber flap on the bottom of the boat the evening before, and Tony had bolstered the mast repair, which had held for the day but didn't appear to have long legs. It was going to be almost five hundred miles before we would pick up the new mast in Cairns.

I walked automatically toward *Southern Cross,* which was positioned directly in front of the entrance to my bivvy sack or so I thought.

As I approached the spot where I thought the boat was, I was struck with a wave of disorientation. *What was wrong with this picture?* I rubbed my eyes, which traced the path from where I stood to where we had approached from and landed the night before. I scanned left and right. The beach looked smaller in the daylight.

Hmmm . . . the beach is smaller.

My stomach dropped. I quickly calmed down when I remembered that evening tides are higher than morning tides. I told myself not to worry.

Yeah, but where's the boat?! Ahhhh, of course . . . Australian humor . . . just to put me in my place for the tiffs we've been having.

"Tony, where's the boat?!" I called out in a you-got-me-this-time voice.

"What, mate?" mumbled Tony from his blue cocoon.

"Where's the boat?"

Tony poked out his head, "What do you mean, mate?!"

Tony came to the spot where the boat had been and proceeded to do a similar rundown of events. Scanning left, scanning right. Taking a step here and a step here.

"Tony, where do you think the boat is?!"

Then I saw the terror in his eyes, and the third, unstoppable wave of angst rose up about the same time the sun did over the rocky shore to the east. It wasn't looking good. There were only twenty yards of beach to the west and if the tide had come in from east to west, *Southern Cross* was surely gone. We both peered out to sea in all directions and saw nothing. We started running barefoot as fast as we could over the rocks toward the sun, toward the last stretch of land *Southern Cross* could be on. It was our last gasp.

We ran and ran. Nothing! *This can't be!* We ran toward the last cluster of rocks before the end of the beach. I hoped I saw something wallowing precipitously. It looked like another rock but it was moving . . . or was it just my eyes trying to assuage my fear. I ran faster. I felt the nail tear off my big toe.

Yesssss!! There she is!

"She's right here!"

Southern Cross had not abandoned us. She had resisted the ocean's temptations, gripping the last rock between the sea and us. The sun lifted off the horizon and I was temporarily reborn!

Joy was short-lived as the gravity of the situation dawned through the shimmering vital signs. Just about everything we had was in the boat. This was more than usual because we had used the boat more like a closet that particular night because of its proximity to our camp. We had taken the opportunity to leave almost everything, including water, food, extra clothing, and the EPIRB inside to make for an easy launch. So we were silently pickpocketed by some of Neptune's pranksters only to be reprieved by something looking over our own shoulders. I rarely rose as early as I did that day. I am glad that I did.

The mutual realization of our folly, stupidity, lack of protocol, and the potential results—the best of which would have been ending the trip then and there, and the worst of which we didn't want to think about—showed me we were naked without *Southern Cross,* and *that* realization was discomforting. We did not have more than a quart or two of water. That means we would not have had much time. We would have been at the mercy of a passing ship or plane that would have to see some type of distress signal that would have been tough to produce from this barren coral shell island. We had even put the cooking gear back in the boat. Moreover, we were at the end of the cruising season and off the beaten path.

Tony proceeded to berate me for taking a couple of pictures of Gloucester Island, looming in the distance.

"Mate, why are you taking a picture of nothing?!"

"Tony, it's the landmark to recall today's events."

"You're always wasting film. If you take a picture, you should take a picture of something meaningful."

"What do you mean by wasting *film? We haven't taken anywhere near enough pictures for the two months we've been out here."*

"You're always taking pictures of nothing!"

"Tony, I have taken maybe eight or ten rolls of film at the most and purchased most of them myself."

"Wasting money that could be spent for other things."

"Fuck you, Tony!"

"Fuck you, too!"

We solemnly packed the rest of our gear into *Southern Cross* and headed off through the Gloucester Island gap. The sea was gracious today and provided a steady twelve-knot wind and three-foot seas. We methodically sailed in open, featureless water once again. Somehow, the clear green water had mottled, and the lush sights we had feasted our eyes on for two days were gone.

After half a day, the outline of an appendage stretching out from Abbot Point became visible. I wasn't sure what it was, so it became a curious carrot at the end of an imaginary stick. *Like we needed a mystery to keep some level of intrigue up.* I chose not to worry about it.

At one point, *Southern Cross* had found such a nice steady groove that I was able to start reading a thick book that I had been kicking around since Brisbane. *The Great Circle* was about an international yacht race around the world, based closely on the Whitbred Cup. I knocked off a good seventy-five pages and felt a special presence from the writing, a necessary inspiration to shake the recent doldrums.

Racing sailboats had intrigued me ever since the 1983 America's Cup, when David and I watched the breathtaking shapes of Dennis Connor's two training boats leave Newport Harbor from the seats of our kayaks. The twelve-meter yachts that are used in the race have to comply with a complicated series of dimensional formulas, yet designers maximize them to squeeze that crucial half-knot out of a vessel.

The Great Circle set up an interesting drama between a maverick, hell's bells Australian, a steady-as-she-goes Englishman, a chance-of-a-lifetime regular-guy American from Maine sailing for an exceptionally pretentious East Coast yacht club, and an ultra-high-tech California boat with a celebrity cocaptain. It also included a daring and competent women's team. All in all, just the right yarns to key me in to our trip again.

The book engrossed me for the next couple of hours, until I looked up and saw more clearly the carrot at the end of the stick. It now appeared to be a long dinosaur tail extending off of Abbot Point. It looked like some very long bridge someone had started to build to go to New Zealand but then abandoned out of futility.

We paddled a mile past this middle-of-nowhere mechanical travesty and found a nicely tucked-away beach. There was still some daylight left, so I went to explore a clearing beyond the beach vegetation where I saw some kangaroos bounding about. My face cracked a smile. It had been awhile and the sensation felt new. I sadly realized that I hadn't been smiling much.

The throb of the missing toenail interrupted the moment, reminding me to tend to it and my bruised feet from this morning's rock sprint. I don't know how many times I've heard of some nick, cut, or scrape going septic in the tropics and flattening the adventurer with disease. I was not going to be macho about the toe. I had sixty-eight hours of "wilderness medicine" for God's sake. A more familiar frown rounded the corners of my mouth when I remembered that Tony had neglected to bring the recommended antibiotics, but I still had the tea tree oil.

Be sure to clean and wrap the toe. Clean and wrap. There's no insurance policy if it goes bad. Lose your boat, lose your head. Lose your toenail, ignore it, get infected, get sick in the middle of the ocean loop. No thanks!

That night we made sure that *Southern Cross* was well beached and that all of our essential life support systems were with us. Water, EPIRB, clothing, food, and desalinator. This wasn't the time to learn to become an Aborigine. No "native skills" tutors were around to give us a crash course. And the Australian terrain was only going to get harsher. We'd have to make sure to have our gear with us, if at all possible.

Today Cape Upstart was challenging us to reach her. If we managed the twenty-mile crossing in short enough time, we planned to ticktacktoe as close to Cape Bowling Green as we could. The wind was off to a slow start, so we paddled with prejudice to give us ten miles in two hours. The wind started to pick up as a storm approached. We passed Cape Upstart in five hours. That was good . . . *next cape.*

The wind increased to a solid twenty knots. Then it gusted over twenty-five.

We had to beeline to the mainland and make our exit. Rough weather closed in, pelting us with squall after squall. A sea fog was blowing in with it. A village seemed to lie well inset from a tiny gap in the low-lying sand and shell coastline. It was exactly what we needed if some unknown weather system was going to sock it to us for a while.

"There's some buildings in there. I think we should try to find some shelter. It's looking pretty bad," I said.

"I agree."

We paddled through the gap. It was like we were in the foyer to a *Journey to the Center of the Earth* excursion cruise. We were in some sort of Paleozoic swamp. Old vegetation, rotted stumps, new vegetation. The perfect breeding ground for some fossil fuels a few hundred thousand years from now. Moreover, this had become a bit of a maze, as the tide was hastily retreating and we were trying to stay in the deeper channels to get to the cluster of shanties at least a mile away. The pelting rain and dreary skies added a last touch of surrealism that we couldn't really appreciate at the time.

"Isn't this place weird, Tony?"

"Look at that bird over there, mate!"

A pterodactyl? We had to keep our eyes peeled for deeper channels if we were going to make landfall and not be stuck in some pre—oil field in a storm system that looked like it was going to hang around. We found an end run that took us close, made a quick left and a few zigzags, and we were . . . *where?!*

There were a dozen shanties in various states of abandon. *Surely this could not be the good side of town,* so we worked ourselves into another channel that took us deeper into the ghost complex.

Still nothing!

Why would a thriving fishing village be completely abandoned?!

Upon sliding *Southern Cross* up some, we saw:

WARNING—ESTUARINE CROCODILES INHABIT THIS AREA! followed by some clever symbol of a massive croc head with its jaw open in a triangle and a swimmer with a large red diagonal international cross-out symbol over him.

Terrific.

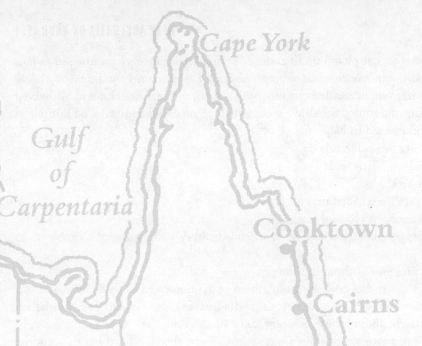

Hell Hole

A field filled with mounds of manure—thick clumps of it—dominated the area like a D Day minefield. Croc manure? *No way . . . no way! There would have to be dozens of them and don't they shit in the water?*

"Whose shit is this, anyway?"

"Looks like cow shit, mate" Tony said.

"Where are they?"

"Couldn't tell ya."

"You're the one who wanted to be the vet."

"Became a model instead, remember?"

"Probably pays better."

"More-flexible hours, too."

After "securing" *Southern Cross* by tying her off to some heavy metal scraps, we tentatively wandered on the one and only street, a potholed dirt one, to boot. I thought I saw a head in a window. A vintage Mad Max car or two were around. *A leper colony. Crazy farm?* Those were not better options than Reptile World. A go-through revealed no shop of any sort and no takeout dining. On our way back to the boat, we spotted a nicely covered porch that looked like it would make a good shelter if the rains were going to continue. I made a mental note of it and went to get our gear.

Just as we returned, we heard the low murmur of an engine. A modern pickup with a roll bar was pulling into our perfect little parched house. *Damn!*

Then another car pulled up to another house. *Well, maybe we got here just in time for the party or maybe the window people had called out a posse,* I thought.

Another vehicle headed our way with a small motorboat behind it. We waved a greeting and smiled for all we were worth. A nice bloke introduced himself as Troy and greeted us back.

"What's this place called?"

"Hellhole," Troy said.

"You're kidding?"

"No, it's been called that for a longtime."

"Where is everybody?"

"Most people come here on weekends from Ayr about thirty k's away to go fishing."

Hell Hampton? I thought jokingly.

The manure was cow shit from a herd of (you guessed it) feral cattle, and yes, the local crocs are large, numerous, and aggressive, usually sunning themselves midday right about where *Southern Cross* was.

"Best to move yar boat up a ways. Crocs'll sort through anything to get some food. This is a great place to do some crabbin', too."

Troy listened to the explanation of our visit and offered the covered porch of his father's house for shelter that night. More rain was forecast. He showed us the place, took out a very large covered pot, and indoctrinated us into his techniques for mud crab cooking. He gave us a few mud crabs to eat—very much the honor in those parts.

"Make yourself at home."

He wished us luck and bid farewell. He would be fishing into the night and then making his way back home. He had opened the house just for us. *This angel certainly took his time getting to us.*

Troy's hospitality offset the stewing feud between Tony and me. I withdrew to attend to my toe and listen to some music on a still functioning Walkman. I even managed to read a few more pages of *The Great Circle* under a porch light. Dinner was quiet. It was easier maintaining silence in the water because we didn't face each other. I wrote in my journal: "It's interesting and therapeutic out on the water. Even as the wind picks up and the waves and rain slap my face from the shoal surf and squalls."

I was still in a foul mood about the relationship thing, and what really ticked me off was the fact that I wasn't shaking it off completely. It chose land to creep back into my mind, when the action had settled down. It was particularly good at using music to get deeper.

I was finding it hard to run away from my storehouse of emotions and memories. Tony got the fallout from it, like any partner would. It seemed to me that women would always wait for Tony. For me, women only waited long enough to leave at the worst possible time. *Not too early. That wouldn't drive the hook in deep enough. No, no, no, no . . . Let that hook get set nice and deep and then cut the line with the hook still in the mouth without even garnering the honor of being hung at the weight stand for all to see.* You ever wonder what happens to those hooks? I was wallowing in self-pity. And it felt good.

Cape York

Gulf
of
Carpentaria

Cooktown

Cairns

QUEENSLAND

Hinchinbrook and Cairns

 We shoved off into a nasty head wind and lingering sea fog. As we wound our way through a deeper series of maze channels, I was comforted in the thought that at least the wind would not be in our faces when we made the left at the channel entrance.

Wrong!

The wind continued to stay directly in our faces, coming from the northeast. The channel had only redirected the main stream of the wind to greet us early, and it was a lot stronger. It was not beach blocked anymore. We continued to battle-paddle into the fray. It felt good, really good, to be feeling the tug of the blades and the driving rain in our faces, but we were using a lot of energy and Cape Bowling Green was still miles off. It was important to get far up this long sandy finger leading out to the cape in order to stage the shot for Townsville the next day. *A short day today puts the crossing in limbo.* We continued to paddle hard, staying close to shore to keep our bearings and paying the price of shoal surf in the face every now and then. *Between fog and a hard place.*

An unexpected turn in the terrain changed our course farther north and took some of the head wind away. The sea was now angling in off our starboard bow and skipped more than a few wavelets into our chests. We took our penance quietly and kept paddling. The squalls kept up for most of the day as we brailled the coast, which went on and on with no end in sight in any direction. By midafternoon the fog had blown away but the skies threatened, and delivered more and more rain. We had no idea how far we had gone, so we trudged on.

In the late afternoon we had better visibility and saw a radio tower. I thought it surely must be near the end of the cape. A couple more hours in some fish-net-phalanxed coast became frustrating. Rows and rows of fishnets and their half-visible trestles extended from the beach like the baleen teeth of a whale try-ing to filter out its food from as much area as possible.

We had to steer at right angles for hundreds of yards to get around them, yet the drama of the storming day in the relative security of the shallows let us enjoy the show. The quest for constant rhythm and more distance kept us focused. I concluded that the waters near the Manhattan Battery displayed simi-lar drama but with quite a few more witnesses, as more fisherman were actually attached to their fishing lines.

We found a tin hut a couple miles short of the end of the cape. It had seen a nomad or two. They were probably more Robinson Crusoe types, not Airlie Beachers. There were primitive attempts for some kind of extended living arrangement. It was remotely possible that someone still minded these parts. For now, we rearranged the rusty box springs and loose tin siding panels, hunkering down for another stormy eve. It would do. We'd done well for shelter during these days of inclement weather. Proper shelter equaled better sleep, which led in theory to better moods and better days.

Tony and I still had little to say except to express our mutual disdain at two sub-par-distance days.

"I can't believe we've only gone forty-five miles in the last two days!"

"The bloody fog made us go the long way."

We had actually paddled more miles than this but the "distance made good" was what it was. We had had to follow the coast too closely. We had become good at crossings to minimize the distance between two points. Our average dis-tance from shore was usually more than five miles. We were only closer than this in the first and last hour of the day. This was due to the shape of the coast. It was like a continuous series of twenty- to twenty-five-mile-long ice cream scoops with islets sprinkled on top.

"We've *got* to get earlier starts," Tony added.

"We could also use some better winds," I said.

We got our early start, finished off Cape Bowling Green in less than an hour and made the hard left turn toward Townsville or Magnetic Island, whichever came first. It would be a mixed paddle, sail, paddle day with the wind puffing out its last variable breath as a new fair-weather system settled in. The trade winds' steady breath had been punched in the diaphragm by some unseasonable weather.

The final crossing was a long one, and the sailing was not giving us the speed we needed to reach our destination before nightfall.

"We have to hit the sticks, mate."

"I know, I know," I said, as I was striking the jib sail and stuffing it into its pocket on the foredeck in front of me.

We paddled hard with lingering hopes that a sea breeze would kick in soon. Paddling wasn't fun anymore. The head winds had sapped some starch out of me, yet the prospect of civilization just ahead spurred me on.

The sunset was rich with coral hues. It looked like the inside of a conch shell. Magnetic Island had us in its sights. The tiniest ripple of wind billowed up and I re-hoisted the sail in eager anticipation of a free ride in. Moments later, the wind died and it was back to paddling. *Maybe we'll get into some kind of gravity field,* I hoped. We were still four miles out.

As day yielded to night, we watched spots of light dart across the island. I was looking for a thicker cluster of lights to lock on to. We were still a good hour away and the right trajectory would save us a lot of grief. It was also getting cold. The combination of a clear night sky and a sweat-cooled body made my desire not to make a wrong move all the more intense. I wanted to get this day over with and not have to rummage about for more clothing, but I wanted to be sure to land near some good food and maybe a beer. Tony seemed content just to make landfall.

"Where do you think you're steering to!" I snapped.

"I'm just trying to get to the fucking island. Why do you keep stopping and looking around?!" Tony said. "It looks like you're trying to find a town or something."

"Yes, yes, I am. I'm trying to see exactly where the ferry is going to," I said.

"*Don't bother!* We're going straight in." Tony paddled harder, I backpaddled.

"*No* way! If I've come this far, I'm not getting stuck on some pebbles or tin hut if I know there's a burger and a beer on the other side of the island!"

"Why didn't you say something earlier!" shouted Tony. "I always have to interpret your little bullshit silent mannerisms. What do you think I am, a mind reader. *I'm sick and tired of it!*"

"*I'm sick and tired of your lack of respect!*"

We "went around the house" a few times, emptying all the closets and shaking out the rugs. All in all we covered a lot of resentments. An hour later, with *Southern Cross* drifting aimlessly, we'd cleared a lot of the air.

"Mate, you've just got to let me know what you're thinking so I can understand where you're coming from," he pleaded.

"I know, I am sorry for being a silent jerk to you. I hope you have a better idea why."

A combination of self-acknowledged reproach and a warm elation at confessing my anxieties with the only other person who could possibly understand them overwhelmed me. At about that time, ferry traffic lights lined up to guide our way in. Near the ferry terminal was a nice tropical beach.

Magnetic Island became a day off to depolarize. It lay five miles north of Townsville. It had been founded and named by Cook, who said that it fouled the compasses aboard his ship. It was the better choice according to Tony.

"When I was growing up I went to Townsville to see my grandparents. I didn't find it very interesting."

I figured any town that actually had the name town *in it was not going to be high on his list.*

We emptied *Southern Cross* to dry and clean her. We walked to the post office and small shop complex to reprovision and send off some correspondence. It was pleasant to sit and write with Tony today. We started talking. Really talking. At one point my mind raced beyond talk of "the trip," visualizing some type of satisfying out-of-office career path, using my hands, partnering with Howard and Lookfar expeditions, a VW Campervan . . . *yeah . . . that's the ticket* . . . or so I thought in that momentary bubble.

"You boys seem pretty interesting." A woman one table over was smiling at us cheerily. She must have been amused by our pontificating. "Would you like to come up to my house for a pot of tea?"

Tony looked at me with an "I told you so" expression.

The "happy thought" bubble floated both of us toward Allison's house, up and down a winding dirt path, toward an airy tropical compound. A blue Austin Mini-Cooper sat parked outside. I knew a Klepper owner named Sir Alex Molton who'd helped design the suspension system for this famous English rally car with tiny wheels, box shape, and uncanny handling. Sir Molton also arguably perfected the first working suspension for bicycles. He even managed a pedal-driven propeller in one of his Klepper kayaks.

We walked in to a well-lived-in, very personal establishment that was definitively Allison. Although her outer spirit and glee were keen, I could sense a woman lonely with the dawning reality that the trade for independence had been made at the price of profound loneliness. No husband, no children, and an ever more humbling fight with time and the power of gravity. But maybe I was projecting my own insecurities onto her?

Tony babbled incessantly, simply tickled by Allison's generosity. A very special exchange was evolving as Allison opened up to TB more and more. I took the liberty to browse through the eclectic household. Her house had become her partner in life. A placard on her wall read:

THE SEA IS IN HIGH SPIRITS TODAY PROMISING ADVENTURE FOR THOSE WHO WOULD CUT THEIR MOORINGS AND BOLDLY FOLLOW.

An extended chill went up and down my spine.

Later on, Tony and I had to get some serious tucker. We were getting really hungry and asked Allison where we could get the most filling food on the island.

"I'll take you there," she offered.

We piled into her Mini-Cooper and she adroitly zipped us to a beautiful and romantic outdoor/indoor Italian restaurant. We asked her to join us.

"No, no. I really have to get back. Early morning tomorrow. Thank you any-way."

Somehow Tony and I knew arguing the point wouldn't be appropriate. We bid her a fond and thankful farewell. This angel came quickly. I thought, *How many of these do we get? Are we using up luck tickets for them?*

Tony and I sat down to a candlelight dinner in the outside section of the restaurant where many handsome couples savored each other as much as their food. Many thoughts and feelings emerged as I remembered many of the pretty faces I'd sat across from in the years past. All that glitters was not gold, though. NYC seems to tarnish the best of them and can corrode the worst *fast*. If a woman fully adapts to the NYC lifestyle she becomes a fish more and more confidently able in those waters, often swimming circles around the typical manfish.

The more comfortable and confident in NYC, the more she realizes how accessible the "country" home in Colorado, the flat in Paris, or the beach house in Amagansett become. These getaways are among the menu of offerings made available by the men who swim those waters with dollar-shaped fins.

We woke up early and set off to bag some great distance. The next big desti-nation was the internationally known Barrier Reef resort town of Cairns over two hundred miles away. First, we would have to pass what was rumored to be an impressively beautiful Hinchinbrook Island. Cairns could take a week to get to, but Hinchinbrook should be a two-day affair from the Palm Island group. Therefore, the Palm Island group, a thirty-mile open-water crossing, was today's target.

The day started off with just the right amount of breeze to fly automatic pilot in the first few hours. I blazed through the rest of my yacht-race book, caught up in the fictional conflicts between good and evil, storms on the high seas, honor in the midst of corruption, the extreme highs and lows of taking extreme risks. The Aussie captain put up *more* sail when a storm system arrived, while the American captain reefed his in, causing an initial loss of ground as the Australian boat pulled away. Just as it appeared that the Aussie was going to pull off this daring technique and the American captain was going to be blackballed from sailing for the rest of his life, the Aussie's mast broke clean away, leaving his boat limping to the finish. Along the way, the British captain had saved the other American boat, with the celebrity and camera crew aboard. It was high drama on the high seas.

Suddenly, *Southern Cross* lurched on her side. Higher winds arrived. I went back to our own drama.

A fresh breeze filled our sails. *Southern Cross* started to gallop. I watched the bow rise and fall through the waves, listening to the *kaaa tissssshhhhhhh* of waves being parted by the V-shape our craft. I mentally cross-referenced images of the yachts in the book with our reality. I was now in the Great Yacht Race with

Palm Island as our finish line. *Oh shit, I have that Australian onboard. He doesn't think he's the captain?*

It didn't take long to settle into the new angle of the boat, the pattern of the waves, and the trim of the sails. It was coming more and more naturally. The new shot of excitement ignited a series of talks. We could now converse at Force 4. We covered the woman situation:

"Your woman is a model," I said, "constantly surrounded by men, and would drop everything to be with you." I grumbled sulkily, "Mine lasted two whole long months."

"Well, mate, T and I have been together for a while." He sighed. "I did think Nikky would wait for you, though."

It was clear that Nicole and I had not developed enough of a history together to transcend the time and distance, whereas Tony and his lady had. They had been through many months apart on different continents and had gone through breakups and reunions, finally getting comfortable with the rhythms of their lives. Tony switched subjects.

"Dad doesn't want me to cross the Gulf of Carpentaria."

"What are you talking about; how does he know?"

"He and my uncle have been talking and my uncle has started to convince him that I'm serious about doing the whole trip."

"You mean that uncle you saw in Brisbane? What did he *think* you were doing?"

"He never thought I would make it this far."

The wind picked up to Force 5 and the conversation ended. Many miles had evaporated and the low silhouettes of the Palm Islands had just come into view. I looked at my watch, it was almost 4:00 P.M. and it would take every bit of this wind to get us there.

An hour later, the wind did us one better. It picked up another couple of knots and I was doubly pleased to fall into the protection of the first chain of islands a mile to starboard. The islands were cutting the waves down to size. The combination of high wind and low waves thrust us quickly into the center of the island group and I was giddy with overchoice.

"Pick an island, TB. Any island."

We got choosy, and started island shopping. With minor changes in the rudder, *SC* would snap to and speed off on a new course. The wind was holding into the eve and did not show signs of letting up. We could veer toward and away from our potential choices with impunity. As the sun set we saw a very uniform series of lights notched into an island, also to our starboard. In fact, it looked like a town, but our maps and charts did not mention any towns there at all.

When we reached the end of one of our islands, we felt compelled to chase down another one. We were skipping through this chain quickly and felt obliged to use the gift. We sailed from the first to the second and landed on the northernmost island of the chain. We got out and after a short reconnoiter, we ran into a trio of Aboriginal fishermen finishing their fresh fish dinner.

These "modern" Aborigines were dressed in Western-style clothes and well set with a late-model motorboat to scoot around in. We exchanged pleasantries and they offered us a spot of fish. We politely turned it down upon seeing the hungry youngsters. It was a short meeting. They remained huddled as a family, and we went about making camp. Later the motorboat roared back to her base, which we had passed earlier. *It was an Aborigine town. I guess they don't have to list them on Western maps.*

We got a good night's sleep. Hinchinbrook Island was thirty-five miles away and there was no wind. After an hour of blissful speed-paddling, we encountered a light head wind. It felt great—wind in the face, cooling the heat of the rising sun. As the sun rose higher and higher, the little abrasions and pressures become more obvious. No way to ignore them. The wind became more insidious. I started counting paddle strokes to take my mind off of it.

First hour: Three thousand, six hundred seventy.

Second hour: Seven thousand, three hundred eighty-five.

Hinchinbrook seemed closer. Its lush, massive presence awaited like the fabled island in *South Pacific*. Mt. Bowen, on top of it, is 3,500 feet high. It is theoretically visible from sixty miles away. Right now, it was still over twenty miles away, five hours, and almost twenty thousand strokes. I knew the latter based on my practiced hour-to-stroke conversion. I became dubious of this mantra, but at least it helped nine miles disappear a little easier.

On days like this, there was no point in taking extended breaks for lunch, snacks, water, and the like. We ate quickly and pit-stopped the water breaks. The longer we broke, the farther we drifted behind, and the more strokes we had to take, the longer we were out on the water, the hotter we got, the more blisters, the more aches and pains.

The tailbone is the real pain. It is hard to escape your tailbone in a kayak. This is where all the pivotal energy of the stroke converts to the boat. The more strokes, the bumpier the conditions, the more tailbone awareness. Imagine balancing your backside on the business end of a jackhammer. The idea of putting our sleeping bags in waterproof bags for seats had been a godsend. These seats facilitated hundreds of relatively comfortable hours in the boat. But there is a breaking point. A simple pressure equation that equals annoyance. We spelled ourselves for a minute every half-hour by doing a parallel bar press off the coaming of the boat. The respite provides relief for about fifteen minutes and then is replaced by "tailbone fever." We knew that landing on Hinchinbrook would cure "tailbone fever," so we paddled harder, only to suffer more from the time/distance illusion. *Don't look up,* I told myself. Instead, I started counting strokes again.

We arrived an hour before sunset in a repentant mood. All we discovered was a long flat beach leading to a high sandy bluff. *Southern Cross* had to be moved up the beach and now up the bluff as well. We lightened our load and set what seemed like the first footprints on the moon. After a couple trips back and forth from the kayak I felt like we had desecrated sacred ground. When we finally moved the boat, it left a bobsled trail on a formerly undisturbed canvas of sand. I reminded myself that the beach had its own ground crew—the tide—the same ground crew that nearly took *Southern Cross* a week ago.

By the time *Southern Cross* was moved to higher ground and camp was made and food on the burner, we were allowed a final glimpse of Hinchinbrook in golden red light. I was glad I'd looked up, yet the effort-to-time-to-appreciate-goal ratio was less than perfect.

Fatigue settled in quickly after our gruel refuel. This is the difference between a long day of paddling and a long day of sailing. Sailing facilitates a couple hours of cognizance at the end of a day. Paddling allows a few minutes. Journal writing is a joke with stiff, half-crooked hands scribbling arthritic-cryptic text, driven by a half-baked brain still counting strokes . . . thirty-eight thousand, two hundred . . . thirty-eight thousand, two hundred six . . .

Nine and a half hours of comatose sleep's not enough. I got up earlier than Tony to make sure we had breakfast for another paddling day. We'd already lost all the weight we should have. I was at my college "fighting weight" and Tony at his optimal climbing trim. I was under 150 pounds and Tony was under 180. This was twenty-five pounds gone in two months. Tony had told me that at 175 he had been his most agile in climbing the rock faces of the Alps. The trip was taking its toll: we were climbing a ten-thousand-mile rock face.

The previous day had burned over six thousand calories. The body starts emptying all its cupboards looking for any source of fuel. It is likely that our bodies had become more economical and shifted to low-burning fat sources from wherever it could find them. Therein lay the problem, our percentage of body fat was going down, down. Lean muscle is the next target. After that, the body will scavenge anything including organ meat and eventually bone itself.

Most people would stop being physical, at the very least, to conserve what was left, but we kept going. Internal organs are ignored to keep the muscles functional, to keep the arms and trunk paddleable. The net effect is like running your internal engine without oil. I prepared a big pot of oatmeal, splooched half a tube of condensed milk and some raspberry jam in it.

Tony added even more condensed milk to his portion.

I had bought some time for my internal engine, but still sensed a warning light about to blink. The first task was to move *Southern Cross* back to the water's edge, a hundred yards away. Another glimpse of Hinchinbrook in the brighter spotlight of dawn before the sea claimed our souls for the rest of the day was still not enough. A magnificent national park was just another landmark on our left that told us continental Australia was still there and it confirmed that we had completed that "distance."

We launched into a hazy stillness. There was no wind from any direction.

Within a couple of hours I was wishing for head wind like we'd had the day before so as to paddle the duration . . . again. It was the first day in weeks when I was feeling the full brunt of heat, salt, sand, and abrasion; my sweat glands poured more salty water onto my skin in a desperate attempt to keep the engine from blowing up. The sun rose higher—nowhere to hide. Nuclear fusion had us at its mercy from 93 million miles away. The calm sea bedeviled us with her silence.

Tailbone fever picked up where it had left off from the day before, near blisters became blisters and the holes in my lower back reopened. Only the steady rhythm of the paddles and the steady glide of *Southern Cross* slicing through the stillness provided solace. Counting had lost its magic and only reinforced the magnitude of distance. After four hours we really wanted some wind. Any wind, from any direction. It was too easy to be cranky and impossible to be pleasant. So we both stayed quiet. I listened to Tony's intermittent sighs. After a couple of hours, he said: "Stick up your hand, mate."

I responded like a dog trained by Pavlov as he put a cracker and some salami in my hand. "Here's some more." This time a little more salami and half a Power Bar.

I took out some water and washed down. We sat dead in the water and I said, "You *know* we're not eating enough!"

"*Mate,* our bodies *adapt.* Here's another piece to keep you happy."

We weren't eating enough, and had lost too much weight too fast! I continued to think. Who's fault was that in my baking brain? Tony's. My thoughts continued to digress into the "prisoner in someone else's destiny" syndrome. The trip was *his* idea. The spartanism was *his* fault. He hadn't wanted to spend too much money on food. The lack of humor was *his* fault. *Welcome to another pity party.*

It was frustrating to know what my low blood sugar and dehydration were doing to my resolve and attitude. I hated this type of pity party. The hate refueled the pity, and anger was at best a Band-Aid for mental laceration. *I shouldn't be this way!*

It's at this point that the "Siamese" kayaking can hinder more than help. When a trip like this is done solo, as the vast majority of these kinds of trips are, there is no one else to blame, project onto, or in any way dump these less than noble feelings on.

"Open your hand, mate."

He gave me another slice of salami and biscuit. I huffed an acknowledgment, choosing to feel like a slave dog rather than a partner. I kept my mouth shut but I knew my mood was being read like a billboard. *I'm being an asshole again and there doesn't seem to be a damn thing I can do about it.* It didn't get better, even as the breeze began to stir. *Probably won't last.* There really should be a pity *prison* for people like me today.

Eventually I traded pity for expectation. At that point I knew we'd make it to

Dunk Island, home to a very exclusive resort. I conjured images of a red carpet welcome for famous adventurers. *Tony probably won't want to go,* I thought. But Tony surprised me.

"Ya think we'll see your Swedish Bikini Team on Dunk, Epic?"

My face cracked a reflexive half-smile and I said, "I sure hope so, but I'm mainly looking forward to a big burger or steak."

The nuclear fusion was subsiding and the afterglow bathed the palm-covered isle as a steady breeze lifted us to it. A full moon started to appear on the opposite horizon when I heard Tony say, "Stop for a second, I want to take a picture."

As *SC* approached Dunk Island, it looked like another camping park with picnic tables and barbies blazing. We landed on one of the beaches and were greeted by some very chipper tourists keen to witness our arrival. The sun-bleached boat and salt-and beard-encrusted occupants were novel and brought out questions:

"What are you doing?"

What do you think we're doing?! (I wanted to say)

"We're paddling around Australia."

"Awwwwright."

"How long ya been going?"

Too long.

"Over two months."

"Can you take me for a ride?"

You're out of your mind.

"Not today."

"*Come on, mate,* we've got to finish moving the boat," Tony said, verbally evacuating me from the assault.

It was hard to be instantly pleasant after another long day in the kayak. However, Tony's apparent resort enthusiasm and the balmy air were perking me up.

We secured *Southern Cross* and headed from the "commoners" day-stop toward the resort through a manicured path bordered by two long rows of equidistant trees. The first telltale sign of "resortism" came in the form of the aircraft landing strip that had seemingly sprung from the bush. The "bush" was cleverly landscaped. The vegetation was thick and varied enough to block initial glances at the airport and maintain that "jungle" feel and yet it was just a few inches away from each and every light.

Past the airstrip we got a moonlight glimpse of the resort's harbor cove, where the yachts and ferry were stationed. We popped out into the first courtyard—complete with fountain and inset hot tub—then down some steps to the first building that looked like a place to get something to eat. It was the Brasserie, but nary a soul was in it.

We approached the colorfully uniformed and name-tagged hostess, a deluxe version of the kind you might see at Denny's, and asked if we could get some tucker. She glimpsed back at the empty dinning room and then into her virtually empty reservation book.

"Ahh, hmmm. If you come back at eight forty-five, there might be something opening up."

Tony and I looked quizzically at her and then each other, simultaneously calculating the two-hour wait. She hastily said: "You might want to try the restaurant farther down the path."

We wandered through the nearly vacant, thatch-roofed, hut-style "open" bar inside a less obvious high-ceiling-protected environment. Rain, wind, and bugs were not allowed! We saw a few brightly dressed, tactically tanned resortee's getting an early start with their cocktails.

Next stop was the entrance to the resort "restaurant" and the luxury appointments that come with it. We perused the beautiful hand-drawn calligraphy on the "specials" board, which spelled out numerous names for fish with pasta.

I asked to be seated in the main dining room. I followed the maître d's eyes down to my feet. My shoes were wet, holed, and dirty. Our light pile pants, although a bright blue, had holes, burn marks, and some loose threads. Working up, we both had long-sleeved T-shirts with spots and stains leading to drawn, salty faces with thick and threatening beards. *Feral and Feral at your service.*

Soon a bevy of colorfully shirted and golden-tagged employees were near us trying to smile the awkward situation away, desperately trying to remember how they were taught to handle a situation like this. It was apparent that the hungry, washed up, slightly dazed, long-range-sea-kayak-expeditioners looking for food in their restaurant was not addressed in the manual. They called the manager.

The manager's shirt matched the others' but his tag had MANAGER inscribed on a thicker tag. He smiled at us uncomfortably while more subtly looking us over. He listened to our story and even pretended to empathize with us.

"True blue?! I wish I could help you out but people not staying at the resort have to make reservations for this restaurant a day in advance or the morning of the same day."

"But there's hardly a bloody soul in there," I said.

"It'll be filling up soon," he said as his eyes rebounded from me to Tony, who had cleared his throat.

"I'm sure they'll have room for you back at the Bistro."

"We've just come from there. They said come here."

"I'll give 'em a call and ya'll be all right."

It was clear that complaining about our earlier brush-off from the Bistro would do no good, so we took whatever meager ammunition we had from talking with the manager at the restaurant back to the Bistro.

"Yes, I can fit you in at eight o'clock now." That was over an hour away. There were two people in the bistro.

"Let's get out of here, mate," Tony said.

"It's only an hour." I pleaded.

"We're getting out of here!"

I walked dejectedly back to a table under some fluorescent lights in a "closed for the day," "day visitor" area. Tony heated up another pot of pasta stew that was leaner than usual on ingredients. I rolled my eyes.

"Mate, you carry an anger about you that is getting tiresome and boring."

"Tony, we don't eat enough. We have lost too much weight and I don't like it!"

"Mate, I told you our bodies will get used to it."

I knew he'd say that.

I continued on a sarcastic vein until Tony said with painful sincerity:

"I am tired of traveling with an unhappy person."

I explained my disappointment at not eating a substantial meal at the resort and my real concern about not having enough fuel to get the job done, thus leading to a less than cheery disposition.

"You can be a real 'bore' to be with. Your sighs and frowns and that thing you do with your shoulder."

"*Today,* I'm just fucking pissed off that those assholes treated us like that over a fucking hamburger!"

"That's more like it, mate, let it out!"

"I am truly sorry you have had to deal with this shit."

He cracked a smile and I felt some relief. Once again, Tony got a difficult situation out on the table, unprotected by bugs, wind, and rain. That night I wrote in my journal.

Dunk Island was bitter disappointment for me. We were treated like bums scrounging for food. Tony seemed much less bothered, but I think he was less thrilled about it than he had let me know.

The message to Tony about provisions had struck a chord. He said early the next morning, "We're going to Mission Beach to resupply."

"A brilliant plan," I said.

We paddled the three miles to the small but popular town of Mission Beach on the mainland. I saw huge nets suspended from long metal booms in a number of locations along the beach.

"Look at the giant shark nets, TB!"

"They're not for sharks, they're for the sea wasps."

"What are those?"

"Giant jellyfish. See this?" he said, pointing to a long, faded scar on his neck. "That's from one broken piece of tentacle. It wrapped around my throat. Got a bit hard to breath for a while."

"What did you do?"

"Had a friend piss on it and went to hospital."

"Does that really work?"

"It seemed to at the moment."

Basically, box jellies make the Portuguese man-o'-wars seem like a gunboat compared to an aircraft carrier. Their tentacles can spread many meters underwater
and kill fish the size of tuna. Moreover, the box jellies seem to migrate and kill
with a unique "intelligence," although science would say they are just a co-op of
independent cells. But sometimes science doesn't get these things exactly right.
Experts recommend that one: Avoid all contact with sea jellies as most give a
nasty sting. Try not to swim in murky water in tropical Australia from October
to May. . . . Hundreds of people have died from the sting. . . . If unlucky
enough to be stung, apply cold packs or crushed ice wrapped in a thick towel to
area. Seek immediate medical assistance. Apply vinegar to reduce pain. Nobody's
said anything about pee.

We wandered into the low-key town of "lifestylers" (Aussies who have chosen a
more serene slice of life far enough away from the activity of Cairns, and who
keep the place beautiful and quiet). There weren't more than a few people walking the main beach and most of them were locals. Mission Beach was where we
were supposed to meet Tony's friend Moz, the bloke that helped us get launched
in Bondi. We were supposed to spend a few days with him, like a stop on a vacation. But Moz never made it to Mission Beach. And we were not on a vacation.

Mission Beach was named after an Aborigine mission that was founded there
in 1914. It was the starting point for the ill-fated 1848 overland expedition to
Cape York led by thirty-year-old Edmund Kennedy. In 1918 it was wiped out
by a cyclone.

We found a bakery and a milkbar, and loaded up a number of bags of groceries. As the morning waned, the uncomfortable feeling that we were wasting
precious time dawned on both of us.

"Boy, I would love to stick around. It seems like a nice place but I know we
gotta go."

"You can come back on the second lap," Tony said with a grin as he rose from
our outdoor table with two plastic bags filled with groceries in both hands.

A couple of days in Mission were summed up in a couple of hours. Cairns
was three days away if we pushed it. Tony's mum was going to be there then.

"Let's go, mate."

The day went smoothly across the board. We paddled for a couple of hours,
caught a nice breeze with the sails, and unexpectedly found another small village
called Fishing Point that evening. It also had a milkbar. Neither of us were complaining, while we ate a half-gallon of ice cream after a chook or two. We were
living large and our tanks were filling. We left Fishing Point with the intent to

get as far as Fitzroy Island, so we could be within a comfortable day's paddle to Cairns. Thirty miles, then twenty-five the next day.

The day brought a sea in high spirits, "promising adventure for those who would cut their moorings and boldly follow." We sailed on a strong steady breeze that kept clocking *Southern Cross* at four-to-four-and-a-half knots hour after hour. We reached Fitzroy before four-thirty leaving us with an hour and a half of daylight. Fitzroy was a known stop, with a known landing. We'd have had to play it by ear if we'd bypassed it.

The sun was setting and we were in that uneasy, neither here nor there situation. No islands, no clear look at the mainland, and over twenty miles from Cairns.

"Well, mate, what do you think!?"

"I guess we'll be in Cairns a day early."

A twinge of adrenaline ran roughshod over any indecisiveness. The new agenda recharged me. I've always liked night paddling but the old primal warnings started to go on again. It had been a month since our last "long" nighter. I figured we'd better start warming up to the idea. We had a potential eight-to-ten-day crossing looming just around the corner. Half of that would be at night.

Sailing through the sunset into twilight and finally into darkness is hypnotic. All other senses sharpen as man's "first" sense is reduced to silhouettes, shapes, and shadows. It was time to sharpen those vampire eyes again.

It is amazing how the mind adapts. Night seems normal after a while. We saw the domelike glow of Cairns as we started to make a left at Cape Grafton. However, as we sharpened our left to establish a west-southwest course, our breeze diminished and our pace slowed. We eked out another mile.

"Tony, do you think it's time to hit the sticks?"

He reluctantly agreed. Our free passes were void after 8:00 P.M. We hit the sticks and enjoyed the change and the warmth produced from the motion. An hour later the lights of Cairns peeked out from a sheltered bay even farther to our left. The wind caught and recoiled directly back into our faces. It started to rain. It felt as if Cairns didn't want anything to do with us. The seas picked up and we had to reapply for our next entry pass.

"Feels like the Manhattan paddles, mate."

"What!?"

"Feels a lot like the Manhattan paddles, mate!"

"Yeah, it sure does!"

We were well practiced for the particular scenario. Urban assault. I flash-backed to the last couple miles of a spontaneous sprint we'd done around Manhattan for which we hadn't planned the tide very well. As we turned the corner at the Battery and headed up the Hudson River we were hit with wind and tide in a misty rain. The last three miles felt like we'd added another lap around the island.

Here we go again.

It seemed the closer we got, the more difficult it became. We were probably meeting outgoing tide as well, so we paddled harder. I could feel *Southern Cross* lifting a little higher with each combined stroke. This was the beauty of having two motivated turboprops in one boat. Tony's energy fed mine and mine his. The paddling became fierce. We were too close to be cranky. It was too dark to determine how far we really were from the harbor so we just paddled harder and changed the angle of our boat ten degrees to the west to deflect the tide and use it to help ferry us closer.

The harbor was on the southeast side of town and made a logical destination. It was a busy place. We started to see a string of very bright lights running near the harbor to the north for miles. We saw airplanes waiting to land at the Cairns International Airport on the north side of town. It was a pulsating place and marked the last "city" we would see till Darwin—well over fifteen hundred miles away.

Almost two hours later, we arrived in a harbor overflowing with boats of all sizes, most of them looking like shiny white porcupine beetles, their bristling lances and antennae prepped for every possible type of fishing. The other part of the harbor looked like a space port with megayachts more streamlined than the space shuttle, and engines to match.

The spaceships were apparently self-contained, with an occasional helicopter interrupting the aerodynamically perfect forms. Many of the sailboats looked like they were on a waiting list moored outside the enshrouded part of the marina. The ones that did make the grade seemed to require the same low-drag coefficient to be given priority docking. I started to wonder if we would find a place to put our thirty-four-inch-wide kayak, which actually looked sleeker than many of these multimillion-dollar machines. We found our place with the bouncy inflatable dinghies. *Southern Cross* wedged its nose between two of the gray hippolike craft and we were able to pry one far enough away to get to the dock. We had been on the water for over sixteen hours.

"It's out best day yet, TB!"

"How much distance?"

"Almost sixty miles."

We secured *Southern Cross* with the inflatable freeloaders and sauntered into town without a town conflict. Cairns was a city of mutual consent for us. We questioned some curious onlookers from a charter company. They pointed the way to go.

We headed to the strip of lights called the Esplanade after passing a shopping annex. I made a mental note of the bookstore. I also noted the gate closing time that would seal us off from *Southern Cross* if we let the hour pass.

My eyes struggled to adjust as we entered the luminous yellow-brick road. We had our town bests on again, none of which had seen a real washing in weeks. Our beards were fully developed. Many well-dressed, nicely groomed tourists composed mainly of Western Europeans strolled about casually and sipped various beverages at the outdoor cafés. Hair, perfume, after-tan lotions, colognes, and food blended in an intoxicating sensual array. Food still remained the prime signal.

We were faced with tremendous "over choice" and were choosy enough to shop around. Pasta got the call when we found a $5.99 (Australian) special that appeared more than generous. We proceeded to eat, and then eat some more. A beer made all the lights, sounds, and smells blend together and ignited a series of positive feelings from days of lesser concern, when the most pressing thoughts were which bar or party to go to next.

I didn't fight it, except for the nagging thought that we had to get back to the marina before the gate was locked for the evening. Midnight was that hour. It was eleven-thirty. We gave ourselves a quarter-hour of luxury and floated from the table back into the Esplanade. We stepped out onto the main drag.

A group of younger German tourists came up and said to Tony: "You look just like Jesus."

I must be an apostle by default, I thought.

On the way back to the marina we scouted some areas in the park that paralleled the esplanade along the break wall bordering the bay. We noticed other vagrants being questioned by patrols. Accommodations for the night were looking dodgy. We both approached the break wall at the same time and noticed that the tide was receding.

"I think we can put our bivvies down here, TB."

"You reckon? What about the tide?"

"I think we've got at least seven or eight hours before we would get soaked. The tide is still going out."

I didn't think the authorities would look there. What idiots would sleep in muck and risk getting soaked by the morning tide? I don't know why the thought of checking into a local lodging never entered Tony's mind. He seemed compelled to be part of this nomadic scene a little longer and I didn't want any more hard feelings.

We made it back to *Southern Cross* just in time. She'd acquired a little more breathing room when one of the dinghies had gone back to its mother ship. We got our gear and disappeared into the park, over the wall, and onto our places in the muck. Fifty feet away cars were honking, tourists were sipping lattes, and bands were well into their sets. Fifteen feet away, the slow pacing and hushed tones of couples arm in arm passed us by again and again. My heart raced with each approach, desperately not wanting to be discovered or tampered with. I was afraid we'd get peed on. All in all I felt put out by everyone's all-night party even though it was Friday night.

I trusted my knowledge of tides and figured we still had a solid seven hours before we had to be concerned. The sun would be up by that time and normally we would arise with it, anyway. Besides, I could not afford to worry. I needed sleep.

Thump, thump, patter, patter, patter, tsish-tshish-tshish-tshish, tetetetetetete-tetetetetettetete.

What in the hell is this?! The warm glow of the sun was striking my bivvy sack. So was heavy rain.

Thump, thump, patter, patter, patter, tshish-tshish-tshish-tshish, tetetetetetete-tetetetettetetet.

I was afraid to exit my bivvy without having a clue as to what was going on. Then a suburban flashback took over—seventeen years old, putting in water sprinkler systems. We were getting pissed on by water sprinklers!!!

I heard the murmur of people discussing our blue-and-red-colored pods. We had been discovered. I for one chose to startle them by arising from my red pod—bed head, beard, and all. This could only have been a warm-up act for Tony's efforts to extract himself from his body wrap. People did not wait around to ask questions after seeing a 190-centimeter "Jesus" aka Rasputin come out of a blue cocoon.

My rebirth into "civilization" had been as aggravating as my "little death" the night before. Reentry wasn't going well. The sprinklers shifted to another sector and we grabbed our wet pods, threw them over the wall and then slinked over the wall ourselves.

I draped my pod over a tree branch to dry.

"I'm going to across to the street to get a room. Mum should be arriving this afternoon."

I had not seen this side of Tony before. He was suddenly concerned about comfortable lodgings. He left and I kept an eye on our normal accommodations drip drying on the grass. A half-hour later he returned.

"We're all set, mate; you've got your own room."

"Thank you, Tony."

"We can move in anytime after one P.M."

"What should we do with our stuff?"

"They have a storage room."

"Excellent."

We checked in our bags and shared a quick breakfast. Tony had to pick up his mum at the airport. He was clearly excited. I looked forward to his distraction. I knew his focus would be concentrated on his mum for the rest of the day, allowing me free rein to explore Cairns on my own with no pressing deadlines to worry about.

My first stop was a café to catch up on my journal, where I met a man from Dallas. His name was Bill, and he said he was on sabbatical from his politics-related work in Washington, D.C. Bill was thirty-five. We started sharing values like fish share water.

"Can you believe the race riots back home?"

"It's awful, makes me sick to my stomach," he said.

That's exactly how it struck me. I heard about it on the radio on Point

Palmerston in the middle of nowhere. I thought I was listening to an H. G. Wells *End of the World* story.

I suppose it was a pang of collective guilt at the American dream not turning out just right since it was *our* job to make it all work.

"Why did you come here?"

"To come to a simpler place. Washington is so intense. I like to think of Australia as a bit like the U.S. was once upon a time," he added.

"From what I've seen so far, parts of it seem to be catching up pretty damn fast. Hell, Sydney reminded me of a combination of L.A. and San Francisco," I said.

"Well, the population is limited by access to water. There just isn't a hell of a lot it."

"Sounds like that might be a blessing in disguise."

We discussed both countries' careless handling of the Aboriginal cultures. In the case of Australia, some of the Aboriginal people got educated, got grievous, and were now getting some precious land rights back. The Aboriginal Land Rights (Northern Territory) Act in 1974 and the Tjarutja Land Rights Act in 1984 (South Australia) have given conditional rights to the land in these states, but they have made only marginal progress over the rest of the country. In the case of South Australia, mining rights are often preserved for the company with arbitrated stipulations on monetary payments made to the Anagu tribe.

"In the U.S. most natives will not see the land of their ancestors in any form that their ancestors would recognize," Bill said.

"Many Native American tribes' idea of 'getting it back' is by manipulating laws to create massive casinos," I said.

"I am sad to say that investigations show that just a few tribal 'leaders' are getting the windfall from it," Bill added.

Bill and I parted and exchanged addresses, which would become moot in the dilution of our return, but for the moment it was a precious exchange between two mirrors reflecting on the land Down Under.

My next stop was the postal god, where I was secretly hoping that I would receive some type of "I can't live without you" response from Nicole after the battery of last-ditch letters I had been sending every chance I could. If not, maybe there was some consolation prize.

Nothing.

Once again I felt alone in the busiest city we'd seen in a month. I made a call to Nicole, making sure to deposit the bag full of coins necessary for three minutes.

"Hello, you have reached Nicole and Amy. If you would like to leave a message . . ."

I tried three more times at ten-minute intervals. Same result.

That takes care of that.

•   •   •

It became a sunny day, I flipped the Ray-Bans down and headed toward consumer land looking for the unique gift that would turn her around. Aboriginal arts and crafts dominated the boutiques. Rich-colored paintings, boomerangs, didgeridoos, carvings of animals, brooches, and more, using dots, circles, and lines. Most of the artwork was bathed in a full range of earth-based ocher, brown, yellow, orange, and red, often interspersed with black.

Most of the stores were trinket based, but a few of them were art galleries. I walked into one and was awestruck by the size, quality, richness, geometry, and simple intricacies. I gravitated to a section where deep shades of blues, greens, and purples were intermixed on black. Some images included sea creatures, and others, ethereal stick-figure man-forms among countless stars and streaks in space.

I kept being reminded of Van Gogh and his work in the last few years of his life, particularly his landscapes and skyscapes, where the environment clearly predominates. His *Starry Night,* painted in 1890 in Saint-Remy, being the most comparable. This, along with his final painting, *Crows in a Wheatfield,* seems to exude the same "consciousness" as most of what I was looking at.

I picked up some pamphlets and a book of Aboriginal stories. According to the author, early Aboriginal art was based on ancestral dreaming about "the Creation," when the earth's features were formed by struggles between powerful supernatural ancestors often related to elements of nature (sun, moon, lightning, floods) and to animals. These were the "big" omnipresent dream themes. There also is more regional and personal dreaming.

These images were first drawn on rock or on the ground using stains from various plant and rock sources. The other "canvas" for Aboriginal art was the human body. The current renaissance in Aboringal painting began west of Alice Springs (central Australia) in a town called Papunya ("honey ant place") in the 1970s. Local children were given the task of making the *Honey Ant Dreaming* mural amid some resistance from local elders. This was the first time Aboriginal art was painted on something other than traditional surfaces—in this case the school wall. This opened doors to small boards and finally canvas and acrylic paints.

I was witnessing the mature result and saw more pieces than not without price tags. Small (chart-sized), less impressive pieces were selling for thousands of dollars. I can only imagine what the wall-sized versions were going for. I exited back to the trinket shops and purchased a couple of "dolphin dreaming" T-shirts for my mom and Nicole for about $20.00 (U.S.). I could not justify spending more money than my whole budget on a midrange painting no matter how much the gallery owner described the popularity and the "investment" potential. Hell, I did not have a home to put it in. *It would be sitting in a thick cardboard tube for a long time as far as I knew.*

I started feeling better about my purchase and turned my attention to finding knickknacks for my other friends back home. Often we give what we want to receive. It felt good to think of them, imagine their faces, what their interests were. It brought them back to me.

As I canvased the town in search of perfect gifts, I was blessed with a sight that generated spontaneous laughter. The sight was flawless in its metaphor. The Jeans West store I came across had Tony's very clean-shaven face plastered all over the place. The outside posters guided me in. It was evident that Tony and a female counterpart were this national store's poster children. The advertisements ranged from five-by-seven counter cards to half-wall-sized megaposters. I turned and looked at the bearded Tony standing only three feet from me.

The image haunted me throughout the day. These people didn't know the Tony I knew, the man in the boat, with the beard, who made garden hoes into masts, the one who was driven, focused, skilled, thrifty, and irascible.

I ventured back to the post, used the very handy built-in stationery store, and sent my trinkets of affection homeward because I shared Tony's bottom line. Cairns was to be my attitude switching station. I don't know if it was a spontaneous switch or a premeditated one. I think it was a little of both.

Cairns was the town that was supposed to end the preconceived, "easy" part of the trip we were supposed to have had so far. Sure, there would be a couple of towns after, but the Western world unofficially delineated the northern wilderness from southern Australian civilization with the minicity of Cairns. We would be going into the bush for a while (although I'd like to believe that the term only applied to those mainly traveling by land). I always thought that if we got past Cairns we'd be "legit" and not on some type of vacation. Cairns was the place I had to leave the last of my fun, "in town" expectations. I had to believe that I could.

As the day went on, I did more window shopping, had another cup of cappuccino, some gelato ice, a falafel, and other fast food. I gorged like a pig at a trough and headed back to the digs. I had an uneasy feeling going to meet Tony with his mum. Maybe it's because I had been privy to some of the darker and sadder parts of her life.

I caught up with them just as they were about to head out for a bite. The greetings were warm and sincere. Mum told me that she had brought a package for us and that she had put it in my room. My heart raced for a moment. *From who? What was it?*

"Any letters?" I asked.

"I think so," she said.

I excused myself to my room and saw the package. Long and narrow, wrapped in paper. The masts! Disappointment and relief swept over me. It was a long-awaited necessity that I was glad to see. I received cards from a number of good friends, but I guess I was still hoping that by some miracle, I'd get a letter from Nicole.

When I opened up the package with the masts, I realized they were missing the adaption pieces. We needed adaption pieces to fit the foot or bottom of the mast onto the foot receiver of our boat.

We'll worry about that when we come to it. Thus far, the mast we'd had still worked. Somehow we'd get the piece of that one when the time came. I couldn't be bothered with the thought just then. I was under the spell of a room with a bed and a chest of drawers with attached bath.

When Tony and his mum came back, it was down to business. It was time to arrange the logistics of "Mum's Week" in Northern Queensland. I had told them that we had excellent accommodation possibilities in Port Douglas at a place called the Coconut Grove Hotel, compliments of a friend of a client named Michael Gabor. The call was made and that was taken care of.

From there Mum would explore the Rain Forest National Park at Cape Tribulation and then venture onto Cooktown, rumored to require a four-wheel drive to get there. Cooktown brought back our experience with Phinny at Cape Palmerston and the idea of rendezvousing with him for a Captain Cook Festival. I think we were far too early.

All in all, it was clear that Mum was on a mission with us and we had to get our sleep to get ready for it. Lights went out early that night. The desire to party the night away was subdued. Cairns was not an ending point. It was a new beginning, one where we would have our emotional training wheels on, for a few days.

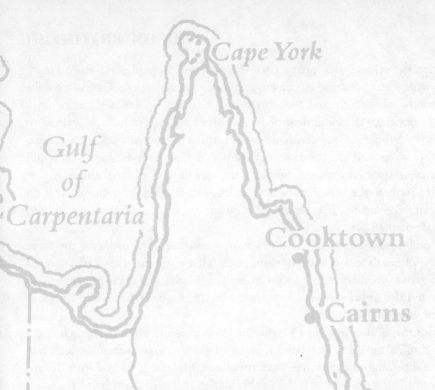

Off to Cooktown

Leaving Cairns was not difficult. It was more like a catharsis. Cairns had become too much, even for me. I still believed that some mail would come for me and asked Mum to check one more time for me before she left to catch up with us. Loading and launching *Southern Cross* was easy from this premium marina. I took a photo to show that the smallest boat in the marina was the one traveling the farthest in the ocean. Our situation here was a living oxymoron. Old-fashioned exploration in a canned-adventure bazaar. A place where well-heeled tourists megaboat out to the reef for the day. It was their "big" deal, their reason for traveling halfway across the world. In all fairness, I had not participated in any such tours. I imagine the underwater life is spectacular, but adventure is relative.

We paddled toward Port Douglas, which actually sits on its own highly developed peninsula and can be thought of as Cairns North. It would only be a ten-mile paddle day, and therefore the shortest distance we had traveled in the boat. It felt that way. We peeled our eyes for Mum pacing the prescribed location and finally spotted her. She was ecstatic to complete the first official beach-point rendezvous.

"It's a bit difficult to get a take on you. I saw a flicker of red for a while and then it was gone," she said.

That corresponded to when we took our sails down. We weren't even traveling very far offshore and she was looking for us specifically. To those onshore we were less than a speck on the shimmering horizon.

We landed on the very pretty, very tropical, and very pleasant Palm Grove Beach, which was bordered by the large jellyfish net deployers. The palms were very orderly, too orderly, and probably not indigenous to the area but rather a necessary detail for the fulfillment of tourist brochure expectations. It seemed to me that this whole setting was made for Disneyland and put back in Australia. Add a few koalas and kangaroos with a couple of Croc Dundees and you could have an even more Australian Australia. I am sure they would make sure of that for their venues in the U.S., France, and Japan. Matching reality with expectation amounted to dollars in the entertainment business. I wondered if "Australia" had been trademarked yet.

Jan had found a nice hotel for us to stay in where there was room for the three of us and places to sprawl and sort things out. That night the trio of us operated in our separate worlds, reading and writing. Jan brought me another package.

"I found this at the post in Cairns yesterday afternoon before I left. I hope it has what you're looking for."

It was from Eddie Anderson, David Lee Roth's right-hand man. It included a host of musical tapes but interestingly none of his Van Haalen music, which had rocked me through my freshmen year at college. The music ranged from Kitaro to seventies Top 40 to Motown. The package also included many batteries. I was grateful and touched that these guys had had the time to think of me, but I still had a flat tire.

I wrote another letter to Nicole and one to my friend Don. The latter included bittersweet lashings about Nicole, entertaining the conjecture that she "may not have the capacity to really love" (as if I somehow had more experience, greater depth and endurance in these matters).

In the midst of this, Mum brought up some fun fact about crocs, saying that they bite with a force of two-to-three tons per square inch, eat only two-to-three kilograms of food per week, and do prefer fresh meat to some of their stored specimens. It was not Tony's first choice of things to hear.

I excused myself to mail my letters and make a call to my own mom.

"How's Dad?"

"Your father is making the best of it." She sighed. "He keeps himself busy but it gets so quiet in the store. Mr. Hoyt has been a tremendous help. Anyway, how's the trip going?"

"I'm thinking of doing a cycling trip by myself."

"What? What's happened?"

"Nothing specific, but we just finished the 'easy' part of the trip and it feels like a huge trip in and of itself. I cannot fathom that we are only a quarter of the way done, much less that we have to repeat it three times over."

"Is there a problem with you and Tony?"

"I think he and I are probably doing as well as two people in our circumstances could, but it has been tense here and there. He tends to blow up and I tend to boil inside."

"That doesn't sound like you. You and your father certainly went at it."

"Dad and I were different. The disagreements were confined to black-and-white business issues, this situation is much more nebulous."

It was good to hear her voice. More and more, it felt like we were just starting our trip all over again. There just weren't any more highways going into this territory. Dirt roads yes, highways no. There weren't going to be any real villages, towns, or cities for over four hundred miles. This last bit of the brochure was a last illusion. I had to tell somebody else firsthand about my solo adventure that was brewing if this Siamese partnership continued to strain. I suspected Tony was venting my transgressions and difficulties to his mum and I had needed to do the same.

That night, I woke up to a cold realization that I had put the letter criticizing Nicole—that I'd written to Don—in the envelope with the letter I'd sent to Nicole. It would be the relationship equivalent of bombing Hiroshima. The "lack of a capacity to love" line probably wouldn't win back a lot of distant hearts. My heart pounded and I paced about in a loss. *Break into the mailbox,* was the first thought. I had to call her and pretend I had made a casual mistake and kindly ask her to pass the letter on to Don. I went to the phone with a boat-load of coin and hesitantly made the call.

"Hello."

"Hi, Nicole."

"Oh. Hi, Eric."

"Have you received all the letters, trinkets, and stuff?"

"Yeah, the blah, and the blah, and blah," she said in a monotone.

"Any feedback?!?"

"Well . . ."

"So what's been going on?"

"I'm going to stay in NYC. I got a new apartment and got chosen for a commercial."

"Listen Nicole, I put a letter for Don Jr. in with a letter I sent to you. Could you please pass that one on to him when you get?"

"Sure."

"So, is there anything else?"

"Nope."

"Is that it, Nicole?"

"Yep. That's it."

"Bye. I love you. . . ." *(click)* ". . . Nicole?"

Just before she hung up, I thought I heard her hushing someone in the room. Her tone had been arctic, finally making it clear to me that it was over.

I must have been clearly disjointed, because Tony's mum took note of my return and the look on my face.

"It looks like you've seen a ghost, Eric."

"Well . . ."

I then proceeded to fill her in on my side of the story, which transferred some of her motherly instincts to me for the moment. I tried to deflect them.

"I'm all right. It's better this way. It was bound to happen anyway."

"She was young," Mum offered.

The lights went off and I tried to sleep. Tony had managed to sleep through this crisis.

I skipped from one negative thought to the next. *Nicole is with another man.* Always a good thought to start a spiraling descent. More immediate concerns added to my gloomy disposition. I had heard from a local that the Gulf of Carpentaria can have torturously high winds. *So, I do the trip, lose the girl, and get to challenge death to a duel all at the same time. Meanwhile, I have my partner's mother seemingly escorting us to some point near the end of the earth as we know it so that we can jump off.*

Superego countered with a resounding: *You needed to lose the emotional burden of the woman, anyway, and it is better that her tone was cut-and-dried instead of in-between, which might have kept an inkling of hope in your heart. A "that's it click" with hushing tones to someone close by in the early morning hours should be enough to set you free. Besides . . . she was young.*

The next stop was Wonga Beach, adjacent to Port Douglas, thirty miles away. A real day on the water again! There is a very different feeling when you know someone is up ahead. Mum could reach our final destination in an hour or less and it would take us the better part of eight hours to get there.

Modern transportation has really taken much less time away from the journey and boiled it down to many destinations. We end up missing most of what exists between point A and point B. For millions of years we traveled more in rhythm with the earth, her seasons, her contours, her light. We have created new rhythms, travel to our own seasons, and light our own way. This has all happened in relatively recent years. Are we really geared for it?! Should we be?! The very latest technology keeps us in one place and allows us to connect with the whole world. Is the journey left out or are we redefining its meaning?

It was a good sailing day—sunny, welcoming, and mild. Neptune was giving us the red carpet ride to Port Douglas. I had a chance to read a bit from the book of Aboriginal stories, in preparation for the leap off the end of the earth into dreamland and the domain of the Aborigines. The land north of Cooktown was relatively untraveled by the "white" man and therefore was subject to the mystery therein.

I flipped to a story about Yhi. According to it, "in the beginning" nothing existed in a dark, silent void. No animals or flowers or trees or any sign of life. Not even wind or rain. The world lay quiet, in utter darkness. There was no vegetation, no living or moving thing on the bare bones of mountains. No wind blew across the peaks. There was no sound to break the silence.

Yhi—the spirit of the sun—slept and waited for Baiame the Great Spirit to come to her and wake her from her stony slumber.

When Baiame awakened her with a whisper, Yhi's eyes fluttered open. All at once the brilliant light of her eyes dispelled the darkness. She floated down to earth and began her wanderings. And where her feet touched, life sprang from the ground—literally the flowers and trees spiraled from the dirt, and reached up from the dark earth to the ripe light.

Reading this story reminded me of Native American myths I had read. I was not surprised that the mythology of the Aborigines would be so closely allied with respect to the earth and things that live. It made me wonder why Christian religion seems so distanced from nature. Was it always that way? Or have the myths of Christianity been rectified by a culture dominated by commercial interests?

Another myth reminded me of the story about the Amazons from Greek mythology. Beyond the mountains where Baiame lived was a land inhabited by a colony of warlike women. Their land was remote and was defended by a vast dry plain and—closer—a deep lake. The women were renowned for their skill in manufacturing weapons. Offerings of meat and skins were left beside the lake, and when the traveler retired out of sight, an emissary from the land of the women would paddle a boat across the lake and leave weapons in exchange.

The stories were beautiful and wonderful and haunting and—at least to a white American thousands of miles from home—remote. I was frankly bothered by more immediate concerns. For instance, what kind of reception might we expect from the Aborigines? After all, we were entering their land, not ours. The facts were not clear and frankly I did not want to know them. I did not believe we had to share the fear Edmund Kennedy may have had before he embarked on his ill-fated overland Cape York expedition, which had left Mission Beach 150 years ago. Thirteen departed and only three returned. He was not one of them. The natives had killed him. What lay in store for us was still much more of the "unknown" than we had experienced until now.

Although born to land we were exiled from her. We were not walking on terra firma. We were floating with the sea, sea separated from us by a few millimeters of rubber and a centimeter of wood, bending and flexing with its rhythm. Myths have more punch when one is in the midst of unbounded natural settings. From this perspective, it was not hard to visualize the Aboriginal stories. I had already been introduced to Baiame, the Great Spirit, and had been up close and personal with Yhi, the sun goddess, on this journey.

The winds picked up and I put the book down and settled into the rest of the day, finding and feeling the right line through the water. In a sailing kayak, this is a constant series of adjustments. The idea is to find the line that minimizes the extent of those adjustments. We were blessed with very pleasant sea conditions.

"Brilliant day today, wouldn't you say, Epic?"

"Fantastic, we're moving really well. Your mum seems thrilled."

"She is! She hasn't been up this way in her whole life. It's been like finding a new country without having to leave her own."

The weather from Cairns to Port Douglas had been very hospitable. I couldn't help but fast-forward. *Is this the proverbial "calm before the storm"?* Yhi was well on her way to disappearing for the night when we finally arrived at Wonga Beach near Port Douglas.

I found the Coconut Grove Motel and Michael Gabor, my distant contact there. Mike immediately reminded me of the restaurant managers at the Coffee Shop in NYC. He had that pace to him, eyes registering all moving people and things. Mike, who it turns out was a transplanted East Coast "Yank," was hustling, almost maniacally so, in a very uncharacteristic Australian fashion. Admittedly, the restaurant was abuzz and running smoothly.

His hobby was flying "Trite" ultralights, which were essentially motorized hang gliders. Pictures of and from the craft adorned the hallways of his establishment. The photos emphasized mountains, sea, sky, openness, and freedom. It presented an interesting contrast—polished hustle in a low-key atmosphere. In this way, he was part magician. His ultralight was his magic carpet.

Mike arranged for us to use the barbie outside to cook up a host of steaks, chops, and chicken that Mum had brought for us. We ate to our hearts' content in a tropical courtyard with soft lighting, tables, and chairs. I started to feel the clinginess of "luxury" in the context of what lay ahead. I started to feel the loss of edge, of readiness. Three nights in a row with a pillow were unprecedented. My body was expelling waste three times more frequently than in recent months. I was starting to feel heavier again and part of me didn't like it.

The destination was Weary Bay, in the vicinity of Cape Tribulation ("Cape Trib"), adjacent to Daintree National Park, which is a magnificent rain forest next to the Atherton Tableland, a volcanic-soiled plateau with tumbling waterfalls, mountain streams, and jungle-fringed crater lakes. The sail/paddle was beautiful. Rain-forest-covered mountains met the water, and the mass of Cape Trib proudly presented itself in the distance. People have spent weeks and months exploring the landmass that we were bypassing in a day. Mum was going to see more inland sights and sounds of the Australian coast in two days than we had seen in two months.

We managed to get to Weary Bay on the northern side of Cape Trib and enjoyed this long, crescent-shaped, beautiful beach for a couple of hours before Yhi did her sunset number again. She rose from the earth, the story goes, then shrank to a ball of light in the sky. According to legend, all the creatures mourned because with the departure of Yhi, darkness rushed back into the world.

But I was mourning far more mundane inconveniences. My Walkman was dying. The tape was playing a third its normal speed, and my attempts to recharge batteries via small solar rechargers on the decks of *Southern Cross* were futile. Moreover, one of our waterproof cameras had called it quits with a high-pitched whining sound. Waterproof, shock resistant, and dustproof. It was not sandproof. During one of our capsizes water must have seeped into the camera.

Electronics don't belong on this trip! I screamed to myself. This was a fact Tony had understood all along. I took out the Global Position System and reset the triangulation coordinates to our latest position.

Tony shook his head as if to say, Will he *ever* learn.

The next day was Cooktown. On June 11, 1770, Captain Cook was sailing only a few miles farther east of where we were.

Cooktown—215 years after its discovery. After sailing thirty-five miles in pleasant eight-to-twelve knots of wind and enjoying the most amicable week of sea conditions we'd had, we landed *Southern Cross* on the banks of the Endeavour River, where Captain Cook had been forced to land and make repairs.

There were a number of other boats in the river, mostly motor driven. There was a modest dock, yet we chose to land at a small strip of beach where we felt we could spread out our gear for the long day of cleaning, maintenance, and repair. The most pressing of these was a two-inch hole that had been gnawed into the top of the bow by a feral pig the night before. *Southern Cross* was suffering and I spent four hours straight in the operating room.

A passerby stopped with his little girl and I informed him of our plans.

"Hmmm, crossing the gulf, huh? Ya know, I've been across once and it was pretty rough."

"What were you on?" I asked.

"A sixty-foot shrimper."

There was a noticeable pause as I tried to compute the new information. I wanted to ask more but I could not afford to hear it. I think the man could see the dejection on my face. I knew I certainly felt it.

"I'm traveling in that boat over there. (It looked like a fifty-foot houseboat, only more streamlined, with a V-shaped seagoing hull design.) I might just escort you across if I see ya up there."

"That would be great! How long does it take you to get to Thursday Island?"

"About five days, but I think I'll slow down and take a week."

"The fastest we can get there is in two weeks, and that is if everything goes perfectly."

"Well, good on ya. We'll see how it goes. Look me up when you get there."

"Where will you be?"

"At the oil company docks. Hey, can you take a picture of me with my little girl near your boat?"

"Sure."

Cook's journey in the area had become a minefield for his crew and the *Endeavour*. The shoals and reefs were maddening and unpredictable, and his keeled ship was at the mercy of the area that Cook would later label the "Labyrinth." With no charts (he was there to make them), a strong sailor's intuition about shallows (the likes of which were unknown to any sailor of the time), an approaching monsoon season, and a profound sense of duty as a discoverer for his country, Cook felt an underlying sense of terror.

When he eventually left Cooktown almost two months later, he would reluctantly choose to leave the coast and go safely outside the reef into deep sea. A
couple hundred miles later he would barely make it back through the reef to the
coast through what he named the "Providential Channel." Cook underwent a
serious reevaluation of his sense of self, his competency, his confidence, and his
soul.

Jan had secured another nice motel and I knew this was the last bed I would
see for a long time. It got me to think far ahead to the antithesis of this final eve.
I started to think heavily about crossing the Gulf of Carpentaria. It was over
four hundred miles as the crow flies. Up to now, I was partially anesthetized to
the scope of this by a yachtie who had said, "It'll be fair winds and two-meter
seas the whole way. You'll have no worries." My experience on this trip had
shown that well-meaning prophets were wrong more often than right. I realized
we would be responsible for ourselves.

"We're going to need leeboards to cross the gulf," I said.

"What?"

"I've been looking at the charts and we have to sail on a southwest course the
whole way."

"So?"

"The trades come from the southeast. I originally thought the route was
more due west. If we sail we will be reaching the whole way. If the winds shift
to the south we will be close reaching. The leeboards will help prevent SC from
drifting north. If we drift to far north we will miss the one and only village at
the end and not be able to paddle or sail against the trades to get back to it!"

"We'll rig something when we get to Thursday Island."

"I'm going to have my dad send us some leeboards from the States."

"I'm *sure* we can rig something."

"I don't think so and this is not the time to experiment."

The facts were that the Klepper leeboards involved three pieces of matched
wood (a sturdy ash-wood crossbar and two seven-ply triangular-shaped verticle
pieces). Moreover, it had specific metal fittings that allowed the pieces to come
together. There were two special clamp bolts with star nuts that allowed the rig
to attach securely to the coaming. As it was, they were primarily designed for
recreational day sailing. Anything bigger could overstress the coaming and anything smaller could be ineffectual. The basic design had not changed much in
forty years.

My journal for this last section of the trip, the section that nearly lost the
Endeavour, read simply:

> Purpose is back to doing this trip to the end. It's what we came here to do in the first
> place. The Nicole fallout helped clarify the purpose. That is good. Unfortunately, there
> is not much social camaraderie with Tony . . . mainly a get the "job" done

approach . . . Find no real need or desire to speak. I believe there is a silent, mutual
understanding that we're really just beginning the trip all over again. Now there is
"only" 7,500 miles to go, two major open sea crossings, 2,000 miles of croc-infested
coast, a couple thousand miles of absolutely barren coast, severe surf . . . again . . .
the Bight, the notorious Bass Strait, and then a 1,000-mile home stretch!? I want to
keep the pace hard now . . . easier said than done . . . Something seems so unreal
about it all. Oddly enough, it is harder to visualize it now after 2,300 miles traveled
than it was discussing it at the briefing clinics in NYC.

Captain Cook and the *Endeavour* had problems we were not nearly as concerned
with as a kayak team. Our boat drafted less than a foot of water at her heaviest.
The second set of air tubes in *Southern Cross* could shave three-to-four inches
from that when inflated. We could travel happily in shallows of a few feet. Less
than three feet of water adds appreciable hydrodynamic drag, but it will not tear
a keel off our boat. Moreover, if worse came to worst, we could paddle our low-
silhouetted vessel into winds up to twenty-five knots and still make some kind
of progress.

The *Endeavour* needed favorable wind and tide to get the mile or so out of
the Endeavour River. Ships did not sail terribly well to windward in those days
and larger tacking maneuvers were not going to work in the narrow and shallow harbor. Captain Cook fretted over the amount of time they had been
docked (almost six weeks) and his choice between heading north through a
"labyrinth" of islets, shoals, and reef or heading back south against "relentless"
southeast winds.

To us, the reef and islets represented a modicum of protection from the size
and power of the open sea. It cut down the surf at its knees and made our
prospects for landing more agreeable. *One less variable to be worried about.* This
chain of islands could also facilitate a form of nautical hopscotch and a more
direct run toward Cape York. The relentless wind could mean a fast passage.
However, we did share a sense of no turning back coupled with the feeling of
going into the unknown.

May 26. We left Cooktown on a steady southeast breeze and headed toward
Cape Flattery. Cook's method was to sail northward closer to the land, past the
shoals, reefs, and islets. The twenty-six-mile paddle from Cooktown to Cape
Flattery was the closest *Southern Cross* came to exactly retracing the *Endeavour's*
course. If we were to superimpose time onto space we would have been within
a couple hundred yards of her. It is likely we would have been passed off as any
one of the native canoes that they had already come across. Obviously the
natives Cook encountered had seen nothing of *Endeavour's* size before. It must
have struck them as a floating village compared to their dark canoes. What were
these massive trees rising from the decks with great swaths of white apparently
catching the wind? Where were the paddles, or the paddlers, for that matter?!

Alas, no ghost ship appeared and in its place came the outstretched metal arm and lights of a modern-day mining facility right off Cape Flattery. We spotted an island a mile or so offshore and headed toward it.

We landed on *our* island, disquieted by the fact that our trip to the other side of the earth already had visitors, as the lights of the mining facility outshone the earliest stars at sunset. *Was our quest for wildness going to be an illusion, too?*

Tony was very comfortable on the island, where the sea crocs would not be. This was *not* a mangrove island, the kind a croc likes. A little brackish water hole, a little vegetation, and a beach to slide across and sunbathe on. However, sea crocs have been found up to fifty miles offshore. Apparently, those crocs found that far offshore have no interest in eating but are desperately concerned with finding a new home.

I felt good about that part of the journey. My main fear (giant surf) was likely absent for a few thousand miles. The crossing seemed unreal and crocs didn't really bother me much, for I knew no better. A croc spotting to me seemed as unlikely as finding King Kong from our perspective on the coast. I just could not associate crocs with coast. I associated crocs with swamps and jungles. I still gave myself the luxury of fretting about my recently lost love life. The more Tony seemed concerned, the more I felt confident about our trip ahead.

I am not sure I would have felt the same affinity to sailing mariners past, present, and fictional if we had not already sailed so much in rough seas with *Southern Cross.* This was in contrast to a purely paddling adventure like Paul Cauffyn did a decade earlier. *Southern Cross* had proven to be a very able sailing vessel to all downwind and off-wind angles—the relatively silent surge of a wind-powered vessel, interrupted only by the bow piercing a wave or the sound of a roller breaking on or near us. There was the magical effect of angling two modest swatches of Dacron a few degrees and finding twice the power. *Southern Cross* was a missing link between all paddled vessels and all sailing vessels, I figured.

That night I wrote a mantra of sorts to myself in my journal:

Rhythm of trip, rhythm of trip, rhythm of trip—positive, positive, positive.

Today our path diverged from Captain Cook's. He would aim the *Endeavour* east-northeast back out through the reef to find open sea. We would bear straight for Murdoch Point, well inside the reef.

I pondered the dramatic beauty of Hinchinbrook and the grandeur of the rain forest. Cooktown seemed like the road at the end of the universe. All the history got me thinking about pirates. I wondered what a modern-day nautical pirate might be like. I knew that quite a few land pirates were found in merger and acquisitions companies back home, where the plundering was more bountiful.

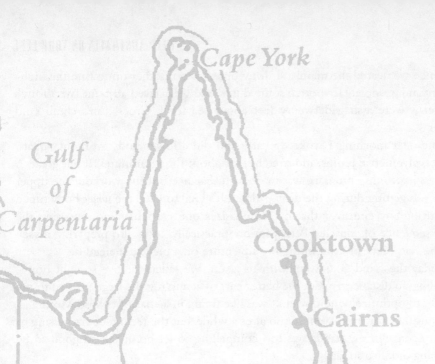

Cape York and Thursday Island

We traveled fifty nautical miles on a steady and strong southeasterly. This was the trade-wind freeway I had been waiting for! Although we had to pay close attention to waves and wind gusts, the NNW course was perfect for Howard's wing-on-wing sailing design. Tony had fashioned a hard rubber drainage plug into the square shape necessary to use the new mast. The straight, full-sized, no-bend mast worked with an efficiency we were not accustomed to. It had been seventy-five days since our first aluminum alloy mast broke. I could sense the difference. I think Tony secretly missed the garden hoe, patchwork and all.

Ten hours of comfortable paddling later, we approached Cape Murdoch. I searched its southeastern face for a landing. Tony expressed serious concern about where we put *Southern Cross*. It was the crocs.

"This is just another night I want to get over with. This is really stupid."

From my perspective we were many miles from any river mouth. The coast looked sandy and relatively barren. Tony started steering to the right toward an island offshore.

"Tony, I don't see any beaches on that island."

"Mate, you've got to be patient, there is sand there you can't see yet."

As we got closer, no sand appeared.

"I really don't think there is anything on the island. We should probably go over there." Tony steered *Southern Cross* to the left toward the mainland.

Once we neared the mainland, Tony opted to go farther on to find the highest ground possible. He spotted some dunes and we arrived an hour later. Tony's concerns were assuaged twenty feet above sea level. Crocs don't climb sand dunes . . . yet.

The next morning I woke up early and did a lower body workout: squats, lunges, plyometric jumps, and stretches for about fifteen minutes. It felt great. A modest leg-toning program was in order to balance out the workout the upper body was getting during the daily paddles. It's vital to keep the *whole* body tuned up during any endeavor that overemphasizes one particular motion using the same sequence of muscles. Perhaps more practically, I was also preparing myself for the possibility of continuing my adventure on a bicycle if need be.

Today the wind gods were with us again. We sailed for five straight hours, gobbling up distance. I spent the better part of it angling the large jib, tied to my paddle, to optimize wind power. It was like flying in a chariot behind Mothra all day long. My forearms went numb after a while, but the feeling of harnessing so much energy in my hands was too compelling to let go. It felt so good to be covering distance so fast!

We passed Cape Melville in the early afternoon. We elevatored up and down on the largest waves we had encountered in weeks. The Force 5 and 6 SE winds had generated four-to-five-foot following seas. Cape Melville was in their way and the collision and recontouring had caused the waves to swell, stack, and fall. Tony was getting submarined again but was prepared this time.

"What do you think of these numbers, mate?" I turned around to see Tony's eyes widely framed by a large pair of dark-rimmed eyewear.

"What are those? You look absolutely mad as a hatter."

"WWII motorcycle goggles. Working rather well, I might add."

I chuckled under my breath and said, "The next thing you'll want is a box car."

"Yeah, so I don't have to look at your furry little head all day."

We rolled and surged past the large cape.

"Look over there, mate!" Tony said.

A dozen booby birds broke us out of our spell when they swooped and glided all around. They occasionally hovered directly over our heads, cocking their heads off to the side like the pilot of a Sopwith Camel.

"Brilliant," he added.

They accelerated fifty meters ahead and did spectacular dives to the tops of the waves and skimmed the water's surface perfectly for another fifty meters along the crest of the waves. Finally, they would all peel out to the left and bank a hard turn and start all over again.

The whole presentation was augmented by the Joshua tree look of the cape itself. Cape Melville was an unusual "pile" of rocks. Big ones, little ones, little ones on big ones, big ones on little ones in tenuous balance. A complete aberration from the rest of the coast provided the perfect theater for our troop of boobies.

The cape was also the closest we had been to the actual Barrier Reef boundary, which lay a mere five-to-ten miles to starboard. It had been the proxemics to the reef that had minimized the "fetch" (open-water distance) that had kept the waves modest and allowed us to talk and sail simultaneously, but now the cape was directing the show.

Eventually we rounded Melville and started a WNW course toward what appeared to be an endless series of islets. We were now paralleling major bits and pieces of the actual Great Barrier Reef. There was not a continental (chip-of-the-mainland) island to be found. These were barren coral and sand mounds. They appeared like dunes in an oceanic desert. The most distant islets looked like a hazy mirage. Shoals surrounding one islet merged into the shoals of others and seemed to connect all the dots. Some of them would have to be our home, as we were leaving the mainland behind and starting to make a sixty-mile crossing of Princess Charlotte Bay.

The second half of the day brought sports stories. Tony discussed the raucousness of English soccer matches and how the local populace supported their teams fanatically. If you lived in the neighborhood of a particular team, attendance at the matches was mandatory. Of course, the après match activities at the pubs were epic.

"I lived in Chelsea and would go to most of the matches. Afterwards the whole stadium would get into drunken brawls. You should've seen it! I mean, just like the movies—punching, kicking, people going through doors head first."

"And yourself?"

"I always managed to find a corner someplace to have another pint and watch the bouts."

This led to comparisons with Tony's beloved "Aussie Rules."

After further explanation it sounded to me like a center versus a guard in basketball. Aussie Rules players are tall compared to soccer and rugby players, although not quite the height of most basketball players. Tony talked about leaping high to make a "mark" and retain possession of another player's long punt or take possession from the other team.

Most posters in Australian pubs show players' feet somewhere around other players' shoulders as they leap and climb simultaneously for the ball. Tony explained that on one occasion he was knocked out cold when his head smashed into another player's in the middle of such a leap. The following flip fall was quite spectacular and was talked about for years. There are no protective pads in Aussie Rules.

I discussed my kamikaze youth, in which I always related to the strong safeties of American football. I would throw my body in, at, and through players with reckless abandon.

"When I played forward in soccer, I would never stop charging the goalie. I got quite a few warning cards for that."

This led to a discussion of martial arts and then boxing.

"I've always wanted to learn a martial art but I just don't think I would have the time," Tony said.

"You have to be willing to give up at least one full year and dedicate it to learning the basics. After that you can practice on your own and be OK, but mastery takes a lifetime and unless you practice regularly, it won't help you in most fights, anyway.

"Bruce Lee used to say: Before learning Jeet Kune Do, a punch is a punch and a kick is kick. While learning Jeet Kune Do, you do not know what a punch or kick is. After learning Jeet Kund Do, a punch is a punch and a kick is a kick," I added.

The night I won my match at the University of Colorado's boxing "Smoker" in front of my fraternity and friends was a tremendous high. I relayed how I had no hate and no anger in the match. I had taken the "art" of boxing seriously and had learned the trade with professionals. By the time I had reached "the match," I had sparred countless rounds with some very good boxers. Boxing at the amateur level did not seem to involve the viciousness of other field sports even though the objective of the sport is to hit the other person rather than score a goal.

We talked of erotic dreams. I had actually dreamed of that French femme fatale "friend" of mine whose motto was: Lovers cannot be friends.

"Tony, she was like a dream. I used to stand on a curb to be a tad taller than her and when I held her in my arms she would purr. I wish it could always be like this."

"In your dreams, mate?"

"No, that really happened once upon a time."

"I'm sure it did," he said dubiously.

"She used to say that 'lovers' always carry the biggest daggers and know the 'best' spot to use them on each other."

Six more hours had passed and our chattering sobered as we approached the mangroves of King Island. Our eyes squinted in the dimming light to find any patch of land. As we got within a half-mile, I spotted a thirty-meter stretch of beach through a corridor of thick mangrove. We paddled through, landed, and even *my* croc warning lights started to blink.

"Mate, a croc has got to be around here someplace!"

"We should build a wall between that spot back there (he pointed to a dark hole in the middle of this tiny island where the beach funneled to nothing amid thicker and thicker vegetation) and the beach."

"I think you're right this time."

We wasted no time in constructing a fortress of wood, rock, and debris as thick as we could in the failing light, which was bolstered minimally by the

microbeam of our Maglites. We figured the barrier would deter, at least temporarily, one of the long-nosed fiends. If he tried to come through it, we would
hear the ruckus and promptly run. Though, *where,* was another question. *Perhaps
a mad dash out in the kayak?!* Anyway, I felt better about our predicament. Sleep
fitfully arrived.

Predawn. I rose alert and realized that there was not enough time to go back
to sleep. I did another workout and started some porridge. Once Tony woke up,
we ate quickly and shoved off. No sense in overextending our welcome. I knew
that crocs liked to warm their cold-blooded bodies in the sun.

The trade winds had diminished some and we started the day paddling. It felt
a little odd and it took a few minutes to get into the swing of things. Hours later
it had become all too familiar and we were reprieved by an afternoon sea breeze.
King Island had been the last vegetated island of the bunch. Now it was which
pile of sand or coral. The weather was deteriorating, a gray curtain was falling,
and visibility was poor. The sea breeze was bringing in a sea fog.

"Tony, we can't afford to get lost out there. There's no mainland within
twenty miles."

"What do you suggest, mate?"

"We should head toward that light tower on that islet over there. It looks like
the highest ground in the area."

We took down the sails and paddled to the somewhat higher pile of sand
amid a low-lying string of islets that appeared to come and go with the tide.
The place we chose was actually adjacent to the strip of land with the
medium-size light beacon on it. *It didn't look like two islands just an hour ago,* I
thought to myself.

It was three o'clock.

"When did you say high tide was?" Tony asked.

"I'm not sure but based on how much of these islets have submerged already,
I can't imagine that we are not past midcycle."

"So what does that mean?"

"A couple hours, three at the most."

"We better dig a trench, mate, just in case."

We dug a deep seven-by-five-by-four-foot trench with our paddles and
packed the displaced sand onto the perimeter to add another foot of protection.
The penalty for choosing the highest point in the bay was the total wind exposure that incessantly roared and blew sand in our ears. But we felt secure that the
tide would not envelop us. When we had begun the digging, the islet was the
size of an aircraft-carrier landing deck. When we had finished, it was more like
a junior league basketball court, and the adjacent light beacon had gotten
noticeably shorter. *Hmm. Can't get higher than this. The sand was not wet up here.*

We huddled ourselves in the trench and did some reading for an hour or so.
At five-thirty, we started dinner. While Tony started some bizarre mustard,
corned beef, and pasta concoction, I was more concerned by our disappearing

landmass. The adjacent landmass had disappeared and the light tower was rising straight out of the water. We still had the company of a couple of shrimp trawlers that had used our islet as a windbreak to hold on to for a while. We hadn't seen a stir on those boats all day. Shrimpers sleep by afternoon and get ready to work at night.

As evening arrived, their lights went on like those on a well-adorned Christmas tree. A clear line of lights, spaced approximately a kilometer apart from each other, extended as far north as we could see.

"We're lit up like Piccadilly Circus," Tony remarked.

At seven-twenty I wrote in my journal, "We're safe. The tide isn't going to come up to our camp."

I assumed that high tide had come up as far as it was going to. Five hours had passed since we had landed and I presumed that the normal six-hour tide-cycle bell curve had run its course. However, the tide continued to climb and our basketball court had become a Central Park sandbox.

"Tony, I think we better start shoveling more sand onto the wall."

"Why, mate?! I thought you said the tide was done."

I shrugged. "I think I might have been wrong."

The tide crept higher. Water lapped over the berm and then under our bags. We had to raise our bedding onto the tops of paddles staked in the ground. The dreary and miserable thoughts of standing in seawater in the middle of the ocean for hours was fast becoming a reality. A tired shrimp trawler captain might mistake us for an apparition or perhaps become reborn at the sight of "Jesus" walking on water. Perhaps, we would just sit in the boat and float it out.

The tide was up to our wall. We dug more sand.

At eight-thirty, the tide crested, then slowly began to recede. Our trench was dry! We must have arrived at the island at low tide. Once again the patient and relentless forces of nature had surprised and humbled me. I drew some satisfaction about stopping at this islet and putting our camp on the very highest part of it. We were learning. But, were we learning fast enough? *What was the next semester going to be like?*

The islet scare enlivened Tony a bit, and he mentioned an ominous secret from the night before.

"Mate, there was a fiberglass kayak split in half in the mangroves at the end of the path."

"What?"

There were two halves of a kayak hung up in the mangroves on the island we'd been on the night before. *How the hell did that get there and why was it split in half? And where was the paddler?!*

The wind had blown all night and the wave tops looked more like the darting tongues of serpents than the more symmetrical rollers. We decided to paddle first to get a feel for the new field. We still had over twenty miles to go to cross the bay and now the farther we traveled, the more fetch the wind and sea had to build up waves. The bay was relatively shallow and it appeared that waves were already bouncing back from the other side, interlacing with the predominant easterlies.

"Stop a second, Epic, I have to adjust my seat." I paused and felt the boat teeter-totter from side to side as a wave leaped onto the starboard side of the boat.

"OK, mate, I'm ready."

We paddled for about two minutes and I heard Tony scream.

"The chart, the chart!"

"What is it, Tony?"

"Do you have the chart?"

"No, I haven't touched it since this morning on the beach."

"Then it's gone."

"No way!"

"It must have gotten swept off the deck by that wave."

"We've got to go back and look for it!"

One of those serpents' tongues stole our then current chart, leaving us blind in our bay crossing. The chart was now lost in a field of whitecaps. We circled and circled to no avail. We were now chart blind all the way to Thursday Island. Moreover, we were in the middle of the "labyrinth" that the good Captain Cook chose not to enter.

"Well, we're just going to have to angle towards the mainland earlier than we wanted to."

"Mate, why can't we just keep following the islands?"

"We have no idea if there are going to be any high enough to stay above the tide line and this weather is looking pretty bad. It's also getting close to the new moon. That's why I think that tower island disappeared last night."

"We might as well raise the sails then, mate, because the wind will be right behind us!" Tony said.

Tony steered toward the mainland. *Southern Cross* was back in her wing-on-wing groove and stampeding westward with the three-to-four-foot predominantly following sea, slicing right through the convoluted backs of the white-tongued serpents.

"Better put on those goggles, TB!"

"I already have!"

After a while, *Southern Cross* had found a precious line and I let my mind wander back to New York, New York. The immense tribe of friends and acquaintances I had amassed between the Klepper shop, Live Bait, and the Coffee Shop were sorely missed. I missed the variety of people, thoughts, problems, and solutions. I could not imagine that the Klepper shop was gone after over thirty years at 35 Union Square West. It was like hearing about the race riots. It was unthinkable, yet it was true. I started to feel banished, banished from my tribe and left to wander with a verifiable nomad in these desolate environs.

Luckily for Tony his mum was bringing him a brand-new Gore-Tex bivvy sack—complete with mosquito netting. I was more concerned about the feral boars Tony had talked about in this area.

"Yeah, I hear they'll run right through camp, goring anything in their path," he had said.

I got up and "Radued" again before dawn. *What has gotten into me?* I was the vampire, the late riser, the night person. Early morning had been an abomination to me. There I was, rising an hour before Tony. *Something inside is telling me "condition those legs."*

Once on the water we reached NNE on a favorable wind. We slowly angled out toward the chain of islets that had in turn angled closer to the mainland. We were past Friendly Point heading toward Cape Direction, a place where the Barrier Reef practically touched the mainland. In the late afternoon the wind quickly digressed into a nasty northeasterly that got progressively stronger until our last two-and-a-half miles took an hour and a half. We needed those miles because our first-choice island, so promising from the distance, turned out to be nothing but a pure mangrove. The island beyond was pure white with a channel marker (mini-unmanned lighthouse) on it. It looked more promising.

The paddling felt good but became progressively more tedious as we got closer to the island. Finally the wind was blocked in the shadow of the islet, the force shield was broken, and we landed amid a circus of birds reconnoitering our movements and diving in to give us a scare. It looked like a stage for the Hitchcock film *The Birds*.

I walked to the top of one of the channel lights and saw a set of tire tracks. I also saw a larger area with a number of large trees. All the trees were absolutely filled with birds of all varieties. I came back to camp and told Tony of my discoveries.

"TB, there were tire tracks near the channel marker!"

"What did they use to get here with, a lunar landing module or something?"

"Oh, and you thought there were a lot birds in that tree over there—you should see the ones back in reserve."

"Must be a special rookery. I think we are in the middle of their migration route," he said.

Night was approaching and a tremendous happy hour appeared to be under way. We made sure to park *Southern Cross* as far from the water as we could, but we did not have much real estate to work with. The beach was nothing but a graveyard for millions of pieces of dead coral.

What about those tire tracks? The Volgons?

The birds ruled the island. In our early attempts to sleep, it sounded like the birds were not only aware of us, but in fact, were mocking and taunting us.

I remembered a favorite Monty Python bit: "We are not frightened of you, you stinking humans. We wave our private parts at thee!"

An hour later a number of birds actually gathered within a few meters of Tony's tent and began squawking furiously. Had the Volgons taken the shape of birds?!

No need for an alarm clock. Thousands of birds welcomed Yhi from the other side of the earth. The celebration was magnificent! It was as if the birds were not totally sure that the sun was going to rise for another day.

We had to leave the party early. As we headed north, the usual thoughts arose. *Is there going to be a beach? An island? A safe place to land? What's the wind going to do? Will the mast hold? Do we have enough provisions?* Those were the standard prompts when we booted up each day.

Tony dropped a bomb.

"Mate, I think I may have gotten enough from this trip." I was incredulous. "If the next part is the tough and painful part, I don't know if I'll get any more from it."

My thoughts were stopped in their tracks. Derailed, more like it. I searched for the rewind button. *Is Tony saying this? Or am I hearing my own voice coming back to haunt me?*

"I have to start thinking about what I want to do next."

"Like what?"

"A new career. I have thought about it hard and I do not want to go back to modeling."

"Tony, I've told you, you don't know how good you have it with that job."

"I've had enough; it's not challenging enough for me."

"What would you like to do, go back to becoming a vet?"

"Maybe, but that is going back to do a lot of schooling. Actually I am thinking of becoming an anchorman for a news program."

"Come on, TB! An anchorman? Do you know what the politics in a newsroom is like? You would have to start out anchoring the news in Cooktown or something."

"Mate, I really think I'm going to do it."

"Yeah, sure, more likely, you could be a weatherman in Bundaberg and call out the cyclones like a sportscaster calling the bowling shots for cricket. You think the journalists who have been waiting out the pecking order for all these years are going to take kindly to a pretty-boy former model stepping in front of them?"

"I have an uncle in the business in South Australia. I've thought about it a lot and I've always been very keen on politics and economics. I think more about those things than about local bank robberies and the lot."

"Ahh, more like *World News Tonight* with Ted Koppel."

"Yes, something like that."

Forty miles later we bypassed Night Island, where three sailing yachts were anchored for the night. We had daylight and we needed distance, so we converged with the mainland a few miles farther on. Tony's doubts about continuing the journey had dovetailed with my own. So where did that leave us? Where did it leave me?

I awoke the next morning with mixed feelings. At our current rate of travel averaging over forty nautical miles a day, we could make it to Portland Roads a little after lunchtime. We were told by our mud neighbors in Mackay that Portland Roads would treat us right. It was a place known to "insiders," where some "yachties" stop over when traveling the length of the Cape York Peninsula. The only place for white Australians and others. I had thought we would have to stop at the Lockhart River Aboriginal community for provisions at that point in the trip. As it was, we were moving farther faster than I had imagined, and our provisions were holding out just fine.

The foreknowledge of Portland Roads was going to save us at least a day of traveling deep into Lloyd Bay and then west to the community, with no guarantees we would have access to what we needed. But we'd also be deprived of an experience with the Aborigines on their home court. An Aboriginal flag was stickered to my compass mount as a gesture of kindred spirit. *We were silently segregated by logistics first and desire for like-kind familiarity second*, I told myself.

We crossed Lloyd Bay straightaway with a steady, strong wind to Resolution Island adjacent to Portland Roads. We covered the twenty-five miles and saw a small compound on the island. I figured it must've been some type of ranger headquarters or out-of-the-way pub/milkbar for the few yachties who stop by.

We landed *Southern Cross* in a calm lagoon and were immediately greeted by a couple of dogs. Then we walked to the compound, where we woke up the station innkeeper.

John took our noisy intrusion in stride. I told him I'd hoped we weren't interrupting.

He shrugged stoically. "I wake up *then* decide what I want to do that day." We told him about the trip, and about the loss of the chart. He went to his desk.

"Take mine. Just return it when you get to Thursday Island."

"Thank you! How should we send it back?"

"Give it to the boat company that stops here once a month on its run to Cairns."

John gave us a tour of his station. The bunk-style bed hadn't been washed, much less made, in a great while. Light green was the color of choice for the interior, highlighted with college-beige tapestries like you would find in a college dorm room. A detailed butterfly identification chart was positioned on the wall bordering John's bunk and was among the very first sights for him every morning. More books on birds, flora, fauna, science, and by Stephen Hawking dominated a middling-sized bookshelf. A *Conan the Barbarian* comic book appeared to be the current read and a B-52s tape had recently been ejected from the tape deck. Some notes on plants and weather were scribbled on his desk.

John told us about other kayaking visitors who had traveled the route before. He was particularly keen on a letter he received from a Scottish couple who had done the route in a month. They thanked him profusely for inside knowledge about some of John's "neighbors," whom the couple visited. These neighbors totaled about three and were located on their own private-island retreats.

"You can use my name when you land on their islands but please be courteous. They are private people and trust my judgment."

Apparently, the advice worked brilliantly and the Scottish couple had a grand adventure. There were notes on weather, wind, and sea conditions. I read them carefully, but less gullibly now, knowing that every voyage for every sailor is different regardless of whether it is along the exact same route.

The other kayaking visitors were a threesome from Mission Beach who had some very "hi-tech" kayaks and some big plans to travel all the way to the Solomon Islands. Tony and I took the news with a certain smugness and the awareness of a couple thousand miles under our belts.

"They've got long way to go," Tony said.

"When did you say they were here?" I said, thinking of trying to overtake them with our "low-tech."

"Over two weeks ago."

"Hmmmm?"

This was "our" coast and I remembered how Howard had felt when he had heard about the French expedition group who were trying to circumnavigate the Horn, as well as Jorn Werkman, who had come down to beat Howard to the punch. A shot of adrenaline made my hair stand on end. *That's what we need, a chase!*

John told us about his once-a-month "deluge" of visitors from the Cairns–Thursday Island express and where he held court for them. He provided a live Discovery channel for them and they gave him a month's worth of company in one sitting.

"It's really a busier place than it looks; fishermen are dropping by every couple weeks. I can also keep in touch with the radio." He walked us to the back of the room.

He pointed to his WWII vintage communications empire with a heavy, handheld radio mike and various tuning dials that kept him in contact with the world.

"Do you know anybody near Cape York that we can look up?" I asked.

"I know some folk at the ranger station. I'll dial 'em up now."

"Any idea where we should stay tonight?" Tony asked.

"You're welcome to camp here but you might enjoy a little hut around that point and a couple miles up the coast." He pointed to the north. "Keep your eyes open as soon as you get around the point."

Tony seemed reenergized by our visit with John. So did I.

"Johnny boy was quite the find, mate!" gushed Tony.

Less than two hours later, we had rounded the point and were on final approach for what looked like the hut John had described nestled on the north end of a sand beach outlined by mangrove and forest.

"TB, something was moving near the hut." I pointed. "It looked like pretty tall. It wasn't a kangaroo." I figured John would have known if anyone was staying there.

"It could be an emu," ventured Tony.

"A what?"

"A nasty bird that's taller than you are. It's like an ostrich, can't fly and has a bad disposition about it. Strong, too, like a bloody sumo wrestler."

"This can't be its nest?"

"We'll see, won't we. I suggest we put *SC* on the other side of the beach in case we have to make a quick getaway."

The closer we got, the less likely I thought what we had seen was an emu.

"Shit, it's some guy with a beard."

We still landed *Southern Cross* on the far end of the beach and debated who would approach the being.

"You better talk to him, TB."

"He's already coming over here, mate."

Soon, the slight, smiling, long-bearded man approached us and introduced himself. "G'day, my name's Dave and welcome to our humble abode. How far have you come?"

"Sydney."

"Nooo!"

"Yep."

"Come in and meet Sue. I'll have her make a pot of coffee and see what she's got cookin'."

After securing *Southern Cross,* Tony and I put on our finest and joined Dave and Sue for a nomadic get-together. The hut was a combination of a nicely fortified large-rock perimeter and staircase covered with a giant wooden beam that supported a dark green canvas tarpaulin. This disguised the cavernous interior. The hut was complete with cast iron cookery, oil lamps, old chests, a cast iron makeshift stove, homemade wooden spoons, spatulas, and other utensils. A lounge chair throne positioned to catch a couple hours of late afternoon sun had obviously been added post-1970. It looked exactly the same as the one Archie Bunker sat in for his TV series. Someone had put a serious life-sustaining effort here.

"Did you guys build all this?!" I asked.

"No, it pretty much came as is, ready to live in," Sue said.

"Did you know the previous occupants?"

"No. Dave found it, called me, and he drove me here in a tinnie [motorboat] full of staples."

Shells, driftwood, and other beach relics were the backdrop to our gathering.

The talk became fast and furious over a pot of particularly potent java. We provided new ears for old tales.

Dave had found the beach hut first through some nomadic hotline, while living for two years in an elaborate tree hut in the rain forest. Sue had joined him sometime later to keep him "in reality" to some degree. Dave had been writing poems about magic, and a book about the various creatures of Australia banding together with the tree frog as their leader, who were going to repel man's destructive nature. His green eyes lit up as he enthusiastically described his characters and the philosophy of his book. As I looked at his long, thin, reddish beard and pondered his biography, he reminded me of an elf.

Sue had well-groomed dark blond hair, large-framed eyeglasses, a well-worn, untucked canvas shirt with no bra support, and she was barefoot. Her feet were thickly callused and looked like she rarely wore shoes anymore.

"Yeah, I was at university in Sydney and was getting tired of the urban rush in the Big Smoke."

They sustained their alternative lifestyle, at the beginning, with periodic staples of rice, beans, and flour to supplement the fish and plant life. Gradually, they weaned themselves from the staples.

"You mean you live completely off the land now?" Tony asked.

"Almost, we grow our vegetables and catch fish, even make our own flour."

Tony had suggested that a local might describe the pair as a couple of "hippies." Dave and Sue both frowned. They appeared more productive than what the term *hippie* might imply. There were no modern conveniences or crutches in their world.

An excellent fresh vegetable and rice dinner marked the middle of the evening. Between coffee and the meal, Tony turned his full attention to making the wooden foot fitting for the new aluminum mast. Tony's hard rubber insert had failed just moments before we landed. I wondered why it had been wobbling throughout the day. I watched him start to diligently fabricate the new piece under a iron kerosene lamp and I was sure I had seen the same scene as this in an illustrated *Robinson Crusoe* book someplace.

I continued to jabber away about the soul ages of the planet and the earth-change prophecies of the Hopi Indians.

"They say when the sign of the bear [the bar codes on consumer products] is found on the wrists and forehead of man then the third earth shaking will be imminent. The next sign is when man lives in a house in space on a permanent basis." The first two earth "shakings" had been found to correspond with World Wars I and II.

"Before the second earth shaking they said that the Hopi sign of life (the swastika) would be found to the east and the sun would rise west (Japanese Imperial flag) of Turtle Island (North America)."

Tony, impatient with my long-winded lecture, sighed wearily and decided to take a walk. Later, he joined us for after-dinner tea and some "peace piping" with some homegrown. This spun a new and mystical atmosphere as the reddish-yellow glow of the few lanterns darted off the rock walls. And it brought up more philosophy concerning the state of the world, particularly big cities.

Dave had not been to a big city and said he would be far too trusting and would need someone to show him the ropes for a long time. We suggested that with his relative purity and skills in the wilderness he probably shouldn't spend too much time in a big city. No sense in spoiling a good thing. Susan agreed. The banter continued for a couple of hours before fatigue and sleep settled in.

We woke up to more coffee and a massive kettle of porridge, consisting of muesli, dates, milk, and more. The jump start was escorted all the way to launch by Dave and Sue. It was back to the sea for us. Outdoor cave huts were too permanent a domicile for our intentions.

A half-hour into our voyage, Tony said, "Wasn't that brilliant, Epic? Maybe I'll bring Tash [Tony's girlfriend] up with me and live here a few months." We had learned that Dave and Sue would soon be moving on.

"Tony, do you think Tash would be keen on a couple of months? I could see a couple of weeks but it's a bit of a stretch to go from NYC-model lifestyle to a cave hut hundreds of miles from a town."

"I think she would enjoy it. We would learn a lot about each other."

His confidence in this experience coming to fruition was such that I had to believe that Tony could make it happen. I figured he'd gotten me to come on this trip with him; how difficult could it be to sell the Tarzan and Jane routine. I still believed that two weeks would be about enough for both of them. I felt a little melancholy that I couldn't even entertain the option anymore. Tony went on and on about the anticipated experience for the bulk of the morning.

Most of our attention for the rest of the day was on the larger than expected seas and the steady fifteen-to-eighteen-knot winds. The chart showed that the reef had cut down a bit and, in fact, was the area where Captain Cook reacquired the coast after spending a couple of weeks outside the "labyrinth." Apparently there was enough deep water here to get the *Endeavour* closer to the coast.

We made forty-five miles in eleven hours and landed hospitably on a beach in a small cove on the north side of Cape Grenville. It wasn't long before the stars joined us en masse, not quite with the same clarity as that of a mountain sky, but still with a horizon-to-horizon presence. That night I wrote in my journal:

I basically like Tony. However, this hip-to-kayak Siamese link all day, day after day is inherently difficult at best and unbearably frustrating at times. Any relationship needs a certain amount of space to remain productive. Much more than we are allowed.

Shelbourne Bay was on the menu today, and *Southern Cross* was more than up to the task. The strong southeasterly trade winds sailed us another forty-four or so miles to the northeast side of False Oxford Point.

"Mate, I think we're finally getting the hang of this," Tony said.

"Took long enough," I joked.

Southern Cross stayed on a near-perfect line and was on virtual autopilot. I verbally drew an analogy to a 747 cross-oceanic flight.

"Flight 964, coming in for a landing," Tony joked.

Shelbourne Bay was the final deep dent in the cape's complexion. In fact it was the last deep dent on the whole east coast. Most of the day was spent out of sight of land but as Flight 964 started to make its final approach, we saw a series of sparse undulating white sand dunes. The area geography had changed considerably from one side of Shelbourne Bay to the next. Nearly all signs of elevation had disappeared.

However, geographical drama had been replaced by four 4WD's armed with tinnies. It soon became obvious that we were their "catch" of the day. As the vehicles stopped, bearded and bellied buddies jumped out and started videotaping us. A few waved to us. We waved back, trying to keep out of hailing distance. The fellows were not Phinny, and we both wanted another night under the stars before Thursday Island and the beachless void of the Gulf of Carpentaria.

"Well, mate, looks like our last night on this section of the trip."

"This section has been impressive!" I said.

"Best so far, I reckon," Tony added.

We traveled a few more miles in the waning golden light to put us that much closer to the next day's goal. Distance still outweighed a full appreciation of the area. The past couple days had been the fairest travels we had had in the past week. A blending of wilderness, wind, warmth, and manageable sea conditions had allowed the forty-five-mile-or-so average per day that was eating up this relatively pleasant part of the journey faster than we had hoped. Getting to its end, I already had begun to miss it.

The relative ease of travel was as much a matter of rapport with Tony as anything else. This past week had given me a sense of amnesia regarding the rigors of the previous 2,200 miles, to the point where I was obviously deluded enough to write in my journal:

> *I was almost thinking that the 2,500 miles is no big deal, don't really feel challenged by it all just yet. Need more grit and effort to feel fulfilled in some way, shape, or form . . . this going with the flow is taking the form of the boat smoothly gliding from one wave to the next with the silent hand of the wind pulling us along throughout the day.*

That night we were granted the most beautiful sky so far. We saw the Big Dipper, but at our latitude we were a little too far south to see the North Star. Instead we saw a perfect view of the "Crux" constellation, better known as the Southern Cross. A fair sign? Cape York was next.

"Well, TB, it looks like we'll be out here another day, after all!"

"Why, mate?"

"We've been traveling so far so fast that I've misgauged the chart. Instead of our regular forty-five miles we would have to knock out seventy to get to Cape York."

"No worries. We'll go as far as we can."

Forty miles later we beached *Southern Cross* on an island in Newcastle Bay. The sea and stars cradled us for yet another night. This time I was startled awake by a sickening thought. The kind that you get when you really, truly consider the fact that you are going to die someday. I wasn't sure if I had been dreaming or just thinking in the twilight of sleep. I was drenched in a clammy sweat. I thought, *We're going to be on the water day and night for at least six days, maybe ten.* The potential—the *probability*—of disaster was very high. Capsize. Drowning. The scenarios bounced around inside my head like pebbles in a tin cup. The Gulf. The Gulf. The Gulf. I slept fitfully.

The last twenty-five miles of the mainland approaching the top of Australia were magic and were passing in slow motion. The wind was variable, undecided, so we were paddling again until it could make us come to some conclusion. *Have we gotten used to a totally different speed to make it feel this way or is it just the labor?*

Tony became ecstatic and yelled,

"*Look,* look to the right!"

A spectral shape of enormous size skimmed just under the surface of the water just off our starboard bow. Then I saw a spout of water and heard a gushing sound.

"What is it?"

"It's a *dugong,* mate! Like your sea manatees in Florida. They've my favorite creature on the planet."

"Don't they call sea manatees sea cows?"

"Actually they started the mermaid myth."

"Get out of here."

"True, they are very gentle and very intelligent and often get torn apart by the props of tinnies and other boats."

"*There it is!*" I said, as I saw it rise just a few meters from my right paddle blade.

The increasingly rare brown dugong, close relative to the manatee, surfaced intermittently and paralleled *Southern Cross* for nearly a mile.

The magic broke when I spotted a tinnie full of dark-skinned and dark-haired people gaining on us from astern.

"See that motorboat coming right for us, TB?"

"I see the boat. I can't make out its direction."

The dugong disappeared and its fluid peace was replaced with the sound, downwind smell, and unknown intent of the approaching motorboat.

"I've heard that they have pirates in these parts, TB."

"*Relax*, mate!"

A minute later it was clear they were heading right for us.

"Do you think they see us, mate?" Tony asked.

"Come on! How could they miss us. Are they all asleep?"

"Better put your paddle up just in case!"

It felt like a premature surrender to me. Now I could see the whites of their eyes. None of them were smiling and I started to feel helpless. I wanted to say "lock and load" but even the flare gun would take too long to get to. They were now seventy-five feet away and I tried another technique. I waved.

Instantly I saw half a dozen gleaming white smiles and waving hands. Seconds later, they were past. They did not look back but just continued motoring northward.

We paddled closer to shore, and about a hundred meters out, I spotted a blue tent and a few trails going up a small hill for a couple of miles. My eyes followed the trails to the ranger station and corresponding park that John had talked about days before.

"There's the ranger station, TB."

"Little early in the day to stop, don't ya think?"

"Yeah, I'm afraid so. I think we have to cross the straight and push for Thursday Island."

Our day did not leave room for a lengthy pit stop. We approached a narrow passage between a lighthouse-peaked island to our right, and the mainland, tangibly to port. We were twenty-five yards from shore when we were greeted by a medium-size sign that said: CAPE YORK—THE NORTHERNMOST POINT OF AUSTRALIA. We could practically touch it from the boat. The winds were light and the seas were calm, cut off temporarily from the straits by the island to starboard. *OK, who's pulling a fast one,* I thought to myself.

We rounded the cape and ventured into the calm, beautiful, green-hued waters of the Straits of Endeavour. A few sailboats were tucked in a protected notch in the mainland coast. It looked like we would have an uneventful passage across this potentially devilish stretch of water. A necklace of islets was strung one-third of the way out toward Prince of Wales Island, perpendicular to the mainland.

Thursday Island lay to the northeast. Between it and Heron Island was a funnel-shaped gap through which we aimed *Southern Cross*. A short five-mile shoot through the gap and a smooth five-mile dash down the throat to Thursday. No problem. I hoped.

A half-hour later, the strong breeze picked up and we raised the sails. Shortly after that we passed the last jewel in the necklace and smacked into the very agitated waters of the Staits of Endeavour. The sails filled hard, the boat heeled, and we were riding a galloping *Southern Cross*. I could see the funnel entrance splitting two islands. We were lined up perfectly for it. To me, that was a problem. A strong east-west current could conceivably take us too far west of the entrance and cause us a lot of extra work that we did not have enough daylight for. I cautioned Tony: "Maybe we should aim a little to the east, Tony."

"Mate, we're right on course."

"Just aim it a little east, Tony."

"Why, mate? What is it that you're thinking?"

"I read there was a strong east-to-west current here most of the time."

"Mate, it doesn't look like it. I think it might even be coming a little bit from the west."

I had a gut feeling that the current was going to come from the east, even though it did appear that it was coming from the west and colliding with the SE wind.

"Tony, just keep your eye out for any eastern push that is taking us west of our target."

An hour later we were almost halfway across and we were getting battered and tossed by strong winds that now seemed more easterly. I could see that we were starting to veer west, if not from sea current then by wind.

"Point her a little east, TB!"

"We're doing fine, mate!"

"We've already drifted a quarter-mile west. If any sea current joins the wind, we'll be booted to the west side of the big island."

"OK, if it makes you feel better." Tony steered a few degrees east and we quickly stabilized until we were about a mile away. Then we began drifting quickly west.

"See what I mean?!"

The current line became more visible. It was a large eddy line like the turbulence you see running past a large rock in the middle of a fast river, only much longer and much wider. We caught it just in time. It wasn't long before we were in the vortex of the "funnel." The last mile was bouncing us like a basketball, much like the Broken Bay crossing eons ago, only with more power. I started to think capsize was likely if we did not concentrate on every wave and every move we made.

"Steer carefully, it's really squirrelly in here!"

"I got it under control."

Once we were inside the funnel, the random waves were gone but the wind dramatically increased as the funnel became a canyon with the tall shoulder of Prince of Wales Island looming to port and the shallower Heron Island to starboard. The large island bent and accelerated the strong ESE winds toward the north and toward a cluster of islands . . . one of which was Thursday.

For the moment, we were enjoying the rare and exhilarating experience of high winds and almost no waves. The islands, bristling with dense mangroves, passed in a green blur. Replacing them was a series of channel markers aimed at a sprawl of humanity a few miles ahead. Thursday Island had us in its clutches.

We passed the northern extremity of Heron Island. A number of yachts were moored in a cove. We were flying through the most beautiful waters I'd seen on the trip. A kaleidoscope of blues and greens color-coding the variation of depths—the darker the blue, the deeper the water. In moments our due north course toward the middle of Thursday Island was bent strongly to the west. It threatened to take us past the westernmost point, which would've forced us to begin our crossing far earlier than we expected.

The wind shifted to the east as the eastern approach funnel took over from the southern approach. We had a strong wind and a strong tidal current taking us west. Our most harrowing seamanship in days was at hand in the last mile of our approach.

We sheeted our sails in hard and leaned both of our bodies hard to the right to stay upright. I was hanging over *SC*'s starboard side. Halfway across we were in the strongest winds of the day.

"Lean, mate, lean."

I was hiked out as far as possible. I glanced back to see Tony's right elbow touching the water. It was going to be close.

This is exactly where the leeboards would help, I thought. *I am glad I asked my dad to send them.*

Suddenly, we were in very light green water and were steering easily to our course. We had entered the shallows and escaped the clutches of the fast current. We slalomed past a few moored tinnies and headed for a beach in front of a large coral-colored hotel with a veranda and black-shuttered windows. Next to it was a grocery store. As we got closer I could see many people congregating and slipping about in front of the two buildings getting in and out of cars. As we landed I could hear the din of band music, the honking and cluttered chorus of the talking masses.

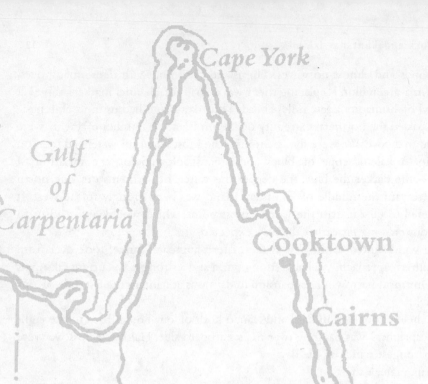

Thursday Island

Thursday Island lies on the southern end of the Torres Strait. Along with Prince of Wales, Big Heron, and seventy other islands, they span sixty miles and are known as the Torres Strait Islands.

We weren't in Kansas anymore.

Moreover, the natives didn't look particularly friendly. In fact, their ferocious appearance confirmed in my mind the rumor that many of these people had been cannibals not so long ago. More recently the inhabitants of this small island were pearlers, a very dangerous occupation where the ability to hold one's breath underwater was more than just a neat stunt on *Baywatch*.

It was the consistency of the scowling expressions that was most disturbing. These were not your Crocodile Dundee Aborigines with thin legs and arms. They were Torres Strait Islanders who came from a different stock altogether. Like Phinney had said, they were more like the Maori in their size of limb and expression. Their ancestors came from Melanesia and Polynesia, long distances over water. They had more ancestry in common with native Hawaiians than native Australians. It was the first time on the trip that I did not feel safe with people. How quickly the euphoria of the day's sail faded into the concern of what to do next.

"Ready to be tossed in the kettle, TB?"

"I think they're going to want your baby-white ass first, mate."

There were still a couple of hours of light left and I was expecting a lot of mail at the Thursday Island post. Moreover, a contact in Cairns had told me that she had a friend named Allison who worked at the Grand Hotel somewhere on the island.

"TB, I'm going to try to find that girl for that hotel connection I was telling you about."

"Awright, I'll keep an eye on the gear."

Previous coincidences told me that this would be our temporary salvation. I headed purposefully to town on a road—the only road—that ran east to west on the island. At the top of the hill I came upon the Grand Hotel. It had seen better days, but still seemed a notch above the lodgings I had seen on the west end. Happy hour had begun and the outside porches and inside pub were full. I asked the bartender if she knew Allison and she told me she was coming on soon. I asked her about a room and she said I should talk to the manager.

The manager smiled politely. "I doubt there's a room on the island," he apologized. "It's the annual inter-island rugby festival this weekend. We're booked through Monday." It was Friday.

"Is there any chance at all?"

"You can keep calling in to see if somebody canceled."

"OK."

"Oh, and it will be fifty dollars per night."

"But the sign says thirty-five dollars."

"Sorry, not this weekend."

Fifty bucks a night? I don't think Tony is going to take too kindly to that. I found out where the post was and I was off.

The hill led into the main street of Thursday Island. An array of shops and eateries lined the way. They clearly lacked the gleam of prosperity and tourist money.

The post office loomed at the end of the street like a dignified but careworn elderly matron. Smaller than most of the posts on the mainland, it was nonetheless one of the finer brick buildings I'd come upon, and it sported a surprisingly fair-sized post-office-box area. The characteristic array of letter and box options was neatly presented on the walls. I felt like a post office surveyor. I had probably been to a dozen of them by now, many of them more than once. The government-run post offices were my only "constant" on a journey where I was rarely in the same place for any length of time. Like an American kid going to McDonald's in Aspen when he lives in Detroit. It's not really home. Just the next best thing.

I impatiently waited my turn in line.

"Post for Eric Stiller, in care of this office, please."

I watched the postmaster shuffle and reshuffle through a small stack of "S" mail and felt the disappointment of his response in advance.

"How about a package?"

Once again, it did not take a lot of package turning to return the verdict.

"No, no packages."

"The late mail hasn't arrived yet. You might want to check at the end of the day," he said, sensing my dejection.

My spirits rose slightly at this slender reed of hope, and I suddenly felt generous.

"Do you have any mail for Tony Brown? He's my partner."

He shook his head regretfully. " 'Gainst regulations, mate." He must have intuited my honesty, however, or was merely anxious to be rid of me, because after a moment he shrugged and handed over a small packet of letters.

As I trudged back to the Grand, I began to wonder what Allison would be like. Hope quickened my pace up the hill.

The hotel was really hopping, and getting to the bar reminded me of the "Best of New York's" competitive drink-acquisition campaigns. After some squeezing, side slicing, and pushing I came face-to-face with Allison.

Long, wavy, blond-streaked hair. Fine features, brown eyes, and a slender chassis. I enthusiastically introduced myself. We chatted briefly and talked about her friend in Cairns.

It was very crowded and I had to shout.

"When do you get off?"

"About one."

I told her that Tony and I might drop by in the course of the night.

She smiled again and said: "That would be great!"

I wasn't sure if we would really drop by again but at that point it seemed that beggars could not be choosers. I felt abandoned by my friends back home. But then I remembered how poor a pen pal I had been to my friend in the Peace Corps. How much a few lines on some wood pulp means when you're far away from home.

"That reporter from *Islands* magazine is coming up to meet us. He asked Mum if there is anything we needed. You apparently told him something about picking some things up from Bruce Easton?"

"Yes! *Yes! Southern Cross* needs two gunwales from the sister boat."

"Can't we just fix them here?"

"If we can get some new, less fatigued pieces it will be a lot better, the warpage on one of them is really severe."

Soon after, we met a white local named Dennis. He had neatly cropped short hair, a big smile, an earring, and a gleam in his eye. Dennis lived on Prince of Wales Island and offered to put us up. The thought of the three-mile paddle into the wind, and separation from the town, did not overjoy us, so we respectfully declined.

He understood. "I'll see ya in the Federal tonight! It's ladies night and it's always sure to be a big one!"

"Where's the Federal?" I asked.

"It's right there." He pointed to the red coral-colored building we had seen first, before landing.

"By the way, a new crop of nurses arrived this week." He practically smacked his lips.

It was Friday and Dennis was getting warmed up. He told us he was assured a steady supply of nurses because a new supply was rotated in every few months. Not too many decide to stay, I guess. Dennis was originally from Cairns, but had moved to Thursday Island and seemed to be thoroughly enjoying his role as a big fish in a smaller pond.

"Quite the ladies' man, our Dennis," said Tony with a sly wink. The sun was dimming and we still had the problem of deciding where to store *Southern Cross*. I had seen a fenced-off and gated apartment directly across the street from us. I had no idea who it belonged to but it seemed the perfect defense against the inquisitive or *acquisitive*.

"I'll give it a go, Tony."

I jogged across the street and cautiously opened the gate and headed to the stairs. Pausing, I took a deep breath. Instantly the door at the top swung open and my heart skipped a beat. A well-built, marine-cropped white man headed down until our eyes met. His eyes narrowed suspiciously.

"Howdy, mate!" I squeaked, attempting to quell his anxieties.

We shook hands. I explained who I was, what we were doing, and where our gear was very quickly.

He said his name was Andrew and he worked at the butcher shop in the grocery store nearby.

"I'll open the gate. Ya can bring your gear in here. I got a tarp for yar boat and you can put your personal stuff under the stairs."

He would be back in a couple of hours and suggested a beer at the Federal. He also confirmed our fears about security on that particular weekend.

"Generally thar awlright, mate, but this weekend brings out the worst of some of them."

It was good to feel an innate, like-kind camaraderie with him. Tony and I felt like unwelcome foreigners. While we were shuttling our gear back and forth, Andrew's wife, Janet, graced us with her presence, not quite sure what we were doing. A rapid recoup of our story and relating Andrew's approval put her at ease. "You can put your personal effects in the laundry room and use it to clean anything you want."

She was friendly but reserved and soon retreated upstairs back to her home. I couldn't blame her. Two feral sorts aren't comforting to the uninitiated. Janet was attractive. I'm sure we let her know that in the way men's eyes do sometimes.

Southern Cross and our gear was safe! Once again, luck was with us and now an enormous hunger took over. We donned our finest and trotted off to the milkbar for a *big* feed. We walked through a park to get there. Our smiles and hearty hellos were welcomed with smiles or frowns. A half-hour later we had engulfed curry chicken, pork, veggies, chips, dim sum, ice cream, and some type of pastry. It was good that we laid a solid foundation. The next stop was the Federal Pub for a big night with a few beers.

"I think I'm ready for a pint or two, how 'bout you, mate? Tony said.

"Don't mind if I do." I opened the door for Tony.

"After you, sir." I added a bow.

The Federal was packed. A raw, untamed tension cautioned me. It was a local bar and the message being boomed from the floor was, Tourists are not invited! A very colorfully dressed group of large black women rocked the house while pool warfare was going on. Two comparatively attractive barmaids kept the bottle caps flying as beers transferred from bar to barfly faster than the securities at the N.Y. Stock Exchange.

It wasn't long before more than the beer caps began to pop.

For no apparent reason, a once smiling native pool-hound turned around, lost his smile, and rushed a blond-mustached man that Tony and I referred to as "Klaus." Klaus was very casually standing near a wall and remained nonplussed while being rushed with a pool stick. Soon we saw why. Just as "pool man" had gotten to Klaus, a large individual that we dubbed "Waldheim" headlocked the "pool man" and promptly, with a smile on his face, escorted him outside. Waldheim was not a bouncer for the Federal. I don't believe there were any. He was Klaus's bouncer.

Later we saw the two circling the rugby field in a *Hogan's Heroes*–style infantry truck. Tony and I took that opportunity to conjure up a story about the two being part of some type of continuing Nazi Germany racial census mission. We scripted them as a hapless duo assigned to the island of cannibals, their high command intent on losing them. Yet, as fate would have it, they didn't even know the war was over and continued to cluelessly count the natives. They had finally figured out that the interisland rugby festival was a more efficient method. Characteristically Klaus never smiled. No one told them that the Torres Islanders got ownership rights in 1967.

The night continued, and we met a couple of people named Adrian and Dave along with some of their friends, leading to more beers and then last call, which involved most of the patrons purchasing six packs of VB's (Victoria Bitters) and premixed rum and Coke in cans. Then everybody left the bar and went to the street and beach (exactly where *Southern Cross* had landed) to drink them. This in turn, led to a party on a shrimp boat. Beyond that the details become hazy. Somehow, we ended up at Dave's flat for some "after party" libations. Instead, I found a piece of floor and fell asleep. Tony and I then managed to get back to our gear and find a deserted boathouse courtyard where we crashed fast and hard. The tone for Thursday Island had been set.

"How ya feelin', Epic?"

What I had expected to happen did not. No hangover! I don't know why but it was not there. I didn't even have that hangover-in-waiting where the body is still fully inebriated after many hours of sleep because the blood alcohol content is so high. No, this was different. It was like my body had expelled all the toxins with unusual efficiency. Tony seemed nearly as nonplussed. I do believe the outdoor/fresh air/clean living we had been engaged in for over a month had flushed out and tuned up our internal organs. Thursday Island was going to try to change all that.

We packed up our hobo camp and headed back to town. On the way, we passed a rugby team warming up for their match. I offered an enthusiastic and sincere:

"Good morning and good luck!"

It was met with a team glare. We had obviously interrupted some type of tribal-warfare preparation ritual. All their previous movements stopped. We moved on.

Perhaps a century or two ago we would have soon been stewing in a large pot with coconuts in our mouths but the modern day had diluted old-time inter-island rivalries into "civilized" rugby tournaments. Instead of war paint there were uniforms. Cleats replaced spears. Leather rugby balls instead of heads. Moreover, there was a referee and rules. How far we have come. Let the games begin!

First, we were going to fuel up on something that I could smell coming from the local bakery a block away. It wasn't long before a pot of tea and a plate full of the best donuts I've ever had were right before my eyes. They were not those big, sticky, glazed kind, making up for lack of substance with sugary exteriors, but rather hearty, well-baked, flour-dense medium-sized wonders with just a dusting of powdered sugar and cinnamon. An enchanting young girl named Kelly kept them coming. I ate a dozen. *This bakery was going to become a staple in our TI diet.*

"Let's get to the games, mate!" Tony said, not quite as smitten as I was with the bakery find.

It was midmorning and the crowds had gathered all around the field. On the north end of the field were the umbrellaed matriarchs as keen to see a hard hit as any, if not more so. Once again there were the large, colorful dresses covering ample bodies. The respect for them was indisputable. They sat in a neat row of beach chairs next to one fence. They were in the optimal viewing position, like heads of state watching an army parade. They were an imposing lot, outsizing most of the men, including many of the rugby players.

There were kids of all ages. Extended families gathered together in team colors forming clusters of tribes representing all the different islands with only a few yards separating each group. All in all, the mood was friendly and festive. The only *blues* that started involved domestic disputes, with a matriarch giving the final word. In one instance there was a physical confrontation between one of the women and an older drunk man that was leading to blows. At first, the family stood behind the woman, until the police showed up, and then the family came to the aid of the man, and the dispute ended altogether. Blood was clearly the deciding factor.

I noticed a large degree of American influence among the younger crowd. T-shirts shouted "Harley Davidson," "49ers," "Michael Jordan," "Orlando Magic." I got the feeling that they felt that U.S. African Americans were their role models and heroes. TV had not missed these islands or islanders.

Tony and I sat in with the Imagi Baw team dressed in red and black. Beneath the name of their team, "We Are the Future" was printed on their jerseys. They were our favorite team because of their quick, slashing style. Though much smaller in bulk, the team's aggressive, spirited team play made them seem larger than they actually were. In the course of the day Tony mended an injured player, we cajoled and cheered with the family, and I got choked up when a little black girl cuddled up to me in total trust. A flash about Nicole and a child came to me, nearly bringing me to tears. Thursday Island was not a place to forget about a black girlfriend. My journal entry: "Almost feel like I have a biological clock of my own."

Then the calamitous reminder of that deep-chill phone call blazed back as a hard reminder of reality. The impossibility of the communication resounded. There was no way to go on "as usual" with phone calls or letters and no personal contact. No eye to eye . . .

I will continue communication and knowing myself have great *expectations when I see her again.*

At halftime the field became a vast children's playground with hundreds of kids running, laughing, screaming, smiling, and making sounds that only they can make. It was a joyous release of pent-up energy. It took many announcements on the intercom system to displace the crowd once the game began again. It was beautiful to watch and listen. Unbridled whirling dervishes loving life!

"Children Off the field! All children off the field!!"

The children did not seem to see any uniforms.

The day was a fulfilling one. Our team reached the semifinals. But it was a big, bruising, punishing team named Badu that won. It was the second year in a row for them.

"There's Klaus and Waldheim, mate."

"Must be making their final count, TB."

Klaus and Waldheim made their final count.

That night there were big winds and rain. I was wide awake and went out to scrub *Southern Cross* with a brush and soapsuds. My mind turned again to the gulf crossing. I tried to commit my anxieties to my journal in a vain effort to allay my fears.

Dangers: big storms, nighttime boat separation in event of capsize, person separation. Solutions: umbilical cord to boat. Problem: entanglement/drowning.

Solution: quick release line à la carabineer or knife handy to cut line with. Danger: sickness at sea—exposure, Ross River syndrome, severe fever, stomach flu. Solution: cover up, have proper clothing, antibios, proper water intake, cloggers-lomotol (an anti-diahrrea drug), charcoal. Danger: freak-out, seizure. Solution: if mild—space blanket, paddle for exercise, calm talk; if severe—EPIRB.

The following day TB received and enjoyed faxes from his friend Sam, and talked with his mum concerning gear acquisition from Mr. Easton in Sydney to be delivered by Tony Perrottet, an *Islands* magazine writer. Somehow he had managed to fit it all in with a friend's wedding plans in Queensland.

I was a bit flustered about the cumulative damage to the boat and would've felt better if a few key parts from our sister boat in Sydney had made it up. In particular, there was a warpage near the side center joints that I had never seen before. It first became evident when we hauled *Southern Cross* half-loaded up the beach into the compound. I wrote:

And an ugly green ooze formed on one side of the deck. Wet frame, etc., etc. 3,500 kilometers, eighty near consecutive days, over 200-kg loads constantly, an average of six foot seas, and 100-meter-plus tide pushes. . . . salt, tropical sun, continuous exposure, constantly wet. . . . She's still good on the water, flex is more pronounced but contact with water is excellent. Might be losing some efficiency into head winds when paddling but that is hard to say for sure.

The wind was really pumping. The funneling effect between the islands amplified the prevailing twenty-to-twenty-five-knot winds. Some gusts stopped me dead in my tracks. I was concerned about our course across the gulf. Further review of the charts showed more of a southerly course to our trip than I had originally thought. It meant we would be reaching—the wind angle 90 degrees to the boat—as much as we would be broad reaching—the wind to the side and behind the boat. And there would be a much stronger leeward drift than any we'd had. Why was that a problem? Reaching puts the boat directly sideways to the wind and waves. Instead of getting the momentum of riding waves from astern, you get knocked sideways. It's harder to find a "groove." Moreover, the boat is getting slowly pushed away from the direction the wind is blowing. It makes it much harder to hold a course.

We could not afford to lose mileage to leeward early in the crossing because we would have a near impossible job of making it up against the wind. *Southern Cross* could sail windward but not at a speed to compensate for dozens of miles of drift. I just hoped the winds would stay as easterly as possible. The more they turned southerly, the more difficult our crossing. Westerlies were unlikely and unimaginable.

Tony heard that the *Who Weekly* article had come out in Sydney and the rest of the country. It was titled, "Kayak Kings."

"Mum got a copy sent to her from Ron. She says there's pictures of me in my skivvies and you brushing your teeth."

"Oh, that's just great, really great," I said sarcastically.

"I'm going to the newsagent, TB. See ya later."

At the news agent there was no *Who Weekly*.

I picked up the *Australian* and returned to the bakery, where I met Dot (Kelly's mom) and the other kids, Tara and Jason. I told Dot how great I thought the donuts were and she credited her husband, Rex. I found Dot (a Solomon Islander) a strongly beautiful woman. Her hands were delicate but the muscles in her forearms coiled upon picking up a dish. Lines around her eyes hinted of travail but the warmth of her eyes whispered of love earned through time.

"Rex and I have lived on a lot of boats. I even had Kelly on one of 'em."

Tony and I would befriend Dot and become quite close to her in the days that followed. She had raised all three of her children on boats. Rex was a white Australian and Kelly was considered a white girl in a predominantly black school on the island. This had its complications. Rex was a horribly driven man whom Dot would have preferred to slow down and live more life, instead of working till all hours of the night at his endeavors, particularly, the bakery.

I countered that the bakery was "his baby," and that he might ease up if and when the bakery had fully established itself and he could hire someone else to do the bulk of the work. She was more grim and said it wasn't his nature. When I mentioned some things about my boat she said that Rex also did fiberglass repair work as a side business and might be able to help. I made a mental note of it.

In the paper that day I read an extensive five-page report on the world environment. It emphasized too much and too fast an increase in population, particularly in Africa; too much CFC's resulting in ozone depletion and greenhouse effect, compounded by timber burning and rain-forest destruction; loss of biodiversity at an alarming rate.

The article indicated that Australia seems to be much more aware and responsive to the problem than the United States (obvious to me after only a few months there). It said the United States *must* lead the way. It *must* show that enviro–economics is "it." It needs to use its powerful world-reaching media to disseminate the message.

Later that day I ventured to the far-eastern end of the island. I discovered the Chandlery! A boat shop! Home away from home . . . sort of. I carefully perused all the goods. I found stainless steel screws and bolts, various tapes, a can of varnish and one can of canvas antimildew paint and protectorant. Violà! This is what I needed for that ooze! My purchases for *Southern Cross* put my heart at ease. It was like finding the right medicine for an ailing friend.

Further, I found different wires and wood panels at various construction sites along the way and toted them back with me to the compound. I stopped by the post without success. *Today it didn't matter. I had the medicine to heal* Southern Cross.

Finally I stumbled upon the oil company docks and looked for Jeff and the black houseboat. No houseboat, no Jeff, no note, no escort. We're going across the Gulf of Carpentaria alone.

Later that night Tony and I stopped to watch a movie on TV at the milkbar. It was an Oliver Stone movie starring Tom Cruise, about a star high school athlete who joins the marines and goes to Vietnam. It was depressing, addressing the life-and-limb issue. The movie pointed out the "repercussions" of hubris and the result of following it without thought to all the ramifications. Cruise's character gets shot and is paralyzed. During the movie I was reminded of something else in the article in the newspaper. In the summary, about making a better world, it said, "First make oneself happy. Then you will be doing best to make Australia happy. Happiness is contagious but it must start from the individual."

Before I go to sleep I continue with contingencies.

Danger: blown off course, Magellan fails or is lost. Solution: head ten-to-twenty degrees more southwest; use the constellation Southern Cross as reference; keep sun at back in daytime; tether GPS Magellan always; tape borders to keep water from getting in; keep in safe yet accessible spot! Danger: sharks. Solution: avoid, sail versus paddle as much as possible to avoid paddle splash, minimize time in water (thinking of swimming), keep bodily waste and loose food out of boat; attack aggressively with paddles if confronted; if boat is bitten, capsize boat, Aquaseal or sew and tape bottom, wait on boat until patch is dry.

We slept under the stairs and in the washroom of the compound last night. Andrew and Janet were warming up to us. It was rush hour on TI and the bakery was packed with at least a dozen people in line. I felt like my space had been violated. But business is business, and I'm glad Dot, Rex, and the kids have it.

I did another beach workout. Calisthenics, climbing a rope that was attached to a tire swing hanging from a tree, a few beach sprints, and the like. *Feels good!*

Thoughts of the impending crossing came spontaneously and unannounced and soon butterflies exercised their wings in my stomach. The moon was becoming half-full. We would leave within four or five days, weather permitting. Tony had talked with his mum the night before. She was positive and encouraging about the trip, but he held his head lower than usual and his face seemed despondent.

"What's up, TB?"

"My father says that going across the gulf is suicide and has told me not to do it."

"He really won't let this one go?" I said carelessly.

"He might have a point."

The next day I called my mom and dad and they were both very positive and encouraging.

"I am very proud of you both; now here is your mother."

"Bye . . ."

"Well, I *was* going to worry about you, but so many of your friends believe you are going to do the crossing with no problems that I've begun to believe them."

"We'll do fine."

"Mr. Arias sent the 'Kayak Kings' article and the front picture is very impressive."

"Really? What does it look like?"

"You and Tony in *Southern Cross* on some big wave someplace. Only one thing that disturbed me a little but I don't think its anything."

"What?"

"Well, Mrs. Brown called in the middle of the night. I think she was upset and said a few derogatory things about you. I didn't get into it because I figured she's just terribly concerned for her son."

"What kind of things?"

"Oh, oh, I shouldn't have said anything."

"You gotta tell me."

"Something about you not appreciating nature and only wanting to go to towns . . . that kind of thing."

Goddamnit, Tony . . .

Later, I dropped by the post and *got the leeboards*! I was aglow with a feeling of trust and confidence in my dad for his logistical support. Of course, they arrived with extra pads covering any sensitive spots so there would be no snafu.

So far, two for two!

I tried the newsagent next, and the magazine was in! Tom Cruise and Nicole Kidman were on the cover. I immediately flipped it open to "Kayak Kings" to see the picture my parents were talking about.

Pretty damn cool!

Clearly the story leans toward the Australian model turned intrepid adventurer. The pictorial contrasts Tony posing in his Calvin's to his feral self, using a fish-cleaning hose to shower off in his Speedos. Tony was described as a "handsome 1.9 m." I was described as a "muscular 1.7." I felt a little better after having read about the 1.7-meter Tom Cruise.

For the most part, the story was right-on, but the actual encounters with crocodiles and sharks were aggrandized. It did not go so far as to have us wrestling them with knife in mouth, but we hadn't even seen a croc yet. It was fun to read. But, the "stretched" factoids, making us look more prolific than we were, gave me some insight into journalism. Basically you have to filter an article by subtracting at least 25 percent of the shine. For the time being, we were local "heroes." The newsagent ladies appreciably changed their manners with me from the moment I walked in. They had already seen the article. The smiles and the body language were far more receptive and engaging.

Ahhhh . . . the power of the press and the domain of celebrity. I must admit . . . I like it.

I bought several magazines with the intent of sending them to friends. I showed Tony a copy later in the day, and his reaction was initially positive but turned grave upon a complete reading. A frown dominated his face for the last page.

"I can't believe Ron wrote some of those things. I know I never said any of them." I thought I heard a hint of insinuation.

"I didn't either."

He simply did not like being misquoted or portrayed differently from how he'd conveyed himself to the writer (even if it was more flattering). He lightened up after we talked about it, but he was not as elated as I was.

Then I saw it!

His thick Rasputin beard was *gone!*

The face I saw then was nearly the same face I saw in the model photo of the magazine article, minus a pound or so.

One of the girls we had met last night had done an outstanding job of shaving it off! Wendy was her name, and she worked at the bank. Unbeknownst to me, they had made an appointment. Although Tony is not much for general celebrity status, I had noticed that he wasn't being eyed as voraciously by the opposite sex as he had been in NYC or Sydney. Moreover, I noticed that he noticed. Hence, no beard! A short walk down the block displayed the power of his face. The few ladies that we passed held their gazes on the unveiled one. *The Volgons would soon hear about this.*

Later Tony casually mentioned that he had talked to the Mission Beach Kayak Expedition team near the post office.

"You talked to them?! What did they say?!"

For me, *this* was a big deal. Tony seemed nonchalant about it. He had talked to them for over an hour. Out of all this he had gathered that they had been around for two weeks and had run into weather and customs glitches that had prevented their departure.

"You should have seen there sleek yellow boats, mate—gorgeous. The guy said he'd heard about Kleppers and called them 'tugboats.' "

Tony seemed smitten, judging from his tone of voice.

I felt a hot flush of resentment in my face. Tony let a couple of brand-new, shiny boats lay a shadow over *Southern Cross* and her efforts so far.

"What did you say?"

"I said she was a bit heavy and we've had to do quite a bit of mending."

Surely, *Southern Cross* had seen better days but we had put nearly four thousand hard kilometers on her on the trip alone. *I can't believe he's saying that.*

"What about the sailing?"

"Their boats can use some small sails but it doesn't look like they are doing much of it."

"There ya go then," was about all I could say. I wasn't going to get into it but I certainly stewed on it in my own mind.

We had loaded Southern Cross *heavy . . . we had pushed her in all conditions . . . and she had received modest maintenance at best. The once olive-green deck was heading toward khaki and the hull had some uniform wear along the keel. There were cuts and bruises . . . there were infield quick fixes, and the frame had a lot more flex. I had felt that Tony was all too willing to leave old faithful for a new fling, but then again, he didn't have the history with the Kleppers that I had.*

The group apparently consisted of two women and one man. They intended to cross the Torres Straits to New Guinea and then follow the New Guinea coast and cross over to the Solomon Islands. It was a five-thousand-kilometer trip that they were attempting in five months. My curiosity was piqued.

Woke up feeling lousy. I didn't get up right away. I lay awake in the pain of a hangover from a night with Wendy, Brenda (a customs airplane flyer), Fruity, and Frenchy, two guys who worked in customs. During the course of the night we had mentioned our intent to cross the gulf in a kayak.

They laughed.

Frenchy said, "That's the best one I've heard in a while!"

Fruity said, "A fifty-thousand-ton tanker just came across and said it had a very rough go of it!"

"You wouldn't have a chance in a kayak," he added.

I knew a vessel that size cut six-foot seas to nothing. It would take waves double that size to make it flinch. We didn't pursue it too far, so as not to call similar problems to us that the Mission Beach kayak team had been having. If they took us seriously we might run into trouble when they were sober.

The immunity to drink had worn off in less than a week sans water travel, and in town. The toxins had made their presence obvious with imaginary jack-hammers pounding near the bridge of my nose.

Tony and I had a disharmonious walk to the bakery. I cursed under my breath about having left my journal at Brenda's. I opted for my silent sulk routine, which Tony hated. He called me "selfish." I tried to explain that I try to keep my "agroness" to myself so that it does not burden other people. Tony went on to point out that my silence showed the "agroness" loud and clear. Just before we were about to take the issue too far, we ran into the Mission Beach kayak team.

I met Stewart, a five-foot-eleven, 155-pounder with a big beard and dirty blond, thinning hair. I learned that he had been kayaking since the age of twelve, that he surfs, kayaks a lot, and repairs and builds his own boats. The expedition was his idea and he had put an ad out locally to solicit two companions.

I don't think he counted on two women—one of whom had been his girlfriend, "now a good friend." *I don't see how that will work.* He admitted to being "tactless" on the water. It was "his" trip, but he wished he'd had another "experienced" mate on the trip to confer with . . . or so he thought. The two women were in the double seater and he in a single seater with the logic that it would even out.

Eventually, I met the two ladies, who had been flirting with the beardless wonder. They were both fair-skinned blondes and well educated—one was a veterinarian. They both seemed strong willed and I could see that Stewart was going to have his hands full. Talk of their trip included the acknowledged like-lihood that the women could be raped in Guinea. They seemed to take it all in stride.

"The men in Guinea think it's practically their duty," one of the girls said.

Stewart asked me to come see his boats later on and then expounded on ideas for building a specially enclosed sailing kayak to make a direct ocean crossing from the Australian mainland to the Solomons or another Polynesian island chain.

I saw his eyes light up as he said: "I'm definitely going to do that trip solo!"

I could see that his current expedition was going to need some CPR.

Later in the day, I got into a funk about the Nicole thing again when a cou-ple of young ladies befriended me in a local park. They reminded me of her. *I want to know what really happened!* Was it just another guy, or did she lose respect for me as I poured out some of my most vulnerable thoughts to her in letters and cards? The latter possibility gnawed at me voraciously and the French woman's words whispered invisibly "lovers cannot be friends."

I took my mind off of it by sending a couple of magazines off to my friends. Later, I did another thirty-minute sweat-it-out workout and I felt better for a time. *I've got to keep the legs fit.* There was a chance that we could be in the kayak for over ten days without seeing land, much less standing on it.

The big leg muscles involved in standing, walking and running, namely the gluteus maximus (butt), hamstrings, and thighs, were going to atrophy. Although sprint kayaking and fitness kayaking can incorporate a a substantial amount of leg drive, ultra-long-distance kayaking has to use those muscles conservatively because of the energy loss. Moreover, if we sail a lot, the isometric leg bracing alone will not be enough to stave off the muscle loss.

A less productive visit to the post set me back a little further, so I went back to the compound and worked on the boat. I spent the rest of the afternoon and evening fixing, mending, varnishing, inventing, and customizing. *Southern Cross* had to stay in shape as well.

The most important customization was the rigging of dual rudder capability. That is, the ability to shift from the normal backseat steering to front seat steer-ing and back again on the water. I had specifically thought of it in NYC and had brought a smaller foot-pedal assembly to be able to clamp onto the narrow wooden keel board under my feet. I had also brought extra chain link and small U-clamps to connect to the existing chain. The idea was to allow for one person to go to sleep and the other to steer in shifts.

Each man could now steer, set the sails to automatic pilot by cleating them to their respective control panels, and read his own compass. I switched from one seat to the next and practiced the rudder-change maneuver in the relatively empty boat. It took a more delicate touch than I'd figured to take off the cables from Tony's pedals and trace them up and attach them to mine. The end of the two pinky-nail-sized chain links had to be unattached from the highly bent, one-karat-earring-sized receiver hooks that are designed to hold the chain firm. I practiced the maneuver over and over with *Southern Cross* sitting on the ground as steady as a rock.

I now dared to take my stainless steel Leatherman pliers, encrusted with lithium grease and salt residue, and pry the hooks open just enough to make the task of hooking and unhooking a little easier. I had to be mindful of not over-fatiguing the metal hooks on Tony's footpad that were well past their prime. A midcrossing rudder failure could only be mended in becalmed seas. Apparently we could not count on that anymore. The winds had been roaring all week as if TI were the end of the earth.

That night I wrote:

General Precautions: Have all critical—lights, flares, knives, repair materials, food, water, clothing accessible and secure! Preferably on person. What about a radio? Keep lines clear to minimize entanglement. Have storm sail ready to go. Have and test drift stopper. Attach additional paddle holder. Have spare rudder components accessible. Made dual rudder capability easy to engage in boat to spell each other.

Sometimes you just *know* when some days are not working right.

It all seemed to start off OK: I had a great shower! Our morning trek to the bakery had a bounce in it. I was going to install the "waypoints" in the GPS to give us subgoals and checkpoints for the four hundred nautical miles of empty sea ahead. They would be electronic lighthouses, detectable only by this wondrous piece of technology. An instrument of technology put into full play by our Pentagon in order to navigate the deserts of the Middle East and the open plains of the former Soviet Union. It was now made available to the adventurous citizens of the planet Earth. I think I qualified as one of them.

Until then, the hand-held GPS had been mainly a curiosity and a fancy toy to play with at camp. It had helped us make one very critical decision in the approach to a treacherous river bar, when Tony and I had come to a standstill in "knowing" where we were. Besides that, it had patiently waited for "the big show": the crossing.

Australia would be so far to our left for so long that it would offer no reference points for comparison. The stars and wave patterns could conceivably guide the experienced Polynesian mariner. A sextant could help the experienced sailor of a generation ago on a relatively stable ship. The GPS allowed us minimal deep-sea navigational skills for survival. The GPS could tell us where we were within three hundred feet of a destination (less than fifty feet for the military) as long as we had a chart marked with lines of latitude and longitude.

A *chart* is essentially a miniaturized overhead view of the sea and its shores, emphasizing natural and artificial obstructions to safe sailing and anything that the sailor can use to find his way. However, the earth is round and the chart is flat. Inevitably, there will be distortions when going from 3-D to 2-D. Moreover, the longer the distances to be covered, the higher the distortion.

We had a chart and we had the GPS. TI was approximately 11 degree-minutes south latitude and 142 degrees 30 minutes east. Our destination was Nhulunbuy (Gove) 12 degrees 20 south and 137 degrees east. The distance was four hundred nautical miles as the crow flies, albeit on a curve. There were no real islands—landmarks—along the way. In the middle of the gulf we would be at least two hundred nautical miles from any point of land. This much I knew from the chart.

A crossing without the GPS would be a very rough guess, possibly placing us more than fifty miles off course—an error to the north of that distance and we'd miss our target completely, possibly sending us into the "Never Never Land" of the Arafura Sea. Next step Indonesia three hundred more miles away to the north. The GPS was a combination crystal ball and magic wand. I thought all we had to do was make sure we didn't lose it overboard or wear out the batteries.

I sat at my favorite table in the bakery and anxiously awaited my opportunity to "dial in" the way points. I also wanted to seriously discuss the crossing with Tony. Tony came and I explained the technology.

"Way points" guide points along our course described in degrees of latitude and longitude. Since there were no landmasses at all en route, I was inventing them. I was making dots for us to connect. En route the GPS could use the points and tell us with sound signals when we were approaching them, how close and how far off course we were. I wanted to put eight way points in every fifty miles or so. The way points would be the optimal course and we would always want to be sure to be south of that course as much as possible. All I had to do was play the keypad on the GPS like a calculator and be sure to enter the right numbers.

Launch was only a few days away to take maximum advantage of the full moon. I quickly plunked a donut in my mouth and took a swig of coffee before laying down the GPS and chart on our "usual" table at the bakery. I pushed ON.

I pushed ON again.

And again.

The characteristic high-pitched ON acknowledgement and blueish-white back-lit boot-up code did not happen. I stared at a lifeless gray screen.

It must be the batteries! I thought. It had been weeks since I had "played" with the wand. It was possible some of the cool nights we'd had had drained the batteries. Luckily, I had brought the extra battery pack with brand-new batteries. I nervously fumbled with the battery casing, made sure all the batteries were facing the right direction, and wiped off the perfectly clean contacts. I put the new battery pack in, made sure the casing was closed just right, turned the wand around, and pressed ON.

I pressed ON again.

No sounds.

ON, ON, ON, ON, ON, ON.

Nothing.

Tony had finally taken notice of my spastic behavior. He looked into my eyes wide with horror. I could feel my face go white and my mouth desperately open with no words coming out. Our magic wand was not working.

"Hand it over here, mate."

Tony took it out of my hands and I imagined him saying, "Open sesame," and making it all better. No such luck. It did not work.

The moments that followed were a blur as my mind unbooted with the device. Handheld GPS's were relatively new to the civilian market in America, much less Australia. Getting another one on Thursday Island was not an option. The technology was not in the local TV repair shop's bag of tricks. This was a specific problem. Minutes later, I readjusted the battery pack and tried again with the same hopeful angst that the stranded car traveler has when his car won't start.

Shit! Now what! Damnit!!

Tony offered a conciliatory "it will be all right." Somehow, I just didn't see it.

"No, no I gotta fax and call the GPS people right away!"

"Take it easy, Epic. I'll talk to some of the people at the customs house. Someone will be able to sort it out."

"I'm still going to make the calls!"

I had to actively work to solve this problem immediately. I was not going to be stranded on Thursday Island for weeks on end like the other kayak expedition. I did not want to be swallowed by TI's black hole in space. I took the manual and headed for the post. I sent the fax to the company and called my father to give him our contact's information, and I also faxed him the specifics. If anyone would be able to help us it would be Dieter Stiller. He was the only person I had confidence in. I asked him to fax the post with the results.

Meanwhile, Tony had gone to the Federal, run across Brenda, and mentioned our situation. She said she was flying to Cairns that afternoon and would take the GPS to their technical person at the airport. Tony seemed annoyed that I had gone all-out with the overseas support when he saw that the solution was right in hand. I was relieved that we had two solutions working simultaneously.

However, it didn't seem likely that we would be leaving in a few days. We needed a reliable GPS to responsibly attempt the crossing. I did not want to entertain thoughts of following the coast of the Gulf of Carpentaria, which would more than double the distance to our travels, as well as place us in some of the hottest croc and shark waters in the world. A large number of rivers drained into the southern gulf. The mouths of the rivers are predatory havens. As I understood it, Paul Caffyn was "bumped" by sharks there, while other kayakers had had their rudders bitten off. Somehow, five to ten days crossing an open sea seemed like the better option. The small lead on our timetable, which had been generated by racing by Cape York, was slipping away.

A fax from my dad came in late the next afternoon acknowledging the problem and indicating that another GPS was on its way direct from the rep. He had paid $146 to have it express shipped. However, the fastest express shipment money could buy was still going to take nearly a week to get to Thursday Island. There were simply too many connections and too few flights. I called him back to make sure. I also had a chat with my mom that I regretted a few minutes later.

"Tony's just too casual about things sometimes and wants to have it his way."

"Maybe he's getting a little nervous."

"Yeah, yeah, yeah, he thinks the GPS is some kind of toy that I'm playing with. He thinks that he could build his own leeboards. *He's like a goddamned precocious child.* I feel like I have to placate him all the time."

"Just be patient with him."

"Yeah, I'll try, thanks, I'm glad I got to talk to you."

Tony had been nearby, and apparently had been passively eavesdropping on what I was saying to my mom. I was not aware that he was around. When I came out of the phone booth I was greeted with:

"You selfish little shit!"

His look of hurt, hate, and surprise stabbed at me like a pitchfork going through my heart. It appeared the gods were frowning on us and that the crossing was looking more and more inauspicious.

Expeditions and relationships have ended on less. This had to be our lowest point of rapport yet. Tony took off and I watched him walk away with a spinning head and wobbly legs.

Later in the day, I offered another apology.

"Tony, I apologize for what you may have heard. I am just frustrated by the GPS and nervous about the trip. I wanted to make sure we had moonlight and now it looks like we won't. I'm truly sorry that you heard me take it out on you."

"It's OK," he said frostily. "I got another letter from my dad today," he added.

"Same stuff?!"

"Yeah. You've got to understand that it's a two-way street, mate. I know the Nicole thing hurt you and the GPS put you over the top. Just watch your mouth. You can be a selfish shit sometimes!"

Tony sympathized and we had patched the dam by the end of the day, but it was a deep wound that struck at the core and would leave us estranged for days to come.

Brenda returned and told us that the GPS worked as soon as the technician pushed the ON button. I felt like a complete idiot, but then less of one, when I learned that the technician had kept it to give it a thorough lookover and testing. He had experienced sensitive on/off switches on units before and could not yet return it to us in good conscience. He had kept our wand for observation and would return it when Brenda returned the following week.

I couldn't believe that it had turned on. I was expecting an "I told you so" from Tony but none came. I still had a few bonus ones that I hadn't used and I think he knew it in a vague way.

In the following week, Tony spent a lot of time with Karen, one of the bartenders at the Federal. She turned out to be an English teacher who had ended up on TI with the same illusion the other teachers and nurses had. Perhaps, the same illusion that made it such a "must get to" destination for us. The last Australian outpost in the far north, I suppose.

She was very attractive. Thick ash-blond hair framed a Donna Reed face. She was witty, intelligent, and keen on TB. She was his blessing and they had many a "harmless" eve together as only TB could have with a lady. It wasn't long before I had one of my "Father Armadillo" sessions with her.

"Father Armadillo" was a subnickname Tony had coined for me in my relations with women. It is best described as my special personality phenomenon. One that inevitably turns a potential date into a cross between a confessional and a psychotherapy session. For me, the process could completely erase a potential romance in less than half an hour. A few of these ladies I had Father Armadilloed were secretly (sometimes not so secretly) interested in Tony and would be trying to figure him out during our sessions. "He loves me . . . he loves me not?" was always their dilemma.

Tony *liked* each and every one of them very much. He enjoyed their company quite a lot, yet romance was, more often than not, an inconvenience that he could do without. He would take them to pubs, he would show them a great time, he would have them doing things they never imagined. Inevitably they would fall deeply in love with him, which he often chose not to be aware of. I had been privy to three of these encounters in NYC.

I saw the pattern redeveloping. Karen came to me "to talk." That was the first sign. I cautioned Karen to try to keep her heart secure, but it was evident that it was already gone when she said hopefully, "But we had the loveliest little walk and picnic yesterday and he was so sweet."

That was the second sign. Her educated English manner tried to keep it all on the up-and-up.

"Well, I'll be just a little harder to find then," she said in a temporary salvo of strength supported by an underlying layer of mush.

Father Armadillo had done his best.

"He's a very good man. I could be wrong. Good luck," I added.

With Tony ensconced with the Englishwoman, I'd hoped for a miracle romance for myself. However, I felt out of my jurisdiction in TI. I felt off stride. I felt overshadowed by the interest in Tony. It was as if I had put all my social masks and tactics in a messy closet and I was desperately rummaging through it ass up in the air. My mom once told me that I was not as "sweet" as Tony. I think she was right. All of this added up to one thing . . . *lose the beard!*

I arranged for Wendy to take my feralism away. It wasn't long before Mr. Hyde turned back into Dr. Jekyll and a couple of "you're not so bad yourself" lines started popping up. I was back in the game.

The danger with the pretty-boy look, while hanging around on the island, was the risk of a coldcocking for no apparent reason. A fair-haired Scot in his early twenties had been coldcocked seven times before he'd been properly initiated, accepted, and then protected by the islanders. I was convinced that our combined feralism had averted a conflict in the Federal.

One night four island lads approached Tony, who promptly asked them if they wanted a drink. They said they wanted money. He said no, pushed one away, then pointed to my scraggly psychopathic form, and said: "See that guy over there? He's my mate; he's rather mad and loves a good blue, so if you would like to step outside."

I arrived on cue and the conflict dispersed without a scuffle. Feralism is a form of protection in an unstable human environment. For now the beard was gone and we had an interview tomorrow.

Tony and I had to put our best media faces on for Mr. Tony Perrottet, who was doing a story on us for *Islands* magazine.

"Thursday Island is a hard place to get to—so many connections, I felt like I was going around the world or something."

"Well, you've come to the end of the world for us," Tony said.

"So I understand. I brought you those parts you needed; they're in my room."

"Excellent," I added.

Perrottet arrived in good spirits and got a "suite" in the Federal. We met him there and he interviewed us until sunset. Later we shared dinner and drinks and then did a morning photo shoot. The retelling of our tales brought a truce between us. I believe it helped put ill-placed feelings back in perspective. All in all, Mr. Perrottet had relit a pilot light that had gone out.

We gave him some other boat parts to take back to Sydney, including a beautifully repaired side panel that Rex's fiberglass shop had handled. Once again, Thursday Island had delivered a certain resourcefulness, which I kept underestimating. Soon Mr. Perrottet had to be on his way. I don't think we were aware of how much of our tension he had diffused.

As days passed, it was getting harder and harder to keep the crossing out of my mind. This extra week felt like an opposing football team calling a time-out just before I was attempting a game-winning field goal. It was giving me too much time to think about.

Tony and I were living separate lives and didn't have much to say to each other when our paths crossed. I know I needed the space to sort it all out and I imagined Tony needed the same. I oscillated between the distraction of the Thursday Island soap opera and thinking of more ways to prepare *Southern Cross* for the voyage ahead.

I had no file for a multiple-day open sea voyage in a small boat. I had not been on sailing boats or yachts in such circumstances. I had gone across the Atlantic on an ocean liner called the *Bremen* when I was five years old. The most I remembered from that was my father giving me a small model of the ship in one of the cabin rooms. Tony had not spent much time at sea either. He had been more of the farm boy and then the mountain man.

The full moon was waning, and daily checks with the Air Express package center kept coming up fruitless. Neither GPS had arrived. It was almost a week.

Omens and "vibes" have been part of adventures since time immemorial. The sea has been man's outer space long before *Apollo*. Although man, theoretically, evolved from the sea, it had been millions of years since our DNA was used for fins, gills, and the like. Not so long ago, mankind believed the earth was flat and that travel by sea could lead to falling off the planet. Sea monsters dominated the architecture of man's mind long before alien abductions did, yet man was compelled to go to sea, into its vastness, its mystery, and its power, knowing that a challenge to life and limb was inevitable where stable footing was impossible.

I had often felt that my father and I had been on a ship together in a past life and that one of us had made a fateful decision that the other one did not agree with or had tried to change. Instead, stubbornness, ignorance, and pride had stepped in the way and let the ship sink.

This karmic thing with Tony was in another league altogether. Tony had helped me escape the father-son reruns only to plunge me into a more dynamic one in which the action played out in minutes rather than years. Wills colliding, occasionally joining, often repelling, with their respective souls on the line.

On Thursday Island, Tony came across as more buoyant, more lusting for life. I—more solemn, more intense, more awkward amid laughter. If this was maturity, I would rename it "curse."

Tony had the innate ability to lead. He had the looks and the genuine charm to gather his flock. Once upon a time, BDS (before Dieter Stiller), I might have been part of the flock happily riding on the comet's tail. Alas, I had already spent too much time with someone who I had once perceived to be invincible and all-knowing, only to realize he was human and fallible.

No, I was not a big believer in human omnipotence anymore. I was still ultimately alone and responsible for my lot. Although I had given up center stage, I was learning a hell of a lot about the importance of the backstage. *I still wanted those luck tickets to be transferable, though.*

One day, I got a letter from home that included an article in the *Folding Kayaker* newsletter by Ralph Diaz. It was a memorial for the Klepper Shop in NYC. He described how many clients and neighborhood residents considered it "an institution." Any emotional wind I was building up in my sails left me. *One emotional punch after another.*

My home theater was closed for real! The long-running Klepper show was now off Broadway—way off Broadway. *Arghhhhhhhhhhhh!!* One of the presumptions before leaving on grand journeys is that the "tribe" will still be there to come back to. The knights of the Round Table left on their search for the Grail relying on the people of Camelot to be there to share their stories and their finds. My temporary exile was turning into a permanent one. Why does one type of life have to fall apart when you choose another?

In the course of the day I brooded and reflected on all those years and people. It was mainly the people! I wrote a long list of all the people I'd met there. So many coincidences and overlapping lives. Old friends, college friends, clients getting to know each other and then forming their own bonds at some wonderful gathering that I had helped engineer. Yes! The Klepper Shop on Union Square was an institution and had become my own personal monastery, my own spiritual home. It was there that I could work my own magic, work the boats into people's lives for the positive. *Now it's gone.* I turned to a letter from a friend for perspective on what I had left it for:

> What's the point of reconciling yourself with an uninformed, almost ostentatious, dogmatic promise you made to yourself (if only enforced through its telling to other people) for a journey of a certain length of time when the only reconciliation that holds any meaning at all is that within the bounds of your own soul? *Learn to be a best friend to yourself.* That's all in the world I could ask of you. It will happen no matter how many hours you log. Be flexible and strong but please just don't be stupid. Be wise and respectful of your bonds and the laws of the universe.

Both GPS's arrived on the same day! I picked up the "express" delivery (eight days) and Tony presented the original GPS brought back by Brenda.

They both *work*! They *both* work!

Can destiny be changed completely? I would like to think that it has something to do with the way we think, act, and feel and is not just some high deity's personal Nintendo game.

I did not trust the original magic wand nor did I particularly trust the new one. They were man's best efforts to consolidate thousands of years of intuitive navigation into something much less than the size of a bread box. It was about the size of shaving kit. Typically, just when we think we've got it, we find there's that much more to learn.

My faith in science was nearly lost, my faith in God was being explored, my belief in "self" was forming. That wasn't a lot to go with. The two GPS's gave science and me a fighting chance. The countdown to launch had recommenced.

Unlike at Ballina, neither Tony nor myself was quick to suggest a dawn launch. The gravity of the upcoming experience was heavier than that. Moreover, we had promised Janet that we would go to her school and do a show-and-tell for her kids with the boat, a map, and us. The next day we brought the *Southern Cross* Expedition to Thursday Island Public School. It was a beautiful day and Tony and I were greeted with twenty smiling faces—boys and girls of different sizes and demeanors. Janet had prepared them for us and made us out to be a big deal. The children stood huddled close with a respectful restraint unusual for preteens.

We assembled the boat from its bags, had a few kids sit in it. We talked about paddling and sailing and the nature of our journey. We answered some questions and felt greatly enriched for doing so. It felt so great that I could imagine making presentations to all sorts of schools. The euphoria of the presentation started to wilt under the reality of our near future—the crossing—and the fact we had to start the following day, weather permitting. My mind was partially appeased that our first day would be a twenty-mile warmup to Booby Island, twenty miles WNW and not an immediate immersion into the void. We would get our feet wet first.

The rest of the day and night was divided between various good-byes and boat preparation. *Southern Cross* was fully revamped and ready to go. I had tackled every detail I could think of in the past two weeks. Dot, Rex, Kelly, and the Thursday Island Bakery family had emphasized coming by in the morning to pick up some goodies and say our last farewells. I got a strange feeling of motherly concern from Dot. She had become as fond of us as we had of her.

Thursday Island had made a play for our souls. It waved carrots with fair faces and blond hair. It tickled our fancies with a splash of fame on a shifty shoreline. It threw bricks heated by the fire of harsh words. It juggled our technology with glee. It taunted *Southern Cross* with threats of impotence and obsolescence. It cast shadows of doubt from the inside and those closest to the heart. Now it was time to erase the board and start again.

June 20, Happy Birthday to me. The events and feelings of that night are unclear. I have no recollection. All I know is that it was my birthday and I was dressed up in my boat gear to begin a journey that would or would not be conducive to another one.

As usual, when I am this deep in the shit I do not fret much. That would explain the deep sleep of the night before. We were only going to Booby Island. There was still a chance to make a decision.

We moved the newly fortified and much stiffer *Southern Cross* from the "compound" to the beach where we had landed. We methodically brought our repacked gear down and proceeded with the boat loading, which took longer than anticipated. Although familiar with it, we had lost some of our touch.

Kelly and the rest of the bakery gang greeted us with a number of Nalgene bottles, which they had filled for us with fresh coffee, and a couple of buckets filled with baked goods, fresh fruit, and other "surprises." Care packaged with great love. They watched us clumsily squeeze all the unplanned foodstuffs into nonexistent nooks and crannies in and around us.

Dot yelled as we walked away, "The bread and donuts are on the top!"

We shoved away amid Dot and the kids saying good-bye and Rex running back to his bakery yelling that he "wanted a copy of the book." Kelly and her brother commandeered a motorboat and escorted us out the passage between Thursday and Prince of Wales islands. We saw Fruity and Frenchy water skiing and they bid their last high-speed farewell. The island passage was over and I kissed Kelly good-bye. Her beaming face nearly erased all the cynicism I had garnered about women. It was a face of honest feelings, of integrity, of innocence. And I loved her for that.

Gulf of Carpentaria—The Crossing

We split the gap between the two last islands and were out to sea, squinting for some sign of Booby Island. I thought we would be able to see it. I also thought we would have plenty of wind to sail to it. I was wrong on both counts. Tony and I were left with desolation and not a lot of daylight. We made our best guess at which direction to head in and even took one of the wands out for a spin. We headed north, saw an antenna, and paddled as fast as we could toward it. The "cruise" strained every one of our sedentary muscles. *Southern Cross* was heavier than ever and clearly a hundred pounds past efficient. We were sitting low, unsure where the current was taking us, and the veil of darkness was dropping. It all came back to us—what the trip had been all about in the first place. How easy it was to forget and fall into the fun and games of civilization (which seem to amount to a popularity contest with consolation prizes found in green cans of beer that said VB on them).

We paddled and paddled . . . and paddled some more. After seven hours, the island appeared. It didn't seem like the current was taking us one way or another. Nature's lights went out and that forgotten funk of not knowing exactly where we were going to spend the night set in. I knew there was a manned lighthouse. Rumor had it Booby Island was haunted. The geography of the previous islands instilled in me the belief that there would be a number of sandy beaches to put *Southern Cross* and ourselves to bed on.

We followed the beam of the lighthouse to Booby (so called because Cook's men shot a few booby birds and found very few plants there) and found it sur-rounded by cliffs. The lighthouse looked like it was on top of Mt. Olympus, although it sat no higher than a hundred feet above sea level. The winds were light, but the sound of the sea smashing the cliffs was unsettling. The sounds indicated the reemergence of swell coming from great distances instead of a backstop for local chop. We started to circle the island to find a landing spot. I had been clued in on TI about a lighthouse boat launch on the southwest side of the island. I was expecting a well-lit landing facility.

We paddled *Southern Cross* close enough for us to smell the southwest side. We continued to scour the west and then headed back to the south coast of Booby without finding a thing.

"This is getting to be a real bore," Tony grumbled. "I thought you said there was a landing spot?"

"That's what Rex said," I sighed.

It was starting to feel like a bad *Hardy Boys* episode in search of bogus treas-ure. Just as we started to the east I spied a suspicious-looking motorboat floating two hundred meters offshore. The plot thickened.

"Tony, let's go out to the boat and see if they know where the damned land-ing site is!"

Tony didn't debate. I was tired, and the "booby" prize of an island was raising my frustration to rival what Great Keppel Island had done to me. We clearly wouldn't be in time for dinner with the lighthouse staff, whomever they were. As late as it was, we had a better chance of meeting the lighthouse ghost.

We approached the phantom motorboat with a bag empty of choices. There had also been rumors of pirates armed not with rapiers but with Uzis. We pad-dled to the boat in stealth, similar to how we had paddled down the Harlem River after hearing gunshots. As we got closer, the boat and its two occupants looked more benign. We paddled more vigorously and were soon blinded by the boat's spotlight. I let Tony talk in "Australian." The boaters didn't seem terribly surprised to see us.

"G'day, mates."

"G'day. Are you all right?" Didn't sound like pirates. That was good!

"Yes, but we're looking for the boat ramp. Do you know where it is?"

"Ohhh. Righhht. Yeeaah. It's fifty meters north of the sign. Just follow the coast, keep your eyes open for the sign and it's just beyond it."

"Thank you, mate."

"No worries, good luck!"

So, all we had to do was just what we had been doing, only we had to find a sign we hadn't seen in the first place and go fifty meters past it. Back to Booby it was.

We retraced our initial path, going as close to the tumultuous coast as we dared, not knowing if there were any rocks under us, looking for a sign that was not going to be lit. We had missed the moon window and were to be given no help from the heavens.

"There's the sign!" I said exuberantly, as my front seat gave me first sight and first dibs on the proclamation.

"Are ya sure, mate?"

"Well, it's a sign. I'm assuming there's only one."

We paddled even slower so we wouldn't miss the ramp. Waves crashed into the coast. We silently entered the blackness. There were no crashing sounds in the narrow depression in the coast. *This must be it! It better be.*

"Let's go in, mate."

"OK."

Kaaabooooommmmmmmm! the wave echoed.

I could feel swell lift us up as we entered, and I heard the loud echo of the wave in front of us. *Not* a good sign.

The swell gently accelerated us into the void and we saw the ramp as a lighter form of darkness. There was no boat there. It was just a concrete ramp angling out of the cove and we would call it home for the night.

It had become very still in the cove and our eyes had adjusted to the terrain.

"We're here!"

I stumbled out of the boat and found slippery footing on the moss-laden ramp. The reduced friction allowed Tony and me to pull *Southern Cross* up with relative ease until we hit the dry parts. A loaf of wet bread was the first thing we unpacked. The second course was an assortment from Dot's care package. Cooking was out of the question. A sticky bun finished my feast. Oddly enough, I could not treat myself to the comfort of a donut in this new terrain.

At the top of the ramp was a small open shed we would call home. The lighthouse loomed over us up a dark path that neither one of us dared to tread. I was exhausted, the gift of ten hours of anxious paddling. No energy left to worry— sound sleep was on its way. I remembered that just the year before, I had been sitting with a beautiful blonde in a Mexican restaurant in the city, celebrating my thirty-first birthday.

"Good night and happy birthday, mate," Tony said.

The paddle coma gave me a deep, detoxing, and regenerating sleep that was an absolute necessity. I woke up almost refreshed. When we strolled up to the lighthouse, I saw a series of simple, one-level structures, but no one seemed to be around. Doors were open to various buildings and we both—in opposite directions—hailed: "Hello, hello, anybody here?"

Finally, we heard some barking and followed it to the back of a building, where we met a man who introduced himself as Bob, the last lighthouse keeper in Australia. He was tall, lanky, forty-fiveish, and rather chipper, but an individual somewhat lacking in social skills. Not that he was unpleasant or weird, just preoccupied with his routine. We didn't have a lot of time to chat, anyway, and had two clear needs.

First, we could see that the week of low winds had abated and a rough chop had already formed on the sea.

"What's the weather you have for the next few days?" I asked.

Bob looked out to sea and turned his face around, looked up to the sky and said, "Well, it looks like it's blowing about seventeen knots, and once it starts, these winds usually last awhile."

I looked at Tony and back at Bob.

"Yeah, I reckon about the same wind speed but what do the weather reports say?"

"We don't get weather reports here."

Hmmm, no boat at the boat ramp, no weather reports, and the last manned lighthouse in Australia.

"How rough does the gulf get, Bob?"

"Pretty rough."

"Six-foot seas? Nine-foot seas?"

"It can be more than that."

"Twelve-foot seas?!"

"Sometimes more than fifteen. It was about that rough when I went across last year."

The complexion of the challenge doubled in intensity from what I had imagined. I knew we should top off our water supplies.

"Bob, can we have some water?"

"Sure, it's in the green tank over there."

We got the water, bade farewell, and saw a woman I figured to be Bob's wife come out from another building.

"Good luck!" she yelled after us.

Our steps quickened to the boat. We loaded *Southern Cross* with a nervous thoroughness. Sooner than expected she was ready to launch. The question was: Were we?

"Do you think we can make it, mate?" Tony asked.

"Well, we're going to see. I think we can."

Tony got in. I got in. We shoved off.

"I'll see you on the other side, mate," he said.

For Captain Cook, it was the end of his first voyage, as he was to leave Australia and head back to Guinea. For us it was the beginning of our greatest challenge.

We left Booby Island and headed out to sea. The rough chop that I had hoped was caused by the shallows near the island and would diminish a few miles out did not. The chop simply got bigger and bigger to the point where we were in huge swells with the tops breaking at an alarmingly frequent rate. They would hit us with a characteristic *thwack!* But unlike any seas we had been in to that date.

A large swell rolled toward us. The winds were off our port bow. What I thought was an illusion became more intense. Another swell came at us from our starboard quarter.

How could this be?!

It was clear that we were like a tiny toy boat in a big bathtub with a precocious youngster slapping at the water. The Gulf of Carpentaria was and would remain a giant pool of hydraulic interaction. Waves came across *both sides* of the boat and *over the front,* with dump from the back. Sometimes it was a combination of the three all at once.

I had counted on more mileage into "open" sea to smooth out the turbulence. I was soon proved wrong . . . *again.*

The Gulf of Carpentaria is a large body of water (over 160,000 square miles larger than the area of all the Great Lakes in the United States combined, with the state of Michigan thrown in). Two very large bodies of water are funneled into it from the east and the west—the Coral Sea to the east and the Arafura Sea to the north and west—like two large spigots. The spigots pour water in *and* draw it out, sometimes drawing out on one side and pouring in from another.

In addition, swells generated from prevailing winds travel across the gulf, rebound from distant shores, and eventually work their way back across the gulf. Because of its relative shallowness compared to the ocean (a few hundred feet versus thousands), changes in wind direction can quickly change the prevailing swell direction, causing a confused clash between the new swell and the remnant of the original swell. No one along the entire way had mentioned any of this to us. I was still working hopefully from the comment of the yachtie, thousands of miles previous, who had said we would have steady winds, two-meter seas, and "no worries."

The sailing was very demanding in this chaos. It took every skill we had garnered till now to find good lines in those seas and to make the best of the strong winds. The leeboards made noticeable complaints with a numbing vibration that could be heard and felt through the boat as they strained to hold a course closer to the wind than the boat would have otherwise preferred.

According to the GPS, we had to hold a 237-degree (magnetic) WSW course the entire distance in order to reach Nhulunbuy (Gove). Part of the day we'd been able to point to 225 effectively; at other times it was tough to get 260 as the wind shifted from southeast to more southerly. I had learned a bit more how the trade winds worked up here.

Apparently, the engines for them were on the other side of the continent in the Great Australian Bight in South Australia. High pressure (counterclockwise spin) systems that were generated there worked from west to east like giant bowling balls with spin backward aiming for Tasmania.

I was concerned that the west-to-east movement of the high-pressure systems in the bight would gradually shift the winds more to the south. This would make it harder and harder to average 237. Therefore, any chance we had to point 220–225, we would, just to buy some bonus distance southward, in case we needed to cash in the bonus chips later on. If we were set adrift, *Southern Cross* would go northward to Indonesia a bit to the west, or to Irian Jaya, New Guinea. It definitely would not go toward Australia!

When darkness came, I realized that we'd be sailing in the same confusion during the night as we had been during the day. It would be a "first" for both of us. A rough sail. All night. We would average forty-five miles or more during the twelve daytime hours, and less than thirty that night. It was distance made good in the world of the GPS, but following the same compass course, holding good lines on the waves, and adjusting our bodies to every little nuance of the sea was torture.

Adding to our troubles was the poorly lit compass (a glow light taped next to it). It started to look like hieroglyphics. Focusing in on its reading ranged from hard to impossible. It was hard enough following it in daylight because of the constant up and down, left and right, back and forth actions of the boat. The compass was one of the best in the business. It was a Silva UN 70 on a special mount. I was now wishing that the UNB (the one with a lithium light inside) had been in stock before I left NYC. To its credit, the UN 70 was gyroscopic, so the face of the compass did its damndest to stay level. All you had to do was add snowflakes and it would look like those Christmas scenes in the plastic bubble. After many hours it started to look that way.

I shifted to the old nautical trick of following the star that lined up closest with the compass course so that I could simply focus and steer toward it, and I soon found out it was not as easy as advertised. Any star near the course we were trying to hold, near enough to the horizon to be practical, was in an atmospheric haze caused by the gradually decreasing temperature of the air versus the steady temperature of the gulf.

The star of choice went in and out of view and eventually disappeared altogether by the middle of the night. Different stars would have to be used as the earth rotated and the constellations played ring-around-the-rosie. Each star had to be higher and higher in the sky to see at all, so I kept looking from the compass on the deck to a point forty-five degrees off the horizon. I found myself nodding yes over and over again.

I was also surprised by the cold. *Cold at eleven degrees latitude?* It was winter in the Southern Hemisphere and the long twelve-and-half-hour night sent a chill through my bones. Somehow, I gradually managed to put on nearly everything I had, one piece at a time. I had kept the clothing bag very handily secured between my legs. Tony's teeth started chattering after about eight hours. I knew we had one piece of insulating clothing left.

"Tony, you should put on your hooded darlex core-temp top," I groggily suggested.

"Whahahahattttitititit?"

"Put on the darlex hooded number. It will warm you up."

"What about you, mate?"

"I'm OK for now."

The last darlex "hot body" insulating garment we had was made by a company called SSA (Sports Suits of Australia), and it was a breathable four-way stretch fabric, plush-lined and hooded. It was ideal for putting underneath all the other layers of pile and nylon. After Tony put it on, his chattering subsided. As for me . . . well, I had sent mine back to Sydney with Tony's mum, thinking I wouldn't need it.

The night *thwacking* became more disturbing. I could hear the wind accelerating like the launch of an airplane off an aircraft carrier. A few moments later a change in the sound of the sea would punctuate us with a loud *thwack!* sometimes stopping us dead in the water, leaving a ring of foamy lighter darkness all around the boat. Just as I'd warm up a bit, we'd get hit with water all over again. Late at night a quarter-moon would pronounce a very late rising sun. I'd expected, no, I'd needed a six-thirty sunrise. Six-thirty came and it was pitch black. I studied my watch over and over again, not quite believing it.

"Tony?"

No response. *"Tony?!"*

"What, what?"

"What time do you have?" It seemed like forever, and I asked again: "What time do you have?

"I'm trying to see my watch. It's six-forty-five."

"Jeezus! Not a bloody hint of light? Don't you have dawns around here?" I was starting to get very cold and I realized I had not slept for a second. The wind had howled all night, sometimes worse than during the day. The idea of going semiprone in the boat and nodding off for at least half an hour, like Lindemann had done when he crossed the Atlantic, was not to be. *The wind will have to have a slow time sometime so we can sleep.*

Seven-forty-five a.m. The first rays of light peaked over the horizon. *Is the goddamned world fatter over here?*

"It's about time! What took you so long?" I yelled, and the burst of anger warmed me up for a moment, but soon the damp chill kept my limbs stagnant and I simply held the sails in position to get the most from the wind, as I had done all night. There had been about five minutes of automatic pilot all night long. It was simply too rough! *This cannot continue.*

It was noon before I started to finally warm up. This was another downside of sailing. Paddling would keep us warm in the short run at least, but *SC* was on its own maniacal tear to get across, like one of those sea crocs looking for a new home. We'd finally dry out by three o'clock in the afternoon, but then it was time for more darkness and cold again. Day to night to day to night, and back again. The wind blew every minute, the seas got bigger, we both got colder and we still had 250 miles to go. *This is not possible. We've got to have a break.*

On the third day of the crossing, we were hit by a morning storm. Fifteen-to-twenty-knot winds had become normal to us. They now pumped up to thirty-five knots and a gale. The seas built up another couple of feet. We desperately needed sleep. *We don't have time for a gale right now?!* It had been over fifty hours since either of us had slept. I tried to be even more alert in an even more aggressive sea but it all seemed futile.

"Mate, let's try to use that Driftstopper thing you brought. We've got to try to get some shut-eye," Tony said.

"Okay."

The "Driftstopper" was a recently packaged name for a small, "easy to deploy, easy to attach to kayak" sea anchor sometimes known as a "drogue." Essentially, it is miniature parachute that could land a field mouse safely from five thousand feet. A cat would splat. The manufacturer had already prepackaged it in a smart, thick nylon sheath that kept the thin nylon umbrella and all associated lines together and out of harm's way.

The Driftstopper attaches to the bow of the kayak and has its own rip cord, which deploys it from its sheathing whence it is supposed to travel forward, past the bow, billow open completely, and catch the sea. From there, it holds the bow toward the oncoming wind and weather and prevents excessive drift in any particular direction. Up to now I had only attempted it on land, back in NYC many moons ago. I had brought it for this type of situation. Now the situation would decide how it all would work.

First, we turned into the wind as the boat lurched and heeled leeward with the gusts and the now breaking seas. *Southern Cross* resented being pulled off her gallop and strained to not go off course as we yanked her to starboard.

WHAP, WHAP, WHAP WHAPWHHSSPPSSHSHSPSSHPHSPHSPHS.

I tried to tame the sails as they maniacally flapped like a flag on top of Mt. Washington. I got face-whipped by the spasmodic lashings of the jib sheets. At first, my reflexes were no match. I was still in a state of suspended animation, seeing things in a slower motion.

A wave suddenly rolled up over the bow and filled my mouth and lap with water. That woke me up. I lassoed the sails to the mast and secured the lines. I fumbled with the Driftstopper and found that the "easy to deploy" concept was being challenged. After pulling and tugging at the rip cord to no effect, I watched the bundled mass congeal in the middle of the sheath like a rat in the belly of an anaconda.

Each tug compressed it more. I realized that the flexible deck of *Southern Cross* was not providing enough purchase. It appeared that the Driftstopper would work better on the solid decks of a fiberglass kayak. The more I pulled, the more the whole unit brought the canvas deck with it. I crawled half out of my cockpit and deployed it manually. Now, it looked and felt like I was giving birth to a nylon octopus, which I soon had wadded and dangling in my left hand. I tossed it over the side and said, "Be Free!" but did not see it open more than halfway.

"Do you think it's working, mate?" Tony asked.

"I think so," I said, as the bow stayed aimed toward the oncoming waves. But the back surfing and drift seemed excessive.

I comforted myself with the thought that it would open up underwater completely. Certainly the designer had engineered it for this contingency. Absolutely. No worries.

Now we both tried to go about the business of sleeping. Somehow, the idea of sleeping in the biggest seas and strongest winds yet was not as preposterous as it would seem otherwise. I methodically unclipped one of the green caboose bags from one hip area and tried to lie on it chest and face forward. Tony copied me.

THWACK PISSHSSHSHSHSHSHSHH.

"Jeezus! What the hell—"

THWACK-PSISSISIISISISSSS.

Waves were smacking us about and around and running up the front deck and from the port beam. My pillow would rise up under my arms on the buoyancy of the flooded deck, roughly jostling me into consciousness. Then my head went down again, like tumbling into a bottomless dark well. Over and over. One time I snapped awake and saw a small island bristling with trees.

THWACK Psshshhshshshshshh. Nothing was there.

"It's no use, mate!" Tony yelled, "let's just keep going."

"Let's just try a little—

THWACK Pshshhshshshshshshsh.

"Let's get going."

Efforts to get any sleep were hopeless, as the larger waves just kept stampeding us. The drogue had not deployed correctly and we were drifting too fast. We had to try to reel in the drogue, which got fouled up on our bow. I climbed to the end of the boat to untangle the mess. The baby octopus had grown some and was clinging to *Southern Cross* with half her tentacles. It was time for me to do some sea surgery like Tony had accomplished with the rudder repair at Evans Head.

I wrapped my body around the mast like a snake to keep my body on the boat and detangle lines as they bobbed underwater more frequently and deeper the closer I got to the bow. Adrenaline rushed in for the moment. I fixed the line, and we sailed on. The detangling balancing act and the drama of the squall kept us awake for most of the day, which then faded back into night. . . . Again.

"I'm knackered, mate. Your turn at the rudder." Tony finished his six-hour steering shift. Now it was time to unrig his rudder cables blindly and behind my back and re-rig them through a cramped, gear-swollen boat to the tiny foot-pedal hooks at my feet and then attach them through a braille code that wasn't getting easier through practice. A procedure that took me a minute on land in daylight took many minutes on end now as the delicate procedure of draping two two-millimeter-thick chain-link ends off of and onto two three-millimeter hooks.

"Damnit!"

"Ya awright, mate."

"Just about got it that time!" It became clear that there were no guarantees they would ever go on. The tolerances were tiny and I did not even have the benefit of seeing the needle I was putting the thread into.

"Got it."

"Good job, mate! Now, I need to try to get some shut-eye."

"Give it a shot, TB. I'll keep her on course!"

Once upon a time in a kayak shop so very far away, I gave a presentation in front of seventy-five Klepper clients interested in how I was outfitting this trip. I stood proudly in front of them all with a crew cut, a pointer stick, and a map of Australia. I had conducted a "virtual" tour of our route up to the point describing what I had expected to happen along the way. I then reached the gulf we were now in and a client asked: "How are you going to sleep in the boat?"

"No worries, watch this!" I had laid out the assembled skeleton of *Southern Cross* with all the bubble-pack-filled bags lashed in the boat as I imagined they would be. I got into my cockpit and wiggled about; took one of the dry, light, pillowlike shapes and moved it away from my feet and pulled it up to my groin; and wiggled down onto the remaining pillow-shaped bags.

"Violà! A deluxe Klepper sleeper car."

The crowd *oohed* and *ahhed*. Very impressed. Of course, that was then.

Now, in ten-foot seas, the bags were heavy, awkward, and far more wedged in and inaccessible than had been imaginable that night. Going prone or semi-prone to lower our center of gravity without effecting the balance of the boat was a pipe dream.

When one of us would fall to dozing in the boat, it would throw everything off kilter, alerting the conscious partner to yell at the other to wake up. Then we'd have to rebalance. Fifteen-to-thirty-second "timeouts" were taken by the mind regardless of the roughness of the seas, the severity of the circumstances, or the utterances of the disgruntled partner. They were instant dream states with hallucinatory properties presenting comforting images of land, birds, trees, and people with smiling faces.

I wrote in my journal afterward:

It appears that the mind will do what it has to do to retain alertness via systematic intervals of lost "consciousness" or that type of consciousness connected with the visual (eyes open). There are still levels of "consciousness" manifested in senses of balance and hearing which as we know are partners in the first place.

Our minds and bodies were coping. They were on overdrive. In scientific terms they were actually in "underdrive," proving to be purposeful, positive, effi-cient, and unfretting. Scientifically we were gradually spending more and more time in "alpha" consciousness because we could not officially go to sleep and yet we did not make great efforts to focus on anything in particular for long periods of time. But the boat sailed, upright and on course. We had not capsized and that was a not so minor miracle.

When we dropped off into time-outs, we were way past anything adrenaline could do for us. Our minds and bodies knew that a quick rush or quick fix could only be administered in the smallest of doses at the most important times for the most economical intervals. I had asked a pharmacist in TI about the use of stimulants to stay awake for seven-to-ten days. He had said, "No way, you'll crash too hard. You can stay awake for about five days straight but you will pay afterwards." All energy must be conserved. All emotions subdued. All thought processes slowed.

I felt exactly like what I'd once heard about a theory of musical "stamina" by a concert violinist: Once you start concentrating on "how" you are making sounds, it will inevitably all fall apart. I found eventually that "letting go" and letting the mind and body do their own thing would keep it all together, more so than trying to depend on what was left of my conscious concentration.

It was pitch black and my turn on the foot steering. The task of resetting the foot pedals had snapped me out of alpha. It was now very difficult to watch the compass and hold the boat on course. When the eyes focus hard on an object, the mind always sets the brain back to beta.

Now the boat seemed to either slide from side to side, peel out, or not move at all. I searched for tangible signs that confirmed or refuted the boat's motion, to get some bearings in time and space, both of which had become vague, sometimes void. The compass went hieroglyphic. I was reading ancient Egyptian letters inside the blizzard of the compass's plastic bubble. I could not focus on it at all. I tried to focus, but couldn't. My eyes would not focus. I started to panic myself with *plaguing* thoughts. *That's it, I'm done, I can't see, how am I going to continue, I can't make Tony steer another six hours, it's not right, what am I going to do?!*

I deliberated on whether or not to summon Tony to retake the rudder only an hour after he'd relinquished his six-hour shift. Just before I was about to give up, I blanked out for an instant and suddenly came to. Immediately, I had an unforgettable epiphany of motion and mind/body awareness. Mihaly Csikszentmihalyi had coined it: flow. He describes it in his book of the same title as the "optimal experience."

I can only say that for many moments in time everything worked perfectly. The boat felt like a magic carpet air-surfing the waves of the universe. I had stopped making choices and achieved grace! A universal grace took control to show me what it *should* feel like! I was not dreaming although I was in a dream state that lasted for most of my shift that night.

Normal consciousness kicked in again. I needed beta to turn on the GPS to see how we were doing. We were south of and between the third and fourth way point. *So far so good!* I did my six hours and let Tony keep his sanity with whatever cycles he could find.

Things like drinking water, eating food, and excreting waste were a blur. We did these things but not frequently or with a lot of awareness. Pieces of food were handed to me over my shoulder. I'd shovel in whatever he gave me until one day he said, "Open your hand, mate, you'll like this!" I reflexively flipped my hand back as if to receive "low five" and felt a gooey mass plop into my hand. I proceeded to shovel it into my mouth and instantly retched it back into my hand.

"What was that?"

"Spam, mate," Tony said as I stared at the pink, fatty, gelatinous ooze and quickly threw it into the sea.

"Was that a good idea?"

"I don't care, that was horrible. How about cracking another can of rice pudding?"

"Not too many left."

"I'll eat half of it now and save some for later."

Urination was infrequent. I peed in a wide-mouthed Nalgene bottle and Tony threw his hose over the side. We were partially dehydrated, which is harder to decipher when one is cold and wet on the outside. My face was always wet and drinking something cool proved undesirable.

Defecating was a feat. First I placed a soup dish under my bum, elevated myself up on the coaming as if rising from a wheelchair. I attempted to aim the waste into the dish while the boat was lurching and Tony was desperately trying to stay in alpha so he didn't have to focus on it. Hitting the target was not easy and I will leave it at that. The preferred Tony method involved using a large sheet of baking paper and wrapping it up afterward. I think we managed the procedures once each in three days.

Toward the end of the fourth day, I took out the GPS for our daily mileage and course check. I pressed the ON button. Nothing happened. A sick electric chill went into every cell of my body. *No, no no not this again! Not here, not now!* I checked the batteries, changed them, pressed ON . . . nothing. The original GPS had gone on the blink again.

"What's the matter?" Tony said.

"The original GPS is not turning on again."

"You checked the batteries?"

"Yes, everything."

"Let me have a look." I handed him the original one and went for the new one, the spare, the one my father had sent. I hoped Tony would work miracles, but I needed this one to turn on.

I pulled it out, took a deep breath, and pressed ON. It worked! It showed me that we were one hundred twenty-four miles from our destination. It would've been a lousy place not to have the GPS. Back in TI, when we were awaiting their arrival, we'd agreed to leave with whichever unit arrived first. Thank God they'd both arrived on the same day.

Day 4 turned into Night 4, which turned into Day 5. It was all blending together. *Southern Cross* seemed to be keeping pace with a moving Himalayan mountain range. The seas had developed fully over those last hundred hours and giant waves seemed to be moving uniformly in slow motion. I could see snow-capped peaks, deep ravines, and glaciers but as one set of mountains went by, another range moved in, like constantly changing grand scenes at the opera.

I also remember realizing that we had neither seen nor heard any other vessel on the entire crossing. No ships, no boats, no airplanes . . . nothing! We were in maximum wilderness. Moreover, there was a four-hour satellite blackout when the GPS did not have the minimum number of satellites to accurately triangulate from to get our course. I heard a *snap*, the boat suddenly downshifted, and I saw the leeboard system wobbling in front of me like a broken arm.

"What happened, mate?" Tony asked. I looked at the whole assembly and it was intact. The new leeboards were fine but I saw that the left coaming was very loose and feared the worst. *Not a cracked coaming, not here!* If the ninety-six-inch-long V-shaped coaming had broken in half, all the duct tape in the world was not going to make it strong enough to handle the forces working on the leeboards.

I felt the coaming with both hands through the spray cover like a paramedic making an infield test of a broken limb through a ski jacket sleeve.

"The coaming isn't cracked. It's something else!"

A wave lifted the boat up and I saw the coaming lift independently from the main frame of the boat. I felt under the deck and found that the T-fitting that held the coaming in the ski-buckle-like clamp on top of one of the open ribs in the boat had pulled straight out of the wood in the coaming.

"Shit."

"What?"

"The T-fitting screws are stripped out of the wood."

"Can you fix it?" Tony had asked the million-dollar question.

OK, OK, Eric, the fix is larger screws but I don't think that will hold, they'll strip out soon enough. I brought small nuts and bolts for this kind of thing, but damnit, not for out here!

"Mate?"

I'll have to drill out the coaming. How am I going to do that? I can't. What if the coaming snaps because of the new hole? I gotta do the bigger screws and hope it holds.

"Epic?!"

"Yes, I can. It's going to take awhile."

"She's sailing at 250. I think I can hold her there without the boards. I'm going to keep us sailing," Tony said.

"OK."

This surgery was intricate, and I had brought T-fittings with larger holes for larger screws—just in case. But placing the T-fitting in place and screwing it with the slightly oversized Phillips head of the Leatherman tool was exasperating. The fitting, or one screw or the other, kept falling into the boat and I had to constantly feel around the bottom of the boat to retrieve them. *Bloody circumcision in a Jeep!*

Finally, I got it in. Now I had to pull the coaming back toward the left side of my ribs and place the fitting back onto the clamp—a ten-millimeter fitting into fifteen-millimeter clamp head. I couldn't do it. The weight of the gear strapped into the sides of the frame had spread it too wide.

"Tony, ya gotta pull and hold the coaming so I can clamp it!"

Tony cleated off the mainsheet and pulled. The boat lurched and heeled.

Normally I would want to let the sail fly free while we did this but the seas were so big that the boat was now more stable in motion than it would be floundering between the peaks and troughs. I had experienced the latter when I crossed the Chesapeake Bay.

"Got it!" *Now we have to keep our fingers crossed.*

I put the leeboards back on. "Try to point her back to 230."

Tony steered to port and the vibration of the boards increased and hummed. *It sounds like 230.*

"Two hundred thirty, mate!"

"Good!"

Snap.

Shit!

Shit plan two, you gotta use the drill and put it in with nuts and bolts.

"Mate?"

"Plan B. *I know what to do!*" I said with conviction.

I don't know what consciousness I was in, but I had visualized this process while doing the first. I chose to use the sharp punch on the Leatherman, instead of the drill, and to hand drill through the wood, and I managed to get through. I found the 20-mm-long-by-3-mm-wide bolt and eventually managed to push it through the hole. I screwed on the tiny nut and tightened with the Leatherman pliers. I did the same for the other.

"Let's try it again, mate!" I yelled to Tony. He pulled and held, and I linked the fitting and the clamp and reattached the leeboards. *Southern Cross* had steadily rambled along at four knots the whole time. This time it held.

At dusk at the end of the fifth day, I thought I saw a haze of lights. The GPS said we were twenty-four nautical miles away!

Yes! Those could be lights! They could very well be the lights of Nhulunbuy. We're there!!! I said to myself. And that was my first mistake.

In normal circumstances, twenty-four nautical miles is considered a long open-water crossing and a full day of travel. Eight hours of steady paddling or sailing normally covers this distance. It was seven o'clock at night, which pushed our landing time to three or four in the morning. *A mere hop, skip, and jump,* I deludedly thought.

Hours later, confusion set in as we watched two separate banks of light emerge, when we were expecting only one.

"Do you see that orange haze of lights now as well?" I asked.

"Where?"

"Straight in front of us, actually a little off to the right now."

"Yes."

A great distance spanned the two. We couldn't afford to guess which way to go and be wrong. My GPS coordinates were not accurate enough to make the decision any easier. *Do we head toward the bluish light bank or the orangish one?* We traveled two hours more and were seventeen nautical miles away.

"Which way do you want to go, mate?"

"I don't know, I just don't know. Let's just stay in the middle for a while longer."

"Mate, the blue lights are going to get farther away soon."

By midnight, our progress had slowed considerably, as we were unassisted by the wind. We sheeted in both sails as far as they would go and imagined we were still making forward progress. Another check on the GPS showed a mile made good in an hour. I realized we were going to be out all night—again—and this time the sailing party was over.

"Go for the orange," I said.

Every ache, pain, and malady in my body that had been so effectively anesthetized in my dream state returned with a vengeance. I suddenly felt a rash running a ring around my torso and I noticed that my hands were extremely puffy and dotted with septic sores all over them and in between all of my fingers. My hands felt hot, but a splash of water gave me instant chills. The sea had become more confused and "splashy" as we reached shallower water. Seawater slapped my burning hands over and over, sending shivers through me. Spasms fired rapidly through all my major muscle groups, lurching the boat with each ignition. My brain pushed the emergency hypothermia button, commanding every muscle it could to get my core body temperature back up. I was tortured by these uncontrollable gut-wrenching contortions for hours. Tony didn't say a word. He had to have been contending with his own personal house of pain.

The body spasms stopped. Unfortunately, the boat stopped, too. It was time to de-mast and hit the sticks. Shots of pain ran through my hands and body while I attacked the grueling task. I already had quite a sweat going, and we had ten more miles to go to the orange lights, which now looked like some sort of ship dock. I thought I saw the neck of a crane backlit by the orange hues. I couldn't imagine how I could paddle. My hands were now swollen like ham hocks whose unfamiliar shapes I could start to see in the near-dawn light. The wind direction now switched to blow straight into our faces.

Tony quietly helped me shuffle the sail equipment away and clear our respective spaces. With our first stroke, one of Tony's weakened fingernails ripped off. He howled with pain. A nail fungus was to blame.

"Mate, I can't paddle." I turned around to see his bloody finger wrapped in a T-shirt.

My mind swam in a poor soup of options.

"I'll paddle us in, Tony!!"

I stripped off my clothes. For about a hundred strokes, I felt superhuman. Each stroke after that I felt like I was nearly dead. The mind sent the message but nobody was home to respond. I had never felt such fatigue in my life. The paddles barely made it from one side of the boat to the next.

Tony saw this and said: *"Mate, I'll paddle us in!!"*

He had apparently come to terms with his pain, like I had come to terms with my ham-hock hands. We alternated heroics for a while, until it appeared that the tide was starting to move against us. Then we paddled together toward the closest shore, even though no sign of civilization existed there. The orange lights were gone and the more graphic skeletons of machinery took their place. I could see some type of jetty between us and them. It did not feel like we were progressing and it was possible that the tide was active and not in our favor.

Tony asked me sincerely, "When a boat comes out of the harbor, we'll let it take us in, right?!"

I had yet to see a boat or even a hint of one but said, "You bet, Tony. I think we've come far enough."

It seemed to appease Tony for a while. An hour later there was no boat and the jetty didn't seem much closer. Tony said: "I think we're going backwards, mate. See, see, look at the water!"

I stared at the water, I looked back at the coast. I didn't want to see it.

"I don't think we are."

"Mate, we've got to set off the EPIRB!"

Then, as if not quite fully awake from a dream, I swore I turned around and saw Tony with the trophy-size orange satellite alerting device that once activated would send signals to satellites and relay them to emergency stations around the world.

I estimated we were less than five miles from shore. Two or three more hours of slow paddling. But I sensed from the frustration in Tony's voice that any more paddling was simply unthinkable. I thought he wanted to send up the biggest baddest flare we could—the EPIRB! But it wouldn't be as simple as that.

First, the EPIRB signal would have to find a satellite or aircraft. That could take hours. Then that receiver would have to acknowledge and re-acknowledge the signal to make sure that it wasn't a fake. More time. The likely receiver would be the naval station in Darwin. They would probably have to coordinate with the local authority in Nhulunbuy (if one existed) or send a plane from Darwin or Thursday Island. Even then, they wouldn't know what they were looking for.

They would be expecting a shrimp trawler or yacht—not a kayak. The EPIRB can narrow the search grid to a few square miles at best. A kayak is hard to find. A search like that is a serious endeavor and requires mobilization of a lot of equipment. Once found and rescued, we would have some serious questions to answer: *What in God's name were you doing crossing the Gulf of Carpentaria in a kayak? Do you know how much it cost to find and rescue you? Do you know how irresponsible your actions were? Etc., etc.*

I had to talk him out of it.

It looked like Tony was going to pull the pin on a hand grenade. I don't remember what I said or didn't say, but I know a minute later the EPIRB was stowed away and he said: "Hit the sticks, mate. Let's take her in!" In no time, we were paddling fast. The minute of madness had passed.

We started to close in on the first sandy shore we saw. It was less than a mile away when I looked a couple of miles beyond it and saw more alluring digs. I hoped I wasn't hallucinating.

"TB, do you see those palm trees and white houses in a row?"

"Yeah——ah," he said questioningly.

"Let's aim for them. Looks a lot better than that patch of scrubland over there."

"Mate, land is right there?!"

"Yeah, but there is nothing around it. We've got to make it to those houses!"

We rejected the first landfall we saw—I knew it would be a long time before we'd want to get back in the boat, or move it, to find better accommodations. We needed heaven but I would settle for a sanctuary. A landing with palm trees looked like the ticket.

I had renewed spirit. The seas flattened out and the tropical sun massaged our torsos. Paddling became easier as we drew closer to the palm trees. We slipped past the point into a cover and saw beautiful, flat aquamarine waters. *One mile to go!* We paddled for all we were worth. *Southern Cross* got up and galloped again, and with about a quarter-mile to go I heard Tony say:

"This could be the finale, mate," implying the end of the whole trip.

A tear worked itself past some salt in my eyes, and a chill went up my spine. I could hear the steady splashes of our paddles landing in a precise rhythm. I felt like the marchers in *The Bridge on the River Kwai.* Soon we were on the southeast corner of the palm tree–bordered beach. *Southern Cross* ground to a halt. *We made it! We're on land!*

My mind said *get up,* and my body flopped up like a puppet and perched itself in the cockpit. *Get out,* it screamed, and I placed one leg over the side and tried to bring the other one over but tripped backward into the water. I tried to stand up and fell backward again. Tony stumbled and fell as well and we both laughed. He remembered how to walk before I did and strode awkwardly to the beach on his own power. I managed to grab *Southern Cross,* stood up, and let my body figure out which way was front and back. Then I took my first successful forward step, I grabbed the mast and took my second wobbly one and then walked myself up *Southern Cross*'s bow to the beach.

I felt like an organism skipping links in the evolutionary chain to go from water to land. I got stuck on reptile. Higher thought processes would be a bigger jump still.

Tony had already fired up some mammalian brain centers and was scouting around. In fact, he seemed reborn. I wanted to kneel down and kiss the ground, but I did not have the energy. (The last time I had felt this odd was when I'd taken my SAT tests with acute pneumonia and a 102-degree fever.) Tony said he'd wished he'd taken a picture of my eyes at that time. He said it was a look he'd never forget. Taking that picture would have been one of those "higher thought" processes that neither one of us could muster right then. Even if he could have, only one of the cameras still worked, and we had no idea where it was stashed. We had not taken one picture on the entire crossing.

My cold reptilian blood had only one desire. To climb on a rock and warm up in the sun. I was down to my underwear, lying on a rock, while Tony went exploring. I opened my eyes. An apparition! It had to be . . .

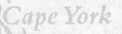

Nhulunbuy

I looked up from my fetal tuck position and saw a white-clad, blond-haired woman walking down the beach. Some latent social instinct wanted me to jump up and cover myself, but my blood was too cold to move. So I just lay there. In minutes her face was a few feet away from mine. Tony returned.

"It looks like you two could use a shower and some tea," she said in a manner that intimated she'd been expecting us all along.

The woman said her name was Claire. This had to be an official, fully decorated, *It's-a-Wonderful-Life*-quality angel, and to this day I still think she is. She lived four or five houses up the beach from where we landed. A former nurse, she'd switched to teaching Aborigine children in town. She was our Florence Nightingale. She told us we had landed on Wallabee Beach. It seemed like only a matter of minutes before we had eaten our first tray of buttered cinnamon toast in her living room, accompanied by coffee and pots of tea.

She had successfully jump-started some higher functions in my brain, which was good, because Claire wanted to know all. She asked, and we answered, a litany of questions. Innumerable words spewed forth from my lips that had pronounced little in one hundred thirty hours. "How far have you come?" Over three thousand miles. "How long has it taken?" Over three months. "What have you seen?" Waves, wind, storms, beaches, birds, dolphins, sea turtles, dugongs, kangaroos, sharks, sea snakes, vipers, tarantulas, fog, islands, reefs, capes upon capes, surf and more surf, mangroves, mountains, jungles, reefs, mossies, crabbers, Aborigines, Torres Strait Islanders, nomads, shrimpers, hermits, the perfect mother, lighthouses, resorts, jellyfish nets, yachties, dingoes, milkbars, and post offices to name a few.

"How was the crossing?" I drew a blank and I let Tony take over.

An hour or so later, I took Claire up on the shower. It just seemed to be time. I went to the shower in a chipper, satiated mood. I went in, looked at the brass knobs and showerhead like they were parts of the control center to a time machine. I turned on the spray, adjusted its temperature and velocity, and stepped inside.

After the first waves of stinging pain subsided from my waist, where there was a Santa Claus–size belt of welted rash going around my midsection, I luxuriated in the soft tickling of these warm healing waters. I turned up the pressure and stood underneath the torrent and spun slowly round and round letting it hit every part of my body. I could feel waves of tension rolling into the drain, when I suddenly heard a voice. I said, "Tony, is that you?" and got no response.

I restarted my rotisserie and heard quite unforgettably these words from outside my head but inside the shower.

"Remember, Eric, I'm always there for you."

I started to sob. It released the rest of the tension and sucked in a newfound joy in one long cry. I had never before bawled from such a deep place in my soul. I returned from the catharsis exhausted, yet refreshed.

"Have a good time in there, mate." I smirked at Tony as he passed me on the way to shower.

I don't know if he cried there. We never discussed it. All I know is that there was another plate of cinnamon toast and more coffee waiting for me. Later, Claire's husband, Harry, returned from the bauxite plant up the road. Harry seemed a little surprised to see two spanking-clean young men at home with his wife in the middle of the afternoon, but soon was briefed as to our "landing" there.

Harry Van Rooy was in his early forties, with short hair and a well-trimmed beard. He sported a modest belly on top of some solid legs. He spoke with what I found out was a Dutch accent. Harry warmed up to us after a bit, and we let it be known that we should check in to the closest hotel to sleep for a day. Harry and Claire understood our insistence on sleep—the kind where you're not to be disturbed—and recommended the best place in town for that. They told us to call when we were ready to return and stay with them.

Harry took us to the Gove Hotel, which was also a restaurant connected to a pub and drive-thru liquor window.

We walked into the hotel with a couple of our bags, clean but haggard, our faces gaunt with dark eyes. The fatigue of the trip had fought its way past the sugar and coffee and had found itself back home in my body and mind. With

Tony's brown fungus nails and my pustule-pocked swollen hands, we looked like poster children for the plague. We went right up to the check-in counter, barely noticing a bevy of bawdy beauties dominating the foyer lounge. However, the bevy noticed us and sent their very cute, twenty-something, auburn-haired, MTV-VJ-looking manager over.

"Where did you come from?" she asked.

"We just crossed the Gulf of Carpentaria in a kayak." We harmonized our monotones and stood with emotionless faces.

The message was quickly relayed to the other girls, who gathered around us like mother hens (in low-cut, high-cut, long-legged, cleavage-laden bodies with lips and hair everywhere). They picked up our hands with concern and affection. *What the hell's going on here?!* Perhaps, *What the heaven's going on here?* was the more appropriate question.

It turned out that the women were the Chantuzzis, one of Australia's top female rock bands, and they were here doing a remote Northern Territory tour. *We were now in Arnhem Land in Northern Territory, Australia. Funny, I did not see the sign in the middle of the gulf.*

"You two must rest up and come to our gig tonight in the hotel."

"What time?"

"Ten P.M."

Normally, this would be an offer that few of the male, heterosexual population could find any reason at all short of death to not respond to. However, we were as close to physical death as we had been in our respective lives. Take the worst flu you've ever had and add a dash of mononucleosis and you would be remotely in the ballpark. The ten o'clock show was exactly eleven hours from when we'd checked in. It seemed possible that we could rise to the occasion. We set every alarm we had and told the desk to give us a wake-up call.

Twenty-one hours later we woke up. We'd paid no conscious heed to any of the alarms we'd set. When I stepped out our door, I was shocked to find out that the Chantuzzis had also been our next-door neighbors the whole night! I found one of the blondes gathering up some of her things and heading to the lobby.

"Are you leaving?" I said hurriedly.

"Yes, we're on to Katherine. We really missed you last night . . . nice meeting you, gotta go . . . good luck!"

My short romance ended with a kiss and a curse at the gods for not allowing me to awaken.

Twenty-one hours of sleep only restored basic life function. Walking and thinking were still not wired up very well for long-term use. The pharmacist whom I consulted in Thursday Island about amphetamines for the trip advised me not to bring any because the duration of time we would have to remain awake far exceeded the short-term benefits of Vivarin or any other product. He said that the human body can go a week without sleep, but that we would pay for it. The body needed to make up *all* of the missed sleep—and then some.

The way I felt the "day after" certainly would not begin to disprove this. Claire had mentioned something about visiting the clinic to check us out. I intended to go before the long sleep. But I'd thought the sleep had begun the deep healing of a systemic infection that had worked its way from my hands and waist into my bloodstream and organs.

I was through the trees, but not out of the woods yet. The idea of doctors probing around my already compromised constitution did not sound appealing. I needed fresh air, an unmoving surface under my feet, low stress, and a beer.

We pushed check-out time to the limit and gave Harry a call. Claire's clinic was the ticket. Harry showed up in a flash and soon we were back to Wallabee Beach. It was the weekend and Harry and Claire were having a barbie that afternoon with Peter and Francine. Peter was Harry's longtime friend from NABALCO, the Swiss-owned aluminum ore (bauxite) plant. The relationship lasted despite the fact Peter was "staff" and Harry was "line" (management versus line worker).

We learned that NABALCO owned and leased all the houses on Wallabee Drive for very attractive rates. They had a great benefits plan, good salaries, long travel stipends, and a host of other incentives to keep their employees in Gove (Nhulunbuy).

The orangish glow Tony and I'd seen out at sea was an ore-loading bridge; the bluish lights were the city of Nhulunbuy. We had made the right choice. It was like a town split in two. The center of Nhulunbuy was lined with Aborigines in limbo—neither connected to their roots nor accepted by the white government and NABALCO-related gentrifiers. People like Claire were trying to bridge the gap. Relations were friendly enough from what we saw during the day, but later on in the evening on the main drag we saw a lot of Aborigines drunk and belligerent among themselves. I am sorry to say that the scene in Nhulunbuy toward evening reminded me of the walking dead in the hit Michael Jackson video *Thriller.* The Aborigines even seemed to walk around that way. Stumbling fights and quarrels crackled in the air. Wallabee Beach had been a good call.

In the course of the next days, Claire fed us continuously, and we watched many a pleasant sunset and tossed back a number of beers with Harry. We met their next-door neighbor Trevor, who looked like Captain Kirk with a perm. He owned the sleek racing catamaran out in the harbor. Harry owned a beautifully restored twenty-eight-foot Hereshoff sailboat. Their personalities were equally divergent, but very complementary. I think they were approximately the same age, but Trevor was single.

The NABALCO "community" promulgated happy marriages for stability in the "system." Trevor was a young man at heart and was less happy in "the system." His fast catamaran was a metaphor for his soul, seemingly on the edge of escape. But the pay was good and the paid travel was hard to discard.

Trevor laid out a giant two-bedroom standing-room tent on his backyard for us to assemble and use as our sleeping headquarters. The Wallabee houses were primarily one-bedroom affairs that would have us sleeping on Claire's living room floor. The giant tent was perfect. We could come and go without disturbing a soul. We enjoyed the diverse company of Harry, Claire, Trevor, and visitors.

A few days later, the rashes had come down, I could see the bones in my hands again, and I could successfully walk down the street without feeling like someone was at each end of it shaking it like a rug. Harry thought we had amply recovered and took us down the road to the Gove yacht club to show us off to some of his yachting pals.

Harry had told us about his most memorable nautical trip from Gove to Darwin, which he had taken the year before.

"That's our next leg," I said.

Tony looked at me and back at Harry and said, "Perhaps."

"It was the most memorable and challenging trip of my life! It is considered quite a trek even by yacht! You really are going to keep on going after the crossing and all the rest?"

"We intended to," I said, as he looked at me, Tony, and back to me.

"Well, then I need to fill you in on all the particulars. Let's start with the chart here on the wall."

Harry enthusiastically bestowed upon us any and all the information he could. The whole time he had that tone and look in his eye that told us we were getting into something that we didn't understand, gulf crossing included.

Nevertheless, we learned from a senior yacht club official that the gulf crossing in the seventeen-foot *Southern Cross* was an unofficial record of sorts for the yacht club. The smallest boat that they had heard of crossing the gulf was an eighteen-foot catamaran. It was nice to be so accepted by the yachties—a result of our success at something they understood and respected. The official added: "The gulf is notoriously rough for vessels under thirty feet in length and bad for really big ships, too! The wavelengths are tighter and the waves can get steeper than in the open ocean."

No shit, I thought.

"Funny body of water that gulf, can be all hell to pay one week and calm as a lake the next. You lads picked a bad week to go across. We just had one of the coldest spells up here that I can remember."

It was during our initial visit to the yacht club that Tony saw something he couldn't take his eyes off. It was a sleek, wooden, twenty-eight-foot green-hulled sailing sloop that was for sale in the harbor. He asked Harry if he knew who owned it.

"I don't know who it is exactly but I heard that it was up for sale."

Tony's eyes lit up and he said, "Really, I would love to hear what his asking price is."

"No worries, I can find out in a couple of days at most."

"Now that would be a fine way of traveling, maybe all the way to Indonesia. Wouldn't it, Epic?"

I suddenly had a jilted feeling, not unlike the feeling I had had back in Mackay after talking to Nicole. I had just seen a spark in Tony's eyes that I had not seen in long time. I had an immediate suspicious sense that this relationship was ending for "another."

Although I had many a mixed feeling about continuing the journey as planned (at the very least, how much farther I wanted to continue), I still felt like Tony was "breaking up" with me first. We had discussed not continuing the journey in the hotel the morning after our last landing. I half-argued to forge on to Darwin. I think Tony took some of that argument to heart and was on the lookout for a way to keep the journey going by other means, much like I had entertained the thoughts of bicycling somewhere earlier on.

The possible death of our kayak journey festered in my mind before expelling itself in confessions of dissatisfaction with Tony to all who would listen. Claire, Harry, and Trevor all got an earful. I was spewing libelous innuendos.

"He doesn't want to go in the kayak anymore. He wants to buy a sailboat. He hasn't even asked me if I would want to go yet."

"Give 'em a little time to sort it all out, Eric. See how he feels in a few days. You lads have been through an awful lot and it might be enough, don't you think?" Harry added, "The trip is a lovely tour by sailboat."

"Harry, I think Eric wants to keep going in their boat," Claire said.

Letters were sent to good mates at home for counsel. I hadn't planned to end the trip quite this early and had always thought I would make it to Darwin if we had managed to make the crossing.

There was the issue of getting permits from some Aborigine leaders to travel through the area known as Arnhem Land. I had never known Tony to have much concern or regard for governmental regulations. Tony had suggested that we were going into a massive crocodile "nest."

"There're crocs everywhere in Arnhem Land. Everyone knows that."

"*If* we keep going, I'm thinking of getting a shotgun," he added.

My heart jumped. There was hope but I felt that I was about to be shoved out of the car ten miles from home, when in fact I would be pushed overboard ten thousand miles from home if Tony did not want to continue. The next day, Tony announced: "Well, that bewdy of a green sailboat is sold but I asked Harry to keep lookin' around. I think I'll go to the gun shop and see what they have."

Tony's case wasn't closed but I had to seriously consider the ramifications of ending the journey and not making it to Darwin. This brought back the issue of money. Where to get it? How to earn it? My concerns extended beyond continuing the trip by bicycle.

What am I going to do when I get back home?

The timing seemed all wrong. I might be headed home much sooner than I had anticipated. The Klepper shop as I'd known it was gone. The void in my life that its loss created became instantly more real to me. My stomach knotted. I was denying its "death" and the lifestyle that went with it. Going home would not let that denial go on. *There really was no NYC mother ship to return to!* It just sounded so implausible. This journey was incomplete and those feelings would not be easy to shake. I had hoped for success, some respect, perhaps some lime-light from the endeavor, but if the journey was incomplete in my heart, how could I share it with others?

Tony seemed to have derived enough from the voyage. He could not have cared less about the limelight. I don't think he wanted or needed any profes-sional recognition from the trip. It had simply been another one of "Tony's Great Adventures." I think the trip had allowed Tony to get back to his core val-ues again. His core values seemed somehow more pure compared to some of my more ego- and price-driven ones. I felt I hadn't dug deep enough to get to the core of mine.

I didn't recognize the Tony that I was with. This Tony was now concerned with permits? I was under the impression that the permits didn't have a great deal of relevance to a one-kayak expedition where our intent was to stay away from people in an already remote environment. Claire echoed my feelings about the irrelevance of the permits to Aboriginal land for our particular endeavor.

Permits were developed to control unsolicited trading and business concerns and the larger vessels potentially involved in such. *Tony should know that!* I thought. He was a man who seemed to have the potential to climb the Empire State Building and parachute off of it given half a chance, and who'd do it with-out the notion of a permit.

Tony seemed different to me in Gove. We had flip-flopped our original per-sonas. Tony was getting caught up in the minutiae and all the limitations to con-tinuing such a journey. I was gathering resolve to get to Darwin in the kayak, even if I had to do it by myself.

One day we went down to the beach to get *Southern Cross* for her biweekly cleaning. We hadn't had any inclination to get near her since we'd landed. *South-ern Cross* was filled with sand and had been noticeably abused by the change of the tides. She looked like a whale that had beached itself and I thought I could hear her crying. Tony looked at her and I saw his eyebrows furrow with concern.

"Mate, we've really neglected the ole gal."

"Very badly, very badly," I said.

"Well, let's get to it then." We proceeded to bail her out.

Harry and Claire let us spread all the gear out in their backyard, and once done, it took up almost every square foot of it. Sand had worked its way into most of our things, and the cleaning process was more arduous than usual. How-ever, with a good hose and Claire bringing us food and refreshments regularly the task temporarily renewed a sense of camaraderie. But our bedraggled gear didn't have the shine of "new" adventure anymore. It shared the same wear and tear that our spirits had.

Once cleaned and repaired, I modified *Southern Cross* for solo seat capability (allowing me to sit in the center of the boat) to optimize paddling and sailing efficiency. I had not exercised in a week and I needed to train. I started paddling three to five miles a day from this position in preparation for possibly soloing to Darwin. *I don't care if he finds a sailboat. I'm going to Darwin by kayak,* I decided. I was mentally and physically preparing for five hundred nautical miles by myself, naively thinking that it would be relatively easy.

I had to face the truth.

Tony and I could soon split.

The next day Tony announced,

"Sam's coming to visit us."

"Sammy from Chadwicks?" I asked.

"No . . . *Sam*—my climbing partner."

Great. I guess that's it.

Sam had been Tony's good friend and climbing partner for years. Sam was a lawyer and Tony took his "adventure" alter ego to get out and play from time to time. Tony had taught Sam to climb. Sam, however, was a great outdoor cook. Tony liked that he could keep them fueled in style. I could boil water.

Sam had that animated Fred-Astaire-in-a-Christmas-special look and apparent personality to match. He would have taken the role of first mate very naturally. They had a long history of working together. Sam was in Australia and was making a special trip to come and see us. *But why?*

Although the idea of soloing to Darwin was starting to gain momentum in my psyche, I think I still secretly hoped I would get my "old" Tony back somehow. When I heard Sam was coming up I first experienced suspicion and then hope.

My sense of betrayal and resultant paranoia made me believe that Sam might have been recruited to some midstream adventure plan change that I was not privy to. My greater intuition believed Sam was going to help Tony shake off some of the doubt demons that had climbed on his back somewhere on the crossing.

We met Sam at a local pub and dance hall. I'd forgotten how personable he was.

"Top of the evening, Epic. Good to see you again!"

I was totally disarmed by his broad smile and warm words. We spent part of the night together. At some point I left Tony and Sam to catch up and have a "big night." They did. They spent the bulk of the next day together, exploring a geographical point of interest that Claire had suggested. Sam was gone nearly as soon as he arrived, but his stay had a noticeable effect on Tony.

"Sammy got me thinking. That I really should continue the trip. Maybe even the whole thing, like we planned in the first place."

"Well, let's take it one step at a time," I said.

My desire to circumnavigate the entire continent had dimmed in the first thousand miles of the trip and had become an oppressive thought at about two thousand. It was then that the bicycle-trip fantasy had presented me the option of a personal escape from what had become much more than a long-distance kayak adventure. It was an initiation journey, presenting emotional and spirtual challenges that I had not bargained on. I remembered a fateful question that a Klepper client had asked me in the last week of preparations before coming here.

How are you going to get along with your partner?

The next day I got a letter from the one and only man to go all the way around. The New Zealander. The legend. Paul Caffyn. I had written to him on Thursday Island and was amazed to get the blue aerogramme from RD1 West Coast, New Zealand. I poured through his letter like a Talmudic scholar. I felt my resolve returning.

But then the $64,000 question: *Is Tony number one, or some modified version thereof?* I needed number one again, I thought. I moved the seats in *Southern Cross* back to a two-person arrangement. We met with one of the Aboriginal leaders. It was a real eye opener.

I half expected to see a wise man in traditional garb with "eternity" written all over his painted face and in his eyes. We met a rotund Don King type in a sports shirt with various gold chains and wrist adornments who was more likely to be seen on Forty-second Street than in Nhulunbuy. He was clearly amused by our request and ceremoniously granted us our wish and said it with a wide grin.

"Our people have motorboats for such ideas!"

The white Australian official then tried to tell us that this man's jurisdiction did not cover the whole distance and that it might be weeks before the other tribal leader showed up. I think "Don King" had put this permit thing in perspective and provided incentive to go sooner rather than later. For me, it added a touch of concern because this type of self-righteous SOB could conceivably make an issue out of nothing if he was in the wrong mood on a particular day.

With clock counting down to resume our journey, I could enjoy the hospitality of our newfound friends more. Harry treated me to a wonderful sailing trip on his Hereshoff. After a few minutes of setting the sails, he let me take the wheel, and although the twenty-eight-footer is relatively demure in yachting size it was leagues larger than what had been familiar to me. All of the mast components, cleats, lines, and pulleys were gigantic compared to the same hardware on *Southern Cross*.

"Make sure to give a wide berth to that island up ahead!" he said with concern.

In a way, the much larger and heavier vessel felt more vulnerable than our kayak. The dimension that I had to be aware of was the same that constantly plagued Captain Cook when he was in the "labyrinth." The dimension was depth—depth of the keel. All of a sudden open water was not free and clear unless sufficient water depth went along with it. I added a new and very important dimension. Harry continued to make sure I steered well clear of any and all depth compromises. I realized, in contrast with this moment, how much more intimate we could be to landmasses as I kept the island five hundred yards to port.

After a while, I made the adjustments and then started to marvel at the maneuverability of this large vessel. This was also a surprise. This twenty-eight-foot, multi-thousand-pound yacht could pivot on a dime in a shorter radius than we could. The wind started to pick up and the four-knot walk in the bay became an eight-knot gallop. The boat responded to the air pressure changes immediately and drove forward purposefully. Harry trimmed the sail and let me continue to enjoy the tiller. Harry wanted to impart his love of his boat to me as directly as he could. He succeeded.

"That was brilliant!" I blurted.

That night we went to the yacht club for some tucker, and I got the chance to talk with Jim Chandler from San Mateo, California, who was captaining his yacht *Nephenthe* around the world. He was a successful businessman with the largest yacht in the harbor. He was taking four years to complete his voyage. Part of the motivation had been a divorce from a marriage that had left him with four "kids," then in their thirties. His next stop was Hong Kong and then he was going to work his way to Greece. The wife had remarried.

After our ten days in civilization we decided to forge ahead, taking it one destination at a time. We would continue, but it was not clear for how long.

The Way to Darwin

A couple of days before we left, we found out that Trevor would be on his way to Darwin to help crew a yacht in the annual Darwin-to-Ambon race. There was the chance that if we moved quickly, we would see him in Darwin before the race began. The idea of getting to Darwin during one of its biggest maritime events was exciting and added a little more incentive to getting back to "business as usual." The race was less than three weeks away. Tony and I had been entertaining thoughts of "touring" the next five hundred miles—maybe even smelling a few roses along the way.

In the two days prior to our departure, I logged in as much of the course as I could. I took a good look at the charts at the yacht club and poured through Harry's detailed guides. I made copies of the complex tidal schedule through the Van Diemen Gulf and into Darwin. Tides in Darwin are infamous. The Van Diemen Gulf tidal/current chart showed arrows going everywhere, with apparent collisions of tide, or at least many overlaps. The anticipation was building again. I realized that I was taking the next five hundred miles of sea travel too lightly.

I was not concerned about crocodiles, sea monsters, or travel permits. I was remembering that there had not been *any* section of the trip that had been "easy" for any length of time. I had offhanded Harry's first comparisons of his yacht trip to Darwin and our trip across the gulf. At the time I thought there was no comparison. Everything was downhill from that experience.

The way not to be safe was to be secure, an old friend of mine used to say.

Six hundred miles or so seemed paltry compared to the thousands of miles we'd racked up to that point. We had not done our launch-paddle/sail-all-day-long-land-in-unknown-terrain number for more than a month. We had been relatively inactive for almost two weeks. *What the hell was I thinking?*

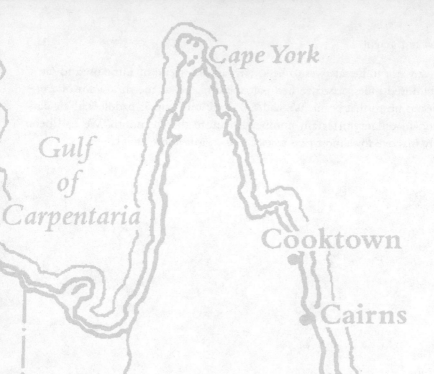

Arnhem Land

July 8. We bid our warmest farewells to Harry and Claire and gave an optimistic "see ya' there" to Trevor. We climbed back into our respective cockpits and headed for Cape Wilberforce. Harry had advised making it to some beaches just west of the cape. The distance was only twenty-five miles, so we felt "secure."

The sea showed her force again. A few miles out of Wallabee Beach we were in the midst of strong winds. Twenty knots made us white-knuckle the sheets and resume the now less familiar hip-on-water balancing act. As the day progressed and the waves and whitecaps increased and toyed with us, the six hundred-mile number began to take on a different perspective.

"I almost forgot about all this, Epic."

"Me, too. It didn't take that long, either."

We were proceeding into Arnhem Land in the state called Northern Territory. Northern Territory is the most barren and least populated area in Australia with only 1 percent of the population living in 20 percent of the country's surface area. Of that 1 percent, 22 percent were Aborigines. The bulk of those Aborigines live in Arnhem Land, which covers most of the land area in the east part of the "top end." The Aborigines have more autonomy in this area than anywhere else in the country although they still battle for more control of national parkland and mining issues.

There are many Aboriginal tribes with their own roots and specialized rituals, but the unifying factor for all of them is called *dreamtime,* when totemic ancestors formed the landscape, fashioned the laws, and created the people who would inherit the land.

Cape Wilberforce was a narrow strip of land jutting northeastward from the Gove Peninsula. It was our destination but we had to finish crossing Melville Bay to get to it. The northeast course from Nhulunbuy had a lot of southeast wind exposure and resultant swells that travel a long diagonal course across the Gulf of Carpentaria.

The seas became larger and larger as we angled toward the cape. Our view changed from long range to short range with the passing of every watery hill. As we closed the gap to about two miles, we saw Chandler's boat, *Nephenthe.* Its long black hull was two hundred meters off our port bow and taking a pretty close line to the point. If a large yacht like *Nephenthe* could cut it that close, I thought we could, too.

"TB, I think we can begin our descent."

"Right behind *Nepenthe,*" I added, knowing he knew the boat as well.

"That would have been a nice ride," he said mockingly.

"It's not part of our reality," I said in jesting response.

We turned WNW and angled in to get closer to shore. We rounded the cape and started heading for the more protected southwest side. The tumultuous east side was tuned down by the dimmer switch of the crystal-clear shallows behind the broad shoulder of Cape Wilberforce. I saw two dorsal fins less than fifty meters to port, zipping in through the surf line like a couple of remote-controlled miniature windsurfers.

"*Look over there!* I think we have some company, TB. Looks like a couple of dolphins."

"Right you are!" Tony said, and the dolphins seemed to pause next to each other.

A pair of surfing dolphins approved our decision and played a team tag "dare you to go under the boat with the two humans in it" game with us. A few seconds later we saw a dolphin torpedo heading full speed for our amidships. At the last instant, a deep dive spared us an extra passenger.

"Mate, did you see that?"

"Yeah, it was huge! I never knew they were that big!"

"It shows how small and insignificant we are," Tony said.

Just before we could finish our synopsis of the fly-by, dolphin number two seemed to flipper-tag dolphin number one, who came hurtling toward us in the exact same fashion, passing just inches underneath the center of our boat. Tony and I remained quiet for a time after that one. Dolphins are traditionally known as "good medicine," and my heart inflated with the experience. It felt like we were making the right decision by continuing on . . . together!

"*Brilliant!*" Tony said.

"Awesome," I replied.

Shortly after that, I started feeling guilty about all the negativity I had conveyed about my partner to our friends in Darwin and the people back home. I vowed to rescind them the first chance I could. I was glad to have my partner behind me again. I suppose it was more the thought of losing him that inspired my lashing out. The playful dolphins had spelled something in those few minutes and had made me deeply appreciate being together again. I vowed that these magnanimous dolphins would be our totem (the link between the ancestral beings and ourselves) in the dreamtime of Arnhem Land.

Upon fully rounding the eastern flank of the cape we saw a narrow channel between it and a nearby island. The tide was with us! We had made it! The funneled water was very bouncy but jetted us through and around the cape in double speed. An hour later we were in the cape's shadow and heading toward one of our most amicable landings—*early*.

The white sand of the beach at the end of this tiny peninsular cape was almost barren and well outside of any active croc territories. It promised a pleasant launch the next day. We set up camp. After our regular unpacking routine came a new element—the shotgun. I turned around and saw the disturbing image of Tony "packing heat." A more macabre state of mind might have generated panic, but the dolphins had taken care of that.

"You got the gun." I said.

"Told ya I would, permit and everthing."

We both inspected the gun. Rust was already starting! Tony went on to clean and spray the gun with rust inhibitors. A former Navy Seal back in the States had told me straight-faced to bring grenades on the trip as a defense against the crocs. *What about humans? Maybe Tony had been thinking about that more than he had led on.* I didn't want to pursue it.

I spent that time doing a little workout for the legs. I went to the top of a small hill that gave me a beautiful view of our trip to come. The low-growing vegetation bent in homage to the harsh wind. I saw a small Wallabee skipping away. It almost looked like an animated cartoon image, I partially expected it to say g'day. I found a group of stones to do some "step-ups" on and get some blood pumping into my thighs.

At first I was frustrated with the lack of stability and level surface for my nature-made step program. I had to remember that nothing was perfectly straight or perfectly round out here. Were they supposed to be? Why are so many of us obsessed with that kind of order? From what I had seen, the perfection lay in the diversity and the harmonious disorder of it all. Nature is filled with dents, nicks, curves, twists, and turns.

"When you're in it you can't find time to put order in your hopelessly disordered lives," Tony had told me earlier that day.

Maybe it is the presupposition of order that is throwing the bulk of us on seemingly disorderly perfect life paths.

Evening commenced with a stereotypical Martian-like sunset—a solid red—over Inglis Island, lying well in the distance to the south and west. Inglis was an eventual destination for us. A mackerel sky draped over us, which Dez had said means "a change in weather is near." A bright star or planet appeared overhead and we listened to the gentle surf lapping the beach. I wondered if I would need ocean surf audiotapes to go to sleep when I returned home.

Tony concocted the first pasta stew in a long while and our paths were officially rejoined. Conversation acknowledged that we were nearing the end of the voyage, and there would likely be a life after the death of our incredible voyage.

Tony made it clear when he said, "You can stop and appreciate the water now, now that we only have twenty days instead of two hundred to look forward to."

I was relieved to hear those words from him. He was thinking Darwin was the final destination and not talking about going all the way around.

"Let's try to really enjoy this next section, TB, there is no need to sprint it anymore."

"I agree."

"Yeah, mate, after this, I've decided I'm definitely not going to do the modeling anymore. I'm looking forward to having a place of my own for a while."

At that moment, I was blindsided by a wave of melancholia. An invisible jukebox selected a U2 track. It started playing loudly for no one else but me to hear.

"But I stillllll . . . haven't found . . . what I'm looking for."

Dancing thoughts bonding with women, not dolphins, precluded sleep.

Have I found any answers yet? Have I broken the pattern. It doesn't seem like it.

The trip with Tony and all that "he" represented by default—models, modeling, recognition, fame, fortune—Tony wanted to shed.

Tony's profession had caught root in my imagination. It had been something that I had once admired if not felt adulation for back in NYC, but I had not been given the anatomy to pursue the profession. The months with Tony had not proved that bad a case for Tony's craft in my mind. It was far from perfect, but so was everything else. It showed me that it could provide great swaths of time (compared to two-week-vacation professions) to journey and explore the world, just like we had. It seemed to offer diversity, travel, recognition, and excitement. Perhaps it was my own personal mirage cloaked from a more insidious truth.

"The great epochs of our lives," Nietzsche wrote, "are at the points when we gain courage to rebaptize our badness as the best of us."

Tony seemed to have rediscovered his core values: love for this country and the outdoors. There was more to search for, but I believed his profession would help, not inhibit him. Tony's "Jane meets Tarzan and lives in jungle happily every after" theory had a fatal flaw. Tony was not Tarzan, and potential Janes have seen too much cable TV. Tony loves people and diversity as much as or more than I do. He's more dollar conscious. I believe he was closer to "settling down" with a woman than he knew, and it wasn't going to be in a tree hut either.

My comparatively stable business life had only contained and delayed the inevitable backlash to instability. I saw the answer somewhere in between— getting closer to where Tony was—but after that journey we would not be equals in our respective quests. The comet caboose had to be detached soon. I did not see any other engines nearby. Deep down my goals were the same as his.

"It would be nice to have a place of my own," he said.

My version would add, "to call home!"

Moreover, the Volgons were going to want a piece of Tony any day now.

Three days later we completed our first game of Arnhem Island hopping ticktacktoe and landed at an Aboriginal barge dock on Elcho Island. We were amicably greeted by a plain-clothed but barefoot Aboriginal man, and a white, neatly dressed government adviser of some sort. It looked like one was given his wardrobe through clothing drives and airlifts while the other made occasional visits to the clothier in a big smoke someplace. I had a nasty suspicion that impe- rialism wasn't dead yet and that poorly disguised double agents were afoot.

They never asked for a permit. Rather, they pointed out the fact that crocs came up the beach on most nights just about where we had docked *Southern Cross*. They suggested that we stay in the cabin of the shuttle barge and move our kayak to much higher ground.

"Thar war two oove 'em, just war yar canu is now dis morning," the Aborig- inal man said.

Tony promptly transferred our equipment to the barge, and I helped him move the kayak. The boat bumpers made it easy. We had come a long way since using driftwood rollers.

The night before, we had made it to the west end of Inglis Island and let our four-month trip anniversary come and go. We talked about repetitive dreams again. Tony talked about one of his "Jack Mason" adventure dreams.

"Let me get this straight, you have another recurring dream where you are the master spy Jack Mason chasing bad guys."

"That's right."

"Bullets were everywhere!" he added.

"Are you getting shot?" I asked.

"They're trying to shoot me but I'm able to shoot every one of 'em."

"Are they vivid?"

"I always dream in color."

"I mean can you recognize your opponents?"

"Oh yeah, they're the same cast of characters except we are sometimes in cars, motorcycles, or even motorboats."

I was just glad he did not have his "eaten by shark" dream again.

I was bothered by a long, all too real dream. The kind where you feel like you have been transported out of body to the scene. I had one of these earlier in the trip, about Nicole. In this one I saw the locked Klepper shop storefront. Neil, the bookkeeper, was nearby, waiting for my father or someone to open it up. I was in the Coffee Shop watching it all.

My father showed up in a blue trench coat, green hat, galoshes, and was smoking his pipe. I heard a police radio say that people were showing erratic behavior in front of 35 Union Square West. All of a sudden I was standing next to my father reminiscing about where we used to work. I felt loss, loss of the shop, loss of my father's pride and dignity.

I woke up and realized that the dream was too close to being real. The water rhythmically massaged the beach nearby but I could practically smell my father's pipe. It would never be business as usual at the Klepper shop, never again would I hear him answer, "Good morning. Hans Klepper Corporation," on the old black rotary after dialing the Chelsea-3428 number.

It left me somber for most of the day's travels and I reflected on it again and on all the people who had made the place through the years. I'd never felt it was "home" until just then. Until it was too late to realize it. Home is where the love is, regardless if it is colored with conflict and strife as well. I had garnered an extended family of common thought and a place where those thoughts could be shared and exchanged and even argued.

The year before my trip had been the halcyon days. "Green Lights down Broadway!" Anticipation by all for the intrepid adventurers going to sea. The classic adventure, epic in its proportions. This cumulative energy would have been hard to muster anywhere else. New York City loves a winning risk taker.

I felt all too human again. Nothing was going to propel me to go past Darwin in *Southern Cross*. I knew it. I just could not "see" it anymore. The two days of travel had quickly removed the novelty of our restart. While the seascape was vast, punctuated by a succession of long bay crossings and devoid of man-made clutter of any sort, it was at the same time pure and unwelcoming to many of my preprogrammed sensibilities. My dreams showed me taxis and stoplights in a city far away. It also showed me people that I knew and loved.

The landscape was low lying, equally vast, and blended seamlessly into the water. Occasionally, I saw a relic of an ancient mountain well inland, along with the plumes of dark smoke from Aboriginal fires much closer. It created the illusion of a far-off volcanic island. So far there had been no roses or bougainvillea flowers along the way.

The Aborigines systematically light fires in areas to burn out old growth and decay to allow new spouts to come up. This apparently attracts more game animals for better hunting. This was their land. Their dreamtime. Their home. I could not relate.

The next day, we traveled thirty miles in Force 4 winds to Mooroongga Island. Along the way, Tony said: "OK, mate, tell me about all this mystical business that you've talked about."

I feigned ignorance. "What do you mean?"

"All that stuff that you were talking to Sue about in the hut and I've heard you talk about to others along the way."

In truth, I hadn't brushed up on my "mystical business" rap as of late and was caught a little off guard about the request to start the rhyme. The events of the last month had been mystical enough on their own. I felt little reason to bathe them in the prophecies and mythos of the ages.

Tony presented the question like it had been a school subject he had procrastinated on and finally had to address.

He told me: "Most of my girlfriends have believed in some kind of mystical business from astrological signs to tarot cards and everything in between. Christ, some of them would hardly step out the door of their apartment without consulting their cards or spiritual adviser. I believe: You live this life, and then you die."

A few months before I left NYC, a fraternity friend—a top athlete and successful Wall Street aspirant—had felt compelled to "have lunch" with me. I was expecting to hear a tale of gung ho support on the "give 'em hell and make us proud" tack. Instead he laid two books in front of me, *The Peaceful Warrior* by Dan Millman, and *Vision Quest* by Tom Brown Jr., and said, "Read these and call me in two weeks."

I had been given my first assignment in broader viewpoints. The source of the task made it that much more compelling. I read the books, gave him a call, and he co-organized a few meetings with some top NYC "mystical" advisers. I figured, what the heck, this trip is big enough to ring on the most tone-deaf spiritualist's Ouija board. Let's see if there is any consistency in their stories or if it is all just bullshit.

Over the next few weeks I saw the astrologer, who only sees so and so and such and such on Wall Street. I saw the channeler and then sat with an impromptu palmist who solicited me in a hole-in-the-wall Mexican restaurant with a witness on hand. The results were unsettling and the phrase "you have a birthright to live out" came up each time. This line arose before I'd disclosed anything about the trip.

Nevertheless, I thought that was pretty standard issue, so I had various friends go to these individuals without saying I had sent them. They came back and we debriefed. None of them was given that line and there was a lot more that jibed with our individual lives than any type of collective. I could no longer disregard the "mystical business."

I then searched for and found common threads of belief in religions all over the world—universal truths, standards of values, and moral conduct that spanned across the globe. I had abandoned my Christian religion in eighth grade after becoming "confirmed" because I figured I had done all the requirements. Then I found that religion compelling again in context with common themes of humanity. Mystical business had become a late "godhead" business for me, as my range of experience was about to have its doors blown open.

Meanwhile, I started talking the talk with all sorts of all-too-eager aspiring actors, actresses, models, musicians working as waiters, hostesses and personal trainers who lapped it up and spat it back to me in spades. There was an epidemic of "mysticism" among the beautiful tattooed youth of Manhattan's hip and trendy as well as in the pantheons of Wall Street's elite.

I knew what Tony spoke of and had even learned their language. Rarely a day went by where these topics did not arise. This was a tribe that needed a common belief system to feel safer and hopeful in a world where the powers that be were astronomical in proportion and where control over these powers was minimal. I felt that there was a movement, a shift in consciousness, with me in the center of it all. Then I came on this trip.

On this day, Tony presented me with a rare chance to "show him," to present my case, to take a stab at enlightening him to what "this business" was all about and how it was all around him.

I was ill prepared for the presentation. *Maybe the student isn't the student after all.* Tony embodied a "follow your own path" persona. He displayed an innate directness of thought and action. He carried himself with a "stature" that transcended his obvious good looks. He had an effect on people that was rarely insignificant. He had been called Jesus in Cairns by a group of German students who were not giggling like schoolkids when they said it. He did not talk a talk but he did walk his own special walk.

He didn't need to figure it out with books.

At that point there was little on which I could lecture him. I believed that he and I were working out "something" from long ago in time and space and that powers at hand were doing a better job than I ever could.

I was in the middle of learning another level of what I had been talking about. I was having trouble meshing "higher meanings" and "action in inaction," "compassion," and the like with what I had begun to feel were personal failings, like "envy," "jealousy," "lusts," "greed," "vanity," and the need for "ego recognition." I questioned my patience and perseverance.

I was a student again, and Tony, in an unassuming way, was a teacher. Together we were sitting at one of smallest desks in one of the largest classrooms imaginable, yet we found a rhythm in the discourse.

"They use all these crystals and symbols and signs to run their lives," Tony said. "I think they are just crutches that will never let them live their own."

"I agree with a lot of what you say—many *do* get way too carried away in the trappings and uniforms, and look outside when the scary answers are inside. A good tribe knows that it needs people who know themselves first. I think that's what initiation rights are all about."

"They earn their decorations and symbols through action," Tony said.

"I hope that the crutches are temporary learning aids and that they eventually take the time to tune in to their own feelings, make sense of them and see how they fit in with the world around them," I added.

"Ahhhhhhhh! What about calling psychics every day and getting words from their dead grandmother, and all that bollocks?"

"Yeah, that's a big problem. Even some of the best 'spiritualists' get high on their own power, especially when they are advising other beautiful or powerful people. They start to forget they are still human. The truly good ones step back for a while until they can advise again from a grounded place. To find a shaman amongst so many charlatans takes a lot of wisdom in its own right."

"So many models fall for it and get in deep!" Tony said.

"I think many of them get out in the world really fast and soon find out they don't know who they really are anymore," I said.

"They never took a chance to find out, they just got herded in one direction," he added.

"They got on a huge wave they couldn't get off of."

Tony asked me if I'd go back to NYC "changed."

"I don't know. There might be too much momentum generated by the way I lived back there. Yet there could be a complete backfire when I return," I said, and added, "I think I will probably find out who my real friends are."

"What do you mean, mate?"

"No Klepper shop for them to hang out in and no quest bandwagon for them to ride."

"Sounds pretty cynical to me, Epic."

The next day was really blowing and the strong winds forced my forearms and biceps to lock at ninety-degree angles. We covered thirty nautical miles and ended up west of Cape Stewart, on a long stretch of flat beach in very flat terrain. An odd tree dotted the emptiness.

We saw some Aborigines walking on the beach about a mile in the distance but they did not continue our way. Instead they uniformly turned around like they could smell us. We still had a couple of hours of daylight and mutually decided to do some beachcombing. Above the tide line, the sand ended and shells of all types began and dominated my walk.

An hour later Tony and I compared our booty. I had found some softball-size conch shells and some unique swirly patterned shells that looked like eyeballs. Tony took the prize with an enormous football-size conch shell and a small crocodile skull! *Yes!* Tony had found his croc at last!

It was clear that this croc had not reached its half-ton-or-more potential before some ill fate had dropped it on our beach. We remained transfixed on it for quite a while. We decided the croc would become the figure head on our foredeck. I assumed this would be a good omen, but I wasn't sure.

"How do I look, mate?" Tony said. I burst out laughing. He had taken the swirly shells and put them in his eye sockets.

"You look like a cartoon figure. I think his name would be Dr. Hypnosis. Let me try."

"I may be Dr. Hypnosis but you are Mr. Madman!" he howled. I wished I had a mirror.

Moments later we were both leaping, lunging, and stooging about trying to make the other laugh harder.

That night Tony mixed up one of his "magic magi" spice pasta dishes, which quickly cleared my sinuses and raised my body temperature at least five degrees. Many small flies joined us for dinner as the winds abated. The orange glow of the Aboriginal fires burned in the background.

We talked of pubs, different foods in different countries, and girls!

"Yes, I will be quite ready to move on to more interesting and enjoyable things," he said.

I thought what we were doing would be considered enjoyable in more modest doses and might be enjoyable in the comfort of hindsight.

We woke up to another one of Neptune's practical jokes. Lulled to sleep by a windless night, we were confident that by anchoring *Southern Cross* fifty meters offshore in the mudflat we would be able to step into the boat and go with the incoming tide.

Our brilliance was way off. The "beach" that we woke up to looked like the Utah salt flats, if you replaced the salt with fine silt mud. *Southern Cross* was sitting low and muddy. The first glaze of water was four hundred meters away. We spent the better part of the early morning pushing, shoving, dragging, and eventually steering *Southern Cross* through a maze of tiny rivulets, and shallow pools of water.

Once out, we paddled and sailed another thirty-five miles, getting variable boosts from a wind that swung around from the south to the northeast. It was a land–sea breeze combination, more typical than the pumping trade winds of the earlier days. We landed in mild surf just south of Point Hawkesbury, west of the Liverpool River. We had landed in a series of shallow dunes in what appeared to be a Dr. Seuss forest.

The water wilderness we faced had often bewildered and bedazzled me. There had been steady madness to it all. A cup of chaos in a gallon jug. It had been savage and dreary. It had also been challenging and sublime.

I had met my shadow more frequently than I'd wanted. It had inspired more bouts with melancholy than anticipated. As Tony put it, "A time to think and mature, I suppose."

As we paddled and sailed the thirty-five miles from Point Hawkesbury, just past Guian Point on our way to Goulburn Islands, I shadowboxed with thoughts of disillusionment and self-doubt about my future. Oscillating energy levels, mild dehydration, and more of the same ol' same ol' kept any "transcendence" at bay.

My Siamese twin noticed my demeanor and presented a case for my staying in Australia. Espousing the merits of Sydney livened Tony up quite a bit, but my self-pity was thick that day, and I countered his enthusiasm with a heavy dose of "poor me."

"I wasn't all that well-received in Sydney. I didn't seem to be able to make your friends crack a smile very often." I went on and on about how my sense of humor and idiosyncrasies didn't seem to fit in well in Australia and that setting new roots in such an atmosphere did not seem likely.

"Mate, enjoy your time here. Maybe you could become a jackeroo [cowboy]!"

It was no use. I was losing the shadowboxing match. I hoped sleep would prevent a knockout.

It did.

Early the next day we saw a couple of eagles soaring over a cliff. The boat was sailing very well. We cruised past the Goulburn Islands at a speedy clip.

Swells began building. The wind picked up. We quickly braced to prevent ourselves from being rolled into shore. We balanced on the top of a surf wave and then suddenly landed near Laterite Point accompanied by a wall of foam. *Where did that come from? Why is there surf here,* I wondered. We rushed *Southern Cross* up the beach, settled down and watched the moon rise early in an amber haze.

A few hours later, Tony said, "Look at the *Cross,* mate, it's huuuge!"

I looked up at the stars spangled in the sky, and found the Southern Cross.

"It's never been brighter!" I said.

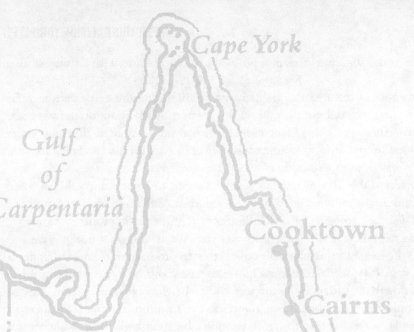

Dawn Launch into the Arafura Sea

Dawn launch into the Arafura Sea. We had traveled over 350 miles and were past the halfway mark to Darwin. The geography was changing. We had left the very low-lying and more settled river plains and mud flats of eastern Arnhem Land and were nearing the more tenacious cut and callused Cobourg Peninsula, one lone finger of northern Australia that had tried to hold on to its Indonesian cousin a little longer only to stretch and almost break off from its Australian host falling south.

Now the Arafura Sea separated the two landmasses forever, with the gap getting a little greater every moment.

Moreover, we were entering the Aborigine-owned Gurig National Park. Entry to this area is by permit only. We did not have one for this area. It was out of "Don King"'s jurisdiction and we were not going to wait another month in Nhulunbuy to see another Grand Pooh-Bah who would wave us onward and act like we were daft and backward in ten seconds. Nevertheless, this territory was one of the more stringent areas about allowing vehicles of any sort per week, none allowed to pass through at night, and most requiring a permit one year in advance. I think the people here knew that excessive traffic in this area would break the stitches holding it to the mainland once and for all.

We were now faced with dumping surf smashing onto the exposed beach we were on. Some of the Australian coast we had traveled offered a shallow-angled gradient from beach to deep water at sea. This creates a relatively gentle spilling surf. Much of the coast, especially in the first six hundred miles, has a moderate gradient and can create the plunging-style surf (*Hawaii Five-O* waves) that surfers like.

Up to now, in this area, the gradient was so slight, and the deeper water so far off shore, that surf did not exist. Now, this section of the coast, on the west side of Aurari Bay approaching Cape Cockburn had no gradient at all. Deep water was a stone's throw away and an easterly wind had built up some hefty six-foot waves. It was time to go kamikaze.

I converted the previous night's fear of having to launch through the nasty, steep, dumping surf into a good hot anger, and since the morning was cool, and I knew we were going to get soaked immediately, the feeling came in handy.

These steep beach surf launches were particularly annoying because we had to place the loaded kayak close enough to the surf to have water roll up under it and lift it so that we could start paddling. Because our bow was pointing thirty degrees down, the proximity to the surf had to be closer than normal so enough water could reach the boat. Then, the trick was to jump into the boat during a small set of waves, so that the boat wouldn't be broached sideways before we could both get in.

Even if we got waterborne, if the waves were big enough, they'd dump us aggressively back to shore like a hapless quarterback who has been blitzed up the middle. Theoretically, that could go on for hours. We had no desire to get caught in the vicious cycle.

"*Fuck you, surf!!*" I screamed.

I, too, was tired of worrying about injury and death all the time and felt we had paid our dues to Neptune!

We went out on the first surge. A huge wave smashed into our chests and faces and stopped the boat dead in its tracks. Another wave was right behind it.

"*C'mon, mate. C'mon!!*" Tony yelled.

I actually felt fond of this previously grating call to action. It inspired me to find another pound or two of paddle pressure to help pull us out of these foamy hands.

We're out! . . . Yesss!!!!!!

This is the benefit of dumping surf. If you get past the blitz, you are in open field.

It was a big day for distance. The big winds and big two-meter-high waves were back. The water was deeper and darker, the swell taller, deeper, and longer. Spectacular geysers of broken surf rose high in the air, fell down, and were funneled through the okra-colored rocks of Bogden Head. One-hundred-foot-high gypsum–white cliffs armored the route to and around Cape Cockburn.

The color contrast between cliffs, sea, and early morning sky was brought to us, made possible, and sponsored by Mother Earth's palette and brushstrokes.

"Check out the helicopter!" I said as I watched a small copter flying just below cliff level and only meters away from the largest plumes of spray. It was less than half a mile away. *I hope they are not a patrol.*

"That must be quite a ride, don't you think, mate?"

"If they see us, they're probably thinking the same thing," I added.

THWACK!

Pisshshshshshshshshhshs . . . BOOOMMMMmmmmmmmmmm.

"We gotta get outta here, mate!" Tony said. We were suffering *clapotis,* caused by the rebounding waves meeting the incoming ones. *Southern Cross* had involuntarily become a bucking bronco. The winds had shifted to ENE and were pushing us more and more.

"Steer us into the waves, I've got to wrap up the sails."

Tony turned ninety degrees to starboard and started paddling while I harnessed the sails.

"I'm good to go!"

We paddled hard to windward to soften the ride past the collision zone. We slowly started a wide turn around the cape. An hour later, I set the sails again and we started to ride the roller coaster.

After twenty-five miles of big water, we finally reached a more protective shadow on the southwest side of Mount Morris Bay. Dead ahead was the long and narrow Croker Island forming the east side of the Bowen Strait. The big swell was gone, but as we approached David Point, on the southern tip of the island, I saw a massive field of white water. One- and two-foot waves were having a good old-fashioned brawl and were breaking the mirrors. I knew we'd be in for a bumpy ride.

"I think there's a tide rip just ahead, TB."

"I just hope by the time we get there the tide will be in our favor."

"Me, too!!"

Within minutes the combination of wind, waves, and shallows produced a steep, short chop that shock-tested our lumbars for over an hour. We were lucky to have caught the proper tide flow going with us. It could've been a very dangerous area in such winds, if the tide had been coming out.

"Reminds me of the ole days, mate," Tony said.

"The only thing different is I didn't get to tell you about them ahead of time."

"That's a relief," he said and we both chuckled.

With tide and daylight on our side, we opted for some bonus miles up the Bowen Strait. The setting changed once again. The backdrop changed from tumultuous seas to a scene out of the *Heart of Darkness*—a flat, calm corridor of water lined by a partially mangroved island to our right and a desolate nondescript shore now a mile to our left. The next big surprise was the boats and people. We passed a few poorly maintained house boats. We saw the occupants scrambling about on their decks.

"Does this look pretty suspicious to you, TB?"

"Yeah, I don't like the looks of it at all."

"It looks like they're smuggling something! I've seen a scene like this in the

Bahamas. Airplane came by, dropped stuff in the water, boats came by to pick it up."

"We better push on fast, mate!"

We felt like we were crashing a party. Only, it wasn't one we particularly wanted to join. *Where's that hundred-horsepower Merc when you need it?* Déjà vu, Harlem . . . again. We paddled out and away from the area, turning our heads back every few minutes to see if we were being pursued. Tony felt for his gun. Crocs? Schmocks. This was a beehive of restless humans that we had errantly surprised.

The newfound fear added another knot to our boat speed and we paddled three miles north in a little over half an hour. We paddled for another mile and I noticed that this island did not have a lot of landing options. Moreover, we were about to leave the strait where the mainland and island coasts diverged radically.

"Keep your eyes open for a landing!" I said.

"I have been," Tony said.

Finally, we passed a point, and a small cove and short yellow beach appeared, bathed in the day's final rays.

"That's the ticket!" Tony announced.

"Ramming speed!" I said.

We accelerated and all of a sudden the boat lurched from the middle up, temporarily buckling its frame.

"*What* was *that*, mate?"

"Must be a rock. We probably should take it slow."

Upon landing, I saw a host of animal tracks and something that appeared to be a croc "slide"—a long, smooth indentation from the beach to the water, not unlike the track made by a smooth-bottomed kayak.

Moreover, as the narrow beach shelved up to a very low-lying, tree-covered mesa we saw feral oxen and their plentiful "deposits" everywhere. I got a déjà vu flashback and truly wondered, *Haven't we been here before?* I made the four-foot ascent up the sandy mesa and nearly stepped into a giant spider web eight feet long by three high. It was a web made by a spider whose eyes were clearly larger than its belly, and it looked like it wanted to catch and eat one of the oxen someday. This was an Australian "nasty" hot spot.

All the "nasties" that we had heard about, but hadn't much experienced on the trip, came crashing down on us. I saw a dorsal fin drawing figure eights in the lagoon we'd just crossed.

"Hey, Tony!"

"Yeah, mate?"

"Remember that rock we hit in the lagoon?" I asked.

"Yeah?"

"It grew a fin."

"That's a dog shark, mate."

We had covered a glorious forty-five nautical miles and had ended up in a comprehensive Northern Territory zoological clinic. Tony seemed oddly nonplussed. He even went to trace the origin of the "slide."

"I'm going to see if I can find the bugger up that crocy-looking rivulet over there."

Now he wants to wrestle the damn things?

"Aren't you going to bring your gun?"

"No, it's all crooked with rust."

Meanwhile, I scouted our tree-protected campsite on the mesa, which did not seem like a croc stomping ground. The short mushroom-shaped trees had crooked trunks and medusa-like branches. Dr. Seuss seemed to get around Australia quite a bit. *But what about the feral oxen up here? Their droppings are all over the place.*

When Tony returned, I asked, "Tony, don't you think these two-thousand-pound oxen might trample us by accident in the night?!"

"Ahh naw, mate. I've told you once before, when are ya going to get it straight? They don't want to get near a strong human scent."

"What if these feral oxen have forgotten about humans. I mean, how the hell did they get on this island, anyway? Aborigines don't farm, do they?"

After finishing our respective biological field trips, we settled down to cooking. The wind was totally gone and I was heavily perspiring. It was hotter than I could remember any evening so far. Then, the mossies entered the camp and made easy work of us. The combination of sweat, blood, and mossie carcasses was not planned on the menu. Sleep was difficult. *Hmmm . . . surf, mossies, clapotis, tide rips, crocs' nests, sharks, feral oxen, funnel-web spiders, suspicious piratelike characters. What is this? A "best of trip" review!*

Yhi returned and I found myself alive. I also saw that *Southern Cross* had not been disturbed. Those were good things. I didn't want to push our luck and neither did Tony. We packed up quickly but were concerned about wading our boat out into the water any more than we had to. We did not want to wake up any of our neighbors. We tiptoed in and quickly jumped into *Southern Cross*.

We paddled and I said: "Prepare for impact."

"What's the name of that point in the distance, mate?"

I looked at the chart and, sure enough, it read Point Danger.

"Oh, brilliant. What's the real name?"

"Same."

It was hot and there was no wind to speak of. We paddled and sweated for a couple of hours. As we got out of the shadow of Croker Island, I detected a merciful breeze.

"TB, do you feel that?"

"I hope it's what I think it is."

Fifteen minutes later, the wind was up and the sails were away but hours later the wind shifted to the northwest, and it was blowing in our faces as we got closer to Point Danger. Once we got past the point we tried the sails again and had to lean out to port as we reached toward Black Point on a NNE sea breeze. We covered almost six miles in the next hour. Two more hours and we were on final approach for Black Point, the eastern entrance to Port Essington. The sea breeze puttered and died.

"Back to the sticks," I said.

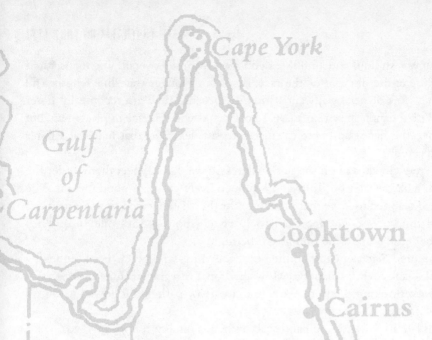

Black Point Ranger Station

We rounded the point and saw a couple of sailboats coming out of the deep fjordlike southern cut in the Cobourg Peninsula. The twenty-mile-long cut had been named Port Essington Harbour by British settlers at Fort Victoria. The ruins of the fort are still apparently located near its south end. I hoped the ranger station was not that far away. As we paddled farther in, we could make out some boats moored together.

"Do you think that's it, mate?!"

"I think it just might be."

We paddled harder and then spotted a bright yellow multihull. There was a beach. There was a tower. It was looking good and then it got better.

A blue inflatable boat with four people aboard was headed right for us. As they got closer, we saw some beers being drawn, and then heard voices.

"G'day!" Trevor said. "We were wondering when you would get here."

In moments we each had a beer and confirmation that we were at the right place. It had been over nine days without contact with the "white man" and all the color and noise he brings about. We were glad to see these very gracious people.

It turned out that Jersey and Marianne (husband and wife) owned the bright yellow Trimaran called *Omni* and were racing in the Darwin-to-Ambon race. Tracker and Maze were their crew. Apparently, they had been given a minimal handicap because they were considered one of the fastest boats in the race. The handicap was an hour and a minute deduction from the overall time that a yacht finishes the entire distance of the race. Boats with longer waterline lengths and multihulls do not get significant handicaps because they are technically faster boats. With a handicap system a larger boat could win the race in placement, but lose when the handicaps were calculated to smaller boats that had sailed faster than expected.

The crew clued us in on the station and said we should meet them under the lights for a barbie later on. Tony and I stepped lively with our good fortune. The *Omni* had planned to leave that morning, but they had decided to stay one more day and time a one-day approach to Darwin (about a 150-mile run). They would be setting sail in the middle of the night.

We secured *Southern Cross* on the beautiful white-sand beach, book-ended by two dark black rock formations. We walked up a fifty-meter dune into a grassy clearing overlooking the port. We found a narrow path and followed it toward the small ranger village.

It was late in the afternoon and rush hour was on. Rush hour involved half a dozen people getting food stores at the shed-size market that was open for a couple of hours each day. The hours were dispersed throughout the day because the owner also owned various other concerns in town and was responsible for running them.

We picked up some Rice Bubbles, milk, and a couple of ice cream bars. We then were off to the ranger station. It was everything a ranger station should be. It had corrugated olive-colored tin roofing and siding arranged in a minibarrack efficiency layout with screen doors and a covered barbie area. The office had "visitors" info and warnings about crocs. It had other geographical and nautical information in the waiting area. A chest-high counter separated us from the secretary and the ranger himself, whom we heard talking through a half-closed door farther back.

We finished our ice cream and were considering breaking into the Rice Bubbles when we met the ranger—Bob Angus. Ranger. Black Point Station, Gurig National Park. He was dressed in an orderly olive and khaki uniform with a name tag to match his title. He was the king of that colony, and a teddy-bear-ishly nice one. He wore the commensurate weight and dark beard. We filled him in on our travels.

"The single gentlemen's quarters," Bob offered us.

He opened the screen door and showed us an array of sheetless bunks on steel bedsprings, with open fans overhead and electric lights. There were a laundry and a kitchen with refrigerator. A regular mansion!

The first thing we did was to sit at the outside picnic table and eat our box of Rice Bubbles before the milk got too warm. Once satiated, we chose our bunks and laid out or strung up a lot of wet and dirty gear.

Later, as we were taking advantage of flat, dry surfaces and lighting to read a paper and write in the journals, we realized we had to find the barbie under the lights we'd been invited to earlier. We left the well-lit quarters and ventured out with our tiny Pelican lights into a darkness that lapped up almost all the photons a couple of double-A batteries could support.

After a time in the void, we saw a faint glow on the opposite end of the clearing and then, as we got out of the thicker grasses, we saw the string of lights. I imagined I could hear the sizzle of a barbie.

It wasn't long before we were eating the remainders of what had been a bountiful barbie. The "sizzle" had been long over and we had discovered that a racing yachtie team could rival our bottomless stomachs. The few pieces of this and that and the leftover potato salad left us half-unfull and required a few beers to take up the slack.

The conversation was brisk and bouncy. They were the closest things to kindred spirits we had encountered. They had a gleam in their eyes and adventure in their throats. It turned out that Jersey and Marianne also knew Claire, from Nhulunbuy. They had been sailing friends of Trevor and Harry for years. Marianne seemed like the source of most of this foursome's energy. She was a very well-built woman in her early forties, a cross between Meryl Streep and Candice Bergen gone nautical. She seemed to personify the Australian outdoorswoman.

Her husband, slighter in stature, but well ballasted, comfortably gave the floor to Marianne and added great color at appropriate times. Tracker and Maze first appeared as the quieter, straight folk for the "Stiller and Mira" husband and wife team.

It wasn't long before another grand adventure was brought up by the apparently quieter Tracker Man. It was called "Hash House Harrierdom."

Tracker mentioned that the world championships of the Hash Head Harriers was in Phuket, Thailand, that year, on a particularly difficult course. I listened with mouth agape as Tracker and Company filled us in on this exclusive, international running-drinker society. A situation where moderate-distance running races are held in complex mazelike courses, where the vast majority of participants are lit up like candles before, during, and after the race. They have an official T-shirt that has two pairs of feet facing each other, and the official greeting among Harriers is, "On on."

This is the secret way of finding out who your Hash Harrier kin are throughout the world. Training involves consistent running and consistent drinking. I did not determine whether the two went hand in hand in training as well as in the competition. Tracker seemed to do his running sober during the week, and his drinking separately. I wondered if this was the most efficient method. It seemed like "state dependent" running would prepare you for the series of misleading detours that were de rigueur for Hash Harrier courses.

Hours of cavorting and belly laughing continued until the midnight hour and the *Omni* crew was due to set off for Darwin. They were going for 150 miles in one day. They normally could do 135 miles and more in a day with good winds. We'd heard about a trimaran that had averaged nineteen knots an hour for twenty-four hours and had crossed the gulf and made it to a point thirty-five miles farther west from us in that time period. It had circled Australia in less than a month.

We said farewell to our transient new friends. The Ambon Race was a week away and we had covered about four hundred miles in nine days. We expected to make it to Darwin before the race. At the pace we were going it was a matter of four or five days. It appeared that we were going to cut a week off our initial estimate. I even entertained crossing the Van Diemen Gulf in one day. Our boat-skill cockiness was coming back, bolstered by the enthusiasm of the middle-aged racing yacht team. We *were* going to see these new friends again in Darwin before they left!

The BC (boat cockiness) simmered our desire to jump back into the boat right away. We tended to domesticum, primarily some laundry and more eating. We had meat pies, more ice cream, liters of Coke, chocolate, and the like throughout the course of the day.

Later in the morning, some of this fuel converted into a quick dose of "brain sugar" and I thought I had come up with a revolutionary new board game or computer game. It would be a sea-kayaking expedition game. *I wonder how that came about?!*

It would follow a similar format to that of the military board games I had played as a kid, games where the terrain board could be changed to a variety of configurations. In the SK expedition game one could choose different sea conditions, from an island archipelago to open water crossings.

I had a mental vomitorium of ideas. My creative brain had been awakened out of a deep sleep. I presented the idea enthusiastically to Tony, who was having a good read of the paper, and he acknowledged me with his familiar lounge-chair reading response:

"Oh yeah, sounds good!"

Wasn't that the trend in our society? Make "adventure" a home game, a video game, a documentary to watch on the Discovery channel. Was I falling right in line? *No.* I wanted to break down expeditions to as many of their vital components as I could to educate and inspire others to get out and "do it."

It was great to feel the brain working on something other than daily survival issues again. *What did it take? A bed? Lively conversation with others? Electricity? Food? What?*

I felt mentally productive again. I had missed it. Creating something for other human minds to feed on, to learn from, to enjoy. The process helped me realize how much there was to what we were doing. From the planning to the range of unexpected events that can never be totally planned for and whose outcome is sometimes held in a mysterious roll of the dice. That type of trip cannot be "won" without significant doses of each!

Later in the day I treated myself to the small but well-appointed cultural museum with a very large croc skull marking the entrance. There were a number of artifacts, paintings, maps, and descriptions of the last time that this area had been frequented on a consistent basis—long ago, by a couple hundred years.

The area had been frequented by Indonesians called Macassins who'd brought spices and various finished goods to the Aboriginal locals in trade for the Macassar trepang, or sea slug. The slugs were highly coveted by the Macassins' Chinese trading partners, who used it for medicinal purposes, such as enhancing virility. Before the six-inch-long, thick, purple, cigar-shaped creatures went back to China, the Macassars put them through an extensive refining process. They would boil the slugs in saltwater for ten hours with bark for flavor retention; this was followed by burying them in sand for a day, boiling them again, and drying them in the sun.

The Macassars would come over on the northerly winds of the monsoon season and head back with the southeast trades that we were experiencing. The method of transport was by praus (deep oceangoing sea canoes with outriggers) made of all timber and no steel.

I learned that the British started settling here in 1838 with ideas of creating a "New Singapore" called Victoria. They were concerned about the French or Dutch getting a foothold here. However, it only lasted eleven years, as bad cyclones, bad soil, and malaria made their stay incrementally inhospitable. They abandoned the area in 1849.

I finished the day off by trying to calculate the precise course we should take to hop, skip, and jump right into Darwin. I had all of Harry's current and tide tables strewn about on the picnic table near the barbie and had calculated our next four days to the last detail. I had planned the optimal time to cross the infamous Dundas Strait, after passing the menacing Cape Don to Melville Island, which defines the northern border of the Van Diemen Gulf. These areas were inauspiciously preannounced in the yachters' guide.

Very strong, six-to-seven-knot currents frequent Cape Don at the western tip of the Cobourg Peninsula. It is advised to pass by in the dawn hour at slack tide. *Hmmm, where have we heard that before!?* Moreover, the strait should be crossed in modest winds because of the propensity in the area for whirlpools and horizontal overfalls. *Horizontal overfalls?!* If the area is crossed in strong winds, it is most definitely at your own risk, for the area becomes a bloody mess. *At least they didn't add a sea monster to the whole affair.*

When I presented the couple of hours of calculations and deductions to Tony, he responded with a coy smile, "We'll take it as it comes."

Oh yeah, just like we just keep Australia on the left, I thought to myself.

I had figured a route that would get us to Darwin in three days, a course that would cross south and west across the Van Diemen Gulf, using its strong tides. Granted, there wasn't a lot of room for error and there was a risk of being stranded in the gulf overnight, but I wanted Tony to at least acknowledge my left-brain orgasm.

He didn't. He passed it all off as the work of some kind of mad scientist. The days that followed led to more "taking it as it comes" and "for good reasons." The area was not to be so neatly figured out since our craft was more a subject of Neptune's whims than a master.

"Dawn at slack tide just like wide bar back at Fraser Island."

"Are you sure it's going to be slack then?" Tony sounded doubtful.

"Almost certain," I said.

"Alllmossst?"

"TB, could you get the GPS out of your bag?"

"Oh . . . you want *me* to go back to the boat, take the bag out, and rearrange my seating arrangement so you can play with your little GPS."

"Well, not if it's really going to screw up your seating arrangement in the boat that bad," I said sarcastically. "I just want to log in some way points for crossing the twenty miles of the strait to check that we're on course, in case we can't see shore for reference points."

"You're acting like the innocent!" Tony said. "It's always *me* who's obstructing *you* and causing problems," he added, and then screamed, "You never think *you* could be wrong!!"

I was taken aback by the venomous screaming and saddened by the resurrection of ill will in our recent string of copacetic travel days. I didn't know what to say. I assigned most of it to Tony's bad stomach. I also knew that my overactive planning hit a nerve. Yet I was still hurt. I had really wanted this last stretch to be harmonious. Tony charged toward the boat, hastily rummaged through the bags, and came back.

"Here's your bloody GPS!"

We tried to sleep, but the birds berated our behavior with mocking squawks, "The humans are going to try to cross Dundas whirlpools and horizontal overfalls. Hah, hah, hah, hahhah!" The fear of the next day's crossing—whirlpools and horizontal overfalls—had descended upon me.

Predawn. Once again, we rise before the sun, a time not meant for humans. The most intuitive birds had not yet stirred but we rose with an unspoken understanding with Neptune that if we gave to him a few hours of deep-dream sleep, we would be given a favorable crossing past Cape Don and through the Dundas Straits.

It is hard to believe that the big knot I had finally untied after the gulf crossing had in fact retied itself in my stomach. These situations *do not* get appreciably easier over time. Experience only seems to help me recognize the knot a little earlier. I'd referred to this trip as using up a finite book of "luck tickets." The cardboard backing of the ticket booklet was thicker than the number of tickets left.

We packed the dark silhouette of *Southern Cross* in quiet tension. I now wondered if *Southern Cross* was friend or foe.

By 5:30 A.M., a few birds squawked, "Good riddance," and we were on the water. The wind had started before we woke up and had increased by the time we left. It was not a good sign. The unmanned white house, standing tall on Cape Don, flashed its roving cyclops eye in a haunting, even rhythm that beckoned us like the Grim Reaper.

We reached Cape Don with the first morning light.

"What do you reckon?"

"We gotta go."

Decisions like those always wrench the heart. It is the closest tangible thing to jumping into a void that one would care to volunteer for. Some might say sky diving's closer, and they'd have a good point. Others might say space walking, also strong. But the open sea to a kayak is not a cruise liner. There is no parachute or high-tech umbilical cord. Pick your pleasure. The sea, like space, implies a time commitment that is beyond any quick burst of adrenaline.

It implies more variables than space as a combination of all the forces begotten by gravity and the rest of it. Loss of the parachute, the umbilical cord, and the boat equal the same fate, give or take a few hours. The sea will probably keep you alive a little longer than the ground or deep space, so you can savor your demise.

Crossing Dundas was like going into the hall of mirrors in a fun house. We got a smorgasbord of all the ghouls. Early on, we would see and then partially spin in whirlpools that were large circular rotations of water with lots of little spinning vortices inside them. Much like a microcosm of a hurricane. I imagined things were spinning contrary to the way they would in northern latitudes, so it would be more like a cyclone Down Under.

As one went, another came. Then we hit patches of mini-overfalls. These are broken fields of water colliding together and splashing themselves every which way. Because we had encountered them early in the day and left on a mild tide we did not witness the mother of these fledgling rippers.

The whirlpools and small overfalls alternated off and on, occasionally combined, but all in all we were well prepared for them. We lost sight of Melville Island, the opposite shore, for almost an hour. An early morning haze caused by the sun heating up condensation on the vegetated island put a veil around the landmass. *Do I dare ask Tony for the GPS? Damnit, why did I give it back to him?*

As I was about to ask the fateful question, a breeze started to pick up and dust off the island. We were still on course and had covered a more respectable twenty-six miles in seven hours. That was all we were going to get, though. The tide built up strongly against us as we closed in on Melville and forced us to an early retirement in the afternoon. We found a nice long, narrow beach with pre–Jurassic Park vegetation and proceeded to explore until dinner.

According to Aboriginal lore, Melville Island is home to many evil spirits. After worrying about the Dundas Straits for two days, I was not terribly concerned about evil spirits. The water, wind, and tide seemed far more alive to us than any land-ridden spirits. However, Tony "not really keen on mystical business" Brown and I were to get a dose of something a little different. Make of it as you wish.

After eating another pasta special, Tony and I sat back-to-back on a rock. I saw a flash of white light fill the entire sky all the way to the ground. It was as if someone had put a large, bright white bag over my head. There were no clouds, so any type of lightning that I was familiar with did not seem like the logical explanation.

"Did you see that, mate??!!" Tony said.

"Do you mean the white light that lit up the entire sky and horizon?" I said.

"Yes!"

"Yes, I did, TB."

"The whole sky was white!" he said.

"I know."

We deliberated on all the logical explanations. Lightning, city lights, rocket launches—but they all were equally inapplicable. We were on the eastern end of Melville Island. There was no electricity, no rocket bases. There were no boats or ships. It was possible that Darwin had been nuked but we imagined there would have been an afterglow of some sort.

"I suppose we'd best leave it as a random atmospheric phenomenon," I said.

We'd been officially welcomed to Melville Island and the Van Diemen Gulf.

It had been an exceptionally cold night. The lack of cloud cover made for beautiful astronomy but it sucked all the heat from the earth. *It's got to be less than forty-five degrees,* I thought. I had put on everything I owned, gone fetal, but I was restless. To make it worse, the wind started howling and jostling well before dawn. I dreamed I jumped out of my semiwarm cocoon into freezing temperatures. But I comforted myself by saying that this was nonsense—we were in the tropics, not the poles. Then the reverberating bivvy sack pinched me. *Ugghh. It's not a dream!*

Cold and wind can exacerbate anxiety and set a negative tone for the day. Add clouds and waves and it is hard to find any silver linings. The only good thought I could find was that we'd already passed the well-announced "hard part" of that leg of the journey.

We muddled through the morning preparations. We launched into a very stiff breeze, which soon became a right-angle wind, as we turned right out of Napier Bay. We were getting thwacked again, and droplets of water rappelled down my neck, onto my chest, and collected in my belly button before moving farther south.

Within an hour, the seas had built to a nasty five feet, with a few larger sets powered by traveling fifty miles from the south side of the gulf.

"Tony! Let's set the sails!" He nodded OK.

I untied the line holding the four-foot alloy boom vertically to the mast. I unraveled the pair and started to straighten the swizzle stick of red sailcloth.

Thummp! Ta ta ta ta ta ta.

The main sail parachuted open and the mainsheet was snapping at the air like the whip of a desperate lion tamer. I reached to the right to grab it and another gust hit, heeling the boat. Water poured into the cabin.

Tony deftly fish-poled the line out of the air with his paddle.

"The wind's up a little early today, mate!"

I laughed. "Wants to make sure we are wide awake for this one!"

After securing the paddles, I grabbed the base of the boom and U-hooked it onto the mast. Tony sheeted in and instantly a bucking gust of wind surged *Southern Cross* forward. I pulled the equal-sized jib out of a pocket in the foredeck. I untied the jib halyard off the three-inch nylon cleat a few feet in front of me. I kept the jib sheet in my teeth to leave my hands free to raise the jib halyard hand over hand. Another gust ballooned the jib and my jaw felt the pressure. It was like controlling a bronco with my teeth.

I secured the halyard. We we're flying! We sailed southwest toward Point Condor.

I felt exhilarated. I flashed Tony the thumbs-up. We had set both sails with the confidence of experienced rodeo riders on a fierce but familiar bull. Suddenly the boat heeled strongly to the right, meekly submitting to a thirty-knot blast that nearly capsized us. It had been awhile since we had been on the bull, and we had lost our hat.

Adrenaline added warmth and sharpened our concentration. Our hands full, having signed on for the duration, we'd been there before and knew we could handle it if all stayed as it was.

How bad could it get?! It was just trade winds and waves.

Then the trouble began.

The sea was in a violent, angry tantrum. It usually took many hours on a windy day to form waves that double broke—meaning the top of the wave is blown off by the wind, which is followed suddenly by the rest of the wave. It was like a jab followed instantly by an uppercut that made the characteristic *thwack!* on the canvas skin of our boat. The thwacking was more severe than I could ever remember. Holding course became more and more difficult, as the shifting combination of wind and waves would high-low us repeatedly, sweeping us ninety to a hundred degrees off course and placing us in ever more compromised positions.

A day like this requires maintenance of precious momentum to sail a kayak. Usually waves follow regular intervals of peaks and troughs. Today the waves ploughed back and forth across one another in a random chaos of sudden peaks and troughs. But keeping a line—holding a course—can slice a path through a confused sea.

We had plenty of wind. The problem was the radically shifting increase and decrease of wind pressure on the sails. In our roller-coaster ride up and down the steep waves, the sails would belly explosively on the crests of waves, then we would plunge into a trough and flounder. It was a tag-team duo that was putting *Southern Cross*—and us—through the wringer. It would take all we had to stay upright. Holding a course was icing on the cake. In some ways I appreciated the challenge. It was an opportunity to test our skills. I also admired the synchronicity of our adjustment to the challenge. Tony and I knew how to fly this airplane and it was going to take more than a sudden kick-up to swat us out of the sky.

As we approached Point Condor I saw a large expanse of churning white about a half-mile ahead. The way the patch extended out to sea suggested waves breaking continuously over a shoal or reef. I had not remembered seeing anything like this on the charts, but prudence dictated that we angle farther out to sea to get to deeper water and out of such a maelstrom. I yelled to Tony to paddle south around the reef and into calmer water.

"Tony! It looks like surf is breaking on a shoal up ahead."

"Mate, it sure looks like it goes a long way."

"It looks like a mile. We should take a course around it."

"OK."

I was wrong. Suddenly we were surrounded by eight-foot stacking waves that were starting to curl like surf waves—not wind waves. What I thought was an uncharted reef turned out to be a living, moving field that quickly swallowed us. Crisscrossing waves broke all around us and as far as the eye could see. Even when perched atop a wave!

"What's going on?" yelled Tony.

"I don't know!" I yelled back.

This was a bull we were not familiar with after all.

The five-foot waves became six-. They became steeper and started stacking themselves closer and closer together until we were in a massive corrugated field of seven- and eight-footers. I scanned the shore for a possible landing, just in case. But we had reached Point Condor faster than anticipated. Instead of an accommodating sandy beach all that confronted us was sheer rock face and not a beach in sight.

A bailout was not possible.

Well, well, well, aren't we a little testy today?

One thing for sure, at this point there was no turning back.

Tony and I reacted and counterreacted as we—and the boat—were pushed and pulled. When my bow section rose into the solid face of a wave, Tony would be sideswiped by a frothing swat from the side.

Tony yelled that we should switch back to paddles. He was right. But there was no time. As *Southern Cross* was pounded by one wave after another, it was all we could do to keep upright. Hip tilt right. Head tilt left. Hips left, head and shoulders right. We were like a Slinky toy trying to stand atop the handlebars of a motocross bike.

The frame of *Southern Cross* suddenly twisted left in the bow and bent upward in the stern as the sea clawed at the boat from all directions.

Just as we were barely adjusting to this new mayhem I saw something I had never seen before on the sea. The steep, closely spaced sets of waves became highlighted with some waves that would be solid in one instant and then just boiling foam the next. The wave had exploded without the normal curl first. It wasn't long before the statistics of wave frequency aligned one of these explosions with us.

When seas become liquid chaos, a clean line is no longer possible. It is like you are a fleck of oil in a boiling pot of water. We were being spun and counterspun like the needle of a cheap compass. The sails had become a curse. Instead of converting the pressure of the wind into speed and balance, they had become the playground for a troop of invisible monkeys.

Too late. We imploded into an overfalling waved and capsized.

Help, Mr. Wizard!!

Tony and I were hurled out of the boat. *Southern Cross* had "gone turtle." The black hull pointed upward and all the monkeys in the sails were drowned.

My leg became entangled in a coiled snake of a jib sheet. As I struggled to free my leg I noticed Tony lunging for his inflatable comfort pad, which was being blown away. Another wave swiped across us and tore and ripped at the gear harnessed to the deck. *Southern Cross* was a house of cards in a monsoon.

We had to right *Southern Cross.* Tony heaved onto the gunwale. Immediately I felt a sharp yanking on my leg. Damn!

"No Tony, no! Not this side. It's pulling me under!"

We lined up together on the windward side of the boat. On cue we simultaneously reached over onto the far side. This is like kneeling on the far side of a double bed and grabbing hold of the opposite side and then trying to pull it on top of you. We mantelshelved (pulled the boat toward us). The boat hardly moved.

"Damn it!" The sails were still partially deployed under water and were acting like an anchor.

"I got it, mate!" Tony swam under the boat to see if he could untangle it. Meanwhile, I tried to find the pin that would allow the mast to release from its mast step. The next step would be to cut the whole affair. I found the pin and pulled. The mast unstepped. Without the mast as an anchor the boat could come up. Luckily, the entangled lines kept the now-detached sail from sinking.

I managed to untangle my leg and we climbed on top of the boat. We both heaved backward.

"Harder!"

"Jeezus!" I yelled. The boat suddenly righted. "All right!" I shouted. A bit prematurely, it turned out, because immediately the boat was blindsided by another huge wave. It was as if a beautiful kite caught in a branch had freed itself only to become immediately tangled in another branch.

The waves were slowly knocking us back toward the sheer rock cliffs of Cape Condor. We had to get *Southern Cross* out of this mess or I was certain we would be smashed like sticks against the rocks.

Tony grabbed the boat and jettisoned himself over the other side. I held the bow and swam it into a perpendicular position against the onrushing waves. I hoped this would delay the drift into the cliffs by giving the sea less boat surface to sweep toward the cliffs.

I swam into my cockpit and took a seat in the bathtub, trying to find enough friction to not float out. Tony's first attempt to get in ended in his falling over the other side of the boat. I attempted to keep *Southern Cross* headed into the waves, but it resulted in my paddle getting caught in the jib sail, which was still dangling half under the boat, netting my paddle blade, and rendering it useless.

Another wave slapped us hard and turned *Southern Cross* sideways. Luckily it couldn't turn us over. With the water in the boat we were too heavy to "fall-size"—the plunging equivalent of tipping over or capsizing. *Southern Cross* realized that when you can't fight them you join them. She had become the sea. There was no longer a vessel on top of the ocean. We were in the ocean, half like a submarine.

Once I freed my paddle, however, I found that I could maneuver the boat unusually well, even when the waves hit. Luckily *Southern Cross* was designed to maintain neutral buoyancy at sea level. It was a feature that may very well have saved our lives.

Tony managed to sling one leg into the boat. But because the cockpit was so cluttered with scattered debris the other leg dangled half over the side. As he clawed at the debris and did all he could to free up some space, I realized it was the first time our compression-strapped cribs had let us down. Then again, it had been near freezing earlier that morning and perhaps we hadn't given the compression straps that final tug of security. Even in chaos the mind makes notes about "next time."

The sea state was apocalyptic from our fish-eye view. The waves looked like ten feet. We paddled as hard as possible into the sets. We were hammered every few minutes. My full forward body lean would be knocked flush against the deck behind me as one large white paw toyed with me and pinned me heartlessly.

"How are we going to get out of this?" Tony yelled.

There was barely enough time to breathe much less talk.

It dawned on me that we were trapped inside the fabled horizontal *overfalls*. Overfalls are waves that—on account of a peculiar trick of colliding tidal currents angling against a strong wind—stack one upon another in an ever-steepening face and then plunge or fall straight down. Even a single knot of current running against the wind can double the size of a wave. Once the tide dropped we would be OK. I don't remember if I yelled that to Tony or not.

Paddling as hard as we could, we were able to keep *Southern Cross* from being pushed backward into the cliffs. But that was it. We could not make any forward progress at all. We couldn't get any bite on our blades. It was like paddling in foam.

It was possible that we were in some type of freak whirlpool. Maybe it would drop with the tide. Maybe not. We were getting hit very hard in the chest by the overfalling waves.

Our only hope was to hold position and keep paddling into the waves until the tide dropped. I did quick calculations in my head. A six-hour bell-curve pattern. Give or take an hour. *Shit!* We were looking at maybe four more hours of sustained give-it-all-you-have paddling. I knew we could paddle that long in normally rough circumstances, but I did not know how many overfall aqua punches we could take.

For the first time on the trip I thought we were *truly* paddling for our lives.

Two-and-a-half hours later, the overfalls turned back into normal white-capped waves and we started making progress. The wind died down a little and gave us some time to bail out the boat and reset our seating arrangements. We were alive and the danger was over. There was no time for any relief, though, because we had no desire to hang around. We just wanted to get out of the Van Diemen Gulf as quickly as possible. It was an unpleasant place that didn't want our company.

"Let's get as far away from here as we can, mate!" Tony said.

That day we did paddle another twenty-five miles on leftover adrenaline. My theories about its potency could be all wrong! A renewed sense of terror, respect, and humility reminded me that we had not been through everything yet. It's likely that we had used up the remainder of our luck tickets to get out of the gulf. It was time to get off the water.

We arrived at Mujiringa Point on a flat calm sea that was reflected in the red sky above. A perfectly flat sea. Red sky at night, a sailor's delight. Right?

The area was a massive tidal flat, which accounted for the calm sea. We had to shuttle gear a couple of hundred meters to shore, opting to anchor *Southern Cross* where we landed so as to get a clean start in the morning.

The horizon light of dusk silhouetted the Vernon Islands to our south and west. They were about twelve miles away and our theoretical stepping stones to Darwin. However, this phalanx of islands divides the western end of the Van Diemen Gulf and the eastern edge of the Beagle Gulf. It was sure to funnel wind and tide and present us with a series of varying depths. We could only guess at the effect. The strength and direction of the wind would determine the day.

I calculated high tide at 10:45 P.M. and 10:19 A.M. the next day. It was conceivable we could get to Darwin in one long day *if and only if* the wind was favorable. A strong southerly or southwesterly wind would make it at least a two-day affair. It was about sixty miles. *Sounds like two days. I don't think we have luck tickets for two days?!*

Evening turned to night. The dome glow of Darwin and the flickering energy of an Aboriginal burn interrupted the darkness of the sky. It was already chilly. We were in for another cold night. As anxiety joined the cold, I became more concerned about *Southern Cross* anchored 150 meters offshore.

We had seen the size of the tidal flat and had watched it disappear throughout the evening. Earlier, we had waded *Southern Cross* closer to where we guesstimated the beach would be at 6:00 A.M. and had made two rock anchors and tied them to each end of the boat. We had also buried them in the mud. The light wind was blowing to shore.

Did I tie the right knots? Did I dig the anchors deep enough? Will the fittings hold in a big blow? What if we lose the boat here?!

This area was even more remote than Manta Ray Island. At least we had all our food, water, and the EPIRB out just in case. I just didn't feel good about leaving the boat out there, even though I knew we needed a prompt, early start if we were going to make it to Darwin. Convenience versus security. *Is convenience the right choice in these parts?*

"Tony, I don't like the boat being out there. I don't want to lose her so close to the finish."

Tony paused with a nod of quiet thought. We looked out at the disappearing silhouette of the boat as night stole her away.

"It'll be fine, mate."

Darwin or Bust

We were on the southern end of Melville Island, and I could still see a faint white domelike glow in the direction of Darwin. We sat by a small fire and I was soaking up the last of its warmth. As the fire dimmed, exhaustion claimed me for half the night.

A combination of cold and wind woke me at 3:30 A.M. *Southern Cross* flashed in my mind. I peeled out of my nest. It was very dark and very cold, but a panic similar to that which would arise at losing a child in a department store sent me wading out into the water, armed only with a small flashlight.

I rolled up my pants to my knees and forged into the dark, scanning furiously with the Pelican light. *I don't see anything!* I scrambled faster toward where we'd anchored her, taking a few small waves on the kneecaps (which, of course, quickly soaked the rest of my pants). Still nothing.

A sick feeling in the pit of my stomach accompanied me on my search. *It has to be here!* I was up to my thighs in water, yet I could not see her. *I cannot see* Southern Cross!

I started a search pattern right and then left. I ventured farther into the water, up to my navel. Then I backtracked a bit. *YESSS!* I heard a battery of wavelets buffeting *Southern Cross* as I approached her. I pulled her in about a hundred yards, so that the water depth was about midshin. If I'd left her where she was, we would've been wading up to our chests to get to her in the morning. Worse yet, she might have pulled off her bridles and disappeared.

Hoping for a couple more hours of shut-eye, I sloshed back to camp. But my clothes were too wet to get comfortable. I shivered more than slept. The wind picked up. *This day isn't starting out well.*

"They're not going to make this easy, are they?" I muttered angrily to myself.

Tony woke up at about five o'clock. We busied ourselves packing and shuttling the gear back to the boat, which was floating in water above the knee. We brought her in a little closer. *High tide should be here by now.* Ready to go before the sun had peaked over the horizon, we launched into a very stiff wind and an endless series of three-foot waves. I set the sail, the boat heeled radically, and we nearly capsized. *It must be blowing twenty-five knots already! Jesus! What is going on here? There's not a cloud in the sky.*

We needed a 180-degree course due south, or we risked being blown too far east, too early in the day. There was the chance of being rebounded in by incoming tide, but if matched against a strong west/southwesterly wind like the one we were in, we could find ourselves in overfall hell again—in the Beagle Gulf.

At first the boat skated west as much as south. We were going west, faster than we'd hoped, but deeper water and mutual will started giving us more southern ground. Nevertheless, the twelve-mile crossing to the Vernons was taking too long. Three hours later we were still an hour shy and almost on their eastern periphery. The Beagle Gulf wanted us for lunch.

That hour became two. We finally clawed our way to northwest Vernon Island in very confused water. Up and down. Up and down. We bounced and balanced continuously in the field of four-foot overfalls, some of which were standing waves that reminded me of a whitewater river. The wind was strong and trying to push us east but we had the leeboards to direct much of that energy forward. The troughs weren't deep enough to cut too much of our wind. We had momentum and managed to keep boat speed up and plow through them until we reached the shadow of the western side of the island.

The western side of the Vernons was a totally different ecosystem. Everything flattened as the wind was now blocked. It was shallow and miragelike. We had stayed on course—to the western side of the Vernon Island chain! We hadn't moved fast, be we hadn't drifted off, either.

"Great steering, TB!"

"Nice crossing, mate!"

We didn't have any time to celebrate as the challenge changed to staying in deeper water. The tide was in the process of receding and was exposing more and more sandbars. We were in a labyrinth of continuously revealed obstacles. We did not have to worry about breaking our hull apart, but we had to be mindful of not making costly errors in direction and losing precious hours of time. If we could pick and choose our way through this in a reasonable amount to time we could make it to Darwin that night! In fact, I started thinking about getting there before sunset.

We meandered, seeking the darker blue streams in the patch of aqua and white. It became clear that the early morning tempest and mini-overfall patch were very likely the last real capsize challenges we were going to have. Somehow, the winds had either shifted or been funneled by the Vernons to a westerly direction and were not nearly so strong. They were downright . . . nice.

We sailed to southwest Vernon Island. The wind shifted again to the northwest. It couldn't have been better. Maybe we had a luck ticket left after all. The end-of-day sea breeze took us past Gunn Reef Point. I saw tall buildings dotting a hill.

"TB, I think that is the Darwin hospital on top of Lee Point. That means we're about six miles out."

"Brilliant! Can we get out there?"

"Well, I was actually thinking we could use the rest of the daylight and the incoming tide to Fanny Bay!"

"How far is that?"

"Well, the tide is pretty strong. Should get us there in about three maybe four hours!"

About five miles from Lee Point, the wind died. It was late afternoon, and we had twenty more miles to the Fanny Bay yacht club in Darwin. I purposely did not tell Tony the mileage. I knew that would discourage him.

We hit the sticks and paddled strongly toward Lee Point. An hour later, I still detected some residual outgoing tide and so did Tony.

"Mate, I think the tide is still going out!"

"It's got to be turning around. High tide in Darwin is about six hours away."

I figured it would be turning around and soon we'd be laughing our way into Darwin. Another hour of paddling made Lee Point look especially good to Tony.

"Let's just pull out here," he said. "There seems to be a fine little beach and a switchback staircase to the top of the hill," he added.

"Our friends are in Fanny Bay and I think they're leaving any day now. We've come so close. Let's give it a go."

"Ohhhkay!"

"Look! You can see the current coming in now!"

Tony didn't buy it at first, but we avoided any prolonged bickering. I sensed it was our last time in the boat together.

"TB—look over there!" I said, pointing fifty feet off our starboard bow. "Dolphins," I added.

"I believe those are harbor porpoises this time, mate."

The beautiful sunset, porpoises, a calm sea, and a tide at our backs were a gift I wanted to savor.

We paddled past Lee Point and into Darwin Harbour. I looked to starboard and saw the beacon of the Charles Point lighthouse making its rounds from the cluster of humanity to its southeast, past us, and into the void of the Beagle Gulf to its north and west. I almost thought it was trying to tantalize me into following it as it waved its beam over and over again. I momentarily felt that all we had to do was get around that point to keep the trip going.

"I don't think the boat is moving very well," Tony said. "That tide of yours seems to be taking its good ole time in getting here."

That's when the spell broke. We had sailed and paddled fifty miles and had been on the water for twelve straight hours. Who was I kidding?

We're going "home" tonight.

The tide really didn't help much at first. The euphoria of our last sunset metamorphosed into the monotonous rhythm of the sticks. Familiar aches became pains in our asses. Now, our attention was drawn to mankind's other light show. We watched a 747 approach and land at Darwin Airport off our port bow. I looked ahead to various suburban communities of the city lighting up in sync. Hours later, we were still paddling, but moving better, as the tidal push had begun just in time. I was starting to feel the guilt of having made us endure more than necessary to reach our goal.

"We're better now, don't you think?" I said.

"It's not exactly a torrent but it's getting us there," he said.

We passed the fancy suburb of Nightcliff, named for its position on a prominent cliff of the same name. The streetlights had that posh look to them, even from a half-kilometer away. The beams had more yellow in them and were directed downward with their perimeters just barely overlapping. Now, all we had to do was get past East Point. Fanny Bay was tucked in a mile or so past it.

East Point is a substantial reef system that extends well west into the harbor and is marked with a few small buoy lights. High tide covers the bulk of it and our shallow draft would generally allow us to skirt over it without having to go a couple miles out into the harbor to get around it. It was getting on toward eight o'clock, it was already very dark, and at first I couldn't see a thing. I began to think the reef was totally covered by the tide or did not exist anymore.

Suddenly I could see a low, dark, jagged line in front of us. I followed it with my eyes. It seemed to go on and on. At the end was a red marker light that seemed to be in the middle of the harbor.

"Mate, do we have to go out as far as that light?"

"I don't think so. Let's just paddle to the reef and follow it out. I'm sure we'll be able to squeeze through someplace."

I figured that a point somewhere between the end of East Point's silhouette and the light would be just about right. We started to paddle faster. The increased rhythm was a welcome dose of stimulation.

We got closer, saw more jagged silhouettes, and headed farther west. Closer, more reef. More west. *How could this be?* We were almost out by the light. When we could no longer see any contrasting darkness between the reef and the water, we aimed a little farther west for good measure and picked up the speed again until we were at full tilt and practically singing with delight.

THUMP, THUMP-SKKKKKCHCHCHCHCHCHCHCHSSSSSSSSSSS-SS!!!

We hit the reef at full speed and grounded the totality of *Southern Cross* on top of it!

Worse yet, the grounding didn't *sound* very good. Although *Southern Cross* was a Klepper Quattro model, originally designed for U.S. Navy SEAL landings, with a special double-reinforced hull bottom, I was not sure how it had handled the brutal collision. I hoped for the best.

We pried ourselves off the shallow reef with our paddles, spearing the invisible foe and pushing off for all we were worth. We prudently followed the reef westward toward the light. Our prudence evaporated, and we turned ninety degrees to port and resumed our southerly course with increased speed. It looked like all water. *We must be past the fullest extension of the reef. We were home free. Back to full tilt! The hull is OK.*

THUMP, THUMP-SKKKKKCHCHCHCHCHCHCHCHSSSSSSSSSSS-SS!!!

Grounded again?!

The middle of *Southern Cross* was resting on a lone, submerged reef rock. We were seesawing on top of it with each passing wave.

"Well, mate, now what?"

"We've got to scooch off," I said.

"Scooch?" Tony questioned.

"We've got to undulate our hips forward at the same time."

"Ohhhhhh kinky, kinky."

"Seriously," I said.

"I got ya, let's do it on a count of three," Tony replied.

"OK. One . . . two . . . three!"

All of sudden SC was tilted forty-five degrees to port and was about to flip. We simultaneously leaned to starboard and twisted and finished scooching our way off. We started paddling. *What's that water at my heels. Must be some water we took in when we tilted. I wanted to believe.*

But as it traveled up my ankles, I began to doubt it. A bit later, and the lower calf muscle felt its first licks, and then I knew we'd holed SC. And holed her badly.

With *Southern Cross* filling with water, we found ourselves in the outer perimeter of a very crowded Fanny Bay. Yachts of all sizes filled the bay from one end to the next. Their masts stuck straight into the sky and were all crossed by their line spreader bars a quarter length from the top. Most had a small light dangling on them, while others were eerily backlit by the faint cumulative glow. It looked like a restless cemetery. By the time we were able to approach the first live body aboard one of the yachts, our butts were all wet.

"Ahoy, mate! Where's the yacht club?" I asked.

"Hello, hello. You're in a kayak. That's great! The family and I had another group of kayakers onboard on Thursday Island. Anyway, you're almost there. Just head to the left of that strip of yellow lights." I recognized that he had an American accent.

"Where ya from?" I asked.

"Minnesota."

"And you?"

"Originally from Jersey."

Well past the chitchat phase, Tony started paddling the fully laden *Southern Cross* toward our goal.

With no waves coming from above, the design of *Southern Cross* doesn't allow water to get deeper than about midboat (i.e., where the bottom of the internally mounted air sponsons are). That is the point at which we achieved neutral buoyancy. We sat in a half body bath and propelled the half-ton vessel toward the strip of lights. The last mile took half an hour. We slowly navigated past the endless array of nautical crucifixes (the yachts). We made sure our last mile was a memorable one.

We finally scuttled *Southern Cross* onto shore near a group of dinghies. The club looked open. We were hungry. Tony headed up to the club, and as if on cue, I heard: "C'mon, Eric. We've saved some tucker for you!"

Marianne from the *Omni* crew was taking on where Claire had left off in Nhulunbuy. *I knew there was some reason we had to make it to here.* We sat at a nicely lit picnic table with our Hash House Harrier brigade as if nothing had happened since the last time we had seen them. The beers kept coming and our spirits were buoyed, as if unaware that anything had happened.

The *Omni* crew was to race in sixty hours and were not going to get "deep" about our adventure any more than we were in the frame of mind to "be deep" about it. We were in Darwin. We had already gone over four thousand nautical miles. Our desire to live had been challenged just two days earlier. We had sailed and paddled over fifty miles the day we reached Darwin. But it did not matter right then. *Eat, drink, and be merry. On on!*

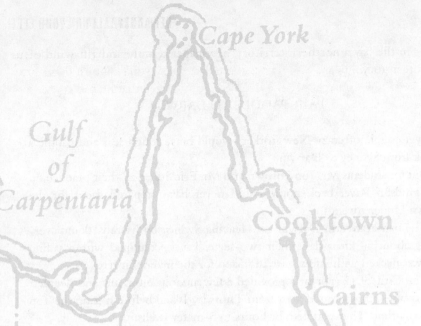

Now Where?

We woke up from our familiar nylon tubes to an unfamiliar future. We had planned to be circling Australia for at least a year. We hadn't covered half of that. There was still adventure in our bones. We seriously discussed the madness of "racing" *Southern Cross* to Ambon, Indonesia. It would be approximately the distance of our Gulf of Carpentaria crossing—five hundred miles—with some additional clusters of islands spread every 150 miles or so. The race would take us significantly off course, northwest and away from the continent we had been clinging to. There would also be all the yachts to keep us company.

"They tell me we can get in if I show them a passport but I don't have one," Tony said. "I called my mum to have it express-shipped last night!"

We would be entitled to one of the best handicaps conceivable in the yacht ranking system. Maybe even win the race because of it. But we would not see our racing-yacht escorts for very long. The slowest of them would be averaging five or six knots in mild wind conditions. We could average only four. There would be a chance of winning outright if there was no wind at all and we paddled the distance with our sails up. But a four-to-five-hundred-mile paddle would require a completely new set of luck tickets. Then, even if we did make it to Ambon, we would still need the passports.

We spent the better part of the next morning assessing and prepping to repair *Southern Cross* in the event that we both felt inspired to race to Ambon. I felt empty and had need of a purpose.

Later in the day a northern territory newspaper reporter caught wind of us and wrote a story.

PAIR PADDLE TO DARWIN

Only a couple of crazy New Yorkers would brave rough seas and paddle a kayak from Sydney to Darwin.

But for students Mr. Tony Brown and Mr. Eric Stiller, all their practice on the Hudson River back home could never have prepared them for the Down Under adventure.

The pair arrived in Darwin after leaving Sydney on March 10 and averaging about 50 km a day. Their two-seater kayak, equipped with a sailing rig, was packed with safety gear and food for the marathon trip.

The Gulf of Carpentaria provided a few anxious moments and sleepless nights when they headed west from Thursday Island before hitting the Top End coastline. They paddled for hours in 5-meter swells.

Estuaries, rivercrossings and strong currents made their journey across the top end a major effort. They intend to rest in Darwin before planning their next move—probably using more conventional transport.

I guess being a "New Yorker" doesn't necessarily mean you're American! Tony didn't seem too taken aback by not being referred to as an Australian. No, he *was* a New Yorker, albeit not in the Woody Allen mold.

Finally, a request to be on the ABC National Public Broadcasting radio station would complete our media trifecta.

It was all very flattering, but still rang a little soft for what we had been through. It was prematurely closing our book of adventure. We still might be racing in less than two days. We got back to the boat and started emptying the soaked refuge of the previous night's indignity. *Southern Cross* was tired, but we proceeded with a certain amount of intensity to get ready for the race.

Tony and I may have foolhardily joined the race to Ambon if we had gotten Tony's passport in time. Our trip to the Darwin post turned up empty. We had been derailed by a technicality. We had a quiet dinner that night with friends. In the morning we launched a gear-free *Southern Cross* and escorted the race fleet off. It was our last paddle together. The boat was light and unencumbered. It reminded me of our early paddles in New York. As I watched the fleet disappear, I knew that our trip together was over.

My thought was to pursue the dream that had arisen in the middle of the kayak trip to bicycle across Australia back to Melbourne. I set about my new plan. Tony and I had been introduced to Dr. Rogen Draper, a local surgeon and kayak enthusiast. He, Tony, and I took long nature walks together looking for birds. I enthusiastically went bicycle shopping in town and made sorties to the post, where letters and cards sputtered in from loved ones.

Tony had given me the adventurer's spirit to travel on. But it quickly dawned on me that a 2,500-mile trip on a heavily loaded bicycle was not something I had been born to do (in contrast to having been in a kayak my whole life). Up to then I'd looked at the bike trip with the same relative lack of concern for detail as Tony had initially had approaching the kayak trip—Just keep Australia on your left. I was now thinking—Just keep the Stuart Highway under my tires.

One day in the post office I saw a young German man with a map of the Stuart Highway briefing a young American about the trip.

"*Ja,* I've just finished. You'll have to leave soon. Otherwise it will get too hot."

"Yeah, I'm planning to leave in a week."

"Dats about right."

A strong urge came over me to introduce myself and merge myself in this trip with the American. I was bending down to speak, then I straightened up and went back outside. That was not what this next trip was going to be about for me.

Little did I know what was stirring in Tony's soul. I hardly saw him that week but soon enough I would find that the same fire was brewing in his heart as well. One day while we were both driving into town in Rogen's jeep, Tony said:

"Mate, I think I'm going to continue the kayak trip. I am looking into having a boat shipped up from Melbourne."

I believe the universe held its breath for a second or two at that point as this bullet ricocheted through every fiber in my mind, body, and soul. Ego, love, destiny, reputation, mateship all collided in an invisible particle accelerator called my head.

All that came out was: "What?"

Tony repeated the part about having the boat sent up to continue the trip and somehow it all came together.

"Tony," I said, "you can use *Southern Cross.* For God's sake, it's already here. I can set it up for solo paddling by putting the seat in the middle."

I think he was surprised. I am sure it was difficult for him to tell me, and I imagine he had been thinking about saying it for a while. I think he wanted to see that I was fully ensconced in my bicycle bubble before telling me. He talked about meeting his mum in Broome on the western edge of the Kimberleys seven hundred miles west of Darwin. No easy task for anyone.

My attempt to circumnavigate Australia was over.

Tony continuing on without me? Did he know that what lay ahead was at least as dangerous as what had nearly killed us? Did he hear the same voice that I did that told me that my original pack of luck tickets was used up and that it was time to get off the water?

Tony dropped me off in town near the bicycle shop and he went to do his own errands. I walked around in a daze for a while. I had assumed that the decision to stop was mutual. I felt ashamed wondering how this would all "look" to friends, families, acquaintances, and followers of the trip. Would I "look" like the one who dropped out, gave up, let down my partner, the trip, and so on and so on. I had to come to terms with this and get back on track for the bicycle trip.

Tony made no indication that he wanted me to join him again.

It was a big day. Maybe this soul search was coming along after all. Maybe the heart rhythms of the Earth herself were finally getting through to me. That night I went back to Rogen's, passed by Tony's room, and saw him pouring himself into a fresh new set of nautical charts. I was tempted to joke: "You don't need charts, mate—just keep Australia on your left." Tony and I had both grown.

Was it crazier to not know the dangers and hardships and go, or to know exactly what was in store and go anyway?

The next day Tony and I gave *Southern Cross* a major shakedown from stem to stern. We put two fresh new keel strips along the two bottom chines of the boat, making the hull bottom look almost as good as new. Tony had a special beach cart made so that he would have a better chance of carrying the boat up to a mile or more if stuck in an outgoing tide.

The cart was made very well but was very bulky. I didn't think it would really work, but it was not my place to interject. I could aid and abet but not change Tony's main course. Getting the boat ready his way and providing it with the accessories he wanted was part of what a solo journey was all about. I simply went about gathering and sorting repair supplies and packing him the equivalent of a technical care package.

Tony would continue to study and calculate with the charts and coastal pilots.

"Good on 'em and God bless him," I said to myself. But I couldn't shake the sinking feeling that it was an *Apocalypse Now* fate that awaited him. Whenever I imagined myself on his trip my mind spun with consequences. Paddling alone from Nhulunbuy to Darwin would have been challenging enough solo. The Kimberleys were another story. *He knows how many crocs there are there. He knows that he could get into horizontal-overfalls hell many times in this area.*

The sad thing was, while I felt rectified and proud about Tony going through all the "details" that he had not had the opportunity to go through before the beginning of our trip, I also felt I had contaminated a pure spirit with the shackles of protocol, details, and discipline. Meanwhile, he had gifted me with the spirit to "just do it."

Something inside me said I wasn't going to see my friend, my comrade, my twin again. I somehow felt Tony might be on a collision course that even he could not avoid this time. I wrote him a long letter a night or two before he left. I confessed my worries, envies, angers, disappointments, and I apologized from the bottom of my heart. I suppose I felt he was attempting some type of unspoken suicide. I finished the letter: "And please don't forget all the people who truly love and care for you. You have to think of them!"

It was a dead calm day at Fanny Bay where we took *Southern Cross* and Tony for the launch. He and I gathered and packed like we had many times before. My eyes triple-checked everything. I found that he was missing some important component and went immediately to the yacht shop to find a solution. I felt like my dad handpicking all the widgets and whatnot for my repair kit before I'd left. I also felt like that German man at our original launch in Bondi who found our spray skirt in the sand, cleaned it off, and handed it to us without a word. *What did this all* mean*?!*

Finally, the boat was packed. Tony made one more round and checked the boat's bow. I could see deep concern on my friend's face as he walked toward me. His voice cracked as he tried to say:

"And in case something happens to me. . . ."

At which point we both hugged each other and burst into tears. It was the first time we had embraced and the first time Tony had cried.

The emotion could not last for long. This was not an end; it was a beginning.

Southern Cross carried Tony out into a completely calm Fanny Bay. I watched him slowly fade into the haze. I rented a small TV from a local mall so I could watch the summer Olympics. For the moment, I was back to watching other people chasing a dream.

Two days later Tony called from a remote phone fifty miles west of Darwin near Port Blaze in Fog Bay, the last bit of Western civilization available for 650 miles before going fully into the void. Rogen answered. Tony asked for me to talk over some "technical details" and Rogen coyly took this opportunity to "stall" for time and implant a seed of reason into Tony's fiery mind. He said I was sound asleep and that "if you want I can still come to pick you up with the Jeep." Tony thanked him for the offer but said he would just try later to speak with me.

Many hours later Tony did call again, apparently queried Rogen on how much of an endeavor it would be to come get him, and received an enthusiastic "only three hours and I would be happy to do it" response.

"You've done enough Tony," I heard Dr. Rogen say. "You've gone far enough."

That night I got to bask in the shining light of two very special men in a magical place near the bottom of the world. We had indeed come very far. That night, well after the other two had gone to sleep, I turned on the Barcelona Summer Olympics. An hour later the K-1 1,000-meter Olympic finals were about to come on. Commentators discussed the reigning Olympic champion, Greg Barton, five-foot-ten-inch, 185-pound American, but felt his chances looked bleak against the six-foot-six-inch, 225-pound world champion, Knut Holmann from Norway. They said that Greg, the mechanical engineer, had the perfect stroke but that Holmann was a phenom and unbeatable at this distance.

The race began, and Knut soon took the lead. At the midpoint Greg started to close the gap. Power versus precision. Seven hundred fifty meters into the race the Australian commentators came to life.

"Yes, it is Australian Clint Robinson who's making the go of it now."

"The young man came from the ranks of the Australian Ironmen and got his introduction to this sport on a surfski."

"He's coming very strong now!"

"He's passing Barton!"

"He's gaining on Holmann!"

"Fifty meters to go. It's going to be close."

"My God, look at him turn it on!"

"He's won, he's won! The Australian Clint Robinson has beaten the world and Olympic champions!"

I smiled. It wasn't a surprise to me anymore.

It was time to go. Tony and Rogen left to go kayaking on the Katherine River some three hundred kilometers to the south. I would try to get there in the next three days. Katherine had become famous of late for providing special croc-viewing boats that have taught these half-ton lovelies to jump clean out of the water and grab tasty slabs of meat from hooks nearly two stories off the water. *Tony and Rogen wanted to do a little paddle on this river!?*

I rode my new bike to Rossetto's bike shop to pick up this and that and to say good-bye to the people who had outfitted me with my new trusted steed for the next adventure. I bade farewell and slowly walked my fully laden bicycle to the nearest road.

And off I went.

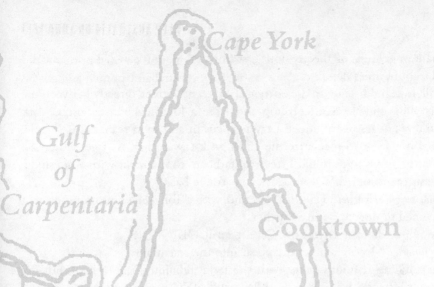

Going Home

Sydney Airport:

Well, here I am! The end of the Oz experience. Hard to imagine this has all happened. An experience of a lifetime. Really have to make way for things like this. I told Mike (the English photographer and Tony's friend, who was there at our send-off) to start thinking about the Congo. Yes, the Congo. This time mountain bike to the boat. Who knows? Perhaps the Caribbean.

I venture back to the old Klepper shop and peer through the locked gates into the empty shell. No boats, no desks, no racks, no books, no people. The 2,500-square-foot floor that I had buffed and waxed many a time was already gathering a thick coat of dust. The ocean blue walls outside, which I had climbed the shop ladder to paint every year with my father holding it steady, were already littered with graffiti. Only my Australian dreams kept this now very real vision from cutting my heart out of my chest and throwing it onto the sidewalk. I was prepared.

I took a last look and deep breath and walked to the Coffee Shop a block south. I had known many dozens of employees there before I had left, many of whom I'd called friends. At first glance everything and everybody looked the same, but closer inspection revealed an almost complete cast change. *It's uncanny how similar the new cast appears,* I thought. Eventually, I was able to trace the

restaurant migrations of the previous cast from a few remaining acquaintances. I
vowed to hunt them down.

I walk out, and I stand on the corner of Sixteenth Street, directly between the
Klepper shop and the Coffee Shop and I see a long-legged, statuesque dark
woman directly across the street. I try to focus in and soon realize it is Nicole.
She does not seem to recognize me and I walk toward her. As I get closer she
takes skirting steps to port and I steer to starboard to intercept with a big smile.
She seems preoccupied. "Oh Eric, it's you. You're back."

"That's right, Epic here, in the flesh!" I said, with a Tony-like boisterousness that
only seemed to disrupt her day further.

"Hey, I'm really late right now. Give me call, OK?"

"Ohhhhkay!" I watched her disappear into the restaurant.

The fulfilling reunions came with the long individual talks I had with my
"old guard" friends. Friends from college and NYC in the early years. Friends
that had gone around the block with me before. The friends that carved out
hours of their time and let me deluge them with my story. It's the telling and
retelling of the story that lets me really see what happened and how it relates to
everything and nearly everyone.

My family was relieved and proud. My mother confessed that the moment I
left in the limo, she had thought she would never see me again. My father said
he knew I could do it, but then brought me back to reality by handing me a
thick wad of credit card bills. "I paid off a few of them," Mom whispered.
"Don't tell your father."

My paddling mate David Lee Roth specifically chose Chumley's Pub in
Greenwich Village for our one-to-one tale-telling session. He chose the place
because it was the sight of many an author's first book celebrations. The book
jackets decorated the walls. It was here after a couple of beers and a celebratory
tequila shot or two that I got to the part where Tony said that we did not need
charts for our kayak trip and that all you had to do was *"Keep Australia on your
left."*

David suddenly lurched forward from his seat and pointed a finger at my face,
"That's the title of your book, Eric!"

I did get a rare chance to meet Dr. Hans Lindemann (who crossed the Atlantic
Ocean in a Klepper kayak) at a West Coast sea kayak symposium where he was
to be the keynote speaker. He was now in his midseventies and, although tall,
was a bit stooped and appeared frail. It was the first time he had been back to
America in decades. Before I met him face-to-face a colleague came over to me
and said that he had told Lindemann that the reason Tony and I had stopped was
because I had felt that the sea no longer welcomed us. Lindemann responded.

"And he was absolutely right, too."

A day later, Dr. Lindemann seemed recharged. He stood straight and his eyes
were gleaming. I met him and he congratulated me on the effort. He signed my

copy of his book *Alone at Sea*. He indicated that he had not talked about the trip to so many people in over thirty-five years. Later he danced the night away with his feisty and lovely wife of that many years. I learned later that after his crossing and before they got married, she had said to him, "It's me, or more long adventures. Not both."

Tony went on to Tahiti to build a full-sized Tahitian seagoing and sailing trimaran canoe from fifty-year-old plans out of all-natural materials and methods of bonding. He spent two straight months, from morning to night, building the boat. Interestingly, this had been the phase of our adventure Tony had been most absent from. I had spent many an intimate hour getting *Southern Cross* ready for the trip, while Tony was already in Oz. *Southern Cross* had been more a stepchild to Tony, whereas she was a blood relative to me. The idea was for Tony to take his boat and sail it to Australia from Tahiti. I faxed Tony a letter to wish him luck, but "suggested" that he give the boat a spin around the waters near Tahiti, or a trial crossing to Bora Bora, 125 miles away, and *then* decide.

After a difficult start and some trying weather, Tony and his partner ended up in Bora Bora, where the fertility gods intervened. Tony received a message from the USA that his longtime lady friend was going to have his baby. Tony immediately and enthusiastically abandoned his boating odyssey. The boat was donated to a school on the island.

I remember wondering what in the world his lady friend thought of "her man" conjuring plans to circle continents in a very small boat. I doubt if she ever uttered a word of dissent, knowing there was a large chapter of his life he needed to write. I received a card that announced the birth of their daughter, Allie Victoria Brown. I guess the Volgons now have a new target to concern themselves with.

Six months after I got back to the States, I was asked to give a presentation to the Explorers Club. A real honor. I was to be given sixty minutes to explain nine months of exploring. I had that generous allotment stretched to seventy-five. I probably used ten more. I prepared extensively to gather the "relevant" points of the adventure. I had less than forty-five seconds to explain each slide. I knew my audience would be tough. I wasn't even a member of the club. I poured through my journals and started compiling "relevant" points on large index cards. I had quite a few index cards before I finished with the first of five journals.

Speed reading my journals was dizzying, as intense images and feelings leaped from the pages and into my heart. The journals were like a crystal ball that presented reel after reel of my experience. I started to panic. *How am I going to present this type of experience in such a short period of time?!*

I couldn't quite explain the real expedition that I was on and I didn't want to convey only the logistical details. The more I looked into my crystal ball, the less I wrote on the index cards. I couldn't see the "Cliff Notes" version. I had to stop. I was redlining, and smoke was coming out of my ears. This type of debriefing was too abrupt and inappropriate. I was either going to have to allow it to fade into vague, pleasant images or I'd have to very gradually readdress the experience step-by-step to see if I could capture more from it. I chose the latter, but managed to whittle it down for my oral presentation.

It went well, I thought. Afterward, a number of people congratulated me on our adventure. A woman came up to me and very seriously said something I shall never forget: "It only counts if you go all the way around."